Morphosyntactic Change

OXFORD SURVEYS IN SYNTAX AND MORPHOLOGY

GENERAL EDITOR: Robert D. Van Valin, Jr., State University of New York, Buffalo

ADVISORY EDITORS: Guglielmo Cinque, University of Venice; Daniel Everett, University of Manchester; Adele Goldberg, Princeton University; Kees Hengeveld, University of Amsterdam; Caroline Heycock, University of Edinburgh; David Pesetsky, MIT; Ian Roberts, University of Cambridge; Masayoshi Shibatani, Rice University; Andrew Spencer, University of Essex; Tom Wasow, Stanford University

PUBLISHED

IN PREPARATION

Morphosyntactic Change

Functional and Formal Perspectives

OLGA FISCHER

OXFORD
UNIVERSITY PRESS

OXFORD
UNIVERSITY PRESS

Great Clarendon Street, Oxford OX2 6DP

Oxford University Press is a department of the University of Oxford.
It furthers the University's objective of excellence in research, scholarship,
and education by publishing worldwide in

Oxford New York

Auckland Cape Town Dar es Salaam Hong Kong Karachi
Kuala Lumpur Madrid Melbourne Mexico City Nairobi
New Delhi Shanghai Taipei Toronto

With offices in

Argentina Austria Brazil Chile Czech Republic France Greece
Guatemala Hungary Italy Japan Poland Portugal Singapore
South Korea Switzerland Thailand Turkey Ukraine Vietnam

Oxford is a registered trade mark of Oxford University Press
in the UK and in certain other countries

Published in the United States
by Oxford University Press Inc., New York

British Library Cataloguing in Publication Data
Data available

Library of Congress Cataloging in Publication Data
Data available

Typeset by SPI Publisher Services, Pondicherry, India
Printed by Biddles Ltd, www.biddles.co.uk

ISBN 978–019–926704–0 HB
     019–926704–9
     978–019–926705–7 PB
     019–926705–7

1 3 5 7 9 10 8 6 4 2

For Mark,
Daan, Joost and Tessel

The history of science is replete with false starts. Scientific progress, however, is not based on a wholesale reputation of old claims with the arrival of new ones. ... It is more constructive when a new theory or discovery embraces old knowledge as a special case under a more general concept

(Goldberg 2001: 46–47)

Our work is based on the strong assumption that linguists and psycholinguists are studying the same object – human language – that their theories and experiments trade in the same notions, and that they will converge at same point (Anshen and Aronoff 1996: 11)

Analogy is the backbone of universal grammar (Anttila 2003: 439)

Contents

General Preface

Oxford Surveys in Syntax and Morphology provides overviews of the major approaches to subjects and questions at the centre of linguistic research in morphology and syntax. The volumes are accessible, critical, and up-to-date. Individually and collectively they aim to reveal the field's intellectual history and theoretical diversity. Each book published in the series will characteristically contain: (1) a brief historical overview of relevant research in the subject; (2) a critical presentation of approaches from relevant (but usually seen as competing) theoretical perspectives to the phenomena and issues at hand, including an objective evaluation of the strengths and weaknesses of each approach to the central problems and issues; (3) a balanced account of the current issues, problems, and opportunities relating to the topic, showing the degree of consensus or otherwise in each case. The volumes will thus provide researchers and graduate students concerned with syntax, morphology, and related aspects of semantics with a vital source of information and reference.

In *Morphosyntactic Change: Formal and Functional Perspectives* Professor Olga Fischer surveys the two main approaches to the study of syntactic and morphological change, namely generative grammar and grammaticalization theory. Her critical examination of these two approaches is firmly embedded in the larger context of the history of language change, and presents insights not usually found in books written from a single perspective.

Robert D. Van Valin, Jr
General Editor

Heinrich Heine University,
Düsseldorf

University at Buffalo,
The State University of New York

Acknowledgements

Many people have contributed, directly and indirectly, to the making of this book. First of all I am very grateful to the editor of the new Oxford series 'Surveys in Syntax and Morphology', Robert Van Valin, for giving me the opportunity to take part in this series, and for his comments and help while writing the volume. I am also deeply indebted to two anonymous reviewers, who, although they may not have agreed with everything I wrote, have substantially improved sections in the book by their pertinent remarks, and have prevented me from making some obvious errors in areas where I was not as knowledgeable as I should have been. One of the difficulties for me in writing this volume was, indeed, the need to be an expert in two rather different theoretical models, and not firmly belonging to either of them.

I would also like to thank John Davey of Oxford University Press for his constant support, his interest in the content of the book itself, and his very efficient and kind handling of all matters connected with its publication.

I owe an enormous debt to my colleagues in the English department and the ACLC Research Institute (Amsterdam Centre for Language and Communication), who have read earlier versions of the manuscript or have taken over administrative duties during my sabbatical, or indeed both (in alphabetical order): Umberto Ansaldo, Anne Bannink, Hans den Besten, Tom van Brederode, Janneke Kalsbeek, Evelien Keizer, Ans de Kok, Willem Koopman, Lisa Lim, Sebastian Nordhoff, Hella Olbertz, Harry Perridon, Jetty Peterse, and Otto Zwartjes. In addition I would like to thank Anette Rosenbach and Guy Deutscher, who very critically read all of the manuscript, and have been a great help and valuable motivators, and Ronny van den Boogaart, Bettelou Los, Muriel Norde, Niki Ritt, Kees Vrieze, Anthony Warner, and Wim van der Wurff, who commented on sections, gave me new ideas, and here and there prevented me from making some serious mistakes. Finally, I would like to thank Chloe Plummer, Jetty Peterse, and Tessel Janssen for their help with the index.

I am grateful to the Nederlandse Organisatie voor Wetenschappelijk Onderzoek (Dutch Organization for Scientific Research) for granting me a generous replacement subsidy enabling me to have a six-month sabbatical in which to finish the book, and to the Faculty of Humanities at the University of Amsterdam for supporting this grant. I would also like to thank the two anonymous referees who have supported my application, and Jacques Arends, Frederike van der Leek, and Kees Ostendorf, who helped me shape it. It is very sad indeed that Jacques Arends died very suddenly in the summer of 2005. He had promised to read the manuscript and his acute insight into matters of language change combined with his, always gentle, advice would have been most welcome and helpful.

I regret that the volume entitled *The Power of Analogy. An Essay on Historical Linguistics* (Mouton de Gruyter 2006) by Dieter Wanner appeared too late to enable me to consider it for the present volume. It provides invaluable discussions of many of the issues I have been concerned with here, most notably with respect to the use of formal and functional models in the area of language change, and the important roles played by frequency and analogy.

Finally, I would like to thank (in chronological order) Richard Hogg, Henk Gons, Barbara Strang, John Pellowe, Frederike van der Leek, David Lightfoot, Roger Lass, and Max Nänny, who each in their own ways have deeply influenced my thinking about language and my professional career.

Olga Fischer   Amsterdam, April 2006

Abbreviations and explanation of technical terms

ACC	accusative case
C-command	a node α C-commands another node β iff the lowest branching node which properly dominates α (this is X in the structure) also properly dominates β, i.e. in the following structure:

	α C-commands β, and also any nodes below β
checking	in the minimalist program grammatical features (such as agreement, case, etc.) have to be checked in the course of the derivation. If the features are interpretable they are erased, if not, the derivation 'crashes' and the construction is ill-formed
control verbs	verbs that take a non-finite clausal complement without a lexical subject. The empty subject is termed PRO, which is controlled either by the subject of the matrix verb as in *John$_i$ promised Mary* [PRO$_i$ *to go*] (subject-control), or by the object of the matrix verb as in *John persuaded Mary$_i$* [PRO$_i$ *to go*] (object-control)
DAT	dative case
ECM	Exceptional Case Marking occurs in so-called accusative and infinitive constructions, in which the matrix verb assigns objective or accusative case to an NP without assigning it a thematic role; it is the infinitive which assigns the NP a thematic role. The infinitive itself, having no tense features, cannot assign structural case to its thematic subject
E-language	External language, similar to 'performance' (language viewed independently of the mind)
fem	feminine gender

GB	Government and Binding Theory (a modular formal generative theory of grammar, identical to the Principles and Parameters Model)
GEN	genitive case
HPSG	Head-driven Phrase Structure Grammar (a theory that contains very few grammatical 'rules' because all important semantic and syntactic processes are driven via the information contained in the lexicon)
I-language	Internal language, similar to 'competence' (language viewed as an element of the mind)
INF	infinitive
INFL (I)	a term used in generative theory for an abstract constituent or functional category, which subsumes verbal features such as person, number, tense (in later versions it became restricted to tense, the other two becoming part of the category AGR[reement])
LAD	Language Acquisition Device (the innate grammar system or UG, which aids the child in learning its native language)
LF	(level of) logical form (representation of the logical form of an expression, which constitutes the initial representation of sentence meaning)
LFG	Lexical Functional Grammar (a grammar in which a syntactic construction consists of a constituent structure and a functional structure, but in which, as in HPSG, the lexicon plays a prominent role in the assignment of both structures)
LMC	Language Making Capacity (like the LAD this refers to the capacity of children to learn their native language, but unlike the LAD it is not assumed to be innate but to consist of operating principles which are simple at first and become increasingly complex, through associative learning)
masc	masculine gender
ME	Middle English (the period *c.* 1150–1500)
MED	*Middle English Dictionary* (also online)
Merge	an operation in Minimalism which combines categories to form higher categories or phrases: it replaces the former projection rules

Move	an operation in which a linguistic element is moved from one position in a structure to another, e.g. by NP-movement or V-movement
N/NP	noun/noun phrase
neut	neuter gender
NOM	nominative case
NP-movement	in generative grammar, this involves the movement of an NP from one argument position to another. The movement leaves a trace, which cannot be filled by another argument
OE	Old English (the period *c.* 700–1150)
OED	*Oxford English Dictionary* (also online)
OF	Old French (the period *c.* 850–1300)
ON	Old Norse (the period *c.* 1100–1400)
OT	Optimality Theory (a model, so far used mainly in phonology, in which filters and wellformedness constraints, ranked in a hierarchy of relevance which is language specific, determine which output form is most optimal of all the candidates available with respect to an underlying input form)
P&P	Principles and Parameters Model (in which a universal set of grammatical principles determines the properties of natural language (UG), and grammatical differences between languages are to be characterized in terms of a restricted set of parameters, which can be set one way or another)
PDE	Present-day English
PF	(level of) phonetic form (representation of the phonetic form of an expression)
pl	plural
PLD	Primary Linguistic Data (the data a child is confronted with in the acquisition period)
PRES	present tense form
PRO	used in generative models to refer to an empty or unexpressed pronominal subject, which functions as the subject of infinitival clauses, and which is controlled by the lexical subject of the matrix clause

pro-drop	a term used in generative models to refer to languages with a full inflectional verbal system of agreement, which enables subject personal pronouns (i.e. 'pro') to be left unexpressed
resumptive pronoun	the term as used here (in a wider sense than in generative theory) refers to a pleonastic element (usually a demonstrative or personal pronoun), which picks up an argument that was left 'dangling' due to an intervening phrase or clause, as in *My aunt, who is such an old fuddy-duddy, she completely forgot to* ... (cf. Crystal 1997: 332).
sg	singular
small clause	stands for an infinitival clause lacking both C(omp) and I(nfl), i.e. clauses like *I painted* [*the door green*], *I saw* [*him do it*], *I consider* [*it foolish*]
(S)OV	(subject)–object–verb word order
SUBJ	subject
Subject-raising	a rule in generative grammar whereby the underlying subject of a complement clause is raised to the subject position of the main clause, the latter being empty when the matrix verb itself is of a type that cannot assign an argument to its subject position
(S)VO	(subject)–verb–object word order
TEP	Trace Erasure Principle (a principle that forbids that an empty node (a 'trace') left by a moved constituent is erased (becomes filled) by another constituent)
that-trace phenomenon	used to refer to constructions which involve extraction of a subject from a clause introduced by a complementizer, whereby the complementizer may or may not be deleted, as in *Who do you believe (that) saw Bill?*
thematic role	also called θ-role; it indicates the semantic function that a verbal argument fulfils in the clause. It is assigned by the predicate to the argument in conformity with the so-called θ-criterion. The latter is a condition which states that at deep structure each argument is in a θ-position and that each θ-position contains an argument
θ-theory	theory about θ-roles
trace	a formal means of marking the place a constituent had before it was moved to another position in the clause. The trace (*t*) and the constituent in the new position are

	coindexed, and the trace is said to be bound by the new position of the constituent
UG	Universal Grammar (common grammatical properties shared by all natural languages)
V/VP	verb/verb phrase
Verb-raising	a generative rule used to describe a process in Germanic languages like Old English, Dutch and German, whereby an embedded clause is unified with the matrix clause (clause-union)
Verb-second	a phenomenon, well-known in the Germanic languages, whereby the finite verb moves to the second position in the matrix clause
Wh-movement	a type of operator movement in generative grammar whereby a relative pronoun/adverb (e.g. *who, that, which, when,* etc.) is moved to the front of the clause
WNT	*Het Woordenboek der Nederlandsche Taal* (Dictionary of the Dutch language)

Introduction

We simply state our position that the rich and diverse body of data thrown up
by students of grammaticalisation is one that advocates of formal linguistic
theory must respond to. At the same time, we reject the view that the
phenomenon of grammaticalisation in and of itself invalidates the project
of formal grammar (Börjars *et al.* 1996: 174)

The main aim of this volume is to consider a number of important issues in
morphosyntactic change by comparing and contrasting two major approaches in this area: the formal, generative (Principles and Parameters,
henceforth P&P) approach and the (mainly functional) grammaticalization
approach. These are at present the two main theoretical frameworks to
offer explanations for morphosyntactic change (cf. publications such as
Lightfoot 1979, 1991, 1999, 2002b; Roberts 1993b; van Gelderen 1993; van
Kemenade and Vincent 1997; Pintzuk *et al.* 2000; Fischer *et al.* 2000a;
Roberts and Roussou 2003, on the one hand and Traugott and Heine
1991; Pagliuca 1994; Giacolone Ramat and Hopper 1998; Fischer *et al.*
2000b; Wischer and Diewald 2002; Hopper and Traugott 2003 [1993];
Fischer *et al.* 2004, on the other).[1] The two theoretical models are not
internally homogeneous, far from it. As far as possible, differences within
each model will be taken into account whenever relevant. I will, however,
concentrate on those aspects of each theory that have been accepted by the
majority of its practitioners, and I will highlight those theoretical assumptions which divide the two schools most. Another problem to be faced is the
fact that the models change continually, which is especially true for the
generative one. The P&P approach comprises both the older Government
and Binding (GB) theory and the more recent Minimalist model. The
basic assumptions are not so different, but they differ considerably in the
mechanisms of derivation. Again, where relevant or appropriate these differences will be noted.

Since the comparison between the two approaches can be seen as a case
of the general formalist versus functionalist distinction in modern linguistics, the investigation is both worthwhile and necessary. (A study of the
differences is made in Newmeyer 1998, but this has a bias towards the

formal approach and is synchronically oriented.) In many ways the two approaches are radically opposed, which proves a hindrance to a proper understanding of the causes and mechanisms of morphosyntactic change. At the same time, too strict an adherence to one or the other theory often leads to a neglect of the philological details (an equally important aim of this volume is to elucidate what constitutes 'good practice' in historical linguistics). A proper understanding of change should also lead to a better notion of the contours of the theory of grammar in the sense that it is generally believed that a better knowledge of the kinds of mechanisms, principles, and constraints that play a role in one linguistic domain (be it language change, language acquisition, the neurolinguistic workings of the brain, or language evolution) should help us to get a better grip on the form and content of the theory of grammar.

The approach will be balanced in the sense that I consider form *and* function equally important.[2] This does mean, however, that I do not support a wholesale acceptance of the idea of a purely formal, innate grammar, as proposed by the generative school (as will become clear from the discussion in Chapter 2). I would like to stress, however, that it is not my intention to use the comparison as a pretext for dismissing either theory. Both theories offer opportunities for a better understanding of linguistic structure and language change. The two perspectives will be contrasted and compared not only in order to gain greater insight into the causes and mechanisms of morphosyntactic change but also to test the explanatory and methodological adequacy of the two theories with respect to linguistic change and to the philological details involved in them. A further aim is to make suggestions towards a model of change which incorporates both form and function in a unitary way. For this model I will rely on work done within other linguistic domains as well as on the traditional notion of analogy, which played an important role in linguistic theorizing in the nineteenth and early twentieth centuries (for a historical overview, see Itkonen 2005).

In general, if we wish to know why linguistic utterances are the way they are (both diachronically and synchronically), that is, if we wish to understand human linguistic behaviour, we need to ask ourselves four questions:

(i) What is it that produces language or what are the principles underlying the generation (including comprehension and production) of linguistic utterances (this relates to the question of 'cause' as well as of 'structure').

(ii) How is language used within society (this relates to the question of 'function').

(iii)   How does language develop within the individual (the ontogenetic aspect).
(iv)   How does language develop over time (the phylogenetic aspect)?

In order to study what is behind language production (question i), we will have to investigate the workings of the brain or mind.[3] A problem here is that we have not yet sufficient means to investigate the mind directly. Consequently, linguists interested in the content of the grammatical system generally study this system indirectly through an examination of the linguistic products of the mind. It goes without saying that it is difficult to study these products separately from the function that they have in society (question ii). Moreover, society itself can be said to 'cause' language production. It is well-known that language in children is not triggered if a speech community is lacking.[4] The study of language acquisition (question iii) and of language change (question iv) are of interest because they provide other angles from which both cause, structure, and function may be studied. A more general aim of this volume, therefore, is to consider what historical linguists can contribute to a better understanding of the language system through the study of language change, in which both structural and functional factors play a role. These results can then be used as input to questions (i) and (ii). In addition, this volume will pay some attention to developments in language evolution and neurolinguistic modelling in so far as this may be relevant to a better understanding of linguistic change.

The two approaches mentioned above, a formal and a functional one, are geared towards questions (i) and (ii) respectively. Thus the diachronic P&P approach concentrates on change as the result of changes in the 'biological grammar' (cf. e.g. Lightfoot 1999), that is to say, it is interested in how change in language output is caused by change in the (formal) grammar system (the top-down approach), while the grammaticalization approach concentrates on how linguistic utterances are used in communication, and how this leads to grammar change (the bottom-up approach). The aim is to show that the two diachronic approaches need to be combined in order to reach a fuller understanding of the causes and mechanisms of language change, and ultimately of the system underlying language.

The first part of the book will address general issues, such as the methodological issues mentioned above, the ways in which the study of morphosyntactic change and the methodology used for it differs from or resembles the study of change on other levels of language, and how the different levels (the level of discourse, the lexicon, the semantic/pragmatic, and phonetic/phonological levels) interact with change on the morphological and the syntactic levels. It will also consider the interrelation between external and internal causes of change (notably the issue of syntactic borrowing); and what the relation is between 'innovation' and 'change' (the terms as used by James Milroy 1992, 1993), or between actuation and implementation/diffusion. This last issue is important since it relates to the controversy of whether syntactic change is gradual or abrupt ('bumpy' according to Lightfoot 1999), and it relates to the *langue/parole* distinction and what the locus is of change, two issues which often divide generative linguists and adherents of grammaticalization. This, in turn, is intimately bound up with the model of grammar one works with, whether one believes in a universal grammar which is innate and which determines, together with the Primary Linguistic Data (PLD), the form of a child's individual grammar during the so-called critical period of language acquisition, or whether one believes in more of an 'emergent' type of grammar, which develops on the basis of an interaction of the PLD with more general cognitive learning principles in the course of language acquisition, and which may continue to change in adult life (cf. e.g. Slobin 1985b, 1997 [2001]; Tomasello 1995, 2003a; Clark 2003; Deacon 2003). This issue is also related to whether one considers change in terms of individual grammars or in terms of what Lightfoot (1999: 79) has called 'social grammars'.[5] The discussion in Part I will also include a brief history of the study of morphosyntactic change (mainly from the perspective of the two approaches), and it will describe the causes and mechanisms that are said to play a role in morphosyntactic change and in linguistic change in general, and more specifically within the two theoretical approaches. Stressing the binary nature of the linguistic sign (the importance of both form and function), it will be suggested that a usage-based, analogical model may prove to be the most fertile model for understanding morphosyntactic change.

The second part of the volume will present a number of case studies, mainly taken from the history of the Germanic languages but, where possible, strengthened with observations from other languages. Central in this discussion will be a consideration of developments that have taken place with respect to modal verbs and auxiliaries, because both schools of thought have had and still entertain very different opinions on both the details of what happened, and on the mechanisms and causes involved.

As such, this case provides a good illustration of the use of methodology and the general factors at work in change, as described in Part I. From the modal verbs and auxiliaries, there will be excursions to the phenomena of subjectification, and clause combining or clause fusion. The former presents an area of difficulty within the grammaticalization model (because of scope problems which go against certain parameters of the theory), which could be solved by paying more attention to form and by scrutinizing the essentially semantic-pragmatic approach taken by grammaticalizationists. This seems appropriate in a book dealing with morphosyntactic change. The subject of clause fusion (here used in a rather loose sense), is of interest because it combines both diachronic and synchronic concerns, and is approached from very different angles by the two theories. Linked to these topics in one way or another are the development of pragmatic markers and the important role played by the fixation of word order (due often to morphological losses) on structural changes elsewhere. Each chapter will present the relevant data and describe and evaluate the formal and functional theoretical explanations that have been offered for the phenomena in question. It will also offer new suggestions for solutions, where possible, in terms of the analogical, usage-based theory of language described in Chapter 3.

Throughout the volume, there will be a bias towards the analysis of morphosyntactic change in English because English has a comparatively well-documented history and a history that has been most intensively studied by both formal and functional diachronic linguists. An additional reason is that it is an area I am personally most familiar with. One needs a good knowledge of a language and its diachronic stages in order to describe and explain the changes that take place therein. Next to English, other Germanic languages will be considered wherever appropriate, and a comparison with Dutch and German on the one hand and the Scandinavian languages on the other will be most useful since they are the closest relatives (or close in the case of the Scandinavian languages) of English. A comparison between closely related languages may throw more light on how similar factors may have different effects because the possible variables are to some extent controlled. Wherever possible and feasible, similar developments in other languages will be considered and tendencies and generalizations (general constraints and principles) noted, but here I will have to rely on the work and intuitions of others. Since it will be emphasized throughout that a thorough knowledge of the various synchronic stages in the history of a language is necessary in order to be able to discover and explain the changes that take place, it stands to reason that we must be careful drawing conclusions about languages that we do not know intimately ourselves. Hence I have restricted myself in this volume to pointing out similar tendencies or generalities rather than providing detailed discussions of other languages. A study that has proved very useful for this purpose, because it covers such a wide variety of languages and because it is a study not tied to either a generative or grammaticalization point of view, is the detailed work on syntactic change by Harris and Campbell (1995).

It is important to emphasize at this point that the case studies only represent a very small selection of changes that could have been illustrated. Lack of space prevents a discussion of other important topics such as the OV > VO change, the rise of *do*, changes in negative constructions, the loss of Verb-second, although some of these cases are touched upon briefly. The selection of topics has been made with an eye to those changes which were either extensively discussed in both models (i.e. the development of auxiliaries) or changes where one model but not the other addressed an issue and where the more formal or functional concerns of the opposite model could in fact have helped to achieve a more balanced discussion.

A final note on terminology, I will use the term 'language' in a number of ways, its specific reference depending on context. Thus, it may refer to a language as a historical object that changes over time. It may also refer to the language output of an individual or a community of speakers at a given point in time. The term 'grammar' presents similar problems. In general, I use 'grammar' to refer to the grammatical or linguistic *system* that each individual possesses, with which (s)he can produce and comprehend language utterances. Whether part of this grammar is due to an innate predisposition for grammar (called core grammar or UG) or whether it is the result of more general cognitive learning mechanisms, depends on the theoretical model under discussion. I do not use the term in order to refer to a 'community' or 'social grammar', a kind of common denominator of all individual grammars. When I use the term 'speaker', it may literally refer to a language user who produces language output. However, in most cases it will have the more general sense of a language processor, including both production and comprehension. A brief explanation of the main terms used and their abbreviations will be found on pp. xi–xv.

Notes

1. This is not to deny that there has not been done a lot of other, most useful work in the area of morphosyntactic change, both in terms of more traditional theoretical models (cf. especially the large amount of historical linguistic work by linguists such as Karl Brugmann, Berthold Delbrück, Hermann Paul, and Otto Jespersen, F. Visser, Bruce Mitchell in the last two centuries), and in terms of sociolinguistic variationist models (e.g. the work of William Labov and his followers). Their influence is felt and their concern for empirical detail is taken for granted throughout this book, and touched upon when relevant, but their methodological stance will not be a central issue in this volume.

2. In this volume I will sometimes use the terms 'function' and 'meaning' interchangeably. When strictly referring to referential (denotative) or expressive (connotative) meaning (i.e. the relation between a 'sign' and its object or referent in the outside world), the term 'meaning' will be employed. When referring to the function that a particular linguistic form or construction has within a sentence or within the system of language as a whole, I will use the term 'function'. In other words, 'meaning' implies some kind of *inherent* semiotic relation between a sign (a word or a construction) and its referent in the outside world, while 'function' expresses what the *relation* is between a sign and other signs (e.g. the relation of subject, object, etc.) or it expresses the use of that sign in the wider context of the discourse situation. However, the two terms also overlap in that both can be used to refer to the significance, the purpose or the underlying intention of some element, and its relational and inherent properties often work together to express the overall use (or function) of a sign. For instance, in functional theories, a syntactic construction itself is said to carry some inherent meaning; this meaning is defined both by the relation between the elements in the construction but also by the referential meaning components carried by each single sign, such as 'agentive', 'animate', etc. It should also be noted that 'function' has a rather different sense in functional grammar than in formal grammar. In functional grammar it is a primitive, while in formal grammar it is derivative, i.e. defined in terms of position.

3. The brain is the physical organism that makes language possible. The mind is different for each individual in that it is the result of a constantly shifting active relationship between the brain and its surroundings. The mind is not something given, like the brain or our surroundings, but it is a dynamic process of discovery which is never completed and which is shaped by its own history. At the same time the experiences that shape the mind, also shape the brain itself (cf. Deacon 1997: 193ff.).

4. Similarly, as Milroy (1992: 4, 223) points out, language *change* is not triggered when there are no native speakers, as is the case in the use of 'dead' languages such as Latin and ancient Greek.

5. Milroy (1992: 165–8) makes a distinction between 'speakers' and (the language) 'system', which he also refers to as 'the community "grammar" ' (p. 169). He has, it seems, a very different notion of 'grammar' compared to generative linguists, not only in that it refers to the system of a speech community rather than an individual, but also in that this system is said to characterize 'the *constraints on the linguistic behaviour of groups and individuals*. It can be interpreted as modelling the effects of the linguistic system on speakers rather than the effects of speakers on the system' (p. 169). In other words, as is clear from his figure 6.1 on p. 170, the system is not a module that stands at the birth of an individual's linguistic production, but it is the property of the language community, which models each individual speaker's production. Social norms and constraints play a more important part in this system than linguistic constraints.

Part I

General Issues in Morphosyntactic Change

1

What is 'good practice' in historical linguistics: aims and methods

> every theory may begin its career as an attempt to preserve the phenomena, but once the theory gets a good hold on life and becomes entrenched in the minds of its adherents, there ensues a drive to sacrifice the phenomena to preserve the theory (Haiman 1998: 172)

> the Galilean style ... is the recognition that it is the abstract systems that you are constructing that are really the truth; the array of phenomena is some distortion of the truth because of too many factors, all sorts of things. And so, it often makes good sense to disregard phenomena ... (Chomsky 2002: 99)

1.0 Introduction

The primary tasks of the historical linguist are to give a *description* of the historical linguistic facts at particular moments in time, to show *how* linguistic utterances change when they are compared over a period of time, to describe what general *mechanisms* are involved in or underlie these changes, and, finally, to provide an *explanation* of the changes that take place in these linguistic utterances. This must be done with reference to the communicative situation and with reference to language users, who, after all, interpret and produce the utterances and are thus in some way responsible for the changes.[1]

A further aim of any study of morphosyntactic change is to abstract away from individual cases and to identify and characterize universals of change (universal principles and constraints), and their possible relation to universals of the language system. This can be done both by means of comparative linguistic research (i.e. comparative linguistics and typology) as well as by using results obtained in other domains, such as language acquisition, sociolinguistics, psycholinguistics, neurolinguistics, anthropological linguistics, etc. For this volume, we will concentrate on the details of individual cases and on how they have been used and explained within two approaches to language, one formal and one functional. Where possible and feasible, we will take into account findings from other domains so that any conclusions drawn in this study will not clash with observations made elsewhere.

In the first section of this chapter, we will consider *what* can be used as evidence in historical linguistic investigations, and specifically *how* the evidence on the morphosyntactic level needs to be approached. In §1.2, I will pay attention to the difficulty of distinguishing between internal and external factors in change and, more particularly, I will concentrate on what role the development of a written standard language plays as an 'external' factor. In §1.3, we will look at *where* we may find our evidence and how the various resources have to be treated.

1.1 What counts as evidence in historical linguistics?

1.1.1 What texts do we use as the basis for comparison?

One thing must be clear from the start: in order to compare utterances from different periods one must have a sense of what is comparable. This is not an easy question because 'comparability' (or 'incomparability', for that matter) exists on a number of different levels. First of all there are external (i.e. not purely linguistic) factors that may stand in the way of a methodologically proper comparison. The biggest problems here are the absence of phonetic records and the chance survival of the historical documents, that is the relative scarcity of homogeneous texts in any one period, region or genre (cf. Labov 1994: 10–11). Ideally, one should compare texts belonging to one and the same geographic region (dialect area), and concerned with the same age group. Sex and class distinctions, as we know from the work of sociolinguists such as Labov, Trudgill, and others,[2] may affect any comparison too. The latter two factors, however, can only rarely be taken into account in historical work in that the earliest documents were usually written by males from the educated classes.

Another external factor in a diachronic linguistic comparison concerns genre and the closely related difference between written and spoken discourse. It is well-known that certain genres, such as for example drama, trial proceedings, and private letters, are closer to the spoken channel than others, while scientific writings, legal documents or philosophical expositions are situated at the written end of the scale. We should restrict ourselves, therefore, to texts from the same genre or written within the same style. An additional problem arises here, however, and that is that the spoken/written difference itself cuts across the genre difference. In most languages there is a clear development *within* its written discourse from a looser, oral style to a tighter, written one. The oldest prose texts, including the more formal documents, are often closer to an oral style. This is because a cultural or speech community only develops a specific (literary) writing style in the course of time. The written mode in our days is usually more 'elaborated', more 'autonomous' than the oral mode because the lack of an immediate context of situation and the fact that a writer wishes to address a larger audience, forces him or her to be more explicit.[3] Such an explicit mode needs time to develop and to become conventionalized; hence it is usually not present in the earliest prose writings of a community. What this means is that one may be wrong in assuming that the genre factor is controlled by a simple decision to compare only texts strictly within one particular genre across a long period. For this reason Biber and Finegan, who have written extensively on how to recognize style/genre differences (cf. Biber 1986, 1991 and Biber and Finegan 1994), have recommended that only purely linguistic indicators (such as the absence/presence of passive constructions, nominalizations, subordination, first/second person pronouns, etc.) rather than genre should be used when one wishes to compare a homogeneous group of texts.

It should be clear that this oral/written parameter also implies that the rise of certain new constructions in the written language may be due not so much to a grammar change in the individual speaker but to the fact that the written standard itself develops a more elaborated code, which at some stage becomes part of the community's 'social grammar', and which, as far as the individual speaker is concerned, may only become part of his grammar as the result of formal education.[4] A more detailed discussion of this aspect will be given below in §1.2.2.

All in all, this means that the situation for historical linguistic research is far from ideal, especially for the earliest periods. There is no real solution to this except that it is important in any investigation to make quite clear which texts have been chosen, why these texts and not others, and to indicate the possible shortcomings in the results due to the paucity of suitable texts.

1.1.2 What linguistic elements do we compare across texts and how?

Comparison may also be difficult from an internal linguistic point of view when we consider *which* linguistic forms are to be compared on each language level. Within phonology or morphology, a diachronic comparison does not require so much effort since the forms to be compared are fairly similar. Here, we can indeed compare cognates. In addition, any one text contains infinitely more information about possible phonological and morphological forms, than about syntactic forms, because not all syntactic structures will be represented in a particular text—this depends to a much greater extent on the style or genre of the text—while not all constructions will appear with equal frequency.[5] The changes that take place in phonology and morphology are therefore relatively easy to discover and describe. We know more or less that we are comparing items that show some continuation in their form, which serves as evidence that they go back to the same form etymologically. The case is rather different for syntax. When we compare two syntactic constructions from two different periods, how do we know that we are comparing 'cognates' so to speak?

Let us look at some examples. If we are interested in the history of infinitival complements in English, for instance, what do we compare? It is unlikely that we will find two clauses that are exactly the same in our data, probably not even simple ones such as:

(1a) OE   Ic seah hie gan
(1b) PDE I saw her go

In a case such as (1), it could be established on the basis of the phonological forms and with the help of phonological and morphological theory that the four words used are indeed all cognates.[6] They are even used in exactly the same order, so that the constructions themselves could be called cognates of one another. But how often do we find such exact forms? And even if (1a) and (b) are the same on the surface (but cf. fn. 6), how do we know that the underlying structure is the same? It is quite possible that the construction was reanalysed in the course of time, or 'abducted' in the grammar developed by a new generation of speakers.[7] This was the case, for instance, with the Old English form *an nædder*, which at some point in Middle English was analysed both as *an adder* as well as *a nadder*. How do we know how any individual analysed it? We only know when that same individual uses the word with another determiner, when he says either *the (that) adder* or *the (that) nadder*. It means that in order to establish what happened we must—beside a knowledge of phonological developments, of course—have a sense of system (in this case the determiner system), and we must be able also to look at other forms or structures that are not strictly cognate, in this case the same form preceded by a definite article or demonstrative pronoun. There was also a change in the grammatical system itself that made the development possible: in Middle English we witness the development of a new determiner category. This category develops via the grammaticalization of an earlier demonstrative pronoun (OE *se* [masc], *seo* [fem], *þæt* [neut]) into a definite article (ME *þe*, later written *the*) and the grammaticalization of the numeral *ān* into the indefinite article *a(n)*. Thus, in order to explain this particular case we need a database of utterances, covering more than strict 'cognate' utterances, *and* a sense of the grammatical system of Middle English. In other words, when looking at developments taking place in a particular syntactic structure, we must cast our net wide and look at all structures which are functionally and formally similar to the one in question (cf. also Mithun 2003: 561–2).

A similar example can be found in the development in English of the so-called *for NP to V*-construction. It is evident that some change took place in this construction at some point in time in that structures such as (2),

(2)   When I realised it might be used in evidence against me, I asked *for it to be fingerprinted* (Online *OED*, s.v. 'finger', **1970** *Daily Tel.* 4 Mar. 17/8)

did not occur in Old English, with *for* used as a complementizer rather than a preposition. In Old and Middle English, *for* immediately before an NP could only be interpreted benefactively (i.e. with the *for* NP functioning as an argument of the main clause predicate), as in (3),

(3a)   ... it were bettre *for yow to lese* so muchel good of youre owene ...
                                             (Chaucer *CT* Melibee 3030)
       '.... it would be better for you to lose so many possessions of your own'
(3b)   Hit bycomeþ *for clerkus crist for to seruen* (*PiersPl.* Skeat 1886: 85)
       'It is befitting for clergymen to serve Christ'

Quite clearly a benefactive interpretation such as found in (3) is out in (2) because of the inanimate NP *it* which follows *for*. We need animate NPs to benefit from whatever is said in the predicate. In order to understand why *for NP to V* comes to be reanalysed, from a structure such as (4) into one like (5):

(4)   [[predicate for NP] [to V]]
(5)   [predicate [for NP to V]]

in other words, from an NP analysed as a verbal argument in the main clause, to the same NP acting as a subject in the non-finite clause, we need to look at many different constructions with *for* in it, and also at other infinitival constructions that are close in form and/or meaning and therefore may have something to do with the change. Thus, we must consider benefactive constructions such as (6), which show a bare dative NP rather than a prepositional NP.

(6)   now were it tyme a lady to gon henne (Chaucer, *T&C* Bk III, 630)
      'Now it would be time [i.e. it would be proper] for a lady to leave'

We must also consider the rise of a new infinitival marker *for to*, which begins to appear in the early Middle English period next to the *to*-infinitive. What looks relevant in the same way, is the appearance at about the same time of constructions such as (7):

(7)   he ded of hys crowne and commaunded *the crowne to be sett* on the awter
                                             (Malory, *Morte d'Artur* 908. 11–12)
      'he took off his crown and ordered the crown to be placed on the altar'

which were replacing Old English constructions found in (8):

(8) seofon nihtum ær he gewite he het his byrgene geopenian (ÆCHom 11 108.556)
    seven nights before he departed he commanded his grave open
    'Seven days before he passed away, he ordered his grave to be opened'

In both (7) and (8), there is an NP immediately in front of the infinitive (*crowne* and *byrgene* respectively). In Old English this NP had an object function; in Middle English, however, this same NP came to be reanalysed as a subject (with the concomitant change of the active infinitive into a passive one). The result of this was that another infinitival structure arose containing a lexical subject, as represented in (5). It seems more than likely that the appearance of the construction in (7) also facilitated the appearance of the one in (2) (or the other way around) since *both* are new types of infinitivals in Middle English.

When these constructions were closely investigated (cf. Fischer 1988, 1989; Lightfoot 1991: ch. 4; Los 2005: ch. 9; Fischer *et al.* 2000a: ch. 7), it was discovered that both new types can be related to changes in word order that were taking place around that time,[8] and to the loss of distinction between dative and accusative case forms (for the latter, see also fn. 6). In Old English, the object of the verb tended to precede the verb in most infinitival clauses, which preverbal position was further strengthened by a frequent parallel order in finite subordinate clauses (in generative studies OV is usually said to be the basic word order of Old English). In Middle English, the verb–object word order becomes increasingly fixed to VO in all types of clauses. At the same time, the subject becomes firmly established in a position immediately before the predicate. This had as a result that an NP positioned *before* a verb became, as it were, automatically interpreted in Middle English as a subject, rather than as an object. It seems clear that for an explanation of developments such as the ones described above and even for a proper description, we must work with some theory of grammar. A notion of grammar is essential, a purely surface description of the data is not enough for morphosyntax.

It is interesting to compare, in this respect, an approach which does not distinguish an underlying structure, but which concentrates purely on surface forms. In Visser's (1973: 2250ff.) discussion of English infinitivals, no distinction is made between constructions such as *I saw him go, I persuade him to go,* and *I believe him to be a liar*. They are all, in his terms, VOSI structures (i.e. a **V**erb followed by an NP that functions as both **O**bject and **S**ubject, and an **I**nfinitive). In other words, it is not considered relevant whether the 'O/S' was originally a dative or accusative, whether the I(nfinitive) is marked by *to* or zero, nor what kind of permutations the constructions allow (i.e. no use is made of substitution tests to discover underlying structures, cf. Chomsky 1965; Huddleston 1971: 154ff; Fischer 1989: 175ff.). Visser does distinguish between eleven semantic classes that take VOSI structures. This leads to some systematization of the data. Such an approach, however, while perhaps adequate as to the semantic (functional) factors that played a role in the changes that the infinitivals underwent, does not do justice to the part played by formal matters. If abduction has taken place (as I have argued above), in which the original object is reanalysed as subject due to general changes in word order, it is form (position) as well as meaning that must be considered. Both have their own role to play, but form and function are also intimately linked on the level of the sign itself (on the importance of taking into account form as well as function in all types and cases of change, see also Chapter 3).

Another danger inherent in the comparison of syntactic structures, which is much less likely to occur in a diachronic comparison of phonological and morphological forms, is that there is a natural tendency to interpret an older construction very much from the point of view of the modern system (this concerns both form and function, see e.g. Lightfoot 1979: 34 ff., van der Horst 1986: 200–2). This happens especially when the form of the construction has remained more or less the same. On the morphological level, we are generally comparing single forms performing one particular function over time so that the interpretative possibilities are highly limited. While in the case of a morphological element its function may shift (in derivational affixes more than in inflectional ones), this is most unlikely to happen with phonological elements: in phonology, function does not come into the picture at all since phonemes do not themselves carry referential meaning but only serve to make a distinction in meaning.[9] In syntax, however, we are concerned with structures containing a combination of elements. This has a number of consequences, which may be relevant to their interpretation, and hence to change. In other words, on the levels of morphology and phonology, there is simply not so much room in terms of stress, intonation, individual meanings and connotations of the enclosed elements, or in terms of permutation of the order of elements to create functional differences as there is on the syntactic level.

First, the individual components within a syntactic structure may each have acquired a different function with respect to the other, even if their position has remained the same (because of possible structural changes or new structural patterns elsewhere). Secondly, the lexical items involved in a syntactic structure may change in meaning and/or phonetic form and may thus have an influence on the function of the whole. Thirdly, each structure, representing a combination of forms, may carry some meaning itself over and above the meaning of the individual elements (cf. Bisang 1998: 14–20; Hampe and Schönefeld 2003). For instance, in English, the two structures *He has to write a letter* and *He has a letter to write* both contain the same elements and indeed they derive from just one structure in Old English, viz. the one with the order *He has a letter to write*. The question then is, are these two modern structures the same or do they perform different functions? If they have two different functions (meanings), did the Old English form contain both these meanings or just one of them? Additionally, if we change the lexical content of the object NP *letter*, does that make a difference to the structure? Note that the clause *He has nothing to do*, with the 'old' order, has a rather different sense from *He has to do nothing*. This was not yet the case in Old English, where only the order *He has nothing to do* occurs, with *nothing* functioning syntactically as the object of *has*, and the *to*-infinitive depending on *nothing*. In Old English this *to*-infinitive represented general modality, and its precise interpretation (of necessity, possibility, etc.) depended on the context. In the modern construction, however, where *have* is immediately followed by the *to*-infinitive, the meaning has been narrowed to 'necessity', *except* in phrases with a NP before the infinitive, where the older, more general meaning current in Old English has been preserved.[10]

I will now briefly illustrate how older syntactic constructions may be misinterpreted because they are seen through the lens of the present-day grammar-system. The first example again involves the new infinitival development discussed above. The clause in (9) occurs in a late Middle English text:

(**9**) God bade the rede See divide (c. 1390, Gower *CA* 5: 1661, Macauley 1900–01)
'God commanded the Red Sea [to] divide'

This particular sentence is ambiguous because it could be interpreted according to the Old English OV structure, that is with *See* as the object of *divide* or as the new, late Middle English VO construction with *See* as the subject of *divide,* making the verb intransitive. Macauley, the editor of this text (the fourteenth-century *Confessio Amantis* by John Gower) indeed reads *divide* as intransitive, that is as a 'modern' construction (as is clear from the entry of 'divide' in his glossary), even though the *OED* indicates that the intransitive use of 'divide' is found only from 1526 onwards. It is possible that the *OED* date is wrong here, of course, but what I want to emphasize is that the editor does not even consider the other, older interpretation, which was still current in Gower's time and hence more likely here in view of the *OED* evidence.

In the case of *divide*, the editor's misanalysis towards a modern construction is not so serious since the mistake is really one of timing. After all, the new construction with a subject and intransitive infinitive does become the rule later (the old one dies out). The editor's misanalysis is also not so obvious since the sense of the clause remains more or less the same, and indeed this must have made the later reinterpretation possible. Often a syntactic reanalysis takes place first in those positions where it does not disturb communication or where both meanings are possible but where by pragmatic inferencing from frequently occurring contextual situations, one interpretation may ultimately come to be preferred, which may at some later stage cause the construction to change formally. Aitchison (2001: 99–100) notes that syntactic changes 'nearly always steal in at a single, vulnerable point in the language', 'in an almost underhand way ... like a disease which can get a hold on a person before it is diagnosed'.

In some cases, however, an editor's misinterpretation is more serious. I described one such instance in Fischer (1991: 146–51), which concerns the translation of the BE + *to*-infinitive construction in Old English. Editors often equate this construction to the modern one where BE + *to*-infinitive can only express necessity, as in *Who is to go next?* ('Who must go next?'), *He is to blame* ('He deserves censure, he must be blamed'). In Old English only a so-called passival infinitive was possible with *beon to* (i.e. an infinitive active in form but passive in meaning, as we still see in the relic structure *He is to blame*), which however carried all sorts of modal shades, and not necessarily one of necessity, as (10a) and (b) respectively illustrate:

(**10a**) ... þæt hi him geræddon hwæt him be ðam selost ðuhte oððe to done wære.

(LS 26 (MildredCockayne)72)

... that they him advised what them about that best seemed or to do were
'that they would advise him what seemed best to them in this matter or what could/should/might be done'

(10b) þæt *is to geþencanne* þeoda gehwylcum, wisfæstum werum, hwæt seo
that is to think   of-people for-each,   for-wise   men,   what this
wiht   sy   (*Riddles* 41.8)
creature   be
'it *is possible* for each one of us, for wise men, *to find out* what this creature
might be'

These examples show how important it is for a correct analysis of historical
syntactic structures to have a sense of the synchronic system of the language at the time in which the structure was used. Too strong a reliance on
the present-day system of grammar of the language in question may result
in the wrong analysis.

We have seen that editors (philologists) may make mistakes because of
their neglect of the synchronic system of grammar operating at the time of
the text under investigation. Misinterpretation, however, also occurs
among theoretical linguists. Too strong an adherence to a theory of grammar, to which synchronic systems should conform, may then blur their
vision. Having one eye fixed on the theory must not lead to neglect of the
historical details themselves.[11] Instances can be found both within the
formal and the functional schools, where 'theory-driven' historical linguists
misinterpret the meaning and grammatical use of a particular historical
utterance because they are too pre-occupied with the hypothesis suggested
by their theory. Thus, one linguist, believing that the theory of grammaticalization predicts that OE/ME *habban/have(n) + to*-infinitive must
undergo a slow gradual development from a full possessive verb followed
by the *to*-infinitive into a semi-modal verb of obligation—because this
happens to be a well-known grammaticalization path in other languages
(cf. e.g. Heine and Kuteva 2002: 243–5)—'forces' Middle English examples
to fit the particular stages dictated by the theory, translating the instances
in (11), as if they already contain a modal verb *have(n) to*, 'must':

(11a) For love and joy I had to se her (Malory, *Wks* Vinaver 1967: 421,13)
(11b) ne hast you nat to faste (Chaucer, *Melibee* 2240)

No attempt was made to check the context, which in (11a) would have
made clear that there is a clause boundary between *had* and *to*, so that the
translation is 'For the love and joy (that) I had, to see her' (i.e. with *to se*
dependent on *joy* and not on *had*), while it would have been clear in (11b)
that *hast* in this case is not a form of *have(n)* but of *hasten*, so that the
translation is 'do not hasten to fast' rather than 'you do not have to fast'
(for a discussion see Fischer 1994a).

Another 'functional school' example is provided by Haspelmath (1989), who argues on the basis of grammaticalization parameters distinguished by Lehmann (1982 [1995]) that in most European (and many non-European) languages infinitive-like forms follow a universal path of gradual desemanticization whereby an originally purposive element becomes a formal marker of the infinitive (for this tendency, see again Heine and Kuteva 2002: 247–8). Haspelmath works this out in detail for German *zu*, implying that a similar development took place with cognate English *to* and Dutch *te*. Even though the developments in the different languages are similar to a certain degree, it is very interesting to note also how different the developments are, especially between German *zu* and Dutch *te* on the one hand, and English *to* on the other. It can be shown (cf. Fischer 1997) that English *to*, which followed the 'German' desemanticization route at first, up until the end of the medieval period, began to move in a rather different direction from the early Modern period onwards. This new direction was steered not by the 'universal grammaticalization path' but by internal structural developments taking place in English (to some extent again related to the new infinitival constructions that appeared around this time, as discussed above), which caused the *to* element to move a step back on the grammaticalization cline towards a more meaningful and syntactically more independent element again. This case, once more, shows that one must be careful with general principles or tendencies dictated by a theory. The synchronic linguistic circumstances of the language in question also play a role and must be investigated.

An instance involving formal theory, can be found in Lightfoot's (1981) discussion of the effect that the so-called TEP, the Trace Erasure Principle (a principle that formed part of the then current generative version of grammar), had on the disappearance of the Old English impersonal construction. Lightfoot's data consist in the first place of the four hypothetical instances used earlier by Jespersen (1909–49, Vol.3) to explain the various stages of the change:

(**12a**) OE   þam cynge[DAT] licodon[pl] peran[NOM pl]
(**12b**) early ME   the king liceden[pl] peares
(**12c**) late ME   the king liked pears
(**12d**) early ModE   he liked pears

For (12a), the Old English stage, Jespersen (and Lightfoot following him) argues that *peran* functions unambiguously as the subject, as can be seen from the fact that *licodon* has a plural ending. At the early Middle English stage (12b), *peares* is still the only candidate for subject—even though *king* has lost its dative case ending *-e*—since the verb still clearly has a plural ending. At stage (12c), late Middle English, this interpretation becomes ambiguous because, with the loss of the verbal ending, both *king* and *pears* could now function as subject. Example (12d) no longer allows the earlier interpretation, that is the earlier dative argument has now clearly been reinterpreted as subject.

Lightfoot concentrates on these four stages when he shows how the TEP, a universal principle of grammar, forces the reanalysis and can thus be seen as the cause of the change. The theoretical motivation for the TEP is that traces which are left by movement rules can only be erased by a designated morpheme, such as empty *there* or *it* (cf. Dresher and Hornstein 1979). In order for an Old English speaker to generate construction (12a), the subject NP *peran* needs to be moved from its base (i.e. initial) position to a position after the verb (according to the theory used by Lightfoot, Old English is an SOV language). A late Middle English speaker confronted with a construction such as (12c) has a problem because his basic word order is SVO. In order to process the old structure, he would have to move the original subject *pears* into a preverbal position and the original object *king* into a postverbal position, that is he must move not only *pears* but also *king*, as follows:

(13)

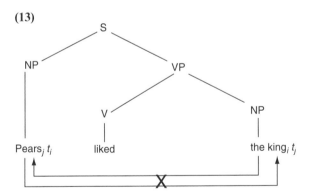

This move would be in violation of the TEP since *pears*, when moved, leaves a trace, and this trace cannot be erased by *king*, when that moves as well. In other words, the Middle English SVO speaker is forced by the TEP to reanalyse the structure to one in which *king* is now the subject and *pears* the object.

In itself, this explanation is transparent and plausible since it is invoked by an independently motivated principle of the theory of grammar. There are two problems, however. One is that the theory in the meantime has not stood still. The TEP no longer plays a role in the Minimalist version of generative grammar because the type of movement rules used in the Principles and Parameters (henceforth P&P) framework no longer exists (cf. Chomsky 1995), and according to at least one Minimalist version all languages are said to be underlyingly SVO (cf. Kayne 1994). In other words, an explanation in terms of the TEP is no longer viable. The explanation would have to be reworded in terms of the strong or weak features that a language is said to possess in Minimalist theory, because it is the strength of the features that now decides whether a language becomes SOV on the surface.[12] Secondly, and this is much more serious, the data that the explanation is primarily based on are reconstructed data. When we consider the impersonal data in detail in Old English documents, the type of construction with a postposed subject (i.e. (12a)) turns out to be not the only one and not the most frequent one. Other word orders and other case-forms (for the two thematic roles involved, i.e. 'experiencer' and 'source/cause') occur with impersonal verbs as well, as illustrated in (14):

(**14a**) Ac him[DAT] ne   ofhreow na þæs deofles hryre[NOM] (*ÆCHom* I, 13 281.14)
        and to-him   not was-pity not of-the devil's fall
        'The devil's fall did not cause pity in him'

(**14b**) For ði him[DAT] ofhreow þæs   mannes [GEN] (*ÆCHom* I, 13 281.12)
        for that to-him   was-pity of-the man
        'Therefore he felt sorry for the man'

(**14c**) Hwæt þa se mæssepreost[NOM] þæs mannes[GEN] ofhreow
                                (*ÆLS* (Oswald) B1.3.26)
        what then the priest   of-the man   was-pity
        'Lo then, the priest took pity on the man'

Example (14a) has the order as illustrated in Jespersen's made-up example, that is with an 'experiencer'-object in preverbal position, and the 'source/cause'-subject argument placed postverbally. Sentence (14b) has the experiencer-object again in preverbal position but here the postverbal source-argument is not a subject. In (14c) the experiencer-role is now expressed by the subject, and placed before the verb, while the source-role is syntactically expressed in the genitive and also put preverbally. It is clear that in (14b) and (14c), there need be no swapping around of both subject and object—(14b) has no subject and in (14c) the subject is already in preverbal position—and hence the TEP does not apply (for more details on this case, see Fischer and van der Leek 1983, 1987; Allen 1986; MacMahon 1994: 129–37).

Thus, when one takes a more careful look at the *actual* data, it is quite possible that the change concerning the impersonals does not so much represent a case of reanalysis as one of loss of some of the variant constructions. This seems to be true not only for the history of English but also for other languages which had impersonal variants such as the ones illustrated in (14), such as Middle Dutch (cf. van de Velde 2004).

1.1.3 The use of translated texts and problems connected with this

Another difference applying to the various linguistic levels in our investigation of change is the way in which we should deal with *calques*. Historical sources are mostly written sources, which are frequently based on other written sources in a different language. In the translation process, it is the lexical and the syntactic levels that may be most affected, but each in different ways.

Spelling and phonology can be affected to some extent, but the effect of this is on the whole marginal. For instance, in Middle English texts the spelling has changed in the case of OE <u>, which comes to be written <u> and <ou> to distinguish short from long vowels on the analogy of the use of <ou> for the long vowel [u:] in French. Other spelling changes introduced under the influence of French after the Norman conquest of 1066 have to do with real changes in the phonological system. For instance, <v> and <f> begin to be used in Middle English to represent the voiced and voiceless labial fricatives, [v] and [f]. In Old English only <f> was part of the alphabet since [f] and [v] were still allophones—hence there was no need for a typographic difference. Spellings therefore are not *directly* influenced by the spelling system or the sound system of the source text; they are mostly inserted systematically in those places where the new spelling is functional.

On the morphological level, borrowing of affixes occurs but again these are usually not direct calques of a foreign affix, taken straight from the source text. Rather they begin to occur only when the foreign language has become so familiar to the native speaker, that he subconsciously substitutes foreign affixes for native ones; this happens only when these foreign elements have become part of his grammatical *system*. Affixes are calqued at first *only* as part of a complete lexical unit borrowed; in other words, this is calquing on the lexical and not on the morphological level. For instance, the late fourteenth-century English author Chaucer uses French affixes frequently in French words taken directly from his French sources. Thus, we see lexical items like *mesurable, servysable, chivalrye, briberye, argument, avisement* quite frequently in his texts. However, the use of a French affix with a native stem is rare: the only examples in all of Chaucer's works are *unknowable, housbondrye, robberie,* and *eggement* (all four occur only once, see Marchand 1969).[13] This shows that it takes quite a few generations for the foreign affixes to become part of the native system (cf. Burnley 1992: 445–6). What may have helped the influx of French affixes (and later also many Latin ones) in the case of English is that many native (Old English) affixes had been lost in the period of the Norse and Norman invasions. This, as it were, created a systemic gap that had to be refilled.

As mentioned above, calquing or borrowing on the lexical level is very frequent, and therefore an important factor in lexical change. It is also easy to spot since the calquing involves the replacement of one native element by a foreign one, which is itself clearly present in the source text. The calquing or borrowing of syntactic constructions is a much more delicate matter, however, because here there is no replacement of concrete and clearly visible elements. Instead, we are dealing with native elements which are possibly arranged according to a foreign structure.[14] This kind of replacement may well occur on a less conscious level in the mind of the translator. In glosses, where the glossator provides an interlinear translation which follows the original text word for word, the calque is likely to be literal and directly influenced by the original. These are not so hard to discern. For this reason, it is advisable to discard such glosses as syntactic evidence of what can be generated by the system of grammar of speakers at that time. The matter is different when the glossator translates more idiomatically or phrase by phrase. This is also the way in which most text-translators work. If such a glossator or translator changes the word order of the original phrase or if he inserts lexical elements that do not occur in the foreign construction, this may be under the influence of his native language. Such (less literal) constructions are therefore of interest to the historical linguist, but they must be used with great care. The linguist must make a careful comparison of the syntactic constructions in the translated texts with similar ones occurring in original texts. He should ignore syntactic constructions which are never found in original prose (cf. also fn. 8 above).

There are two further problems to be noted here. First of all there are languages whose record consists only of translated texts. This is the case with Gothic, for instance. In such a case evidence from related languages may be invoked, but there will never be any certainty as to the type of sentences that the grammar of Gothic could generate. For the history of a language like English, this problem is not so great in that there are enough original texts available for proper comparison.

A much bigger problem concerns those translated syntactic constructions that are close to native ones, and/or which do appear in purely native prose at some later stage. The question then is, are these constructions developments of existing native structures, are they borrowed, or did they become possible because they were available in the foreign source and fitted the native grammatical system somehow? In these cases it is often the linguist's intuitions about the language in question that decide. The more he has read in that language, the better his intuitions will be. It is also important that the historical linguist is not hampered too much by intuitions derived from his knowledge of the same language at the present-day stage (see also §1.1.2). Other factors that may help to decide what is borrowed and what is not, are matters such as: does the text read clumsily in comparison to native texts; does it show heavy borrowing on the lexical level; what are the kinds of (often minimal) alterations that the translator inserts into the structure that the foreign text uses, making the structure closer to a native one? It is interesting, if possible, to compare two or more translations of the same text in cases such as these. This may give a clue as to the quality of the translation.[15] Other help as to whether a structure is native or not may be provided by evidence from sister languages, where available. If none of them have the structure in question, borrowing is more likely.

As to the ease with which foreign elements may be adopted, all linguists agree that lexical borrowing takes place most frequently and effortlessly because lexical items can be easily detached from the donor language, even when a speaker is unfamiliar with this language. It is also well-known that such borrowed lexical items will be closely adapted in the course of time to the receiving language both phonologically and morphologically.

There is, however, much less agreement on the extent of syntactic borrowing. One school of thought maintains that structural borrowing takes
place mainly through substratum influence—which entails the presence of
a large number of imperfect learners mixing the language they have to learn
with structures that are entrenched in their native grammar—or in cases of
prolonged and intense oral language contact. Thus, there is for instance
general agreement about a Celtic substratum in Irish English or about
borrowed structures in the Balkan Sprachbund area. When one of these
two constraints does not apply, for instance in the case of a source language
with prestige, syntactic borrowings are considered to be likely only when
the structure to be borrowed more or less fits the rules of the target language (cf. Thomason and Kaufman 1988; Fischer 1992a; van der Wurff 1990:
139; Aitchison 2001; Bisang 1998: 14, and the discussion in Harris and
Campbell 1995: 121–2).

Harris and Campbell (1995: 120–50), however, are of the opinion that
syntactic borrowing is much more frequent than is generally assumed and
is not bound to constraints such as the above. They state that the 'insistence
that grammatical borrowing happens only in situations of shared structural
similarity [involving structural compatibility, syntactic gaps, as well as
renewal] is simply wrong' (p. 124). They quote a fair number of case studies
to prove their point but do not go into any of them in any detail, which
makes it hard to judge whether these cases do not in fact involve substratum situations or long, intensive contact involving large parts of the
population (where indeed it is agreed that any kind of borrowing becomes
possible).[16] More useful in this respect is the 'borrowing scale' set up by
Thomason (2001: 70–1) (note that a similar plea is made by Lass (1997:
189) i.e. to set up a 'hierarchy of borrowability'), which indicates that
syntactic structures are only likely to be borrowed when a combination
of factors prevails, such as intensity of contact, length of contact, number
of speakers involved, bilingualism and/or quite special social circumstances
or attitudes. The latter is clearly the case in the Media Lengua situation
described by Muysken (1981) and discussed by Harris and Campbell (1995:
124) as an example of the ease of syntactic borrowing. Media Lengua is an
Amerindian contact language spoken in several communities in the Equa-
dorian Highlands. The language is Quechua in its grammar, but its lexicon
is almost completely Spanish. It has native speakers as well as speakers who
are bilingual or trilingual (Spanish and Quechua being the other languages). Muysken (1981: 75) believes that this language came into existence

'because acculturated Indians could not identify completely with either the traditional rural Q[uecha] culture, or the urban Sp[anish] culture', and that it was therefore not communicative needs but special 'expressive needs' that led to the development of Media Lengua.

A good case to show the difficulties and subtle judgements involved is again provided by the treatment of the infinitivals in English. Miller (2002: 179) believes that certain types of ECM constructions (traditionally called 'accusative-and-infinitive constructions'),[17] such as ECMs with *wh*-movement (e.g. *Whom I believe to be a liar*) were already grammatical in Old English and that after some 'reflective' verbs (verbs of mental perception, such as 'know', 'believe', 'consider') ECMs were 'marginally grammatical' (Miller 2002: 172–5). Miller's evidence for their grammaticality comes exclusively from texts closely dependent on Latin (such as the translation of Bede's *Historia Ecclesiastica Gentis Anglorum* ['Ecclesiastical History of the English people'], the translation of the Benedictine Rule, the glosses added to the Latin grammar of Ælfric) and is crucially based on the fact that Old English allowed 'small clause' constructions with these verbs, that is constructions of the type *I believe him a liar*. In other words, Old English did have constructions that could be expanded into true ECM structures by adding an infinitive such as *be*. The question remains, though, why there are no occurrences of ECMs with an infinitival verb after these 'reflective' verbs in original Old English texts. Do we have to accept that these constructions are (marginally) grammatical in Old English *because* they have become grammatical in the late Middle English period? Additional evidence from closely related languages such as German and Dutch, which are syntactically much closer to Old English than Modern English is, suggests that such ECM constructions were not native to Old English: in Dutch and German these ECM constructions never established themselves in original prose, as they did in later English. Other linguists (e.g. Warner 1982; Fischer 1989, 1992a, 1994b; Los 2005) have therefore suggested that the ECM constructions in Old English were the result of Latin influence. They were later 'able to creep in' via vulnerable spots in the language, such as the above-mentioned 'small clauses', and also via complements with a bare infinitive after physical perception verbs (as in, *I saw him disappear*), and via the word order change to SVO in Middle English (see above, §1.1.2). All these facilitated the later change, and turned the ECM into a construction generated by the native grammar of late Middle English. In the end, it is up to the investigator to decide whether the evidence brought forward in favour of or against ECM constructions in Old English is strong enough in each case.

In a similar case studied by van der Wurff (1989), also involving Latin influence, it is shown that a peculiar parasitic gap construction found in classical Latin (of the type, *A man, whom if you know, you must love*) gets a foothold in formal/literary writings in Renaissance English, but never becomes part of the grammar. Van der Wurff concludes that this negative result is due to the fact that it could not be integrated easily into the native English grammar system.

These two instances of syntactic borrowing with rather different results are interesting since the source and target languages are in both cases the same. The fact that one Latin construction became an integral part of English, and the other did not may suggest something about the ease/difficulty of syntactic borrowing in cases of prestige: that is a syntactic structure borrowed from a prestige language seems to become integrated into that language only when it fits its native grammar without difficulty. Van Coetsem (2000: 216–17) suggests as much in his theory of the transmission process in language contact. He notes that in cases of phonetic and syntactic borrowing, target languages apply the 'extended mode of borrowing', which involves the 'extended application of imitation' (i.e. inclusion and integration) rather than 'adaptation', and that instability is an immanent feature of this 'extended mode'. In the case of the parasitic gap construction, the new structure was indeed 'imitated' and 'included' wholesale, but not adapted, and for this reason was short-lived. In the case of the ECM construction, however, the new structure could be truly 'adapted' to the native syntax because the grammar of English had seen the development of similar constructions (cf. examples (2)–(8) above); hence it could become part and parcel of the grammar of the target language.

1.2 Internal and external factors in morphosyntactic change

We will have a closer look at the internal and external factors that play a role in morphosyntactic change in Chapter 3. Here I would like to concentrate on two general questions: To what extent *can* we make a distinction between internal and external factors, (i) in theory, and (ii) in any individual case of change? As to question (i), it is clear that a dichotomy such as this may be useful from a theoretical or methodological point of view, because in that way, one may create order in a collection of seemingly loose facts or data. However, even though we may 'behave as if the notions "internal" and "external" [are] clear-cut terms which [can] be used in a straightforward way', reading the literature on these terms or considering how individual linguists use these terms, soon shows up the 'heterogeneity of conceptions of this dichotomy' (Gerritsen and Stein 1992b: 7).

If we mean by 'internal', anything 'inherent in, or arising out of, any given synchronic state of the language system' (ibid.), we would probably not include 'economic' factors, such as when structures change through the speed and frequency of delivery. Still, a change in speed is said to be crucial to the development of a pidgin into a creole, which by most creolists is seen as an internal factor. For some formal generative linguists, any change that is triggered from outside the central module of syntax, is considered to be not internal, so changes on the phonetic or the lexical level will be seen as external factors (see further §1.2.1). In a similar way, it is difficult to ascertain to what extent psycholinguistic factors, like 'ease of effort' (e.g. assimilation) and perceptual strategies may be said to be internal. This depends on whether they are seen as related to the 'mind' of the individual speaker, or whether they are a result of the make-up of the system itself; and again they may be seen as due to the requirements of communicative economy. In sum, it is not surprising that some linguists see frequency, economy, and perceptual (psychological) factors as internal (e.g. Bresnan and Aissen 2002), while others, generative linguists but also grammaticalization theorists (e.g. Haspelmath 2004: 563–4), consider them external.

If by 'external' we mean 'the forces arising out of the location and use of language in society' (Gerritsen and Stein 1992b: 7), it is clear that all factors of a social nature (such as fashion, language contact, prestige, community norms, etc.) belong here. The factor of economy, when it is related to speaker interaction (cf. Grice's maxims of quantity and manner),[18] may then also be said to be an external factor. Alternatively, if we see internal factors as involving the 'physiology of human speech organs' and psychological aspects concerned with 'the perception, processing and learning of language', and external factors as ones 'being largely outside of language *per se* (outside the human organism)' (Harris and Campbell 1995: 316), then one may wonder under which heading the 'expressive' use of language should be placed; is it psychological or social, or both? It is obvious, in other words, that the notions of 'internal/external' depend to a large extent on the theory within which one chooses to work.

Another point that Gerritsen and Stein (1992b: 8) make, which relates question (i) above to (ii), is whether it is 'possible and useful to hypostasize an abstract, non-observable entity as something logically separate from use, speakers and speech community'. Dorian (1993) stresses the danger of such a position and highlights it as a general problem in all scientific endeavour:

'Dichotomy', writes paleontologist Stephen Jay Gould, 'is the usual pathway to vulgarization. We take a complex web of arguments and divide it into two polarized positions' (1984: 7). Gould was writing with special reference to 'the false antithesis between nature and nurture', but this point is equally well taken in the case of many other simplistic dichotomies, including some which are dear to linguists. [...]

Dichotomies have the effect of nudging us in the direction of an either/or distinction. The responsibility for this may lie with the user of the dichotomy, but it is certainly encouraged when the terms of the dichotomy are themselves antonyms, as is the case with *internal* and *external* in the phrases 'internally motivated change' and 'externally motivated change'. (Dorian 1993: 131–2)

The point I wish to make is that we may use the dichotomy of internal/external factors as a working method but that we must not fall into the trap of forcing each *explanandum* (each case to be explained) in linguistic change—which usually concerns a combination of internal and external factors—into the same dichotomous mould. Gerritsen and Stein (1992b), indeed, warn us against preconceived notions about changes being typically either of an internal or an external nature and draw our attention to the last of the seven general principles drawn up by Weinreich, Labov, and Herzog (1968) in their 'Empirical foundations for a theory of language change':

Linguistic and social factors are closely interrelated in the development of language change. Explanations which are confined to one or the other aspect, no matter how well constructed, will fail to account for the rich body of regularities that can be observed in empirical studies of language behavior. (Weinreich *et al.* 1968: 188)[19]

To help clarify which factors may be at work in actual cases of change, I think it pays to make a distinction between 'innovation' and 'change' as done, for example, by Milroy (1992, 1993).[20] An 'innovation' by an individual speaker represents the beginning of what may but need not become a 'change' (Harris and Campbell (1995) refer to such innovations as 'exploratory expressions'). It seems likely that in most cases such an innovation is carried out with an 'intention' (by which I do not imply that speakers are necessarily *conscious* of what they do); that is, it is motivated 'teleologically' (in the sense used by Shapiro 1991: 10), or 'finally' (in Keller's (1994) terms, cf. fn. 24 below). This motivation may be related to the linguistic system or it may involve social accommodation due to speaker contact. According to Milroy (1992: 200–5), whose work concentrates on sound change, most innovations are due to speaker contact via what he calls 'weak links', and they involve speaker identity and community norms. Hence they are motivated socially. Milroy recognizes that the motivation may also be structural, that is related to the linguistic system.[21]

It is likely that speaker-innovation in the area of sound change is more often socially rather than linguistically motivated, since, as noted in §1.1.2, phonetic elements are not 'meaningful' in the way morphosyntactic elements are. Also it is well-known that speakers are more aware of phonetic, and lexical, variation than of (morpho)syntactic variation, since the former concerns elements physically present, whereas the latter usually involves abstract structures.[22] Lexical and phonetic differences are therefore more likely to function as accent or dialect markers than syntactic differences, and hence are more likely to be motivated socially. I believe that the situation is rather different in the case of morphosyntactic change and that internal systemic factors play a more important role there. In this area, propagation may depend more on an increase in frequency through multiple innovations and analogy than on social attitudes.

Structural motivation in innovation may involve the (originally phonetic) notion of 'ease of effort' (see also fn. 21). In the case of morphosyntactic change, ease of effort could be 'translated' as the 'easy' adoption of patterns that are a slight extension of the original one, that is, it would be an analogical process (for more details, see below and Chapter 3).[23] An innovation may also be motivated structurally so as to preserve a maximal distance to other structures/elements in the system (push- and drag-chains); or it may be caused by the fact that the speaker is an adult learner and produces a new structure through interference with the system of his native language (substratum influence, which is an external factor). In all these cases innovations may spring up spontaneously in different individual speakers (depending on how much less 'effort' it takes, or on how many substratum speakers there are), and may hence cause a change to move faster if indeed the innovation develops into one.

Granted that a morphosyntactic 'innovation' is more likely to be caused by factors related to the language system than to social contact, an ensuing 'change' may also be helped further by social factors. A typical linguistic change follows an S-curve. The first stage of this curve is slow. This may be because only a small number of contexts are affected or the change itself is still in its innovatory phase and restricted to a small number of individual innovators. When the change speeds up and its frequency increases, this could be due to social factors like prestige, normative consensus and imitation, although the factor of frequency itself is also important, as mentioned earlier (cf. Croft 2000, quoted in fn. 20 above). There may be a relation between frequency and the way our brains perceive or interpret language. It is possible that once a change has reached a certain threshold (a point at which an old and a new variant are almost equally frequent), that speakers no longer perceive any variation but perceive only one form, usually the new form. This could be compared to the visual experience we have with typical Escher engravings. In these we can spot either birds or fish but not both at the same time (for illustrations, see the Escher website: http://www.mcescher.nl.indexuk.htm).

Note that when this point is reached, the variation probably has lost its initial motivation, and hence there is no reason for a speaker to be aware of a difference. Thus, he may ignore the old variant even when he hears it, and in fact not even 'hear' it. The spread is now no longer motivated teleologic- ally but 'causally', following the laws of natural systems.[24] Once a change is driven by causal factors, the change becomes law-like and in general unstoppable. It explains why the Neogrammarians saw sound changes as laws, as taking place simultaneously across the board, and as exceptionless. They were looking at the results of a change, at the situation after the change, ignoring the early innovation stage and the stages where variation was still the rule. In addition, innovations that never made it, were simply not noticed. The causal nature of the second part of the change also explains the orderly heterogeneity that Labov found in community behav- iour (cf. also fn. 24). At the innovation stage of any change, there is nothing orderly about it.

Still on the topic of innovation versus change, it is crucial to distinguish between the various ways in which a morphosyntactic innovation may diffuse. It may diffuse gradually across the lexicon working in the same way as lexical diffusion in sound change, with structures 'clutch[ing] on to particular lexical items' (Aitchison 2001: 105). Thus, a new construction may spread paradigmatically from verb to verb-class (by formal and semantic analogy) or from verb-class to another semantically or formally similar verb-class. For instance, Barron (2001) and Fischer (1989) show how the similarity between physical perception verbs (*see, hear*) and mental perception verbs (*see, hear, seem, know, perceive*) accounts for the spread of raising constructions and ECM constructions respectively. A structure may also 'worm' its way in further by an extension of the type of arguments that it may take. This is how the grammaticalized BE + *going to*-expression spread slowly from animate subject agents to inanimate subjects, while the nature of the infinitive following it changed from concrete to more abstract.[25] Bybee (2003) shows in detail how a similar extension spread the use of *can* in the history of English, transforming it from a full verb into a modal auxiliary. Here again this happened on the basis of formal and semantic analogies with other already existing verbal patterns.

So far the discussion has concerned examples involving internal linguistic factors. Further spread of a new construction may take place via a shift from colloquial to more formal styles (frequency again is important for this shift; it makes the new variant less 'awkward'), and from social class to social class (this shift in turn may also be related to prestige and/or the 'formality' parameter). With each type of spread, the frequency of the new variant increases so that in time it is likely to become a fixed part of the grammar. Once in this position it may even oust other variants with which it is layered (for the notion of layering cf. Hopper 1991, and §3.2, fn. 27), or take over some of their properties (cf. fn. 25 above).

What this distinction into 'innovation' (caused, on the morphosyntactic level, mainly by systemic, 'final' factors) and 'change' (caused by frequency, social and/or systemic factors) also shows is that it is not easy to make a distinction between internal (intra-linguistic) and external (extra-linguistic) causes in each case of change. Thus, an innovation may be motivated by internal factors but its adoption may also be facilitated by social ones. Likewise, substratum influence has to do with the system of a second language impinging on a first language (so is of an internal linguistic nature), but the fact that there is substratum influence at all has to do with an external non-linguistic factor, that is the presence of a large number of second-language learners in a speech community.

1.2.1 'Internal' versus 'external': the relation between the morphosyntactic, and the phonological and semantic components

Within the generative framework, sometimes a more narrow interpretation is given to the difference between internal and external factors in change (cf. also Heine 1994: 256). Clark and Roberts (1993: 340), for instance, write: 'In our terms, innovation may arise from one of two sources: either internally, when a parametric change makes new constructions available, or externally, when phonological or morphological change weakens evidence for certain hypotheses'.[26] Internal factors, in other words, refer here only to syntax, the influence coming from all other levels is seen as external.[27] Indeed, in their article on how language change comes about and can be understood (its aim is to develop a computational learning model), linguistic factors are the only ones discussed, no mention is made anywhere of the kind of social factors that have been termed external by most linguists. It is interesting too that the semantic/pragmatic level does not seem to play any role at all. Quite clearly, in the view of Clark and Roberts, only formal (physically present) variation is seen as a possible trigger for change.

Clark and Roberts' position is easily understood from within the generative tradition. From the very start Chomsky distinguished between a central syntactic component and two 'purely interpretive' (Chomsky 1965: 16) components: phonology and semantics. This is still the position in Chomsky's Minimalist program, even though the names have changed and the position of morphology has shifted (see fn. 27): a dividing line is drawn between the cognitive (computational) system of the language faculty and the performance and conceptual-intentional systems, which access information stored in the central computational system. For Chomsky it is therefore unlikely (and definitely undesirable) that the requirements of the PF (Phonetic Form) and LF (Logical Form) levels 'turn out to be critical factors in determining the inner nature of C_{HL} [the computational system] in some deep sense' (Chomsky 1995: 221).[28]

If the phonological and semantic components are seen as interpretive and hence dependent on the central system for their input, it is not surprising that these two components are also seen as external as regards change. Even though generative studies of change now devote more attention to what is called the Primary Linguistic Data (PLD) because they see a close connection between language acquisition and language change, on the whole the PLD is not seen as providing a *direct* trigger for grammar change. Clark and Roberts (1993), for instance, assume that learners, by means of a learning device, match all the potential values for each parameter against the PLD (i.e. the device steers the interpretation of the input, not the other way around), and when the input data do not unambiguously force the setting of a certain parameter, then 'the learner must evaluate its [i.e. of the learning device] hypotheses using criteria that are not purely a response to the external environment' (Clark and Roberts 1993: 301). They assume that the learner will rely on the Fitness Metric to select from the alternatives at hand. In their discussion, it is not quite clear what the status of this learning device is: on the one hand it is separate from the biological grammar (UG), on the other, it must, for its hypotheses, rely on what UG makes available (cf. the way a similar device is used by Lightfoot below). An inherent part of this device is the 'overall elegance of representations and the number of superset settings' (1993: 319). This makes clear that the triggers for change may, but need not be, the PLD.

What is considered to be a trigger in each case, therefore, depends heavily on the content of the theory. Lightfoot (1999) follows a similar scenario. He sees the PLD or the linguistic input children receive as a store of physical, incomplete and often rather degenerate data, from which the child collects 'cues' by means of some sort of partial parsing. These cues are called 'designated cues' because they are specified by UG, the idea being that children match their cues against UG. These cues, then, are said to represent the child's 'triggering experience'. The PLD is not *directly* the trigger in the child's learning process, in other words, but abstract structures or cues derived from it. This point is related to the question of whether the object of study should be grammar change or language change; we will return to this in Chapter 3.

1.2.2 An elusive 'external' factor: the role played by the development of a written standard

A language (or grammar) may also change when a written medium is developed, and this in turn may influence the spoken language. Changes that occur in such a case are less directly related to the historical chronological development of a language, but are mainly caused by the non-immediacy of the context in which texts are written and the different purpose for which they are written. One needs to make a careful distinction, therefore, between these changes and others so as not to attribute such changes in too simple a way to possible internal factors in the system.

A fair amount of syntactic research in this area has been conducted, especially by German scholars, as shown by the references in Feilke *et al.* (2001) (and see also Weiß 2004; Cheshire and Stein 1997). These studies show that languages which have developed a written standard undergo what the editors call a 'Verschriftlichung der Sprache', that is the language is 'moulded' both in its form and in the way it is interpreted by the forms of the written standard: 'Die Schrift ... wird zum Motiv einer weitergehenden Sprachanalyse, sie wird zum Motiv grammatischer Analyse und der professionellen Grammatik*schreibung* selbst' (Feilke *et al.* 2001: 18). It means, in a somewhat free translation, that a written standard influences the language both theoretically (in the way we interpret grammar as linguists) and practically. The influence of *Verschriftlichung* is especially strong on syntax and the organization of text (ibid. p. 19). Feilke *et al.* mention especially the development of complex prepositional constructions, constructions expressing purpose, new conjunctions and complex clauses (ibid. p. 20, and see also Kalmár 1985 and Chapter 5).[29]

I would like to give a brief example of how the oral/written dichotomy may have influenced the grammatical development of English, one that involves the occurrence of initial subject clauses (i.e. clauses functioning as subjects). Bock (1931: 247) and Mitchell (1985: §§1537–39, §1963) both noted, contra Visser (1963–73: §901), that there are hardly any examples of subject clauses (both finite and non-finite) in Old English. The few examples that Mitchell has found with infinitives (finite ones were not attested at all) are either based on slavish translations from Latin, or are characterized by the fact that the subject is not found in its usual position at the beginning of the clause, or by a 'tautologic *þæt*' ('that') being involved. Before we attribute the rise of 'true' subject clauses (so with the subject clause in initial position) in Middle English to a grammar change, we might, therefore, do well to check the occurrence of such constructions in contemporary spoken language first, and the acquisition of such structures by children.

Yngve (1996: 50ff.) shows that subject clauses in initial position would create a 'depth' problem, a problem that is related to the processing capacity of human temporary memory (also called working memory) when encoding a sentence. Without going into too much detail, this means that in the production of a clause such as *To suggest that he can help himself, is not particularly helpful*, the language user must postpone the matrix predicate (keep it in his working memory) while producing the subject clause itself. Yngve (1996) writes:

Nearly all of the previously puzzling complexity of language over and above the signaling function can, in fact, be explained in large part by the depth hypothesis as an adaptation of the structure of language to human memory and processing capabilities and limitations. It provides a *raison d'être* for many of the otherwise obscure details of morphology and syntax (Yngve 1996: 57).

It is not surprising in the light of this that such subject clauses are rare in spoken language or in language close to oral speech, and that, when they occur in those styles, they are usually accompanied by a 'resumptive pronoun' (defined broadly as in Crystal 1997). This pronoun serves as a 'memory aid', as it were, to reduce depth, to make the structure of the clause transparent. Example (15) represents one of the earliest examples of a 'true' subject clause in English:

(15)   ... repenten hym of alle his othere synnes and nat of a synguler synne, may
       not availle   (Chaucer, *C.T., Parson's Tale* 300)
       '... to repent of all his other sins and not of a particular sin, may be of no
       avail'

But most other examples of subject clauses in Middle English given in Visser (1963–73: §898) are indeed accompanied by a resumptive pronoun. There are two types:

(16)   gon & iseon swuche & elnen ham & helpen mid fode of holi lore, *þis* is riht
       religiun he seið seint iame.   (*AncrR*, Day 1952 [EETS os 225] 4.27–28)
       'to go and see such [people] and assist and help them with the food of holy
       learning, this is the right religion, says St James'

(17)   *þet* is ðet beste þeonne, speowen hit ut anon mid schrifte to ðe preoste.
                                              (*Ibid.* 107: 12–13)
       'that is the best then, to spew it out at once by means of confession to the priest'

In (16) the subject clause is given first and then taken up again in the form of a pronoun *þis* before the rest of the matrix predicate follows, in (17) the subject is first announced by means of a pro-form, *þet*, immediately followed by the predicate, and then later expanded into a clause.

Similar cases in which memory may play a role involve the use of resumptive pronouns in the not yet standardized language of Old and

Middle English texts. Such use of resumptive pronouns becomes increasingly rare in written texts after the Middle English period. The following examples should suffice:

(18)   ... it was þat ilk cok,/ þat petre herd *him* crau (*Cursor* (Vesp)15995)
       '... it was that same cock that Peter heard (him) crow'
(19)   Now turne we unto sir Trystrams, that uppon a day *he* toke a lyttell barget
                                               (Malory Wks (Add 59678) 441.27–8)
       'Now let's return to Sir Tristram, who one day (he) took a small boat'
(20)   A knyght ther was, and that a worthy man,/That fro the tyme that he first
       began/ To riden out, *he* loved chivalrie   (Chaucer, *Gen.Prol.* 43–45)
       'A knight there was, and a brave man at that, who from the time that he first
       began to go on expeditions, (he) loved chivalry'

In all these cases, the resumptive pronoun serves to make the structure of the clause again transparent, it 'picks up' an NP mentioned at the beginning, and functions syntactically in the remainder of the clause (i.e. it fills a 'gap' in the main clause).

Corroborating evidence that processing depth is experienced as a problem by both children and generally in colloquial speech, may be found in the fact that pure subject clauses (i.e. without a resumptive pronoun) do not seem to occur in child language data (cf. Diessel and Tomasello 2001: 100, and references there), and in the fact that similar resumptive strategies are used by children, and in relatively 'new' languages like pidgins and creoles. Compare this example from Tok Pisin quoted in Slobin (1977: 201):

(21) Na   pik   *ia*   [ol ikilim   bipo   *ia*] bai ikamap olsem draipela ston
     'And the pig *here* [they had killed before *here*] would turn into a huge stone'

Here the deictic particle *ia* serves to introduce or draw attention to a relative clause, and is repeated after the clause in order to keep the listener cued. Slobin notes that the same device is used by 'Turkish children and [in] Turkish colloquial speech to avoid the complexities of the Turkish relative clause' (1977: 202). In Dutch colloquial speech there is something similar:

(22)   De   tekst *die* ik nu   voorlees *die* gaat   over   taal
       The text   *that* I   now read-out *that* goes   about language
       'The text I am now reading out deals with language'

Here too, deictic *die* (used as a relative) is repeated in order to refresh the memory of the subject of the matrix clause. In some languages indeed such a second marker becomes grammaticalized, as is the case in left-dislocation structures in spoken Italian, such as:

(23a)	*Ci*	vado	domani	*a*	*Roma*
	There	I-go	tomorrow	*to*	*Rome*
(23b)	*Ne*	compro	due	*di*	*regali*
	of-those	I-buy	two	*of*	*presents*

This phenomenon clearly needs further research, but on the whole it looks as if the 'Verschriftlichung' of languages may lead to a dropping of such resumptive pronouns because they are 'illogical'; they introduce unwarranted redundancy in the expression of the argument structure of the *written* text (cf. also Bergh and Seppänen 1994). There is indeed less need for them in written text, because the structure is 'there' and can be deferred to, if need be, when the reader processes the rest of the clause. This is not the case in spoken discourse, where we need to be reminded of the structure. Quite clearly, phenomena such as these are not caused by the linguistic system itself but are due to the 'channel' used. They are also related to judgements about 'grammaticality'. What is considered incorrect in the standard written language, is not necessarily incorrect in the spoken language (cf. van der Horst 1986: 192–3). Strangely enough it is the written language that has often been taken as the yardstick for grammaticality judgements in linguistic theories. If one thus compares constructions in the modern written language with similar constructions in the older stages of that same language—where we, of necessity, deal with written texts but texts that may reflect oral speech more closely—then we may be comparing apples with pears. In the historical linguistic literature, however, this distinction is rarely made so that historically separate developments are presented as directly in line.

Two examples should make clear that too much reliance on the written standard plays a role in both formal and functional paradigms. Chomsky (1981: 240ff.) makes a distinction between French and English on the one hand and Italian on the other, having to do with the so-called '*that*-trace' phenomenon (which involves the absence vs. presence of resumptive *that*). It is quite likely that this constitutes a distinction between written and spoken varieties rather than, as generative linguists claim, between pro-drop and non-pro-drop languages (this is an important parameter in generative theory: *that*-trace violations are caused by the positive setting of the pro-drop or null-subject parameter). The literal English equivalent of the Italian (a pro-drop language) *Chi credi che partira* 'Who$_i$ do you think t$_i$ *that* t$_i$ will leave' also existed in Old and Middle English (cf. (24a)), which was *not* pro-drop, by the side of a construction without *that*.[30]

(**24a**)   grymbert who wolde ye *that* sholde goo and daye hym to come
'Grimbert who do you want that should go and summon him to come?'
(Caxton's *Reynard the Fox* ed. Blake 1970: 23, 27)

The construction is still used colloquially in English. It is not hard to find present-day examples used by native speakers on the web (the following websites were active in October 2005):

(**24b**)   I mean, who do you think *that* will be more incline[d] to make, or to use, an overgeneralization, that is a fallacy of composition?
(http://homepages.nyu.edu/~jmg336/html/fallacy.html)

(**24c**)   who do you think *that* will be buying or selling a house in the coming year?
(http://www.stgco.com/letters/oct01.pdf)

(**24d**)   who do you think *that* does that?
(http://www.ukhh.com/features/interviews/lowkey/index1.html)

An example of reliance on the written standard within the functional grammaticalization approach is provided by Miller (2004), who shows that the *have*-perfect in standard English, which is supposed to be the end point of a grammaticalization cline, is only the rule in standard written English; in non-standard and spoken varieties of English, many different forms, which are stages on the cline are still used. In other words, there is not the perfect kind of unidirectionality that grammaticalization theorists have discovered in this development from *have* as a possessive verb into a perfect marker (described as a 'channel of grammaticalization' in Heine and Kuteva 2002: 245).

What may also play a role is the period in which standardization takes place. Depending on the time of standardization, the results for related languages may be different because 'imminent' grammatical constructions of a colloquial nature may become barred from the standard in one language, while sister languages which standardize later may fully accept colloquial usages not accepted by their 'relatives' because by then these may have become more firmly spread and hence socially acceptable. Detges (2004: 212), for instance, shows that Modern Catalan has a construction called the *perfet perifràstique*,

(**25**)   El   seu   discurs   *va*[3rd PRES SING]   *causar* [INF]   un   gran
The   his   talk   *goes*   *produce*   a   great
impacte   en   l'auditori.
effect   on   the audience
'His talk *produced* a great effect on the audience'

This construction, consisting of the verb *anar* 'go' + infinitive, also developed in French and Occitan with verbs meaning 'go'. Detges notes that '16th-century grammarians in France, in the Languedoc and in Catalonia criticize these constructions as vulgar and uneducated' presumably because 'their use in literary discourse reflects an oral technique of story-telling' (2004: 218). He further remarks that the construction was abandoned in French during the first half of the seventeenth century, whereas in Catalan it supplanted the old synthetic past simple and became the default marker for the aoristic past tense. He believes that this process may well have been 'favoured by the absence of a written standard' because in the sixteenth century 'Catalan was ousted as an official written language by Castilian Spanish, and when a new Catalan standard was promoted by the nationalist *renaixença* movement in the 19th century, the grammaticalization of *anar* + *inf.* was already completed' (2004: 220).

1.3 Where to find the evidence

The first thing that needs to be pointed out is that all evidence we have for past stages of a language is indirect. This is true even for our primary evidence, the manuscripts themselves. There are various degrees of indirectness. In order to give shape to the evidence and to be able to do anything with it, we depend heavily on drawing correct inferences. I will first discuss the problems that exist with reference to the primary evidence, the written records, and the methods we can use to clean or firm up these data, and secondly I will discuss what tools we have to make the inferring process as successful as possible.

A first stumbling block for the linguist is deciphering the script. Some scripts are unproblematic because they are still used today, but others have been lost and may pose enormous problems; some have not yet been deciphered at all. Even if the script is known, we still have to be able to read the handwriting, which may differ according to place, period and individual. Linguists interested in morphosyntactic change, usually employ edited texts, not manuscripts, but we have to be aware that the editors of these texts have made inferences about the script they edit; in other words, an edited text is always one step removed from the original.

A second problem concerns relating the spelling to the sounds by sorting out what spelling conventions were used. This may constitute another type of indirectness in that editors before the 1980s were in the habit of normalizing the spelling, thus causing the text to be two steps removed from the original. Looking at spelling, we have to distinguish variations from errors, and, next, meaningful variations from meaningless ones, phonological variations from morphological ones and grammatical variations from stylistic ones (cf. van der Horst 1986: 202; Lass 1997: 6, 68).[31] In this way, we try to build up the linguistic system and the spelling conventions used to express it, that lie behind the text, or rather we try to establish the grammar of the author who has produced the text. (Note that there is another snag here in that the manuscript may have been copied by any number of scribes, each with their own grammar, whose copies may differ both geographically and diachronically from the text of the original author). Once we have established the relationship between the spelling and the phonemes that the letters stand for (most alphabets are phonemic rather than phonetic),[32] we are still far removed from the original language in that we miss allophonic details, while information about stress, intonation, rhythm, and tone is missing.

It is clear that on this rather basic level, we already have to do quite a bit of inferencing. What can we use as a basis for this? There are various sources. We can make use of metalinguistic commentary provided by contemporary grammatical treatises if these are available. We can also use contemporary poetic texts for more information on rhythm, stress, and accent.[33] Another useful source is linguistic genetic information, which may be tapped via either internal or comparative reconstruction. If no daughter or sister languages are available, typological evidence is another source upon which we can draw. In a similar way, word divisions or contractions may tell us something about suprasegmental tone groups.

Because the edited texts are, as it were, an interpretation of the primary material, it could be said that they constitute secondary sources rather than primary ones. In practice we will need to work with edited texts because, as I mentioned in §1.1.2, we often need a large amount of text in order to find enough evidence about specific syntactic constructions. Another reason why we need more data for historical syntax is the lack of grammaticality judgements. Unlike linguists working on contemporary speech, historical linguists have no access to native speakers' competence. To make up for this, we rely more deeply on quantitative information. One way to find out whether a particular construction has become or is becoming grammatical in the course of time is by doing a frequency count. What is important here is the relative frequency of constructions compared over a number of periods, not their absolute frequency; the latter would not mean much if the structure under investigation is rare (cf. Fischer *et al.* 2000a: 33).

In order to do quantitative analyses within a reasonable amount of time, it is advisable to use computerized corpora and concordances. However, the use of these brings along another risk because the examples as they come up on the screen are divorced from context. Ideally, one should check every example in context, which is hardly feasible. In general what one does is to check a good part of them contextually, work out what the problematic cases may be from there, and what kinds of factors may play a role in the variations noted. On that basis, we may go through the rest of the examples more quickly. It must be clear, though, that using corpora or concordances really represents a third degree of indirectness, not only because the context is not immediately available, but also because these concordances and corpora have been typed in from editions rather than manuscripts, as a result of which further mistakes and further interpretations may have been introduced. Finally, an ideal source and tool for historical linguists working on morphosyntax are the 'tagged' and 'parsed' computer corpora. These can be searched for strings which are not tied to lexical items. Obviously, this represents yet a fourth level of interpretation because the morphological tagging and the syntactic parsing are based on the analytic skills of the linguists (or, more dangerously, the automatic programs) behind these, and in some cases the parsing is based on earlier tagging, providing yet another intermediate level.

It is obvious that there is a lot of room for disagreement about the eventual analysis of even the primary material. For this reason the reconstruction and typological tools mentioned above are important; we need lots of checks and balances in this work. Another kind of help may be provided by older monographs and handbooks. These are often based on a more intensive reading of the texts in question, and come from the hands of thorough and dedicated philologists. They may provide us with useful data and insights that can be used as tools in our own analysis.

1.4 Concluding remarks

The above considerations show that the study of morphosyntactic change is not easy and straightforward but fraught with many difficulties. These difficulties, as we have seen, are related first of all to the nature of the data itself: the greater abstraction of the (morpho)syntactic level (in comparison with the phonological one), the various degrees of indirectness of the primary material, and the lack of sufficient homogeneous data as to space, time, and speakers. Secondly it is hard, if not impossible, in the study of linguistic change to separate intralinguistic or internal factors from extra-linguistic, external ones, and even to define them. A clear categorization of these factors may be possible within a *particular* theoretical model, but this doesn't provide much help for the historical linguist investigating an *actual* change, because he may well need to look at more than one model to explain or understand the change. The amount of attention paid to each of these factors also differs per theoretical model. The path provided by a linguist may seem strewn with roses but may also turn out to be a 'garden path'. Each linguist has his own story to tell, which he believes is coherent, but as Lass (1997: 3) so aptly puts it, linguists are like 'time travelers':

we manipulate our landscape, and we do it in different ways depending on the kind of pictures we happen to be interested in seeing. This book [about historical linguistics and language change] is about just these two things: the adventure of linguistic time-travel, and the manipulations we perform on the scenery to make it 'scenery' rather than just confused images whizzing by.

What I hope to do in this volume, is look a little more closely at the 'manipulations' by linguists in the hope of making clear what these involve and how reliable they are in the analysis of linguistic change. In the end, however, my story here is a personal one too, which has grown out of a life-long experience with morphosyntactic change and the various theories used to explain it.

Notes

1. 'Responsible for the changes' must not be taken in too literal a sense. As far as linguistic 'innovations' are concerned, it can be said that a particular change originates with a speaker or hearer in a particular communicative situation (i.e. the context in which communication takes place). When an innovation becomes a 'change', i.e. when an innovation is implemented elsewhere in the speech community, other factors begin to play a role as well, such as the frequency of an innovation and factors of a social nature, which need not be directly linked to the cause or origin of the innovation. See also below, §1.2.

2. Classic studies in this respect are Labov (1972a) and Trudgill (1974). These studies on change-in-progress have deeply influenced historical linguists occupied with changes in the past. Through their work, the effects of social-economic variables on linguistic change have been studied much more intensively. Books on socio-historical linguistics begin to appear from the early 1980s onwards, cf. e.g. Romaine (1982), Milroy (1992), and, on English, Rissanen *et al.* (1993), Nevalainen and Raumolin-Brunberg (1996). Related works on socio-historical pragmatics can be dated from the early 1990s, cf. Jucker (1995), and the *Journal of Historical Pragmatics*, which was initiated in 2000.

3. Milroy (1992: 39) following Brown (1982) refers to this difference in functional terms as 'message-oriented' vs. 'listener-oriented' speech. Listener-oriented speech is 'characterized by inexplicitness and vagueness, with primary attention to the feelings and attitudes of conversational partners', while message-oriented speech is interested first and foremost in the propositional content of a text. Tannen (1985) refers to this difference as 'involvement focus' vs. 'information focus'. For linguistic differences produced by differences between speaking and writing, see Chafe (1985).

4. Cf. also Janda and Joseph (2003: 17), who advise 'to use extreme caution in generalizing from formal [written] documents'.

5. For the problems connected with this, and how frequency itself impinges on the correct interpretation of historical linguistic signs, see van der Horst (1986: 198–200).

6. Strictly speaking, the PDE 3rd person sg. *saw* is derived from the OE past tense pl. *sawon*, so it is not a direct cognate of the OE 3rd person sg. *seah*. Similarly, the direct ancestor of PDE *her* was not OE *hie* (the accusative fem. sg. form) but OE *hire* (originally the dative). So even in a simple example such as this, two of the lexical cognates are morphologically indirectly connected.

7. 'Abduction' is an instance of analogy because it is based on the recognition of a *pattern*, cf. Itkonen (2005: 35), who writes, 'every abduction is ... more or less analogical, namely in the sense that it is necessarily based on some pre-existent model'. It was first discussed as an important factor in linguistic change by Andersen (1973) (for Andersen's use of the term, which he had taken from the philosopher Peirce, see Deutscher 2002). Andersen focuses on phonetic change brought about by abductive processes during language acquisition. The occurrence of abduction or 'misassignment of constituent structure' as an important factor in morphosyntactic change had itself been noted by many earlier linguists, e.g. by Jespersen (1940), who termed it 'metanalysis'. McMahon (1994: 122) describes the relation between abduction and analogy as follows: 'when the patterns of a language become confused [by changes taking place elsewhere], they will in time be reorganised. The force generally thought to be responsible for tidying-up is analogy; and *one way of implementing analogical change is innovation by children using abductive reasoning*' (emphasis added). Since children do not receive a fully-formed grammar from their parents but have to base their grammar on the output they receive, they may draw the wrong inferences

and thus 'abduce' a different rule or different pattern compared to their parent's rule. More discussion on this in Chapter 3, where it will also be argued that reanalysis in fact involves replacement induced by analogy.

8. Lightfoot (1991) investigates the simultaneous appearance of these infinitivals, but he offers a rather different explanation for their simultaneity, which is only laterally related to the word order changes suggested by Fischer *et al.* 2000a and Los 2005). Crucial factors in Lightfoot's account are changes in the status of infinitival *to*, which coalesced with the governing verb enabling it 'to transmit the head government and case marking properties of its governing verb', and the assumption that 'children are degree-O learners' (1991: 96). For more details and problems that this account creates, cf. Fischer *et al.* (2000a: 239–41); Miller (2002: 161–2, 184). Miller (2002), who deals with these infinitivals in his chapters 7 and 8, only gives a very small role to the word order change in the developments (see p. 186). In his view the two new infinitival constructions developed more or less independently, each helped by factors already present in the language. Thus, the *for* NP *to* V construction developed out of an earlier (indirect object) NP *for to* V construction (cf. the example in (6)), which became transposed (pp. 205–6), while the construction found in (7) was already marginally grammatical in Old English, and fully grammatical in w*h*-constructions in Old English. A problem with Miller's account is that his examples of the Old English construction exemplified by (7) almost all come from Latin translated texts (more about this problem in §1.1.3), and that his account sheds no light on the facts that both Dutch and German, the closest relatives, did not develop constructions such as those found in (2) and (7)—in other words these languages remained at the Old English stage—and also did not undergo the word order changes that were crucial to the English development.

9. This is not quite correct. In phonology we may distinguish so-called phonæsthemes or sound symbolic clusters, which carry some referential meaning, often based on an iconic relation between the sound (through its acoustic, articulatory, or kinæsthetic characteristics, cf. Sapir [1929]1963; Fónagy 2001: 2–8; Bergen 2004) and the notion it refers to. Likewise, some inflectional morphemic variables (e.g. in English, biblical 3rd person-*eth* against the much more regular-*s* ending), which are often relics of earlier dialect differences or diachronic relics, may carry prestigious or stylistic overtones conveying a different social meaning (cf. also Milroy (1992: 44), who refers to the fact that certain pronunciations express community norms, which are associated with taboo, 'face' and politeness). Derivational morphemes, indeed, do carry referential meaning, but on the whole there is just one morpheme for each possible slot.

10. For a detailed description of the change involving *have* and the *to*-infinitive, see Fischer (1994a). For the exceptional behaviour of quantifiers and negative phrases in this position, see van der Wurff (1999); Moerenhout and van der Wurff (2000).

11. Van der Horst (1986: 198–204) and Lass (1997: 56 and passim) emphasize again and again that a struggle with the primary data takes up a lot of research space

in historical linguistics, much larger than in synchronic linguistics because of the fact that the elementary facts are much more difficult to formulate, and because of the anachronistic risk mentioned above that may lead to a misinterpretation of the facts because we tend to see them through a 'modern lens'. Lass writes that 'without this nitpicking we would have no sound basis for saying anything interesting about the ... linguistic past, and therefore no historical background for talking about the same aspects of the linguistic present' (1997: 56). He adds that it is rather strange that in most studies of language change the necessity of 'nitpicking' is either ignored or simply assumed.

12. A possible minimalist analysis of OV and VO word orders in Old English is given in Fischer *et al.* (2000a: 151–60). Under this analysis Old English would be underlyingly SVO, but AgrO (now often referred to as *v*) would have 'strong features', forcing movement of the object to a preverbal position in order to check AgrO's features. This movement happens before Spell-Out (this is the phonological component which interprets the syntactic rules to produce the actual pronunciation). When AgrO's features are weak (as is argued to be the case in late Middle English), checking will also take place, but *after* Spell-Out. The point at which checking takes place thus decides the word order of the surface structures, checking before 'Spell-Out' resulting in OV, after 'Spell-Out' in VO. If the loss of impersonals is to be explained within this framework, it will need to be tied to the strength of 'features' not to movement per se.

13. *French* stems with similar suffixes appear in English writings from about 1200 onwards, cf. *lechery* (first attested according to the *OED c.* 1230), *prowess* (*c.* 1290), *ornament* (*c.* 1230).

14. Benskin and Laing (1981: 95) note that in dialect translations performed by medieval scribes 'the units that a scribe takes in, glance by glance at his exemplar, are too small to encompass the larger syntactic structures, and that the syntax [or for that matter the discourse structure], though not the spelling and morphology of his copy, remains essentially that of his exemplar'. This entails, in other words, that constructions invoking successively larger spans of text may be more of a reflex of the grammatical system of the language of the original text than of the native language of the translator.

15. The Old and Middle English translations of Boethius' *De Consolatione Philosophiæ* is a case in point. King Alfred produces a version in the tenth century that has only a loose relation to the Latin original. Chaucer, on the other hand, produces a most awkward text in the fourteenth century that can be shown to be rigidly faithful to the French text that he used, itself a translation of the Latin (cf. Fischer 1979). Another interesting text is the translation of the *Gregory's Dialogues* in earlier and later Old English (cf. Los 2005: 179–90).

16. For instance the borrowing they discuss of English constructions in American Finnish (p. 125) is a rather doubtful case since American Finnish spoken today is characterized by English-dominant bilingualism, involving Finnish words but, as it were, native English syntax (cf. Hirvonen 2005), while the influence of

Spanish on many Amerindian languages is due to long and intense bilingual contact of these speakers with Spanish.

17. ECM or Exceptional Case Marking constructions is a term used in generative grammar to describe constructions where a verb exceptionally governs case across a sentence (S-bar) boundary with the result that an argument which fulfils a syntactic role in a non-finite subordinate clause receives case from the predicate in the matrix clause (cf. Chomsky 1981: 66ff.). ECM is necessary in clauses such as *I believe* [*him to be a liar*] because infinitives as non-tense Vs cannot assign case to their subjects, and therefore the syntactic subject *him* needs to receive case from the matrix (tensed) verb. ECM was earlier (and also later) described as Subject-to-object raising.

18. One of the maxims of quantity runs: 'Do not make your contribution to the conversation more informative than necessary', and of manner: 'Be brief (avoid unnecessary wordiness)', cf. Grice (1975).

19. Cf. also Vincent (2001: 7), who writes: 'In sum, it may be difficult to understand the way in which change in the external community feeds into change in the internalized linguistic system, but the conceptual problem is a genuine one, and must be faced and not avoided by an arbitrary limitation of the domain of inquiry'. Similar views are expressed by Pintzuk *et al.* (2000: 9–12), to which Vincent also refers.

20. Cf. Croft (2000: 3–5), who emphasizes that a *theory* of language change must distinguish between 'two processes of change', which he calls 'altered replication' and 'differential replication'—and which others have called 'innovation' or 'actuation' vs. 'propagation' or 'diffusion'. He adds that this distinction 'is very rarely recognized in models of language change' resulting in some linguists taking up 'apparently contradictory positions'. Croft continues to say that *innovation* 'occurs in speaker action' and hence is 'a synchronic phenomenon', while *propagation* is a 'diachronic phenomenon' which is not directly related to a speaker but to 'shift[s] in ... frequency of variants of a structure'. Note that more philologically inclined linguists (e.g. Saussure 1983[1922]: 167–68; Bloomfield 1933: 405–8; Samuels 1972: 138–44—I owe these references to one of the unanimous reviewers) and sociolinguists (e.g. Trudgill 1983: 72ff.) do usually refer to this distinction.

Formal generative linguists have a very different notion of 'change'. Thus, Hale (1998: 2) sees change as something that takes place only between grammars of different generations, i.e. it is solely a matter of I-language. Change involves individual grammars and is always instantaneous. Lexical and phonological shifts are not seen as changes relevant for the system (altered replications), even though they may be prerequisites to a syntactic 'instantaneous' change. The diffusion or differential replication of a change (which he admits is usually gradual) is the concern of E-language and therefore lies outside the concerns of this model (see further §1.2.1)

21. Thus, 'ease of effort' may play a role in phonetic change involving cases of assimilation, reductions in unstressed position, etc. Possibly, the avoidance of

homonymic clash may be an internal factor too in sound change (cf. Samuels 1972: 67–75, but see Lass 1980: 75–80), since this involves *phonological* distinctions, where meaning differences do play a role.

22. It is probably not an accident that syntactic variation has been called the 'Cinderella' of dialect studies (cf. Benskin and Laing 1981: 98).

23. An innovation in the *interpretation* of a speech sign may also occur by pragmatic inferencing from a particular speech situation rather than by analogy (see also Chapter 3). Such an innovation does not manifest itself by means of a new form (that only happens when the interpretation leads to further changes) and is therefore quite difficult to detect by an investigator because he would need to look at the context of the discourse and the speech situation that causes the inference, in great detail. It is to be noted that even formal innovations are difficult if not impossible to spot. It is unlikely that an investigator is present at the right moment, and even if he is, he is unlikely to see it as an innovation because he can only realize afterwards, if/when it becomes a change, that it *was* an innovation. It may simply have been a performance mistake.

24. The notion of teleological (or 'final') vs. 'causal' change is well described by Keller (1994[1990]), who argues that languages are 'phenomena of the third kind' (like all cultural or historical systems). This means that they are neither a purely natural system (such as physics or chemistry) governed by natural laws, nor an artificial system (such as logic and mathematics) governed by the human will, but they partake of the characteristics of both. The process of change, according to Keller, consists of a micro-level and a macro-level, the micro-level representing the intentional ('final') actions of individual speakers, and the macro-level the non-intended, 'causal' consequences of all the individual actions. Milroy (1992: 206–22) also distinguishes a micro- and macro-level with reference to innovation and change but in the social domain; the former comprising individual consensus/conflict of norms in social networks, the latter involving patterns of social stratification (having to do with class, status, economic wealth, etc.). On the micro-level, innovations are unordered, while 'orderly heterogeneity in speaker-behaviour' (p. 170) exists on the macro-level. It is not clear, however, whether Milroy also links this to 'final' actions vs. 'causal' consequences. My impression is that he does not.

25. Thus clauses like *He is going to fetch me some water* are early, whereas clauses such as *You're not going to like this* and *It's going to rain soon* are later developments. Once fully established as a new 'future auxiliary', the new construction may rival and even oust other future auxiliaries such as *will/shall*.

26. Note that Clark and Roberts (1993) do not distinguish, as Milroy does, between 'innovation' and 'change'; the two terms are used interchangeably to refer to Milroy's 'change'.

27. It is perhaps surprising that morphology is seen here as external to syntax since in present-day generative treatments morphology is usually seen as part of syntax, not as a separate level. Work within the Minimalist program indeed 'posits a tight connection between syntactic operations and morphological

features' (Lightfoot 2002a: 3). However, in the P&P and earlier generative frameworks, there was still a clear-cut distinction between deep and surface structure, with all inflectional morphology relegated to the phonological domain; the principles and parameters themselves were strictly syntactically oriented (having to do with binding, C-command, types of movement, X-bar theory, etc.).

28. Cf. Schlüter (2003: 70), who shows in an interesting article how phonological forces do in fact determine the nature of the computational system in a number of changes that took place in the history of English, involving the variants of the indefinite article, and restrictions bearing on attributive constructions and sentence adverbs negated by *not*.

29. Cf. Mithun (1988), who shows how the development of written language leads to explicit grammatical marking of coordination, which in spoken language is most often done by intonation, pause, rhythm, pitch, etc. Harris and Campbell (1995: 308–10), however, quite rightly warn against too easy an attribution of subordinate clauses to the development of a written standard. Cases which are suspected to have been influenced by this development should be checked against studies of language acquisition and studies of oral languages in order to find out which types of subordinate clauses are frequent outside the written medium (see also below).

30. The diachronic development of the construction is discussed in Bergh and Seppänen (1994). They show that the *that*-trace was found from Old English until late Modern English in their corpus, that the use of it decreased at the same time when other superfluous uses of *that* were dropped, and that the development is closely linked with the use of and the later dropping of resumptive pronouns, which they describe as the result of the rise of the standard language and normative influence. For Old English, see also Gorrell (1895: 351).

31. For instance, what looks like phonemic variation but is indeed a morphological one, is the spelling of *aanraadden* 'advised' in Dutch, which is the past tense pl. of the infinitive *aanraden*. The pronunciation of both words is the same but the form *aanraad-den* shows that the stem is *aanraad* followed by the regular inflection of the past tense pl. *-den* (cf. the infinitive *halen* 'fetch', past *haalden*). Another example could be the expression *to hande* in Middle English, where the *-e* could be a silent sound or an old dative ending.

32. If we are dealing with a logographic system (such as Chinese), we have an even greater problem in that we have no direct information about how that language was sounded.

33. Poetry may also be useful in that poems often preserve in their diction archaic expressions, so it may give us information about earlier stages of the language (cf. Taylor 2005). Van der Horst (1986: 193), in addition, acutely remarks that poets work with the same language system as prose writers but they often use it in a more original fashion. This may also open our eyes to specific characteristics of the language in question.

2

Conflict and reconciliation: two theories compared

The truest and most complete theory would not enable us to solve all the difficult problems which the whole course of the development of life upon our globe presents to us   (Wallace, *Darwinism*, 1890: 7)

A theory is often nothing else but a contrivance for comprehending a certain number of facts under one expression   (Playfair, *Nat. Phil.*, 1819: I. 3)

Were a theory open to no objection it would cease to be a theory, and would become a law   (Grove, *Corr. Phys. Forces*, 1850[2]: 105)

2.0 Introduction

Both grammaticalization and the various generative models, among which is the P&P approach, are seen as 'theories' by their practitioners.[1] In spite of this, Newmeyer (1998: 240) states that 'grammaticalization is not a theory'. It may therefore be appropriate, before we compare the two approaches that are the subject of study in this volume, to consider what is meant by 'theory'.

It is clear from the definitions given in the *OED* that the term 'theory' is conceived of in different ways. This is not surprising when we consider its origin, viz. the loanword θεωρία, taken from Ancient Greek (Aristotle) and borrowed via Latin *theoria*, meaning 'contemplation, insight'. It still had the general meaning of 'contemplation', when it was first introduced into the various European vernaculars during the Renaissance, beside the already more specific reference it gained within the emerging empirical sciences of 'a mental scheme', 'a scheme or system of ideas'. A general, modern description of 'theory', which also makes reference to the *empirical methods* used to set up such a 'mental system', can be found in the *OED* under definition (4a), where it is described as

A scheme or system of ideas or statements held as an explanation or account of a group of facts or phenomena; a hypothesis that has been confirmed or established by observation or experiment, and is propounded or accepted as accounting for the known facts; a statement of what are held to be the general laws, principles, or causes of something known or observed.

Some further definitions in the *OED* show at the same time how the reference of the term has undergone a certain degree of narrowing. In some fields of science, the term came to mean the principles and methods of a subject 'as distinguished from the practice of it' (cf. *OED* senses 4b and 5) thus sharpening the divide between the empirical data and the system behind it and opening up the way to a much closer association of 'theory' with two specific domains of science, that is mathematics and logic. Through this, the notion of theory came to be linked to 'a set of theorems forming a *connected system*' (cf. *OED* 4c, emphasis added). This latter interpretation is palpably present, for instance, in Meillet's (1903 [1937]: 475) description of *langue* as 'un système où tout se tient et [qui] a un plan d'une merveilleuse rigueur'.[2] It is this more narrow interpretation of 'theory' that seems to be the norm within the structuralist and generative schools of thought (to which Newmeyer also belongs), where the *system* of grammar became more important as an object of study than the actual language data. The theory of grammaticalization is less well-organized as a logical system; the part that deals with change does not cover all the facts of linguistic change,[3] and as an approach it is more concerned with the data themselves. However, because it is data-driven, it is much more concerned with pragmatic-semantic factors that play a role in change than the generative approach which is centralized around morphosyntax. The generative theory of grammar, on the other hand, does present itself as a complete system of language, generating all its possible utterances. However, as we will see below, this completeness is also achieved at a cost.

The idea of a theory is indeed that it explains the observable facts, but this, as is clear from the epigraph to this chapter (taken from the *OED*), does not necessarily mean that the theory *will* explain *all* the facts. Reality is complex and refractory, and totally 'connected systems' are usually only possible in artificial domains. Connected systems can be made to work in natural domains (or partly natural domains, such as language or economics) only when one cuts away some of the facts to be explained, or cleans up the facts in laboratory situations. Skousen (1989: 139–40) brings out this dilemma very neatly with an interesting analogy between linguistics and physics, which helps us to see the difference between data- and system-approaches to language, and which at the same time makes clear the usefulness of both. He compares formal rule descriptions to the description of gases in terms of laws:

Long before the atomic model of gases was developed, various laws were discovered about the properties of gases ... [here he refers to Boyle's Law and Charles' (and Gay-Lussac's) Law]. In actual fact, these laws only approximate the real behavior of gases. For instance, for pressures greater than ten atmospheres or for certain gases such as water vapor and carbon dioxide near liquefaction, Boyle's Law is not very accurate .... It is obvious that these gas laws cannot be viewed as fundamental. Instead, these relationships are derived from the general kinetic properties of individual gas molecules acting in an aggregate. A gas may appear to be following Boyle's and Charles' Laws, yet in actuality these laws have no existence except in the minds of scientists. Such laws are meta-descriptive devices that scientists use to talk about the properties of gases. In no literal sense can it be said that individual gas molecules follow these laws. In a similar way, linguistic rules are meta-descriptive devices that exist only in the minds of linguists. Speakers do not appear to use rules in perceiving and producing language. Moreover, linguistic rules can only explain language behavior for ideal situations. As in physics, an atomistic approach seems to be a more promising method for predicting language behavior.

We will see below that the formal and functional theories discussed here, differ on exactly this point. Formal theory is not interested in the *actual behaviour* of speakers but only in the general properties of the *language use of the individual speaker in ideal situations*, while grammaticalization theory wishes to explain the variable nature of linguistic utterances produced by speakers in communication through time and space. It is not surprising therefore that the pragmatic-semantic aspect of language is treated so very differently by the two frameworks. There is nothing wrong with either approach in that both can help us to gain a greater understanding of the language system, of language change and the interrelation between them. Laws are seen as useful strategies to discover the properties of the object to be investigated. They need not be related to reality. As the above quotation suggests, the 'atomistic' approach may be the more suitable one when one wishes to investigate the factors relevant in the *processing* of language. This is a question we will come back to in §2.2.1 below and Chapter 3.

A well-known Popperian requirement is that theories, in order to qualify as a theory, must make use of hypotheses that are falsifiable. Here I think both theories have a problem. Grammaticalization works often with tendencies, which makes falsification more difficult. First of all, the tendencies themselves are not always 'sufficiently articulated as an empirical theory so that [they] can specify its potential falsifiers'. And, secondly, one has to decide on the 'statistical structure of the universe over which GR[ammati-calization] phenomena are defined' (Lass 2000: 208, and see also 213–15). Generative grammar works with hypotheses that are in principle falsifiable. However, in practice, falsification does not always result in the relinquish-ing of a particular principle because the (data in the) model itself—because of its degree of abstraction—can be 'moulded' to salvage the principle. Haiman (1993: 307–10) describes the situation very acutely in connection with the history of the generative distinction between the empty categories PRO and trace: 'Once empirical evidence appeared which seemed to call the distinction into question, however, it was necessary to do one of three things: abandon the distinction, and with it the theory of PRO; dismiss the evidence as "marginal"; or reinterpret the evidence to conform with the theory' (p. 307). He next shows that the third option was chosen in the case of PRO and that in generative practice often the 'natural recourse is to relabel the data' when 'the data mock the theory' (p. 310).

Considering all of the above, both grammaticalization and generative grammar deserve the label 'theory'. Both make use of hypotheses and propose principles and terms (primitives) with the aim of establishing generalities underlying (some of) the facts of language. In both cases these facts are 'cleaned up' in the sense that some of reality is cut away. In the grammaticalization approach, linguistic facts are considered as if they float freely through time and space, as if the formal patterning of the overall synchronic system of which these facts are part is not relevant. In the P&P approach, the synchronic forms are mostly viewed in isolation. Semantic motivation of syntactic structures is denied because the syntactic system is deemed to be autonomous, downgrading the forms' meaning and/ or function in communication. They are also usually cleaned of any diachronic residues (i.e. variant forms).

It is also important to observe that the way in which the principles and terms are established is not the same in the two cases. As stated, the principles in grammaticalization are 'tendencies': they are of a general nature and formed heuristically, and their formulation has remained more or less the same in the theory over time. Categories are non-discrete and seen as parts of clines and continua. Such tendencies or generalizations are typical of an inductive approach to building linguistic theory (cf. Labov 1994: 13). In contrast, the principles of generative grammar are typical of a deductive approach; they are precise, discrete, and fixed (as in fully man-made systems such as logic or mathematics). They may be altered or replaced whenever new facts arise or whenever a more elegant principle (comprising more facts) can be established. The principles are meant to be falsifiable, with the search for falsification causing modifications in the model. It is to be expected therefore that the model changes over time, ideally becoming more adequate and explanatory, but the ultimate aim is the establishment of 'laws', that is a completely fixed model. In sum, grammaticalization has change built into the terms and principles of the model, while in generative grammar the terms and principles are fixed. In the latter, the genotype or 'biological grammar' provides the blueprint, on the basis of which the child, during the process of language acquisition, fixes the parameters of its phenotype.[4]

Each approach practises a different kind of 'cleaning'. It is usual in the generative model to purify the facts to be explained by reducing them to *written forms* of language. Generative linguists by and large ignore spoken and variant forms and ignore the circumstances under which language forms are used (which shed light on the referential and social aspects of the forms).[5] In addition, generative grammar looks at language as a *product* of the *competence* of speakers; this competence is itself a mental system, and hence does not represent observable facts but native speakers' intuitions. Grammaticalization is concerned with the *processing* of language as it takes place in a social, communicative context (which automatically incorporates a *time factor*, which in the generative approach is fully controlled and thus missing); it is concerned with the observable facts, their *forms* as connected to their *functions*. Note that function is not directly observable from the language forms but has to be inferred from the circumstances (which are to some extent observable) in the situational context as they are interpreted by the human mind (cf. Yngve 1996). We may conclude that both theories have weaknesses (in order to make them strong!), which lie in the not directly observable areas (i.e. 'competence' and 'function'). In both cases, this may result in circularity of argumentation. Still, it can be said that both theories provide satisfactory explanations for some of the facts, if not all.

Summarizing, the two approaches relevant here deserve the status of 'theory' in the sense that they use the apparatus common in theories and are adequate as theories since they are able to provide insightful explanations which we can build upon further. I will try to show in some detail in the remainder of this chapter how the two frameworks differ, and why this is so. Both approaches have long histories ('new' theories do not appear out of the blue), and indeed history to a large extent defines or determines their nature. I will therefore first discuss their historical background (§2.1) before moving on to their aims and methods (§2.2). In a brief final section (§2.3), I will reconsider the main differences between them and explore ways in which the two approaches may be reconciled. Some conclusions are drawn in §2.4.

2.1 Historical backdrop to the two approaches

2.1.1 Grammaticalization

Studies of grammaticalization (e.g. Traugott and Heine 1991; Hopper and Traugott (2003[1993]) generally refer to Meillet (1912: 131) as the first linguist to use the term, but they acknowledge that there was a long tradition before that, whereby reference is made to linguists such as Franz Bopp, Wilhelm von Humboldt and Georg von der Gabelentz, covering the whole of the nineteenth century.[6] Meillet defined the phenomenon of grammaticalization as 'l'attribution du caractère grammatical à un mot jadis autonome' (Meillet 1912: 131), and this is still the most commonly used definition among historical linguists, that is that grammaticalization is seen as a process in which originally autonomous, fully referential lexical items acquire a purely grammatical function in the course of time. In more recent literature, it has been observed that most cases of grammaticalization concern a combination of lexical items rather than single lexical forms. The more general definition given by Tomasello (2003b: 102) reflects this: 'These processes [of grammaticalization] take loose discourse sequences, comprising linguistic symbols for concrete items of experience ..., and turn them into coherent grammatical constructions with various specialized symbols that perform grammatical functions with respect to these concrete symbols'. Tomasello's definition also comprises developments such as clause combining (cf. Hopper and Traugott 2003: 175ff.), which are more difficult to tie to a particular lexical word. The process of grammaticalization takes place on the language-output level and is seen as gradual, in which the lexical item or construction progresses along 'clines', of a formal as well as a semantic nature. The movement along the cline may be partial or complete. In more recent times, grammaticalization also developed into a more general grammatical theory, which has translated the notions developed by historical linguists into requirements for or principles of the synchronic language system. Further details about the theory (its methods, beliefs, aims, and 'machinery') will be discussed below and in Chapter 3; here, we will first discuss its origins (for a history of the notion from the nineteenth century up till now, and its more recent synchronic and theoretical branching out, see also Hopper and Traugott 2003: 19–30).

A renewed interest in the *history* of language started in the Romantic period as part of a search for the roots of a nation. This linguistic interest was intimately connected with the literature, history, and culture of national communities, and was therefore of a philological nature: language forms were described in close connection with language use; form was bound up with function/meaning. This historical angle also explains the diachronic (and comparative) bias of the work of these linguists: they were interested in how their language had changed and diversified from its sister languages. It likewise explains the breadth of the historical linguistic volumes produced in the nineteenth century, which, apart from chapters on language (on all levels), also often contained chapters on literature, art, law, economy, etc., all areas deemed necessary to be able to understand the changing context in which the language was used. Even though these more general chapters were omitted in the course of time, the diachronic or historical approach to grammar and the close relation between form and function remained the rule in all the theoretical books on contemporary grammar written at the beginning of the twentieth century, such as, for instance, Jespersen's (1909–49) detailed description of English, Hanssen's (1910) of Spanish, Riemann's (1927) of Latin, etc. Such grammars had in common that they explained the present as arising from the past, and that they linked the use of structures to the function they had in communication.

Another linguistic development which left its mark on the theory of grammaticalization is the movement of the *Junggrammatiker* (Neogrammarians), a group of Indo-Europeanists associated with the University of Leipzig in the last quarter of the nineteenth century. They turned linguistics into a 'science', seeing language as a purely 'natural object' that could be studied like other natural phenomena, as was done in physics and chemistry. They formulated principles (e.g. sound laws, analogical principles) and postulates as had become the rule in the empirical sciences. These principles were most successful and influential on the phonetic/phonological level,[7] and in the area of inflectional morphology, which likewise carries little referential meaning (cf. §1.1.2), but this does not mean that they did not also pay attention to syntax, especially to questions of word order. An important aim of the Neogrammarians was to provide a genealogy of the Indo-European language family and to show how a common parent language could be reconstructed by comparing all the branches of the tree, thereby uncovering the mechanisms that guide the evolution of different languages in similar ways. Three aspects of the neogrammarian school in particular became part of the legacy they left to grammaticalization theory: the diachronic interest, the search for universal principles and the use of comparative data.

The neogrammarian search for similar tendencies found in related languages and their systematic approach to the phenomenon of language may have revived typological studies in the 1960s, which in turn became a staple ingredient of grammaticalization studies. In typology, *non-related* languages came to be included in a comparative, *synchronic*, enterprise with the aim of finding further language universals, especially in the realm of syntax. The motive behind this comparison on a larger scale was the fact that, as far as syntax was concerned, reconstruction had not been very successful (because syntax concerns abstract structures and not strict cognates, see §1.1.2). The idea grew that, if related languages follow universal paths in the way they change on the phonetic level (this was found to be true even after contact between them was lost), this must also mean that (i) principles found in related languages could be truly universal and hence could apply to other, unrelated languages; and that (ii) the syntactic level would be subject to such principles too. Concerning (ii), the syntactic observations on non-related languages were necessary in order to increase the database so that statistical evidence might contribute towards the establishment of the more abstract (and hence more elusive) syntactic universals.

A more recent linguistic school, which revived pre-Saussurian notions about a diachronic approach to grammar, and which may well have influenced grammaticalization to become a 'movement' of its own, spreading even into the synchronic field (cf. Hopper and Traugott 2003: 2), can be found in the study of sociolinguistics, which itself grew out of a new interest in sociology, an interest in fieldwork describing as yet unknown languages in colonized areas, and perhaps partly as a reaction against the neogrammarian notion of blindly operating sound laws and the simultaneity of change. Sociolinguists in the twentieth century working on change in progress introduced the idea of 'variable rules', of change diffusing gradually through language and society, both socially and lexically (rather than instantaneously as the Neogrammarians upheld), and it re-emphasized the importance of the context (both linguistic and non-linguistic) in which change takes place. Language was no longer seen as simply a physical phenomenon to be studied objectively, separate from its users, but as a communicatory tool in the hands of speakers and hearers. Speakers do not produce language in isolation but are influenced by place, time, social norms, social background, age, style, etc. This notion that rules are variable, that they do not apply across the board, that rules/categories may be flexible rather than discrete, that diachrony is an inherent part of synchrony, led to a *synchronic* theory of grammaticalization, which concentrates on syntax as arising out of discourse-pragmatic phenomena, and sees the language system as consisting of fluid patterns rather than clearly outlined terms and principles.

2.1.2 Formal generative grammar

The formal study of language is also heavily indebted to the neogrammarian school but it inherited other properties from this illustrious forebear.

Generative linguists embraced the notion of linguistics as a hard science, subject to laws, fixed constraints, and principles. They did not adopt the neogrammarian diachronic approach to language, but they followed them in their concentration on language as form. Within the neogrammarian school, the neglect of meaning/function was almost an accident, since they worked mainly on the phonetic and inflectional levels, where referential meaning was hardly significant (except for establishing cognates formally). Within the generative school the emphasis is on the grammar module (morphology and syntax), where the emphasis on form is a deliberate choice, since meaning *is* relevant here. It is only in the later versions of generative grammar that functional roles begin to play a more important role.

Linguistic *comparison* lies also at the basis of the generative theory of grammar, but as in typology, this basis has been extended to all languages, to related as well as unrelated ones. The difference with typology is, however, that while typologists are interested in bringing out the formal *variations* found across the world's languages (to show how a particular function can be expressed by different forms), and thus in dividing the world's languages into a number of language types, generative linguists are interested in finding the deeper formal principles that lie at the basis of all variation and form part of a speaker's competence, resulting in one uniform type, usually called 'universal grammar' (UG).

An important difference from both neogrammarian and typologist thinking is that the proper object of study is not considered to be *parole* (in generative theory termed 'performance', and later also 'E-language') that is the observable linguistic data, but *langue* ('competence', 'I-language'), that is, the system underlying the data.[8] The Neogrammarians, dealing as they did with historical data, could not but compare the written elements as they found them in their sources (studying something like native-speaker competence was out of the question), but it has to be emphasized that the variation possible in their data with respect to phonetic and morphological form was far less complex than the variation the generative linguists would have had to deal with had they chosen to rely on the spoken synchronic linguistic forms rather than competence. The relatively 'clean' data the Neogrammarians dealt with may have attracted generative linguists and may have led them to clean up their data accordingly, paying attention mainly to the forms as used by the idealized speaker; it made it simpler to discover generalities in the system underlying the data.[9]

A way of thinking that had even greater influence on generative grammar was the structuralist approach to language which had developed in the early part of the twentieth century with, or rather after, the publication of de Saussure's *Cours de linguistique générale* in 1915 (notes on his lectures made by two of his students were only published after his death). As is well-known, the structuralist school shifted the emphasis of the study of language radically to the synchronic plane, concerned as it was with the agents that use/interpret language rather than with the language output itself. The assumption was that since speakers have no historical knowledge of their language, it would be wrong to describe or explain the form of their grammar from a historical point of view. What makes it possible for a language user to learn a language is the *synchronic system* that he relies on in production and perception. Chomsky's notion of this system ('competence') further shifted the attention to individual grammars, away from the notion of *langue* as one system of language shared by speakers (cf. fn.8 above). For a grammar to be learnable or for learning to be feasible, the grammar has to be seen as internally consistent: the rules of grammar have to be simple, economic, and elegant. In such a system, idiosyncracies, fuzziness, and variation have no place (but cf. fn.5 above). They are therefore relegated to the lexicon and to the performance level.

For the comparison in this volume we will concentrate on the P&P approach, which has been the most fruitful and most frequently used model in studies of change. Generally this model can be described as a modular and computational system of grammar, which is closely linked to the LAD (Language Acquisition Device). Central in this model is the syntactic component, which is considered to be autonomous and generates the (deep) structures that will be further expanded with information from another component, the lexicon. Lexicon and syntax together provide the base which feeds the interpretive modules of PF (Phonological Form) and LF (Logical Form). The syntactic component consists of categorial (phrase structure) rules and transformational rules, the latter having been reduced to just one type, that is Move-α. The whole system is constrained by principles which may work on one or more of the subcomponents, such as the principles of X-bar theory, government, binding, bounding, Case and θ-theory, and control. The principles always obtain, but there is some room for parametric variation. Parameters will be set on the basis of UG and the PLD that the child is faced with during the period of language acquisition. The setting of the parameters forms the basic mechanism for change (cf. Chomsky 1981: 1–16).

The dichotomies that have often been noted with respect to the two theories—the most important of which are given in (1)—are to a large extent bound up with the historical developments out of which they emerged.

(1a) language vs. grammar (performance vs. competence)
(1b) process-oriented vs. product-oriented
(1c) contiguity with cognition vs. innateness of grammar
(1d) equality of all levels vs. centrality (autonomy) of syntax
(1e) gradual vs. radical change
(1f) non-discrete vs. discrete categories/rules
(1g) motivated vs. arbitrary codes
(1h) diachronic vs. synchronic
(1i) function vs. form

In the following section, we will consider these dichotomies in more detail and explore the different aims and methods related to them and considered typical for the two approaches in question.

2.2 The aims, assumptions, and methods of the two theories: a broad view

2.2.1 What is the proper object of study: language or grammar?

There seems to be a deep split between generative and grammaticalization theorists as to what should be the prime object of investigation: should we take language output as basic or the system of grammar (cf. (1)a above)? It is easy to find diametrically opposed opinions, but we must not forget the many shades that hover in between. Let us look at the more extreme positions first. There is, on the one hand, Paul Hopper, with his notion of 'Emergent Grammar', who writes, 'the term Emergent Grammar points to a grammar which is not abstractly formulated and abstractly represented, but always anchored in the specific concrete form of an utterance' (Hopper 1987: 142). 'Emergent' here refers to a 'continual movement towards structure, a postponement or "deferral" of structure, a view of structure as always provisional, always negotiable, and *in fact as epiphenomenal*, that is, at least *as much an effect as a cause*' (Hopper 1987: 142, emphasis added). The other end is best represented by David Lightfoot, since he has written most explicitly and most extensively about the theoretical position of the historical-generative enterprise: 'our focus here is grammars, not the properties of a particular language, or even general properties of many or all languages. A language on the view sketched here is an *epiphenomenon, a derivative concept*, the output of certain people's grammars' (Lightfoot 1999: 74, emphasis added).

It is clear that a grammar (or a language) as 'cause' or as 'effect' are each other's opposites here. Many, if not most functional linguists, however, believe that there is such a thing as a system of grammar, a system that may steer the interpretation or production of linguistic output.[10] What there is disagreement about is what type of system this is: autonomous (arbitrary) or functionally motivated (cf. (1)g above and see also §2.2.3); how much of it acts as a 'cause' (grammaticalizationists would see its development as a combination of cause and effect); and how much of it is specific to language (cf. (1)c). Similarly, in the early days of generative grammar, most linguists saw the grammar as a *logical* system that *could* be a model of speakers' actual language competence. Such an interpretation of the theory of grammar as a *possible* model can clearly be read into Chomsky's earlier work. (As a *possible* model, it would be less of a 'cause'.) It was only in later generative work that the idea crystallized that the generative model was a 'biological grammar', a *direct* representation of the 'grammar module' in our mind/brain, and therefore a direct 'cause'.[11]

I would like to note at this point that accepting the notion of a genetically endowed grammar, is clearly attractive from a scientific point of view. It means that the contours of this grammar will have to be brought in line with the physiological workings of our brains. It makes the theory of UG falsifiable at another level (in another domain), and would thus avoid the problem of circularity noted above. Methodologically, then, this would be a healthy standpoint. If the ultimate aim is, however, to show how our language abilities are connected to the workings of the brain, it would be more logical to concentrate on the processing and comprehension of speech rather than on the competence which produces language. In the same way, it would be more logical to concentrate on actual language utterances (both spoken and written) than on the isolated sentences produced by the idealized speaker, which resemble most closely only the written forms of language (cf. (1)b above). This step, however, is not taken (see further below, §2.2.2).[12]

Leaving aside the innateness of UG for the moment (but see §2.2.2), what we can note is that there is a real difference of opinion as to how the system of grammar (geno- and phenotype) is to be established. For grammaticalizationists, it is clear that the system can only be determined on the basis of the language output, and hence that it is this output that is the primary object of study. Similarly, as far as change is concerned, this too should be studied first and foremost from the performance angle because here the variation and fuzziness is to be found which forms the beginning of change. In order to explain language change, or rather linguistic innovations that may lead to change, we would therefore have to look at language as it is used in a communicative context.

In fact, it could be said that in grammaticalization studies too much emphasis is laid on context, which is seen as the main engine of change while the role that the synchronic system plays or may play is on the whole neglected. Mithun, who works within the grammaticalization framework, has consistently pointed to this shortcoming. She writes, '[u]nderstanding the process of grammaticization involves not only discovering which categories tend to be grammaticized in languages, but also why these are not grammaticized in every language' (Mithun 1991: 159, and see also Mithun 2003). She mentions a number of factors that may play a role here, the most important being 'the shape of the current grammar'. She notes that '[t]he formation of new grammatical categories is motivated or hindered by the contours of the existing grammatical system' (p. 160), giving examples in the rest of her article. Haiman (1998: 161) similarly notes that 'motivation is not always semantic or pragmatic. It may be entirely syntactic.'

Within the generative school, the study of the language output has been relegated to the lowest possible position. This is because, when the grammar is seen as the 'cause' of language rather than as its 'effect', language performance is not really seen as the primary force that steers the learning child towards the formulation of a language system; the system is prior to the output; it is in fact innate (cf. (1)c above). Here again, there are differences of opinion within the generative community.[13] In more recent years, much attention has been paid to the role played by the PLD in language acquisition (see notably Lightfoot 1991, 1999). It is acknowledged that language-specific phenomena help shape a speaker's 'phenotype'. However, ultimately, this phenotype is 'attained on the basis of a certain trigger [in the PLD] and the genotype', that is UG (Lightfoot 1999: 66, and see fn.4 above). Since the biological grammar or genotype cannot be studied directly, generative linguists are still forced to use language output as a path towards knowledge of its source. Another area which is currently under attack from within the generative community is the centrality of syntax (cf. (1)d above). Jackendoff (2002), for instance, proposes a 'parallel architecture', in which the levels of phonology and semantics should be seen as independent tiers next to syntax (so no longer as mere interpretative modules) correlated to each other through an interface.

The relegation of actual performance data is also seen in the fact that the output data that are eventually considered mostly concern isolated sentences based on native speakers' intuitions; they are hardly ever culled from corpora. These data often resemble the *written* forms of language rather than the spoken. This is presumably because the written language looks more logical, uses complete sentences rather than half-finished ones and is relatively free of fuzziness and variation (in social and stylistic terms, since the written forms used are those of educated speakers) and hesitation phenomena. This in turn provides a link to the assumption that the generative system underlying language must be a logical and elegant system and contain a finite set of elements (see §2.0).

In the discussion of aims and methods, the question of the innateness and autonomy of grammar (cf. (1)c,d above) takes up a highly fundamental position. The autonomy of grammar involves the idea that the syntactic rules and principles of language are formulated without reference to meaning, discourse, or language use. The assumption of the innateness of such a syntactic module is an awkward one because it is difficult to explore empirically. We must therefore look at the issue of innateness a little more closely.

2.2.2 The innateness of a grammar module

What pleads for or against innateness of some type of core grammar?[14] The arguments usually put forward by the formalist linguistic school are of a biological and a logical nature; both are, as yet, based on indirect evidence. We will look at the biological facts first.

Biological considerations

Evidence from brain-damaged patients is often used to show that there is a specific part or module in the left hemisphere of our brain that deals with grammar. Pinker (1994: 45–6) and others describe cases of people with Broca's aphasia (a form of aphasia called 'agrammatism'), whose grammatical processing is seriously impaired but whose lexical processing is left more or less undisturbed. It was at first thought that this impairment was strictly related to Broca's area but further research has shown (see Lieberman 1991: 85; Pinker 1994: 309–10) that this is too simple an idea: Broca's area cannot be said to constitute 'the grammar organ' (Pinker 1994: 309).

The lexical type of aphasia ('anomia') is a still bigger problem since damage to the brain is in this case even less localized, making the idea of a separate lexical module unlikely (cf. Pulvermüller 2002: 116–17; Goldberg 2001: 65). Research has shown that different lexical signs are stored in different brain regions. Pulvermüller (2002: 56–62) discusses experiments that show that signs for objects which are usually visually perceived (such as wild animals or large man-made objects) are stored in an area that is also concerned with visual processing (the occipital cortex), while signs for tools and action verbs (which are related to touch rather than vision), are stored close to a brain region that is also connected with motor activities (the premotor cortex). It was also found that words associated with these objects/activities often activate the same regions.[15]

Similarly, Pulvermüller observes (2002: 116) that no easy distinction can be made in terms of localization between grammatical or 'low-imageability' words (functional elements) and lexical, 'high-imageability' words (referential elements). Their localization is diffuse. In linguistic terms this could be interpreted as a continuum, with word signs referring to concrete objects and activities placed at one end of the spectrum, and signs referring to more abstract qualities and activities placed closer to the purely functional elements at the other end. In a similar vein, Slobin (1997: 282) notes that cross-linguistic studies of aphasia have failed 'to find any support for a "dual-lexicon hypothesis", which postulates that open- and closed-class items are mediated by different mechanisms and/or stored separately'; rather, this research points to 'processing factors alone as distinguishing the two classes', and he adds that it is more likely that both classes of words are handled within a single lexicon. These findings are relevant in connection with point (1)f above, because they pertain to the question of the concreteness of categories.

The neurologist Goldberg (2001: 66), too, found that 'the knowledge of word meaning is not stored in the brain as a separate, compact module. Different aspects of word meaning are distributed in close relationship to those aspects of physical reality which they denote'. More generally, Goldberg (2001: 55ff.) describes how the 1980s saw a revival of 'phrenology' under the term of 'modularity' (cf. Fodor 1985). It was assumed that the cortex consists of distinct modules, each in charge of highly specific functions, which were encapsulated and showed very limited interaction. The 'reality' of these modules would be proven by the existence of strong 'dissociations'.[16] This idea was taken up by generative linguists, who used these dissociations (e.g. Pinker 1994: 45–54, 313–17) to establish the autonomy of a grammar (syntax) module (cf. point (1)d above). Goldberg (2001: 56) writes that this search to identify 'the mysterious modules' is fallacious in that for 'every case of strong dissociations there are hundreds of cases of weak dissociations, where many functions are impaired together, albeit to different degrees. By making an a priori decision that these far more numerous cases are unimportant and only the strong dissociations are important, one inevitably drifts toward a bias in favor of the modular model of the brain'.

There are also reasons to assume that a specific grammar (and lexical) module is not particularly parsimonious in a neural and evolutionary sense. If indeed the different representations of categories of things are distributed in the brain according to their various sensory components, as mentioned above, then the language capacity could be explained as a gradual development from these sensory capacities; that is our knowledge of grammar can then be coupled to evolutionary older cognitive abilities (cf. (1)c above).[17] There would be no need, as Chomsky (e.g. 1982: 23; 1991: 50) and other generative linguists have done, to postulate a language module suddenly appearing, as it were out of the blue, in the course of the evolution from apes to humans (but cf. Pinker (1994: 361–3), who argues, *pace* Chomsky, that natural selection is the only way to explain the complex design of language). [18]

We cannot actually prove that language evolved gradually. All we know is that the evolution of humans stretches over a long enough period for it to be possible that complex systems arose gradually by natural selection. The conflict among linguists in this respect may be seen as somewhat similar to the conflict between biologists and some other natural scientists: the (neo-)Darwinists argue that complex design can evolve by natural selection through small steps given enough time (cf. Dawkins' (1986: 77ff.) description of the development of a complex organ such as the eye), while many supporters of Intelligent Design believe that such complex organs as the eye and human beings in general cannot be explained by an evolutionary process because such a random process simply cannot result in anything so fine-tuned and perfect (cf. e.g. Behe 1996; Johnson 2000);[19] in other words, there must have been a 'designer' to oversee or at least initiate the process. In a similar way, the innate design of UG may have been assumed because it is felt that this is the only way to explain the fact that children can learn the highly complex system of language so perfectly and in such a short period of time in spite of the degenerate data presented to them.[20] Where this design originates remains a mystery.

No one would deny that parts of the language faculty are innate. Carstairs-McCarthy (2000: 252; and see also Hauser and Fitch 2003) rightly points to the biological changes in the human larynx and pharynx, which increased the 'vocalization possibilities' and hence 'facilitate[d] a larger vocabulary of "calls" '. Yngve (1996: 90–1) points to brain mechanisms such as memory, which have also become adapted to the production of language. What is being questioned rather is the very specific nature (and position) of modules concerned only with language, or even more specific, concerned only with the lexicon or only with the grammar (i.e. the *autonomy* of grammar).

The evolutionary aspect deserves a little more attention. Recently a number of studies have appeared on the evolutionary emergence of language, and in particular syntax, with the aim of finding more evidence for a possible biological grammar (e.g. Hurford *et al.* 1998; Knight *et al.* 2000; Christiansen and Kirby 2003). The sort of questions asked here are whether UG emerged as a 'big bang' together with human language, whether it evolved by adaptive biological evolution (cf. Givón 1995a, referred to in fn.17 above) as exaptations of pre-existing, non-syntactic structures (e.g. semantic or phonological/syllabic structure[21]), or whether UG is not innate at all but arises naturally from some type of proto-language. The majority of the linguists contributing to the discussion on the emergence of syntax in Knight *et al.* (2000) and Christiansen and Kirby (2003) (and see also Wunderlich 2004) favour the last possibility. Although there remain clear differences in their approach, the general suggestion is that the proto-language consisted of acoustic signs (which may have been arbitrary or iconic or even random), which are holistically tied to function/meaning. In the course of many generations of learners, who learn 'observationally' from older generations, the link between form and function became fixed, and perceived 'compositionally' (Kirby 2000 and Hurford 2000b show by means of computational models how this inevitably takes place given enough time). Alternatively, some decomposition may have been there from the very beginning given the fact that man (in common with other mammals) has a general disposition towards compositionality (it is present, for instance, also in vision and manual activities) and towards making generalizations. The advantage of compositional rules rather than idiosyncratic rules is that they are more general, and hence are applied more often (cf. Kirby 2000: 319–20; Hurford 2000b: 330) so that they have a greater chance of being replicated. Idiosyncratic rules, on the other hand, are easier to learn, as long as there are not too many of them. But when the vocabulary expands, it is the more general rules which carry the day, even though they are harder to learn in the first instance, because they are more frequent and more powerful. We will return to the issue of language evolution in Chapter 3.

Logical considerations

Other arguments for innateness are provided by the 'poverty-of-the-stimulus' notion. This concept is one of the most crucial assumptions on which the generative paradigm is based, and it is also the most hotly contested one (see the open peer commentary in *Behavioral and Brain Sciences* 12: 334–75 (1989) and 14: 597–650 (1991); the debates in special issues of *The Linguistic Review* 19/1–2 (2002) and *Studies in Language* 28/3 (2004); and Lombardo Vallauri (2004)). The 'poverty'-argument refers to the child's ability to learn the parent language within a relatively short period of time in spite of the following obstacles:

(i)   The PLD contains many incomplete, ill-formed utterances, and yet the child makes the correct choices, it does not overgeneralize.
(ii) No evidence is provided in the PLD for constructions that do not occur; i.e. the PLD is not rich enough to determine the limits to the generalizations that the child makes.
(iii) Very little linguistic correction is offered where it could be offered.
(iv) The child produces novel utterances that it has never heard before.

The basic idea, briefly, is that the PLD is poor and incomplete and that *therefore* there must be some linguistic 'extra' (some innate 'source') that helps the child to acquire language. The 'incompleteness' of the stimuli is of course interconnected with what one selects as data for one's investigation. As we have seen, the generative school filters out most of the contextual and functional aspects of language use, leaving only 'form' (cf. point (1)i above), which inevitably limits the informativeness of the data that they select when they investigate the language that the child is confronted with when acquiring its native tongue. According to more functionally or cognitively inclined linguists, early child learning is heavily context dependent, in which it is similar to non-human communication (cf. Itkonen 1994: 46; Givón 1995a: 428, 434; Clark 2003: 26, 138 and *passim*).

The second 'obstacle' mentioned in the poverty argument also depends heavily on the kind of data that one includes in one's investigation. Children do generalize from the structures they have already heard, and they also *over*generalize, producing structures which are not part of the grammar. They drop most of these again, however, if they do not encounter them frequently in the speech surrounding them.

Similar problems exist with respect to how one interprets the relevance of points (iii) and (iv). Clark (2003: 44 and *passim*), an expert in child language acquisition, does not agree that correction is not offered to children, but it is often implicit rather than explicit. Correction is offered by means of reformulations, which by 'repeat[ing] the same content, ... imply that what the child said had something wrong with it'. '[C]hildren show evidence of attending to adult reformulations: They take up some of them directly and correct their own utterances in their next turn' (Clark 2003: 427). Even positive evidence may provide correction for the child because it emphasizes 'the conventional way to say something' (Clark 2003: 428).

Another point that Clark makes, which is relevant to (i)–(iii) above is that the speech used by adults in their conversation with children is heavily 'child-directed', in the sense that it has specific properties that will help the child to learn and understand its native language. These properties include special pitch and intonation, differences in rate, pausing and fluency, repetitiousness, a virtual absence of errors, and a highly grammatical form (Clark 2003: 28, 38–43). In addition, most of the conversations with young children take place in concrete situations, where the child is directly confronted with the objects talked about. Contextual clues are therefore crucial for comprehension and later production. It has further been shown in many studies that acoustic clues (e.g. Peters 1985: 1033–40; Dodd and Fogel 1991: 617) and frequency (e.g. Braine 1988; Schlesinger 1989: 356; Bybee and Hopper 2001) are very important in child learning, aspects which are often neglected in the data considered by generative linguists (cf. e.g. Crain 1991).[22]

Point (iv) concerns the fact that children produce *novel* utterances, phrases, or clauses they have never heard before. It is clear that such utterances cannot be produced purely by imitation. The child must have acquired certain mechanisms to build new phrases. What is behind such mechanisms is subject to debate, but it does not *a priori* point to an innate grammar of the type envisaged by generative linguists. The novelty consists mainly in the use of already encountered and frequent structural patterns but with different lexical slot-filling, or in the use of the same construction but with a dependent clause stuck onto it or embedded in it. Lightfoot (1999: 60) calls the latter 'iterative devices', devices which 'in principle' may cause 'any given sentence [to] be of indefinite length'. Fairly simple operating principles working on the input, such as analogy—an awareness of 'same' and 'different'—could help children to produce such novelties.[23] Peters (1985) and Slobin (1985a) describe such general operating principles or strategies, which are based on analogy, on recognizing what is *same*, and therefore, what is *not-same*, and drawing conclusions from that.[24] These same/different operations are performed on linguistic utterances in context, on the form as well as the situated meaning of the utterance, in which frequency, too, plays an important role (see Slobin 1985a: 1165–6). Peters and Slobin recognize different stages and different types of operating principles (OPs), beginning with simple ones dealing with extraction and segmentation of the acoustic 'noise' children first receive, later followed by OPs recognizing internal segments (bound morphemes), OPs to distinguish 'frames' (syntactic patterns) from 'slots' (content words), and OPs monitoring feedback. Itkonen and Haukioja (1997) show how similar analogical procedures can account for novel structures in syntax.[25] In sum, children's structural novelties need not be triggered by the grammatical device alone, they are also the result of the environment in which they learn and act, and of their ability to discover patterns through what they have already learned and stored at each particular stage.[26] (More discussion of this particular point will follow in §§3.3 and 3.4.)

A Methodological consideration

One more aspect should be addressed in connection with the innateness of grammar, and that is a methodological one. Derwing (1977: 79–80) writes that we should be 'questioning the value of any linguistic theory that attempts to invoke "innateness" as an explanatory vehicle' because positing innateness 'does not provide any positive insight into either its nature or development, but is rather tantamount to an admission of a *failure* to explain it'. Calling upon innateness is setting the problem aside instead of facing it, which does not advance knowledge.[27] For historical linguistics a similar plea was made by Bybee (1988: 357), when she stated that 'complete explanations must specify a causal mechanism: thus we cannot explain change with reference to preferred types, but we must explain common types by referring to the factors that create them'. It is by doing detailed spadework that we may be able to discover whether typological or statistical universals or 'preferred types' are truly causal factors in the (development of the) language system or in language change.

2.2.3 Further dichotomies

In the previous subsection, we considered the question of the innateness of UG or of some form of grammar. It is clear from the discussion that opinions are still very much divided on this: the functional school argues against, the generative school argues in favour. From an evolutionary and neurobiological point of view, the evidence for an autonomous grammar module seems weaker than the evidence for the grammatical language capacity as part of more general cognitive processing and development. It is also clear, however, that the neuro-scientific enterprise is still in its infancy. Much remains to be discovered. Not surprisingly, neuro-scientists are hesitant in drawing firm conclusions. Pulvermüller (2002: 110) formulates carefully when he observes that '[f]rom a neuroscientific perspective, some assumptions immanent to modular models appear difficult to anchor in brain matter'. In connection with this, he refers to the idea of a one-directional activity (which the P&P model uses for the purely interpretative function of the levels of PF and LF), which is problematic since most neuro-anatomical observations show that 'most of the corticocortical connections are reciprocal'. Another problem he notes for the generative approach is their idea that the processing of different types of linguistic information 'should take place without interaction' (ibid.). Quite clearly generative linguists are responding to these problems (e.g. Jackendoff 2002) and solutions to them within an autonomous framework may still be forthcoming because, as Pulvermüller (2002: 111) also makes clear, a modular approach in itself is not 'incompatible with a neurobiological perspective'.[28]

Most of the dichotomies mentioned under (1) in §2.1.2 were seen to be closely connected to the innateness/autonomy issue discussed in §2.2.2 and to the issue of whether language or grammar should be the point of departure for the study of language (here more specifically morphosyntactic) change, discussed in §2.2.1. Four of the dichotomies mentioned under (1) have been paid less attention to: the issue of the (non)gradualness of change (1e), the issue of arbitrariness (1g), which is closely connected with the form/function dichotomy (1i), and the split between diachrony and synchrony (1h). These too can be seen to be related to the two bigger issues, as I will show in a brief discussion of each one in turn.

Gradual vs. radical change

According to the generative model, all categories are discrete. The system is digital rather than analogue.[29] Intermediate steps are therefore not considered possible, at least not at the level of the grammar. In the analogue grammaticalization model the categories are fluid, containing prototypical as well as peripheral members. It is perhaps possible to introduce discreteness even in fluid categories by introducing features into each category, which may then discretely mark each member within a category (comparable to distinctive features in phonology). What one needs to establish in that case is how many features are needed. This, however, will not be easy since most of these features are connected to semantic/pragmatic functions (which is not the case in phonology!), which are themselves not discrete, and it is hard to give formal expression to them.[30]

As an example, let us look at a typical case of change seen as gradual within grammaticalization theory, that is the grammaticalization of the original Latin ablative noun *mente* into an adverbial affix *-ment(e)* in the Romance languages. We may note that there are some discrete stages in this development of *mente* (cf. Hopper and Traugott 2003: 140–1). Some of these are formally marked. Thus, there is an intermediate stage (still relevant for Spanish, but no longer for French) in which the ablative noun *mente* is already an affix but with enough semantic content still for it not to have to be repeated in cases of coordination. This is formally marked by the presence or absence of repetition. Thus in Modern Spanish, one still finds *clara y concisamente* 'clearly and concisely' (also found in Old French: *humble et doucement* 'humbly and gently'), whereas in Modern French only the structure with a repeated affix is possible: *humblement et doucement*. More difficult to formalize, however, is another, earlier

intermediate stage, in which the ablative noun *mente* comes to be coordinated not just with psychological adjectives like 'humble' (where it is to be
expected, with a noun meaning 'mind'), but also with physical, more
concrete adjectives such as 'slow' or 'soft' in combination with concrete
verbs such as 'walk' or 'touch'. One could attempt to attach features to
the adjectives or verbs in question regulating their collocation, but since we
are now dealing with semantic qualities, all kinds of intermediate stages are
easily imaginable. For instance, the affix may begin to collocate with more
concrete words, only via more abstract metaphorical usages of these words
first. We might end up with an endless list of features (similar to the
problem Katz and Fodor's (1963) semantic theory ran up against). Since
in the formal P&P model, semantics plays a subordinate role, this particular problem simply does not exist, and can therefore be ignored. Without
the semantics, the change can more easily be considered discrete and
instantaneous.[31]

Of course, as is clear, this happens at a cost. The change may be
instantaneous in the individual autonomous grammar but it is clearly
not, or it is less, instantaneous from the point of view of the language
output. There the change may take hundreds of years. In cases such as
mente, the P&P model only considers the change a 'real' change when it is
in its last stage, that is when there has been a discrete *category* change (cf.
also Chapter 4 on the modals, where we are confronted with a similar
problem) or a discrete change in *position*.

This brings us to another point. In generative theory, a change is seen as
instantaneous not just from an internally linguistic point of view related to
formally discrete categories and positions, but also from the point of view
of the model of language acquisition (which is also a model for change) that
is used by the theory. The model shown in Figure 2.1 originally comes from
Andersen (1973) and goes back to Klima (1965).

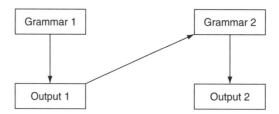

Figure 2.1. *Model of language transmission*
Source: Andersen (1973)

The basic idea is that it shows how the speaker of the next generation (the speaker of Grammar 2) bases his grammar on the output of the first generation (and with the help of UG). The diagram shows that there is no direct link between Grammar 1 and Grammar 2, the link is via the Output of Grammar 1. It also shows that there is no direct link between Output 1 and Output 2.

This looks neat, but there are some grave problems. The schema does not take into account that the output on which the speaker of Grammar 2 bases his grammar, is not just that of the speaker of Grammar 1. In fact the output that Speaker 2 bases his grammar on is the output of various generations, young and old. The output in other words is not homogeneous but has diachronic variation built into it. Another tenet in the generative model of language acquisition (not made explicit in Figure 2.1) is that a speaker fixes his grammar during language acquisition (in the so-called critical period) and that no significant changes are made to it in the course of his adult life (when the output he hears around him will have changed and broadened). This is in fact very much open to question.

To sum up, the instantaneity of change in generative theory is based on the discontinuity of grammars (which is in itself correct), on a rather narrow view of the way in which the output level influences the formation of the grammar, and on the idea that a grammar gets fixed once and for all during the acquisition period. According to this view, a change in a rule or category is not likely to be gradual within an individual speaker's grammar (see also the discussion in §3.1 below).[32]

There is no disagreement between formal and functional linguists that a change may be gradual on the level of the language output. This type of graduality of change is fully acknowledged: it involves the gradualness that can be observed in grammaticalization processes and in the diffusion of a change across a language community (cf. the distinction that was made between an individual 'innovation' and general language 'change' in §1.2). In addition, most functional linguists, in line with formal linguists, agree that the transmission of grammars is discontinuous—at least in theory, if not always in practice—(for a list with full references and a discussion, see Janda 2001: 272–5), and that for that reason a particular ongoing change at the output level may become intensified and rapid between generations in grammar transmission. The disagreement exists elsewhere.

Formal linguists maintain that changes are instantaneous on the individual grammar level. Now this may seem correct when one looks at each individual utterance or interpretation generated by an individual's grammar—because one does not normally produce a mixed construction. Such an utterance or interpretation shows a discrete result of the application of some rule. But it clearly need not be true for the way a rule is present in the grammar itself. A grammatical rule may be a variable one, so that the output of it may vary according to occasion; or a rule may change in a speaker's lifetime. Thus, a Middle English verb may still be impersonal on one occasion (taking a dative NP as subject), and personal on another (taking a nominative as subject) for the same speaker, in contrast to what is presented in Lightfoot (1979, 1981) as discussed in §1.1.2 above. How is this to be represented in the grammar? Does this speaker allow both SOV and SVO order? In the same way, different stages of a grammaticalization process may still be present in the grammar of one and the same speaker (as is for instance true in the case of the grammaticalization of BE + *going to*), and these forms may also be produced by some variable rule.[33] When various outcomes involving the same linguistic sign are possible, it follows that the grammar rule generating them has not undergone an instantaneous shift. One way out of this dilemma has been to adopt the notion of simultaneous, competing grammars (cf. Pintzuk and Kroch 1989 and Pintzuk 1991). However, this does not really solve the problem, because where does multiplication stop? Do we postulate a separate grammar for each variable structure? Another way out is incorporating lexical-semantic features into the grammar on an equal footing as is done in HPSG, LFG, and Construction Grammar (cf. fn. 31 above), which enables one to cut up categorical changes into smaller but still discrete steps.

Clearly a solution that does justice to both the formal and semantic/functional aspects of the language (system) would be preferable. The changes that we will investigate in this volume and which have been studied from both a formal and a functional angle should be of some help towards a better understanding of how formal and functional factors interact. I hope that they will also shed light on the causes behind these changes, and ultimately on the shape of the system of language.

Motivated vs. arbitrary codes and form vs. function

In an autonomous syntacto-centric theory there is no room in any primary sense for the functional (semantic) properties of signs[34] because these properties are part of an interpretative module (LF), which is dependent on the input coming from the syntactic module. This entails that the machinery of the syntactic module must provide enough information for LF (and of course for PF too) to be filled in properly so as to produce the correct output. To indicate, for instance, what function a (pro)nominal or verbal element has within a clause, the machinery relies on principles such as C-command, different types of government and binding, θ-theory, on the position of the element within the generated string, on movement rules—and in the more recent Minimalist version on Move and Merge, weak and strong features and feature checking—and empty categories. The fact that semantic factors and morphological surface features must somehow be accounted for in the syntax, makes the syntactic structure highly abstract and far removed from the eventual surface structure. A corollary of this is that it makes syntactic structure look more arbitrary, that is its high level of abstraction makes it difficult to see the syntax as somehow being motivated by usage (this is in contrast to most functional linguists who consider syntactic structures to be or to have been motivated by their functions, see below, and cf. e.g. Croft 1991; Givón 1995a; Haiman 1998). This degree of abstraction is also problematic in terms of language acquisition and in terms of actual language processing, and it is undoubtedly one of the reasons why generative linguists assume UG to be innate.

We have seen above (§2.2.2) that from a neuro-scientific point of view it is not possible completely to separate form from function. For example, the location of some lexical items is only understandable if one takes their function into account. It is also clear from empirical studies of language acquisition that children learn the meaning of linguistic signs in connection with their function. Clark (2003: 138ff.) notes that children learn their language in a social context, and that the situational context and mutual knowledge established as common ground play a crucial role here. In mapping form to meaning they combine cognitive with social information. Cognitive information consists of universal perceptual and conceptual primitives. Thus, children build up word meaning relying 'on shape first, followed by properties like sound, size, taste and texture' (Clark 2003: 140).

The build-up of word meaning comes first, syntax appears only later, and this relies in turn on the words (and their functions) already learned. Children first produce holistic 'formulas of limited scope' and there is 'little evidence that word order has any grammatical role at this stage' (Clark 2003: 171); order seems to be used pragmatically or is an imitation of the order used by caregivers (ibid. p. 172). The learning of categories like nouns and verbs most likely follows a two-way track. First, children

'draw on the correlations between the entities in the world and the categories at the core of syntactic word-class definitions' (ibid. p. 178), such as
nouns and verbs, beginning with the most prototypical examples within
these categories. As they learn these word classes, they discover the formal
morphological properties that go with them, helping them to distinguish
the classes further. Secondly, 'word classes may also emerge from consistent patterns within the constructions children pick up and extend' (ibid.).
This is a more abstract type of pattern recognition.

Thus, it is clear that both form and function play equally important roles
from the very beginning. Children start off by recognizing and distinguishing acoustic (phonetic) forms and linking them with objects in the world.
This involves a primitive, first stage of symbolic thinking (because these
acoustic signs are essentially arbitrary), which is helped by indexical and
iconic modes of thinking.[35] Once they have developed a symbolic mode
of thinking for words, they will also apply it to higher level constructions,
connecting specific functions to abstract patterns (see further §§3.3 and 3.4).

Considering the close connection between form and function, it seems
likely that *new* constructions in language begin as motivated ones,[36] which
in the course of time may become a conventional part of the language
system.[37] Constructions that are frequent become automated and are
henceforth processed as single units. When this happens, the relation
between the elements in the construction, which was motivated before,
becomes opaque and arbitrary. We can observe a similar process in the
lexicalization of morphological or syntactic constructions. For instance,
the form *methinks* originally had the structure of an impersonal clause
(*Me thinks that* ...) followed by a complement. The structure occurred
frequently, and did not disappear when other impersonal constructions
disappeared from the language. Because it could now no longer be generated by the syntax, it lived on as a holistic unit, it lost the other forms of
the paradigm (e.g. *him thinks*, *us thinks*) and began to appear in positions in
the clause where it did not appear before, its origin being no longer
transparent.

The development from a motivated construction into an arbitrary form
is an important part of grammaticalization theory. The development is
caused by natural forces, which are linked to frequency. It is similar to the
ritualization of actions and activities which are part of everyday life. These
too become conventional through frequent use. In the process of conventionalization they lose their iconic and motivated aspects; by becoming

automatic they lose in transparency and sincerity (for more details, see §3.3).[38]

By taking form as primary, generative linguistics ignores or loses sight of the possibility that the structure of signs may be motivated by their function. It is true that many structures in language have lost their motivation through repetition, and have thus become arbitrary (cf. Haiman 1998). It is therefore important to remember that form by itself may play a role in the linguistic system and in change. Conventional, arbitrary structures that have conventionalized through frequent use and concomitant loss of meaning have become entrenched in language and hence shape the language system too. This is ignored by most or even denied by some grammaticalization theorists, who in general show a neglect of the formal aspects of grammar (cf. the reference to Mithun 1991 in §2.2.1) and see grammaticalization as motivated by semantics and pragmatics alone. But this is just as mistaken as seeing grammar change as being motivated by form alone. Generative linguists have taken too big a step to conclude from the existence of arbitrary structures in language that all structure is arbitrary. Once this step had been taken, however, the road to a syntacto-centric, autonomous theory of language lay wide open.

Diachrony vs. synchrony

The main reason for the strict separation between diachrony and synchrony in structural and generative linguistics is the fact that, in contrast to the past history of linguistics (see §2.1), the attention of the linguist was fully turned to the speaker; the language as such was no longer the primary object of investigation. This was a good decision at the time. Too much attention had been paid to language as if it were an object freely floating in space, which could change, as it were, of its own accord. Thus, it had been common in all linguistic research before the structuralist 'revolution' to consider the present-day language in terms of its past, to think in terms of 'diachronic rules' of the type [p] > [f], as if speakers at some point in time were actually changing [p] into [f].[39] We now realize that many sound changes are in fact discrete shifts (between variants of a variable rule or between grammars, see above).[40] A variant for [p], that is [f], might be introduced into the language (via contact, assimilation in a particular phonetic context, etc.), which would exist side by side with [p]. In the course of time the new variant might become more frequent, and finally may oust the old [p] altogether. It is not the case, therefore, that an individual speaker's grammar possesses a rule [p] > [f]. Rather it contains a variable rule, stating for each variant where and when it is used. To clean up this confusion, it was a good decision to make a sharp methodological distinction between synchrony and diachrony. However, this decision, in combination with the later decision of generative linguists to consider only the core language (doing away with all variable forms occurring in performance) and to concentrate on competence mainly, led to a situation in which most variation was simply ignored.[41]

Since it is variation that provides the seeds for change, possible changes were no longer spotted the moment they started, and in an explanation for a change its initial stages were ignored. It is therefore not surprising that in generative descriptions of change, the changes are always abrupt, because mostly the end point of a change is paid attention to (the point at which a parameter shift takes place) when the variation has shifted to zero in the grammar of a next generation of speakers. Grammaticalization theory, on the other hand, has a strong inclination to see grammaticalization changes as taking place gradually by imperceptible shifts, and being steered only by semantic/pragmatic factors. Any concomitant morpho-syntactic (and phonetic) changes are seen as a (mere) *result* of this earlier 'conceptual manipulation' (Heine *et al.* 1991a: 174, and cf. also Hopper 1991: 19; Rubba 1994; Hopper and Traugott 2003: 75–6). Hence all the emphasis is on the earlier stages, and on the semantic-pragmatic motivation. What we need is a description of morphosyntactic change that does full justice to form as well as meaning, and takes all of the change into consideration. What we need, therefore, is a theory that looks at performance facts, takes account of variation, and gives equal weight to form and function.

2.3 Reconciliation

First of all, I think it is important to realize that the two approaches under discussion here are *both* useful as *heuristic devices*. Indeed it could be said that no theory is more than a heuristic device. The *Scientific American* (July 72/3, 1955) aptly noted that 'Einstein's 1905 paper, for which (nominally) he had been awarded the Nobel prize, did not contain the word "theory" in the title, but referred instead to considerations from a "heuristic view-point" '. Both our models give us insight into language and language change, highlighting different aspects of it. For a fuller understanding of change, therefore, the insights of both theories need to be taken into account. Thus, the primary aim of Part II, the case studies, will be to see what the two approaches have suggested with respect to particular changes and to combine their insights, relating to *both* form *and* function, to achieve a deeper understanding of the changes in question. The expectation is that these case studies will then also advance our understanding of morphosyntactic change in general.

The above could be called rather a pragmatic approach to reconciliation, in that it does not involve any change in point of view from within a theory. Similar in this respect are the pleas coming from both functional and formal linguists for more cooperation, and for more openness towards one another's views. Givón (1995a: xv–xvii) strongly criticizes the reductive tendencies on both sides, describing them as a 'collective smugness', 'an old denial reflex'. He gives a list of all the dichotomies that the two sides indulge in, whereby each school claims the other to be 100 per cent in whatever aspect of the theory they don't like, whereas in reality and taken broadly (i.e. not just concentrating on your pet enemy) the various points of view are much less categorical. He advises the functionalists 'to submit their constructs to the scrutiny of method', 'to the harsh light of analytic rigor', while he warns the formalists that they are in danger of succumbing under their 'own weight of formal vacuity'. Givón opens the windows but remains true to the functional approach (the quotation is from the preface to a book entitled *Functionalism and Grammar*), just as Newmeyer (1998), in his detailed comparison and critique of the methods, mechanisms, and explanations provided by both theories, remains true to the formal approach.[42]

Other ways of reconciling the two views have been attempted within the bounds of theory itself. As I briefly noted above (§2.2.3, fn. 31), there are theoretical models (usually a form of Dependency Grammar), which are committed to 'form' but allow function a full and independent role. In these grammars it is the lexical elements with their formal 'dependencies' that take up a central position, and hence lexical features co-decide on syntactic structures. In the P&P model, the syntactic rules come first, later to be filled in with lexical items. It is to be noted, however, that within the Chomskyan framework, there has also been an increase over the years in the incorporation of functional roles into the syntactic machinery (e.g. the introduction of θ-theory and Case theory in Chomsky 1981, the notion of feature-checking and the more prominent position of lexical features in Chomsky 1995), but the autonomy of syntax has remained a stable ingredient.

Another form of *rapprochement* from the formal 'camp' is the attempt by Roberts and Roussou (1999, 2003)[43] to incorporate the ideas of grammaticalization into a Minimalist framework. Unlike most formal linguists, they take grammaticalization seriously and tackle it head-on, which is a very positive development. They interpret grammaticalization as a regular case of parameter shift, showing how the formal, reanalysis part of the grammaticalization process can be fitted into the theory. There are, however, problems with this proposal. The question of how a grammaticalization process starts is not addressed. Like all generative linguists, the interest of Roberts and Roussou is in the *grammar* 'change', not in the various kinds of 'innovations' and 'changes' (which they would call 'triggers' if they are of a formal kind; semantic-pragmatic triggers do not exist in their model) that lead up to it. According to grammaticalization theorists, it is the earlier semantic-pragmatic innovations (by pragmatic inferencing) that set the ball rolling, and they see the formal change, which is the core in Roberts and Roussou's proposal, as 'only' an accidental result of the semantic-pragmatic manipulation chain (see also the end of §2.2.3). According to Roberts and Roussou, the motor behind the change is not semantic/pragmatic but a case of 'structural simplification', and what one needs to show therefore, is why the structural simplification did not take place at some earlier stage. A serious drawback to their proposal is that the number of empty categories, that is, the number of functional heads, increases dramatically. These are functionally motivated, it is true (all functional heads have a logico-semantic content, cf. Roberts and Roussou 2003: 26),[44] but their obligatory presence considerably widens the gap between abstract structure and surface manifestation. This is in stark contrast to Dependency models, which, with their abolition of empty categories, have narrowed the gap that exists between generative and functional approaches. (More details on 'Minimalist' grammaticalization will be found in §3.1.)

Other formal theoretical models also offer approaches in which variation and gradience are taken into account, and in which the output is taken seriously. One of these is 'Analogical Modelling', which centralizes analogy, and more specifically 'analogical sets'. So far, most of the research in this area has concentrated on morphology and morphological change (cf. Skousen 1989, 1992; Baayen 2003; Chapman and Skousen 2005) but some analogical work on syntax has also been attempted (cf. Itkonen and Haukioja 1997). What makes this model attractive is the fact that its basic mechanism, analogy, is also an important cognitive principle working in other domains, thus providing the theory with an explanatory base. No doubt more space in future will be given to these ideas, what with the renewed interest in the role played by frequency in change and acquisition (cf. Bybee and Hopper 2001; Bybee 2003; Krug 2003), the interest in automatization, and the possibility of syntactic structures functioning as formulaic or holistic phrases (cf. Wray 1999; Wray and Perkins 2000; Bybee 2001). The importance of analogy and frequency in morphosyntactic change will be further discussed in Chapter 3.

Another model that takes account of variation on the output level is 'Optimality Theory', which focuses on the limitations on variability, abolishing derivations and using universal constraints and constraint ranking (which has to be learned on the basis of the output, in which frequency may also play a role) rather than rules. Most of the work here has been done on phonology, where the constraints are still relatively simple in comparison to syntax. There remain quite a few problems with this theory in that it is difficult to see how the constraints themselves will be controlled, while an explanation for change in terms of constraint re-ranking, seems descriptive rather than explanatory (cf. McMahon 2000: 90ff.).

Another important but hitherto neglected means by which reconciliation between formal and functional approaches may be achieved in the future, is via advances in neurolinguistics. Pulvermüller (2002: 270–5) notes that if one understands language as a biological organ (as many linguists within the generative paradigm do), then one should also be interested in brain structures and brain processes: it would be 'advantageous to attempt to connect one's terminology to the putative mechanisms' (p. 272) of a neuronal grammar. He continues: 'Using neuroscientific knowledge and data for guiding linguistic theorizing appears to be fruitful' 'to explore the space of possibilities', adding that 'a neuronal language theory may be a necessary condition for deciding between alternative approaches to grammar' (p. 272).

Pulvermüller (2002) presents a possible model for a neuronal grammar. A highly simplified but I think basically accurate description of the main aspects of his model is as follows.[45] Pulvermüller's (2002: 161) proposal builds upon the idea that the mechanism of 'mediated sequence processing' may be responsible for processing the serial order of morphemes and words. Each word or morpheme (A, B, etc.) is presented by a 'neuronal set' or 'functional web' (α, β, etc. respectively). The information concerning the form and meaning of a word/morpheme is seen as processes within *one* functional system (cf. 2002: 200, 248). In other words, form and meaning are closely linked, and a neuronal set (functional web) contains information having to do with phonological and lexico-semantic features of a morpheme/word (2002: 88). There are four possible activity states that a neuronal set can be in: ignition, priming, reverberation, and rest. Ignition and rest are each other's opposites (i.e. they are in an on/off position, digital), while priming and reverberation are analogue or gradual in nature (for a characterization of the terms digital/analogue, see fn. 29 above). The first word in a sequence is always ignited. Ignition is followed by reverberation, which may prime the next element in a sequence. Priming can be seen as a kind of pre-activity, it may be followed by ignition (provided another priming from another neuronal set takes place) or by non-activity (if the priming is not enhanced). The principles behind 'mediated sequence processing' are 'grounded in neurophysiology and neuroanatomy' and are 'as such, genetically determined, or at least under strong influence of the genetic code'. Everything that goes beyond the neural mechanisms is 'assumed to be the result of associative learning' (2002: 247), that is not innate.

In the processing of grammatical or 'congruent sequences' the first input word A, represented by a neuronal set or functional web α, after it has been ignited, reverberates and primes the next element in the sequence, β (representing word B), which, if it presents a possible successor word, is also ignited. These two elements together, ignite a neuronal 'sequence set' γ (more on sequence sets, below). If a construction is ungrammatical or an 'incongruent sequence', then β, although primed by α, does not ignite, nor does the neuronal sequence set γ, which needs two elements to be ignited.[46] If the sequence set γ *is* ignited and primed, 'processing is followed by a wave of ignitions running from β to the sequence set and back to α, leaving all neuronal sets in the highest state … of reverberation' (Pulvermüller 2002: 183–4). This backward wave of activity is not created by the ill-formed string.

In connection with sequence sets, a number of points have to be noted. First of all, there are two types of sequence sets (or sequence detectors), so that they may detect forwards as well as backwards (2002: 191). Secondly, Pulvermüller assumes that a sequence set is not necessarily a lexical item, but it may also be a set of abstract lexical categories, such as Noun-Verb, etc. The link between a lexical item and a lexical category may be achieved by links connecting two neuronal sets, so that when α ignites, it not only primes β but it also primes a lexical category neuronal set. Thus, the category of a nominative (or subject) noun *bear* in a sequence such as *The bear attacked* would be represented by two sequence detectors. One would detect that it follows a determiner, the other that it is followed by a verb. In a similar way, a homonym such as 'bear' (animal or verb) would be recognized by the sequence it is in and by its lexical category. 'Essentially, for each lexical category label ... a corresponding sequence detector can be postulated at the neuronal level' (2002: 191). The sequence detector stays in a state of reverberation after it has been ignited, whereby it stores the sequence detector in active memory. In this way, discontinuous elements such as 'switch' and 'off' in a structure like *She switched the light off* can still be connected together.[47] Sequence detectors thus function like a kind of checking device, they force a choice which up to the checking moment had been left open.[48]

A neuronal grammar such as that proposed by Pulvermüller works best with a bottom-up approach to grammar. A possible marriage with a dependency type of grammar can therefore more easily be envisaged than with a P&P model. The neuronal model proposed here, like a dependency grammar, offers a straightforward solution to discontinuous constituents, where the generative model has to work with movement rules. Similarly, form and function are seen as linked and completely equal. In contrast, as we have seen, the generative model ignores or subordinates function, while grammaticalization theory pays too little attention to form and especially to formal patterns in the grammar (see, for instance, my comments on Kuteva 2001, in Fischer 2004c: 322). Dependency models and grammaticalization theory work with flat structures, which goes well with this neuronal grammar, in contrast to generative models which have highly abstract structures. Finally, in this neuronal grammar, not much is taken to be innate, which is in line with grammaticalization and dependency grammars but not with generative models. Instead of innateness, Pulvermüller, stresses the role of frequency and associative learning. He notes (2002: 75) that 'two connected neurons that frequently fire together increase the strength of their wiring' and that 'any two cells or systems of cells that are repeatedly active at the same time will tend to become "associated", so that activity in one facilitates activity in the other'.[49] Another advantage of Pulvermüller's grammar is that its idea of mediated sequencing shows similarities to other cognitive systems. He observes (2002: 160) that '[a]nalogous mechanisms of movement detection by mediated sequence processing were uncovered in the visual cortex of higher mammals ..., and a related mechanism of sequence detection exists in the cerebellum ...' (references omitted).

2.4 Concluding remarks

In this chapter the two approaches under discussion have been compared from a number of aspects. I am aware that there is a danger in such a comparison in that the subtle differences that also exist *within* each paradigm tend to get smoothed over so that the two theories in some ways look more opposed than in fact they are. Still, by and large, it can be said that they concentrate on different aspects of language, that is either on the output itself or on the system underlying it, through which they reach different results. However, in both cases there *are* results, and they have to be taken seriously. I have shown that some of the differences can be explained historically, some from different methodological concerns and some from basically different assumptions, such as the top-down vs. the bottom-up approach, the emphasis on language as a product vs. language as a process, the idea of the categories of language as discrete vs. fuzzy. In all these 'oppositions', something can be said for each way of looking at things, with one exception, however, and that concerns the assumption of innateness. It is for that reason that I have devoted quite a number of pages to the poverty-of-the-stimulus argument. I seriously doubt whether this 'innate' standpoint has any advantages at all, even if it turns out eventually that we are born with an innate type of grammatical system, which I doubt. Such an assumption does not bring the investigation of (the structures of) language on a higher or deeper level because it does not adhere to the curiosity that is typical of all scientific endeavour.

I believe that the results of both theoretical models can be fruitfully linked to new approaches in linguistics, such as, especially, analogical modelling and models of neuronal grammar. In Chapter 3, I will take a more detailed look at the factors involved in language change and at important evolutionary and language acquisition findings as far as language development and change are concerned. I will provide a description of how these various factors are used and defined by the two different schools and put in a first sketch to find out how much these factors can be connected to recent analogical and connectionist models.

Notes

1. With respect to grammaticalization, Hopper and Traugott (2003: 1) note that '[t]he term "grammaticalization" has two meanings, one to do with a research framework within which to account for language phenomena, the other with the phenomena themselves' adding that this usage is rather similar to the way in which terms like 'grammar' or 'syntax' are used. For more traditional linguists the term grammaticalization refers strictly to a phenomenon, not to a theoretical framework; the latter is a development that took place only since the 1980s. It is clear that in this chapter we are discussing grammaticalization as a theoretical framework.

2. For the very interesting story as to the ascription of this well-known saying to Antoine Meillet, who may have had it from his teacher Ferdinand de Saussure, see Koerner (1999: 183–97).

3. Traugott and Heine (1991: 3–4) emphasize that grammaticalization is 'a kind of language change', and that not 'all change is grammaticalization'. Similarly, Heine (2003: 575) writes that '[g]rammaticalization theory is neither a theory of language nor of language change; its goal is to describe ... [and explain] the way grammatical forms arise and develop through space and time'.

4. Lightfoot (1999) makes this distinction between the genotype (UG) and the phenotype (the speaker's mature grammar). In Lightfoot's cue-based model children parse utterances, which results in their setting up 'mental representations' or abstract structures which they scan against so-called 'designated cues' in UG. At first some of these representations constitute partial parses because children ignore the more complex parts of the input; only at a later stage do children reach their mature grammar or phenotype (Lightfoot 1999: 57–8, 148–51). The genotype is seen as biologically endowed, innate, and predetermined. There are also generative linguists who see UG not as model of what takes place in our heads, but as a model of what an idealized language user possesses in terms of implicit linguistic knowledge (cf. Klooster 2000). Chomsky interpreted the model as biological rather than logical only in his later writings (see §2.2.1 below, and especially fn.11).

5. Of course there are exceptions here too, especially with synchronic linguists working with non-standard, non-written languages and linguists interested in diachronic and/or dialect variation (cf. the interesting work done on a syntactic atlas of Dutch dialects in the Meertens Instituut, the so-called SAND project (http://www.meertens.nl/projecten/sand/sand.html). On the whole, however, these linguists are less concerned with context and the communicative situation; this is even true for linguists who take synchronic variants and corpus evidence seriously, such as Kroch (1989a, 1989b), Pintzuk (1991), Kroch and Taylor (1997). When variation between written and spoken forms is taken into account, this is often done only to prove a theoretical point. An example of this is the attention paid to the contraction of *want to* to *wanna*, which is used to show the difference in behaviour between PRO and trace. For a discussion of this from both a generative and functional point of view, see the generative treatment of it in Crain (1991), and the comments given on this by functional linguists in the same issue of *Behavioral and Brain Sciences* 14 (1991).

6. Section 2.1 will present a fairly rough overview of the various approaches to language and change that influenced the generative and grammaticalizationist frameworks. For more details see e.g. Lehmann (1992), McMahon (1994).

7. No distinction had been made at that point between phonetics and the more abstract level of phonology. This only happened in the 1930s, under structuralist influence.

8. It has to be noted, however, that de Saussure's idea of *langue* is not the same as the later Chomskyan 'competence'. *Langue* is the language system which somehow belonged to the community, it could be called a 'community grammar', rather similar to Lightfoot's (1999) notion of 'social grammar'. Chomsky's competence represents the system of the individual mind. This notion of a mental grammar later developed into the idea of a 'biological grammar'. Not all generative linguists share this view, however (cf. fn. 4, and §2.2.1 below, especially fn. 11).

9. This is not to deny, of course, that the Neogrammarians were not interested in generalities, on the contrary, after all the famous Grimm's and Verner's Laws were formulated by them, but these generalities are *tendencies* based on the observation of variant phonetic forms on the level of *parole* (i.e. in the case of Grimm's and Verner's Laws on the variations between sister and daughter languages within the Indo-European family). The generalities made, however, are of a different nature: they have nothing to do with the system of grammar. As Lightfoot (1979: 34ff.) argues conclusively, diachronic rules like Grimm's and Verner's can have no place as a 'rule' in a speaker's (synchronic) system of grammar.

10. Consider e.g. Givón (1993: 1), who writes, 'grammar is a set of strategies that one employs in order to produce *coherent communication*. Nothing in this formulation should be taken as a denial of the existence of rules of grammar. Rather, it simply suggests that rules of grammar—taken as a whole—are not arbitrary; they are not just there for the heck of it' (emphasis as in source).

11. For instance, in *Syntactic Structures* (1957: 18), Chomsky uses the words 'device', or refers to 'the theory of grammar' and he talks about the adequacy of this device only in purely logical terms; no mention is made of a biological base. In *Aspects* (1965), Chomsky links linguistic theory with language learning, but his idea is that 'empiricist theories about language acquisition', are not at all helpful: they 'are refutable wherever they are clear, and ... further empiricist speculations have been quite empty and uninformative' while 'the rationalist approach exemplified by recent work in the theory of transformational grammar seems to have proved fairly productive, to be fully in accord with what is known about language [note that what is known concerns only competence, O.F.], and to offer at least some hope of providing a hypothesis about the intrinsic structure of a language acquisition system that will meet the condition of adequacy-in-principle and do so in a sufficiently narrow and interesting way so that the question of feasibility, can, for the first time, be seriously raised' (1965: 54–5). In other words, there *is* a link, but the language acquisition device can only be productively studied from the top down so to speak, and it is quite clear that logical principles only play a role, i.e. reasoning from competence (which does not constitute empirical data!) is the only productive way forward. The model is therefore not 'a psychological model of the way people construct and understand utterances' (Lyons 1970: 85). Only in later work (e.g. Chomsky 1981: 8), do we learn that UG is 'an element of shared biological endowment', but there is still a gap between UG and core grammar, the latter is said to be an 'idealization' of 'the reality of what a particular person may have inside his head'. More recently, judging from his reaction to John Searle in the *New York Review* (July 18, 2002, p. 64), Chomsky's stance has become clearer, he writes: 'The long-term goal has been, and remains, to show that contrary to appearances, human languages are basically cast to the same mold, that they are instantiations of the same fixed biological endowment, and that they "grow in the mind" much like other biological systems, triggered and shaped by experience, but only in restricted ways'.

12. In recent neurolinguistic research it has been shown (see e.g. van Berkum *et al.* (2003) that the semantic analysis of sentences is rapidly sensitive to the wider discourse. A holistic type of *sentence* processing (as is the rule in generative grammar) cannot deal with such facts.

13. It should also be noted that the generative theory of grammar is not a homogeneous entity with respect to how much of the grammar is innate, and what form the terms, principles and constraints take. To give an example: in the P&P approach the assumption was that the choice of basic word order (SOV vs. SVO)—and further word orders dependent on this—was subject to a parameter that could be switched on to either SOV or SVO on the basis of the PLD. More recently, in one version of the Minimalist model, Kayne (1994) has proposed that *all* languages are SVO in the base, i.e. the word order parameter has disappeared and all languages are SVO by principle.

14. For a lucid discussion, see also Penke and Rosenbach (2004), which forms the introduction to a special volume on the question of innateness.

15. These different locations in the brain, as well as the word associations show the importance of the situational context for word learning, as well as the importance of pragmatics/semantics in acquisition.

16. Dissociation is a term from chemistry which involves the direct separation of compound substances into their primary elements, or into less complex compounds; in a similar way it came to be used in neuro-psychology to refer to the decomposition of mental activities into separate centres of consciousness.

17. This is what is suggested by Givón (1995a: Ch. 9, and see also Givón 2002). He accepts as a central hypothesis that 'the human lexical code began its evolution as an iconic visual-gestural system' and that 'two distinct cycles of symbolization took place in the evolution of human language. The first involved the evolution of a well-coded lexicon, the second the evolution of grammar'. He adds that 'the very same sequence of changes—from more iconic to more symbolic coding—is invariably observed in the evolution of coded communication in pre-human species', which again makes evolutionary sense (1995a: 394). Deacon (1997, 2003) expresses similar ideas; he believes that symbolic thinking is a specifically human development from older iconic and indexical modes of thinking, which were already present in apes. For a discussion of Deacon's ideas in relation to linguistics, see §3.3 and Fischer (2004b).

18. Chomsky's position has shifted somewhat in more recent times. In Hauser et al. (2002), a distinction is made between two faculties of language, the so-called FLB (Faculty of Language in a Broad sense) and the FLN (in a Narrow sense). The characteristics of the FLB are mostly accepted as being an adaptation to language, presenting clear characteristics that are shared by many other animals. The FLN comprises 'the abstract linguistic computational system alone' (2002: 1571); it is a component of the FLB but it is 'independent of the other systems with which it interacts and interfaces'. Its principle property is recursiveness: it takes 'a finite set of elements' that yields 'a potentially infinite array of discrete properties' (2002: 1571). The authors hypothesize that the FLN, unlike the FLB, 'is recently evolved and unique to our species', but they leave open the question that the FLN may also be an adaptation. Proponents of that idea, however, would 'need to supply additional data or arguments to support this viewpoint' (2002: 1573).

19. Note that perfection is a relative thing. As Dawkins (1986: 81) writes, half an eye or 5 percent of an eye is better than no eye; even half an eye improves one's chances of survival (1986: 302). It is also clear that the physical circumstances for our language capacity are not exactly perfect, and that its evolvement has left some debris on the way. Lieberman (1991: 54) notes for instance that, because of the changes in the human larynx, its low position compared to that of apes, 'we are now liable to choke when we eat or drink [because] solid objects or liquid can fall into the human larynx'. Similarly, 'the reduced length of the modern human palate and mandible also crowds our teeth, presenting the

possibility of infection from impacted wisdom teeth'. Apes may have less in terms of language but they do not have these problems.

20. For a clear and sensible discussion of all the pros and cons on innatism vs. the gradual evolution of language, see McMahon (2000: 156–70). For a broad-minded discussion on what innateness might include in connection with language acquisition, see Clark (2003: 399–408). Another good discussion of the problems connected with innatism can be found in Dąbrowska (2004: chs. 3, 6).

21. The importance of phonological or syllabic structure is emphasized by Carstairs-McCarthy (2000) and Schlüter (2003), but in different ways. Carstairs-McCarthy suggests that syntactic structure arises out of syllabic structure, for which he finds quite strong evidence, while Schlüter points out instances of syntactic change and syntactic structure which can only be explained by reference to the 'principle of rhythmic alternation', i.e. to the 'alternation of vowels and consonants', and 'stressed and unstressed syllables', which are ultimately 'conditioned by principles of neural action' (Schlüter 2003: 76–7). Cases or developments such as these would be difficult to explain if one upholds the autonomy of syntax.

22. One of the reviewers pointed my attention to Guasti's (2002) generative study on the acquisition of grammar. Unlike Crain, Guasti does take acoustic clues and frequency into consideration but this happens only at the initial stage of language learning when the child is learning to recognize the rhythm, stress, and syllabic structure of its native language before it can recognize words. Some contextual clues also play a role in lexical learning but even here UG plays a central role. When it comes to building up its grammar phenotype, which is done on the basis of UG and via bootstrapping from the phonological on lexical levels, the importance of acoustic and contextual clues recedes into the background.

23. For a description of what such novelties entail in the generative framework, and the problems connected with it, see Itkonen and Haukioja (1997: 133–6).

24. Note that exactly the same principles operate in life in general (cf. Itkonen 1994, Deacon 1997) and in science. Yngve (1996: 134ff.), for instance, shows that in linguistic science one moves from very specific properties obtaining in any situation, to more general properties, by observing underlying *differences* and *similarities*.

25. Itkonen and Haukioja show (1997: 145 ff.) how by means of a simple computer program for analogical reasoning a structure like (2i) can correctly be produced from (1) and how (2ii) is avoided by learners,

(1)   The man who is tall is in the room
(2i) Is the man who is tall in the room?
(2ii) *Is the man who tall is in the room?

Chomsky (1975: 30–2) and Lightfoot (1982: 67–8) use these same examples to argue that only the presence of a rule system like UG can produce the correct result. Itkonen and Haukioja make clear that children can induce

(2i), by analogical extension on the basis of the simpler patterns given in (3) and (4):

(**3i**)   The man is tall

(**3ii**)   Is the man tall?

(**4i**)   The man in the room is tall

(**4ii**)   Is the man in the room tall?

And that they can induce on the basis of general perceptual structure (i.e. they would know from the situational context that 'in the room' goes with 'man' and not with 'tall') that only the construction in (2i) is proportional to (1).

26. Note that the general strategies said to be used by children in the process of language acquisition, are very similar to the general 'dispositions' that played a role in the evolution of grammar according to most linguists in Knight *et al.* 2000 (see above).

27. Von der Gabelentz, quoted in Itkonen and Haukioja (1997: 166), already observed this very pointedly in 1891 (*Die Sprachwissenschaft*, p. 365): 'Eine Idee für angeboren erklären, heisst erklären, dass sie unerklärbar sei' ('to explain a notion as innate means to explain that it is unexplainable').

28. One anonymous reviewer remarks that the problems for generative grammar mentioned by Pulvermüller are not to the point since this 'grammatical model is not an account of processing'. However, as I noted in fns 4 and 11, most generative linguists see the grammatical system as a biological organ, and not as a mere model. If this is accepted, it should also be brought into line with brain mechanisms.

29. An analogue device operates with numbers represented by some physically measurable quantity, such as weight, length, voltage, etc., while a digital device operates on data in the form of digits or similar discrete elements. This difference between the grammaticalization and the generative approaches is not surprising given their bias towards language output and the grammar system as data sources respectively. It has also been suggested (cf. Knight 2000: 6; Burling 2000: 33–4) that instinctive animal calls and gestures are analogue in nature, and that conventionalized gestures, and hence also language is digital, because cognitively controlled. On the other hand, Goldberg (2001: 215–30) observes a difference between the cortex and the neocortex, which may also be related to the digital/analogue divide but in a different way. He refers to two different principles of brain organization, a modular and a gradiental one. The modular one he relates to an old structure, i.e. the thalamus, the gradiental one to a recent evolutionary innovation in the brain, the neocortex. These are 'functionally close' but 'differ radically in neuroanatomical structure. The thalamus consists of distinct nuclei, interconnected with a limited number of pathways as the only routes of communication. By contrast, the neocortex is a sheet without distinct internal borders, with rich pathways interconnecting most areas with most others' (2001: 217).

30. Of course, I do realize that a lot of work on this has been done in (formal) semantics. But even though abstract semantic features have been established with which linguistic signs can be described, it remains the case that the semantic core that ultimately distinguishes one sign from another cannot be established any further in terms of features. There are also many problems with the features themselves, as Lyons (1977: 317ff.) has noted. A further problem is that, diachronically, denotation is not fixed, in fact it develops out of connotation (cf. Haiman 1998: 153–4).

31. An intermediate solution to the problem of semantics, which does not relegate it to a mere interpretative module, is seen in models such as HPSG (Head-driven Phrase Structure Grammar, cf. Pollard and Sag 1994) and LFG (Lexical Functional Grammar, cf. e.g. Vincent 2001). These models possess a formal theory of categories and features, and a set of principles which determine how categorial information may be combined in syntax. Thus the coding of syntax takes place partly in the lexicon; lexicon and syntax are independent, equally important and processed in parallel. It can therefore handle the lexical basis of much change and it has an eye for lexical variation in the linguistic output. Through this, it is not committed to the generative type of instantaneous change, because changes of a more gradual type via lexical features are possible. Construction Grammar (cf. Goldberg 1995; Croft and Cruse 2004), too, will be able to deal with these problems because lexical and syntactic constructions are equal in status, both pair form with meaning.

32. For a far more sophisticated schema and discussion of the transmission of language taking into account the objections to the Andersen schema given above, see Janda (2001: 277). For further objections against a child-based theory of language change and a plea for an utterance-based theory, see Croft (2000: 44–63).

33. Wong (2004) shows how the various grammaticalized forms of *bei* 'take' in the synchronic grammars of Chinese children all derive from a prototypical core, which represents also the oldest stage of the diachronic grammaticalization process. The other meanings are acquired later in the same order as the development of stages on the diachronic language level.

34. By 'signs' I understand morphemes, words, as well as constructions, i.e. all the elements that convey a particular meaning, either by themselves or as a unit.

35. Cf. Deacon (1997, 2003), who argues convincingly that symbolic thinking developed out of iconic and indexical modes, which were already present in apes. Apes can also reach this first stage of symbolic thinking provided they are explicitly taught (and rewarded!). Iconic thinking is the ability to see similarities (and differences) between objects (of whatever type). The most basic semiotic 'icon' is a sign which shares some physical features with another sign. The most basic linguistic icon, is a sign that shares some physical features with its referent (as in onomatopoeic words). These are (now) rare in most languages. A higher form of icon is the 'diagrammatic icon', which shows a similarity of a higher

order, namely a relation between signs that semiotically mirrors a similar relation between referents (first-degree iconicity), or a purely intra-linguistic similarity between two signs concerning more abstract features, as is involved for instance in the formation of paradigms (called second-degree iconicity). Indexical thinking concerns associations rather than similarities, it is connected with locality/orientation, and it provides an anchoring point for iconic (or analogical) thinking. For a discussion of the different types of icon, and the relation with index, see Fischer and Nänny (1999), Fischer (2004b).

36. E.g. the meaning of morphemes in a new compound or construction is motivated by the way these morphemes are used as single items elsewhere.

37. This would be true in early language evolution as well as in regular language change. Note that the structuralist de Saussure (1983 [1922]: 130–2) recognized the importance of 'relative motivation' in syntax and word formation; this is a type of motivation which is strictly of an intra-linguistic (i.e. non-semiotic) kind (similar to the second-degree diagrammatic icon discussed in fn. 35). The basic sign itself remains strictly arbitrary for de Saussure. Considering motivation in connection with new structures appearing in child language, Clark (2003: 171ff.) suggests that these structures may be pragmatically motivated as well as simple imitations of patterns heard. The latter involve conventional patterns, and it is likely that children learn these as arbitrary forms.

38. On ritualization in language and in life, see Haiman (1993, 1994, 1998, 1999). On how seemingly arbitrary codes or rituals (e.g. codes of aggression or submission in animals and humans) can be explained by reference to their origin, see Givón (1995b: 65 ff.). The loss of sincerity and transparency leads to the search for new, more expressive structures, which may then go through the cycle of conventionalization in turn.

39. For a lucid discussion of this methodological mistake, see Lightfoot (1979: 34–45).

40. A shift is most likely in cases of morphosyntactic change. However, in phonetic change it is possible for the sound change itself to be phonetically gradual, which is especially true for vowel changes. Lass (1997: 278 ff.) distinguishes between these two possibilities by using the term 'translative' sound change for the gradual change, and 'structuralist-replacive' for the shift. Lass shows that there is strong evidence for both types, an opinion shared by Labov (1994: 471, 541ff.).

41. This is putting it a little too strongly. In the work of e.g. Kroch and Pintzuk, referred to above, variation is accounted for by means of the notion of competing grammars or internal diglossia.

42. Reception of Newmeyer (1998) has been mixed (cf. Foolen 2002: 90) but on the whole positive. Haspelmath (2000: 253) in spite of various criticisms regards it as 'an excellent book', which he 'recommend[s] ... to every linguist', but he also fears that 'most functionalists will get away with the impression that Newmeyer's main purpose is functionalist-bashing' (2000: 252). As Foolen (2002: 91) in his review notes, Newmeyer offers a few critical remarks regarding

the generative approach, especially some of the later versions of OT, Minimalism and Kayne's (1994) 'antisymmetrism', but the remarks concern on the whole small points. Essential aspects of the theory are defended (cf. e.g. Newmeyer's conclusion on p. 94: 'In each case, I have argued that the [autonomy] hypothesis is correct'); this in contrast to his remarks on functionalism, which ideas are seen as mostly ill-directed. Since, as we have seen in §2.2, it is the autonomy hypothesis that underlies most of the differences between the two approaches, this conclusion precludes a truly balanced treatment, not only in Newmeyer's contribution but also in my own. Although I attach great importance to formal matters, I do not accept that they are fully autonomous.

43. And see also IJbema (2002), van Gelderen (2004).

44. '[F]unctional categories are present as features in the lexicon' (Roberts and Roussou 2003: 6), and 'each functional category has a full phrase-structural status' (2003: 5). Although it is the nature of this feature, F^* or F, which decides whether the functional category or head will be filled (lexically at PF or not), the position of the head itself is stipulated beforehand by UG. In other words, unlike in LFG, the lexical feature itself has no influence on the syntactic *structure* that is generated.

45. This is a very brief summary of the discussion in Pulvermüller's Chapter 10. The refinements discussed in his Chapter 12, concerning clause embedding, word repetition, and obligatory/optional complements/adjuncts are left out of the account for lack of space, but they do not essentially alter the basic aspects of the model presented in Chapter 10.

46. The firing probabilities depend strongly on the context of other neuronal firings (cf. Pulvermüller 2002: 149). Pulvermüller writes that 'the mechanism of mediated sequence detection requires information flow, and therefore connections, from input units (e.g. word webs) to sequence detectors (e.g. sequence sets)' (2002: 181).

47. Provided there is no memory overload. It may be for this reason that resumptive pronouns in (spoken) language are necessary when too many elements intervene, as it were providing *overt* sequence detectors (cf. §1.2.2). Similar reasoning may explain the 'complexity principle' proposed by Rohdenburg (1996, 2003 and *passim*), which asserts that the more explicit grammatical option is preferred in cases of cognitive complexity.

48. This looks similar to 'checking' in the Minimalist program, which also works on features. Notice, however, an important difference. In the Minimalist framework, checking takes place *in the course of* the derivation, and the features to be checked are mostly of a morphosyntactic nature, while in this proposal the checking *coincides* with the sequential processing of the clause and includes phonetic and semantic features as well.

49. And see also p. 163, where he writes that 'frequent cooccurrence of words in linear sequences may be an important factor for establishing neuron ensembles in the detection of word sequences. This allows for an economic representation of word-pair sequences'. On the connection between repetition and

automatization, he notes: 'An important observation is that previously perceived syntactic structures are being imitated in subsequent verbal actions. The phenomenon attributed to a mechanism dubbed *syntactic priming* occurs with above-chance probability in both conversations and controlled experiments' (p. 165, and see also p. 163). More on syntactic priming in §3.3.

3

Principles, mechanisms, and causes of change

> it may take some mental effort to realize that the very concept of *structure*, as
> it applies within a single language, is based on analogy (Itkonen 2005: 8)

3.0 Introduction

In this chapter, I will review the different mechanisms, principles, parameters, constraints, and, ultimately, explanations that have been put forward
for language change within the grammaticalization and the P&P models.
When comparing the two approaches, I will refer to all the factors that
somehow condition change—whether as mechanisms, causes, or constraints—with the neutral term 'factors', so as not to prejudge the issue.
The reason for this is the well-known problem that many of these
determining 'factors' are themselves constrained by the nature of the theory
in which they are employed. In fact, what may be seen as an explanation or
cause in one theory, may not be considered more than a description or a
mechanism in another.

Obviously, when doing (historical) linguistic research, one has to start with a description first (a description of the facts and a description of the theory or theories based on those facts). However, most linguists (theoretically inclined linguists more so than philologically inclined ones) consider a 'mere' description not satisfactory, they would also want to know *why* something happened.[1] It follows that, if the adherents of one theory do not accept the principles established by the adherents of another theory, any explanation based on those principles will only be acceptable to the linguists who established them in the first place.

One of the problems facing us in the present discussion, is that there is indeed a wide divide between the two approaches, which has to do with the dichotomies discussed in Chapter 2, and especially with the question as to what constitutes the primary object of research, the language output or the individual underlying grammar. It seems to me that suggested causes or explanations for change can only truly be such if they can also be shown to be valid outside one's theory, that is if they are not theory-internal. When 'causes' are rejected by another school of linguists, this is often because they are seen as the outcome of a circular argument. In such cases, the 'cause' is probably no more than a description in terms of the theory, providing no explanation beyond that theory. I will first discuss what each theory has proposed in terms of 'factors' involved in change (§§3.1 and 3.2). Next, in §3.3, I will compare and evaluate these in the light of what is known about brain processes and structures, as discussed in §2.3, also taking into consideration research results available from domains outside the narrow sphere of language change and grammatical theory (these two latter fields are themselves rather closely intertwined). In §3.4, I will tentatively propose a model for grammar acquisition and language change that emerges from the evaluation in §3.3.

The close link between language change and the grammar system underlying language is more or less (as in the case of the P&P and the grammaticalization models respectively) accepted by both schools of thought. When one takes the speaker as central, which both approaches in principle do, then one accepts that there must be a direct relation between the grammar system a speaker possesses and his/her linguistic output, irrespective of whether one takes the former or the latter as the primary object of research. Thus, Hopper and Traugott (2003: 40) write:

First, when we speak of language, what is thought to be changing? We speak loosely of 'language change.' But this phrase is misleading. Language does not exist separate from its speakers. It is not an organism with a life of its own; rather each speaker has to learn that language anew.[2]

Opinions, of course, may differ as to how this learning takes place (i.e. with or without the help of some form of UG), but it is clear that *some* language system develops in every speaker in connection with output.

Even though grammaticalization linguists admit the role of the speaker, the fact that most of the factors at work in grammaticalization refer to diachronic processes taking place at the output level, creates the suggestion that, for some at least, the speaker has receded into the background (as suggested e.g. in Janda 2001; Joseph 2001). For generative historical linguists, the link between change and the grammar system is more direct and up-front. Lightfoot (1979: 149–50) proposes an 'impoverished theory of change' because

a restrictive theory of grammar imposes severe constraints on possible historical changes, and ... there is no reason to expect plausible formal restrictions to be imposed on possible changes by a theory of change.

The limits of change are thus imposed by the grammar so that Lightfoot's theory of change contains only four general constraints:

(i)   communicability must be preserved between generations;
(ii)   grammars practise therapy rather than prophylaxis;
(iii) less highly valued grammars are liable to reanalysis;
(iv)   certain therapeutic changes are more likely than others.

Factor (iii) is intimately related to the so-called 'Transparency Principle', which Lightfoot proposed in 1979 (but dropped again in later work in favour of general principles of grammar),[3] but this too is seen as part of the theory of grammar. This inclusion seems fair enough since the child that sets parameters differently would have to be guided by such a principle, which, therefore, must be readily available in his grammar. Roberts and Roussou (2003: 205 and *passim*) re-introduce the 'Transparency Principle' under a different guise; they call it 'structural simplification', which is related to a formal notion of markedness (2003: 210 ff.).

I agree with Lightfoot and other generative linguists in principle that the purely *linguistic* principles that guide change, cannot be different from the ones involved in the synchronic system (see also §3.3. below)—except perhaps in the early stages of language evolution—[4] but what Lightfoot totally ignores in his 'theory of change' (because it is a *formal* theory of *grammar* change) is the way *external* circumstances may affect a language, and hence cause it to change. The interrelation between internal and external factors, and the possible effects it has on the development of a language could well be part of a 'theory of change'.[5] (On the question of whether one is able to distinguish purely linguistic principles, see below.) Newmeyer (2003: 73–5), for instance, mentions changes in society (e.g. from pre-literate to literate) that might influence change, and he even wonders whether the uniformitarian principle (cf. fn. 4 above) can be upheld: 'the shibboleth that grammar and culture are *completely* independent might well be too strong' (p. 73). Here he refers to studies that have shown that more complex cultures may have less complex grammar, and the other way round (cf. also Deutscher 2000). With respect to another external factor, that is contact, Thomason and Kaufman 1988 (and see also Thomason 2001) have shown that interesting general observations can be made, which help us to understand why or how change may occur. Similarly, 'social network' theory developed by Lesley and James Milroy (e.g. L. Milroy 1987; J. Milroy 1992), discusses the kind of socio-cultural constraints that are at work on changes as they spread through a speech community.

An important problem here, which I have already addressed in §1.2, is whether we can separate the internal from the external factors. For Lightfoot, the situational context, pragmatics and communicative needs (e.g. economy, the need to be expressive or polite, etc.) are all external factors, not relevant to grammar, and hence not relevant to grammar change. Lightfoot does not deny that external factors do play a role, but he sees these mainly in the form of 'triggers', that is changes on the level of the PLD that may lead to 'real' change, that is, grammar change. It may not be so easy, however, to distinguish between PLD 'triggers' and 'changes' (cf. McMahon 2000: 123; Croft 2000: 49–50; Matthews 2003). Possibly, some of the 'external' factors could be incorporated into a more encompassing type of grammar system (as happens in functional grammar models), but it is also not unthinkable that some of these functional needs themselves are not constant. As mentioned above, they may change over time or be different for different cultures. It would be valuable, therefore, to have beside a theory of grammar, a theory of change, which would describe the type of external functional, societal, and 'contact' constraints that play a role in language and how these constraints may influence the course of change. Not surprisingly, grammaticalization theorists, who do take account of many more external factors, may consider some of these 'external' factors to be part of a theory of change.

If we follow Lightfoot and agree that the language output is produced and comprehended by speakers in similar ways, then it does not matter in principle whether the speaker lived/s in the seventeenth century or in the twenty-first. That is, the internal linguistic factors involved would be similar for a seventeenth-century and a twenty-first-century grammar, and hence the same principles would play a role in language change. Lightfoot's interest in language change lies in the fact that one can use actual cases of linguistic change heuristically to discover the limits of the individual system of grammar (and of UG) and to choose between competing analyses; hence, via change, one can get a better idea of the properties of the linguistic system (cf. Lightfoot 1979: 79, 154). But here lies the snag. In the P&P model, the changes themselves are considered with these very properties in mind, and changes that do not relate to these properties, are considered 'triggers' and relegated to the language output level. What is discovered about grammar change, therefore, does not tell us much about deeper causes or causes different from the principles already established, that is the facts of change do not tell us why the properties are the way they are, because they are part and parcel of the same research domain. The argument tends to be circular, because the 'theory tells you what you should expect, and the onus is on languages to conform' (McMahon 2000: 116, and cf. also Aitchison 1987: 15–16). That is, tackling the changes with the instruments of the theory, which is at the same time the object that should be improved by means of the observation of the changes, is not going to advance our knowledge of the properties of either.

Grammaticalization faces a similar problem. Its practitioners concentrate on function in language change and not on form, and in their search for the properties of change, they look at the language as it develops from a functional point of view, and they look at what the speaker does in terms of functional and communicative needs (cf. e.g. Kuteva 2001), whereby the *overall* linguistic *system* of the individual language user, with which output is produced or comprehended, is ignored. The only difference with the generative school is that they start with language change and armed with this then look at what the speaker/hearer does, while generative linguists start with the individual linguistic system, and then, with the help of that, look at change.

A theory in which both form and meaning play equal and independent roles, would be a great advance, providing more in the way of explanation.[6] Even more helpful in terms of explanation would be to make use of the investigations of linguistic facts in other domains, such as first and second language acquisition (which relate to immature speakers, and hence present different language facts), language evolution, language pathology, neurolinguistics and also to look at data coming from cognitive domains (such as vision, motor development, etc.). Similarly, results obtained via psycholinguistic experiments and computer simulation programs should also advance further understanding. Tomasello (2003b: 94), for instance, emphasizes that investigating the systems of communication that are simple and not 'full-blown', is important if we wish to make progress. This includes the language of children and our nearest primates, but also the language of pidgins, aphasics, etc. Hurford (2003: 53ff.) notes that using computer simulation is important to probe the evolution of language, which presents another system that is not 'full-blown'.

3.1 'Factors' of change involved in the Principles and Parameters model

We will start with the generative 'toolbox' used for the description and explanation of linguistic change, since of the two approaches, this is by far the most restrictive one. As we have seen above, this limited number of tools is possible, first of all, because the principles and constraints used in linguistic theory are equally valid in change. Each system of grammar at each stage of the history of a language must obey the same principles. These principles and constraints are described in such a way that they are falsifiable. If falsified, a principle must be adapted or changed; if not, it stands (but cf. §2.0). A second reason why the number of tools is limited is because they only concern *formal* principles and constraints. The way in which a grammar changes and how to explain this change can best be described in the words of Lightfoot (1981: 90):[7]

(1)   Any given change will be explained if one demonstrates two things: (a) that the linguistic environment has changed in such a way that some parameter of UG is fixed differently (e.g. that a PS rule $V' \rightarrow N'' V$ is replaced by $V' \rightarrow V N''$), and (b) that the new phenomenon ... must be the way that it is, given some general principles of grammar and the new property of the particular grammar.

Lightfoot here discusses the loss of the impersonal construction in Middle English (discussed in §1.1.2). In this scenario, a change on the output level ('a new phenomenon') is only a 'real' change (i.e. a change explicable from the point of view of the *system of grammar*) *if* it is caused by a parameter shift, and *if* this occurs in combination with some other principle(s) of grammar so that the 'new phenomenon' cannot but arise. According to Lightfoot (1981: 88),

clusters of changes [here, presumably, the 'new phenomenon' and the parameter shift itself] are of particular interest because apparently unrelated simultaneous changes may manifest one parameter of UG that has been fixed differently. If so, a change can be 'explained' by showing that it is related to some other novel aspect of grammar.

A problem in this particular case may be that the loss of the impersonal is both caused by a parameter shift (OV>VO), but at the same time is also a manifestation of it. In addition, it is not so obvious how this change involving the impersonal represents a 'cluster'. Other instances of clusters discussed within this model are clearer because the cluster of changes does not include a parameter shift and the cluster itself consists of more changes, as we will see in Chapter 4 describing the change involving the modals in English, Lightfoot's paradigm case.

There is something very neat and pleasing about this strict scenario for change, and a decisive advantage is that it gives direction to our enquiries. It encourages (historical) linguists to look for a bundle of changes occurring on the output level, which appear unrelated. Their simultaneity would then indicate the presence of a more fundamental shift in the grammar. Because it indicates on the grammar level that the superficial phenomena *are* related to some deeper principle, it vindicates the existence of the principle itself. To my mind, this approach is very valuable if it is combined with detailed corpus research (cf. van der Wurff 2000). It may then have two positive results. It could provide evidence for already posited parameters (and thus strengthen them), and it could unearth new parameters (and perhaps disqualify some posited ones). Secondly, it could inspire historical linguists to look for evidence of further surface-like connections between the 'unconnected' changes that have simultaneously arisen.[8] It is easier, after all, to find connections when a link has already been established.

When this strict scenario for change is combined with extensive corpus study, its idea of simultaneous or radical change may be corroborated, but it is also possible that researchers discover that the new phenomena *were* linked on a less abstract or less formal level (e.g. there may have been functional connections). This would be the case, for instance, when the researchers discover that there were other more gradual (less radical) small shifts on the output level that preceded the postulated grammar change. If these small shifts cannot be directly connected to any principle of grammar, a generative linguist would classify them as mere PLD 'triggers', which serve to build up towards a catastrophic or radical grammar change. On the other hand, if these small shifts *are* recognized as changes within grammar (and this of course depends on the model used), then it would mean that there is no build-up towards a radical grammar change. And if that is so, it would not provide evidence for a parameter shift, nor for the validity of that parameter within the theory.

The following case may serve as an illustration. Lightfoot (1991: 124) links the development of a new indirect passive in English (of the type *He was given a book*), which replaced the earlier dative passive (*Him was given a book*), to the simultaneous development of a number of other new constructions, which according to him are all caused by the loss of dative case in Middle English. Allen (1995, 2001), however, shows on the basis of a detailed corpus investigation that the change involving the development of the indirect passive took place in separate steps, and that there is no *direct* relation between the loss of dative case and the emergence of the new indirect passive, because, according to Allen (2001: 54) dative fronted passives had died out *before* the new indirect passives arrived. Rather, Allen argues, there is a direct relation between the loss of the dative fronted passive (*The student was given a book*) and the fronted dative in active sentences (as in *The student I gave a book*). Due to this positional loss (of the fronted element), the original dative and accusative NPs (Allen does not include the pronouns in this story because they still had distinct case forms for subjects and objects) came to be used side by side immediately after the finite verb (*I gave the student a book/I gave a book the student*). It was when the recipient object came to be fixed in the first position after the verb, that it became reanalysed as an *object*. This fixed position is what enabled the indirect passive to occur: because of the reanalysis to object, a subject position in passives became possible. Note that this scenario would not be possible within a P&P framework because it would not allow two types of object.[9]

Trying to find evidence for simultaneity is thus in itself useful in that it may confirm the existence of parameters, and it is useful as a heuristic device in that it stimulates historical linguists to dig deeper into the historical data. In a similar way, some of the principles of the grammar posited in the P&P model have been used as heuristic devices in neurolinguistic work, and have been found to comply with neural networks. For instance, the X-bar principle and the principle of Subjacency have been found to comply with a simple neuronal network of sequential learning (cf. Kirby and Christiansen 2003: 275ff.).[10] This would mean that these principles are not necessarily language specific but are the result of the properties of neuronal sets dealing with language in sequence.[11] These extra-domain findings may thus vindicate the principles of UG and show at the same time that these are not necessarily inherently linguistic.

Next to the positive effects that the P&P model undoubtedly has (had) on our efforts to understand the way grammar and change work, there are also quite a number of problems. Not all grammar changes can be explained in this way, posing the question of how valuable the machinery is. For instance, in Old English the reflexive pronouns had the same form as personal pronouns, so that a clause like *He wende hine* could in principle mean both 'He turned himself' (i.e. 'he went') and 'He turned him' (i.e. somebody else). In this case there doesn't seem to be a combination of a parameter shift and a general principle forcing the change that must have taken place (the ambiguity is no longer present in Standard English), rather the change seems to be semantically motivated and caused by requirements on intensifiers (cf. Haiman 1998: 61–79; König and Siemund 2000; Sinar 2005). The loss of the personal pronoun as a reflexive seems as good a change as the loss of the impersonal, and yet it is not one that can be easily explained by any principle or shift in the system of grammar.[12] Note also that in the description of the impersonal change quoted above, the parameter shift from OV to VO *itself* is not explained. Can this shift also be explained in terms of some parameter shift in combination with a principle of grammar? I don't think so. Lightfoot (1991: 56–72) himself explains the change from OV to VO on the basis of the gradually diminishing 'triggers' for OV available in the PLD. In other words, a far more important shift in the history of English that had many further repercussions on the language (cf. Chapters 4–6) cannot itself be explained by the machinery given in (1) above.

This leads us to the important distinction between 'triggers' and 'changes'. Triggers are part of the experience that a child has; they 'var[y] from person to person and consist[] of an unorganized, fairly haphazard set of utterances'; 'the universal theory of grammar' and the 'variable trigger' together 'form the basis for attaining a grammar' (Lightfoot 1999: 66). When we look a little more closely at these triggers, we find that they may involve 'minor changes in the relevant childhood experience', which only have an effect on the emerging grammar when they 'cross a threshold' (Lightfoot 1999: 79).[13] On the other hand, there are also *grammar* changes (≠ triggers) which are 'small-scale' and may progress 'in piece-meal fashion', word by word. These minor grammar changes must, like the major, abrupt grammar changes, 'take place in direct or indirect response to changes [=triggers] in the PLD' (Lightfoot 1999: 88).

We may represent these three types of changes as shown in Table 3.1. The division seems clear enough. In category 1, 'triggers', no formal grammar distinction can be made between one pattern (variant) and another. In category 2, minor grammar changes, there is a morphological or categorial distinction: they may involve a loss or emergence of a morphological feature (e.g. inflection) or a change in category; in category 3, the major grammar changes, they involve the loss or emergence of a syntactic pattern.

Since there is little difference between gradual progress and a piece-meal change, the important distinction between categories 1 and 2 is that in 1 there is no pattern (categorial) division visible. If a pattern distribution could be made on semantic grounds, it does not exist within the model, since the model is based on *formal* divisions. Notice though, that category 2

Table 3.1. *Types of changes according to Lightfoot*

Type of change	1 Triggers (on the PLD level)	2 Minor grammar changes	3 Major grammar changes
Characteristics	Involves variables (small changes) on the output level	Involves changes in the grammar	Involves changes in the grammar
	Progresses gradually until threshold is reached	Change is piece-meal, may diffuse lexically	Change is abrupt
	Is haphazard, but may lead to change in the grammar	Involves recategorization (morphological and categorial)	Involves parameter shifts, and clusters of simultaneous changes

Source: Lightfoot (1991, 1999)

includes piece-meal progress by lexical diffusion, which is probably as much based on semantic considerations and lexical features as on purely formal features. Lightfoot gives as an example the recategorization of the modals, which, in his 1991 account moves from verb to verb (see for more details, Chapter 4). Looking at it from a different angle, if the change from OV to VO begins as a category 1 variation in main clauses, as Lightfoot (1991: 63 ff.) shows in detail, then it will have to be established that the gradual changes shown by the OV/VO patterns in the PLD are haphazard. If, on the other hand, it can be established that with certain verbs VO occurs earlier or OV is lost earlier, we might have a pattern: that is structured variation by lexical diffusion. Or if we can establish that certain types of Objects moved to postverbal position before others, again we might have a pattern based on lexical features of the objects. It is interesting to observe, for instance, that the later stages of OV were found to be patterned (cf. van der Wurff 1999; Moerenhout and van der Wurff 2000, 2005). It means that the historical record must be examined very closely indeed before a change can be established as being of category 1 or 2.

A problem connected with the category 3 type of change is the nature of an abrupt change. First of all, a change can only be abrupt, if it involves a parameter shift. So, to some extent, the presence of a category 3 change depends on what are seen as parameters in the model.[14] A category 3 change also depends on the presence of a cluster of changes (i.e. simultaneous surface changes and subsequent chain reactions, cf. Lightfoot 1991:167). Here, the timing of all these changes becomes crucial. Again the OV > VO change may serve as an example. Lightfoot (1991: 42ff.) describes this as a gradual category 1 type of process in main clauses, but as an abrupt category 3 change for embedded clauses. To accept this we have to accept his hypothesis of degree-0 learnability.[15] The fact that this case is used to prove degree-0 learnability as well as that degree-0 learnability is needed to prove this case, makes it difficult to avoid a suspicion of circularity. Secondly, it is not clear what the role of coordinate clauses is in this. They also show a sudden shift to VO like the subordinate clauses; yet, as far as I can see, they do not fall under degree-0 learnability, since some of them must be main clauses.[16] A final problem is that the loss of OV order in subordinate clauses may not have been as abrupt as Lightfoot accepts it to be. OV is definitely still quite common after the twelfth century, the putative date of the abrupt parameter shift (cf. again the studies by van der Wurff 1999, and Moerenhout and van der Wurff 2000) within the grammars of one and the same author.[17]

There is also a more general problem with the nature of abrupt changes. Lightfoot (1999: 18, 84, 231–2) defends their occurrence with reference to the evolutionary notion of 'punctuated equilibrium'. He refers to the work of Eldredge and Gould (1972), who put forward the hypothesis that biological evolution is not necessarily gradual (as was the Darwinian idea) but may occur in fits and starts. Lightfoot (1999: 84) writes:

Discontinuities are the norm, and punctuated equilibrium is overwhelmingly reflected in the fossil record. Consequently, proponents of abrupt change, punctuated equilibrium, derive very direct support from the relevant records.... Evolutionists committed to gradualism need to argue that the gaps in the fossil record are accidental.

Lightfoot does not refer to the fact that this hypothesis is disputed among scientists and has become subject to faulty interpretation in a strongly reductive fashion (see fn. 18 below). Dawkins (1986: 223–52), who admittedly represents the other side, describes the dispute in detail. He argues that 'punctuated equilibrium' in fact supports Darwinian gradualism, if one observes the correct Darwinian notion of gradualism. Gradualism refers to gradual long-term change by small steps; it does not mean that those small steps have to be absolutely equal, some are smaller than others.

In connection with Lightfoot's use of this hypothesis, it is worthwhile to highlight the following points made by Dawkins: (i) the fossil record is bound to be defective since only a very small proportion of living beings will become fossilized. Fossils only tell us something about the *order* of evolution (because they can be easily dated). (ii) No scientists (including Eldredge and Gould) dispute that 'some very important gaps really are due to imperfections in the fossil record' (1986: 229). (iii) Eldredge and Gould did not support the theory of 'saltation', that is sudden jumps that occur in a single generation (but they have been interpreted this way, especially by creationists).[18] Such macro-mutations occur (i.e. freaks are being born), but they do not affect evolution, because freaks normally do not survive in the wild. The kind of gaps they proposed were quite small ones. (iv) Eldredge and Gould's main message was that some real gaps in the record could be explained by speciation due to geographical isolation (1986: 241). This, according to Dawkins, in fact supports gradual evolution in that it explains why some gaps in the fossil record occur when parts of a species get separated due to geographical isolation. The evolution of each division itself remains gradual, that is the gaps only *seem* gaps. (v) 'Even the evolutionary jerks of the punctuationists, though they may be instantaneous by geological standards, still have a duration that is measured in tens or hundreds of thousand of years' (1986: 242), that is they are not talking about jumps but rather about episodes of relatively rapid evolution.

I have used quite a lot of space to expound this controversy, because, although looking at another domain is necessary, as I have argued, it may happen that scientists look at only half the story when taking ideas from another field of science. In a way, this is almost inevitable since it is difficult to be aware of all the issues in some field not your own. No doubt I may err here too, and it is to be hoped that others will set me right.[19] The point I wish to make here is that the analogy that Lightfoot uses, is based on a superficial comparison. In the field of evolutionary biology, gradualism is still the rule, and Lightfoot overstates his case when he writes that 'discontinuities are the *norm*' (emphasis added). It seems to me that gradualism is also more likely in grammars, since grammars are built upon output, which itself changes only very gradually, as Lightfoot himself (1999: 85) admits.[20] The differences in steps observed between the categories in Table 3.1, may be due to the model rather than to the nature of linguistic change or grammar change itself.

As far as I can see, the question is still open as to whether abrupt change exists. As Nagle (1989: 45) aptly remarks, 'the gradual versus abrupt issue in surface change is largely one of theoretical orientation', adding that 'the broad picture of at least surface change is gradual' (1989: 46). What we need to do as historical linguists is to examine more carefully the reputed simultaneity of the changes in a cluster, and the simultaneity of the chain reactions. We also need to look at the (in)divisibility of each change in question, because possibly some of these radical changes are themselves a chain of smaller changes.

Bennett (1981) draws our attention to the various types of gradual changes that can be distinguished, next to non-gradual or abrupt syntactic change. He makes a distinction between lexical graduality (a new construction enters by lexical diffusion), environmental graduality (i.e. the new construction enters via slight changes in its formal environment), strategical graduality (the change in the construction itself is abrupt but the old and the new exist side by side for a while) and socio-geographical graduality. In order to find out whether a syntactic change is gradual in any of these ways or abrupt, one needs to look very carefully at the diffusion of the change in the surface output. As far as the grammatical system is concerned, the first two gradualities are the most important because they are linked with internal causes, the strategic one is a problem and may indeed at closer inspection turn out to be dependent on either social, stylistic, or internal factors, the last one is the least interesting from a grammar point of view. His article makes clear that in-depth study of change is necessary to decide on the issue of graduality versus abruptness. Lass (1997: 288) indeed advises (historical) linguists to look more at the micro-stories (beside the macro-stories) when looking at change, because the micro-stories are of 'enormous *theoretical* importance as well' (emphasis added). Harris and Campbell (1995: 48–9) voice similar concerns.

A problem of a rather different nature is that, although the machinery of generative theory itself may be restrictive, this cannot be said about the way the machinery changes in the course of time (see also fn. 14 above). For instance, the parameter change of OV>VO referred to above, no longer constitutes a parameter in the base in the Kaynian (1994) approach, where all languages are said to be SVO (it would there be tied to the strength of features, cf. fn.12 in Ch.1), and the kind of movement evoking the Trace Erasure Principle has also disappeared from the latest models (see §1.1.2 and fn. 13; the general ban on downgrading, however, has remained). It can also be questioned whether a parameter setting works as firmly on the data as is often presumed. For instance Lightfoot (1991: 11) mentions that the so-called null-subject parameter is set to positive in Italian and Spanish because in the PLD children hear clauses like *Ho trovato il libro* and *Chi credi che partira* [Chi$_i$credi t$_i$che t$_i$ partira], while English children do not hear *Have found the book* and *Who do you think that will leave* (according to the parameter these two features are linked). We have seen in §1.2.2 that this is correct in the sense that English does not have subjectless sentences, but the second example with the *that*-trace did occur regularly in Old and Middle English (cf. Gorrell 1895: 351; Bergh and Seppänen 1994), and can still be found in colloquial language nowadays. In other words, the model may be restrictive at any particular point in time or in the hands of any particular linguist, but it is not in terms of spread in time and spread across practitioners. In this respect it differs from the grammaticalization model, which does not change much across time and practitioners, but is in its very nature not restrictive (see §3.2).

Before we move on to the characteristics of the grammaticalization model, we must briefly consider the work of Roberts and Roussou (Roberts 1993b; Roberts and Roussou 1999, 2002, 2003), who take the findings of grammaticalization seriously and endeavour to reconcile it with a Minimalist generative model. The study by van Kemenade (2000) on the negative cycle, which is a typical case of grammaticalization, has a similar intent, even though it is not carried out strictly within a Minimalist framework. Both proposals have in common that the grammaticalization process as such is strictly morphosyntactic in nature, and in which function/semantics plays no motivating role (so the reverse of the grammaticalization model where function rather than form drives the process). This is not to say that function plays no part at all, but in Roberts and Roussou's model the functional categories are an already 'given' (they are present as universal features in the lexicon in the form of functional projections). They assume that the functional architecture is invariant for all languages (which leads to the adoption of a great number of functional heads in UG) and that it depends on each particular language whether the functional category is expressed or not (this is indicated by the feature $F^{(*)}$, see below). If the functional feature *is* expressed in a language, then it depends on morphosyntactic evidence (on the material the learner has as input) how this function will be expressed. Thus, a lexical element is Merged in its functional head if it has no inflectional morphology marking its function; for example the Modern English modals have merged in the functional head of Mood because they have lost all inflectional verbal features (this also explains the difference in behaviour between modals and verbs). In Old English, Mood was expressed by a syntactic affix (the subjunctive); this merges in the Mood functional head but also needs to Move in order to attach itself to the verb. In Middle English, when the subjunctive inflection was lost and there was therefore no overt Mood element, material from elsewhere (often the verb, as here) had to move to the functional head in order for Mood to be expressed (a movement dependency checked by the Spec position of the functional head).

As already indicated, Roberts and Roussou distinguish two types of functional features, ones that have PF properties and ones that do not (i.e. functional heads that are not spelled out at PF level). A functional category which is spelled out at PF level is indicated by the feature F^* in the Lexicon (i.e. $F^{(*)}$ works rather like some meta-parameter (cf. Roberts and Roussou 2003: 29), there is no longer any parametric variation in the set of functional heads themselves). When the parameter is set to F, it means that the functional feature is zero on the surface and incorporated in the functional head at LF level. Thus, the diacritic * is related to morphophonological matrices. The PF realization of F^* can be done by Move or Merge, or both; the option taken depends on what the lexicon makes available but the most economical one is always preferred, that is Merge. So there are three states in which these functional categories can be expressed: (i) they may merge in the functional head; (ii) they may be visible through a movement dependency; (iii) or they may merge in Mood and then move. These three states represent the auxiliary (i), lexical (ii), and affixal (iii) stages on the grammaticalization cline. The cline is here represented by a change from Move/Merge to Move, and then to Merge only, representing a structural simplification.

In this system Merge is seen as the default, which a learner will set up if there is no suggestion otherwise. Underspecified lexical elements (e.g. when inflectional morphology is absent) will move since their function can only be fully specified by their functional head. In other words, the existence of a movement dependency is a first step on the grammaticalization cline. By making a distinction between three possible settings (a) Merge/Move, (b) Move, and (c) Merge, the gradual semantic cline of grammaticalization is cut into discrete formal steps. It is in the presence of these clear-cut stages that the analysis differs from grammaticalization theory, where no clear distinction can be made between the various stages because they are all part of a conceptual chain (see further §3.2). The analysis also provides a unitary solution to the problem of scope because in this model the moved or merged lexical element always acquires wider scope since it is now situated in a functional head which sits high up in the tree.[21]

There are also a number of problems, however. The model involves a very rich array of functional heads—since the presence of the functional heads themselves has been assumed as part of UG—many of which may never surface in any particular language. It seems problematic to have to assume that all these functional projections are innate. In functional models, functions such as Mood typically emerge in combination with the PLD *and* the (meaningful) communicative context in which the language forms are used. It is difficult to accept that these functions are already conceptually in place in the form of purely formal projections. Their assumption also means that we cannot explain the rise of *new* functional categories, such as the determiner phrase (DP), because in fact the DP must already have been present in UG. Additionally, in the case of the rise of the DP (as seen in the history of many—unrelated—languages), we cannot always fall back on the loss of morphological inflections, which is such an important trigger in other cases discussed by Roberts and Roussou. A third problem is empirical. The trigger for the syntactic reanalysis heavily depends on the loss of inflectional morphology. We will see in Chapter 4, where the history of the English modals is discussed, that the relation between this loss and the reanalysis is often less neat than Roberts and Roussou assume.

So far this model has only dealt with a small number of known grammaticalization cases. It remains to be seen how well it does when it is applied to others. Campbell (2001a) suggests that there are a large number of cases that this model cannot deal with, such as the developments of definite articles from demonstratives (but see Roberts and Roussou 2003: §4.1), and relative pronouns from interrogative, both of which are common grammaticalization processes. A final comment concerns causation. The model presents grammaticalization as reanalysis, and in this way really only deals with the last stage of a grammaticalization chain. In this, it shares the difficulty we have with the P&P approach, in that the changes that lead up to the reanalysis itself, are not considered to be part of the change; again they are seen as mere 'triggers' on the PLD level. Thus, as far as causation is concerned, we do not really understand why the process happens. The functional heads are always there in the grammar in principle, but why one gets lexically filled while another does not, remains a mystery.

3.2 'Factors' of change involved in grammaticalization

In grammaticalization theory a distinction can in principle be made between factors that distinguish grammaticalization as a diachronic process—these could more properly be called diagnostics or heuristic devices—and conditioning factors at work at each step of the grammaticalization process, which are, unlike the first type, related to the speaker. The problem, and the conflict with generative theory, lies in the fact that grammaticalization theorists do not always explicitly make this distinction. For some, the principles directing the process are seen as 'causes', which are said to help explain why and in what way the process takes place, and indeed some linguists see grammaticalization itself as a cause. Since language does not steer itself (but see the remarks on Keller (1994) in §1.2, fn. 54) but is the work of speakers, it seems to me that the conditioning factors for grammaticalization must in the first place be found at the speaker level. I note that this *is* done in the semantic-pragmatic branch of grammaticalization, but here the *form* of the system in which the structure is used is almost totally ignored.

One of the reasons why the distinction between language level and speaker level is not always made within the theory, is the fact that grammaticalization is seen as so gradual that no stages in its process can be perceived. Note that this is rather similar to the neogrammarian claim that change in progress could not be perceived because sounds changed too gradually. Heine and Reh (1984: 15), for instance, describe grammaticalization as 'an evolutional continuum. Any attempt at segmenting it into discrete units must remain arbitrary to some extent' (see also Heine *et al.* 1991b: 68, 165 and *passim*). Because grammaticalization is seen as an insegmentable 'chain', it is also felt that it cannot be reversed, *ergo* it must be unidirectional. Indeed, for some, unidirectionality is a principle of the theory.[22]

The idea of graduality is closely connected with the prominent position of semantic change in the whole process. For most grammaticalizationists, the semantic changes come first, and are only later followed by structural changes, cf. Bybee and Pagliuca (1985), Brinton (1988: 95, 161–2), Heine *et al.* (1991a: 174), Hopper (1991: 19), Rubba (1994: 81), and Hopper and Traugott (2003: 76). Bybee *et al.* (1994: 17–18) even suggest that we can reconstruct the path of grammaticalization with the help of the 'hypothesis that semantic change is predictable'. The emphasis on unidirectionality and on the graduality of the process has in turn led to the idea that the process is mechanistic, that it is itself a mechanism or cause in or for change. Bybee *et al.* (1994: 298), for instance, write: 'Thus our view of grammaticization is much more mechanistic than functional: the relation between grammar and function is indirect and mediated by diachronic process. The processes that lead to grammaticization occur in language use *for their own sakes*' (emphasis added). Similarly, Vincent (1995: 434) writes that, even though he is challenging the 'pre-eminence [of grammaticalization] as [a] source of new patterns', he does not 'wish ... to deny the power of grammaticalization as an *agent* of change' (emphasis added).[23]

Another possible reason for the inability to distinguish between language and the individual grammar of a speaker is that grammaticalization linguists concentrate on the output of speakers (i.e. more than one). Language is studied as a meaningful communication process between speakers, as the interplay of production as well as comprehension, and not as the individual output generated by one speaker.[24] The object of study, therefore, is the *dynamic* process of language and how this dynamic interchange triggers the grammar system that a child develops. The grammar, in other words, is not, as in generative grammar, the result of a stable UG, which interacts with cues coming from the language output (the PLD). In the generative model the triggering experience has been cleaned up, because it is cues from the PLD and not the PLD itself, which together with UG define a child's grammar in the period of language acquisition (and not beyond!).

A third reason why the distinction between speaker level and language level is blurred in grammaticalization theory, is the fact that its practitioners want to explain the phenomenon of grammaticalization itself, which they see as an independent phenomenon. Formally inclined linguists tend to see grammaticalization as an epiphenomenon (cf. the discussion in Campbell 2001a). If only the grammaticalizationists would concentrate on the speaker, they argue, they would see that the unidirectionality and the clines that they distinguish, cannot be part of a speaker's grammar, and hence cannot be real. Grammaticalization linguists, however, argue that regarding grammaticalization as an epiphenomenon, does not explain why such unidirectional processes follow similar clines, why they are the rule rather than the exception. Their task, therefore, is to explain the paradox that many of these processes occur in language in spite of the fact that the kind of clines and parameters suggested in grammaticalization theory cannot be a direct mechanism in a grammar that a speaker builds up or possesses. I think this is only possible if we accept that a speaker's grammar itself is much less fixed syntactically and much more dynamic than generative linguists accept, and, furthermore, that the constraints on the form of a speaker's output not only come from the formal grammar acquired in childhood but from a much wider field encompassing all aspects of the speaker's mind and the communicative situation.

Let us now have a look at the factors (or diagnostics) distinguished for grammaticalization as a diachronic process.[25] The clearest discussion of this is to be found in Lehmann (1982 [1995], 1985), whose 'parameters' can be used to represent stages in the development. Lehmann (1985: 306) presents the material shown in Table 3.2 (slightly adapted in order

Table 3.2. *Diachronic stages in the process of grammaticalization*

Parameters	Paradigmatic processes	Syntagmatic processes
Weight	(Loss of) integrity	(Reduction of) scope
Cohesion	(Increase in) paradigmaticity	(Increase in) bondedness
Variability	(Loss of) paradigmatic variability: increase in obligatoriness	(Decrease in) syntagmatic variability

to indicate the *processes* taking place), where the parameters illustrate the degree to which a particular linguistic item has grammaticalized:

The 'weight' or substance of a lexical item (row 1) involved in a grammaticalization process is reduced (in contrast to similar, but non-grammaticalized items within the same field or paradigm), through both semantic and phonetic erosion (also called semantic bleaching and phonetic reduction). This means that the element becomes syntactically less dominant in the clause, as in the case where a full lexical verb such as *go* in the expression BE + *going to* V, first dominates a purposive adjunct (as in *I am going (to the market)) to get her some fish*), and next develops into a semi-auxiliary, becoming part of the VP headed by the infinitive (as in *She's going to/gonna be sick*). Similarly, in the example showing the development of *mente* in French (cf. §2.2.3), *mente* could at first have two coordinated adjectives in its scope (*humble et doucement*), but at a later stage it needs to be repeated (*humblement et doucement*), indicating that its scope has been reduced to the immediately preceding element; it has in fact become a bound morpheme.

Concerning 'cohesion' (row 2), the more grammaticalized a linguistic element is, the less choice there is formally, that is within the paradigm of forms that have a similar function. Thus, in the expression of a thematic role, an inflection for case is more paradigmatized than a preposition to express the same function because usually only one choice exists within the paradigm of case-forms, whereas often more than one preposition can be used to express the function in question. Syntagmatically, cohesion is increased in that the grammaticalized item fuses with other linguistic elements, for example *mente* in French became a suffix.

Paradigmatic 'variability' (row 3) refers to the degree to which a particular linguistic element is obligatory within the clause. Thus, the past tense marker in English is a highly grammaticalized element because it occurs obligatorily within the clause, whereas adverbial markers of time can occur much more freely, their presence being determined not by the grammar but by discourse. Syntagmatically, a grammaticalized element becomes less variable because it takes up a fixed position in the clause. For example, the tense-marker must follow the matrix verb, while the adverbial marker of time can occur in quite a number of positions within the clause.

Hopper (1991) presents a number of further generalizations (principles) that can be made regarding the process. Most of these can be subsumed under Lehmann's parameters, except the phenomena of 'divergence', 'layering', and 'persistence'. Layering is a synchronic phenomenon that arises out of the diachronic process; it reflects the fact that various stages of the process (i.e. the still lexical and the already grammaticalized forms) occur side by side.[26] When the grammaticalized and non-grammaticalized forms go their own separate ways, it is called 'divergence'. An example of this would be the indefinite article *(a)n* and the numeral *one*, which both go back to the same Old English form *ān* (cf. Hopper and Traugott 2003: 119). When two layered elements (sharing the same origin) diverge, they each develop their own semantic and syntactic characteristics and no longer influence each other. 'Persistence' points to the fact that traces of the original lexical meaning of the linguistic elements that are grammaticalized adhere to these elements. This may be reflected in the way the grammaticalized forms are grammatically constrained. A clear example of persistence is the Present-day English future auxiliary *will*, in which the old volitional meaning of *will* lives on. Since this older meaning is still found in some idiomatic expressions in English, as in the parenthetic phrase ... *if you will* (where *will* is used in its old meaning of 'wish, want'), and also in the negative form *won't*, *would not*, and the noun *will*, it is more than likely that persistence, although it looks diachronic, is in fact based on synchronic knowledge.

It is important to note that grammaticalization linguists have observed that not all of these parameters hold true in each case of grammaticalization. The discourse-pragmatic type of grammaticalization (see Sweetser 1990; Traugott 1982 and many later studies), in which a lexical item moves from the more concrete propositional domain into the textual domain, and from there into the expressive or epistemic domain, diverges from these parameters on almost all levels. It undergoes pragmatic enrichment rather than bleaching, increase in scope rather than decrease, there is no 'increase in bondedness', etc. (cf. Table 3.2). This strange behaviour needs to be explained. It is clear that grammaticalization theory cannot account for this type adequately if its principles do not apply. In addition, Tabor and Traugott (1998) have pointed out that one of Lehmann's parameters—the reduction of scope—may not be a well-defined and proper diagnostic either for other types of grammaticalization. They argue that within a definition of C-command many 'grammaticalized' items show an *increase* in scope. Increase in scope rather than decrease also follows from Roberts and Roussou's (2003) definition of grammaticalization. Another type of grammaticalization, recognized by Meillet (1912) from the beginning is the fixation of word order. Again, not all of Lehmann's parameters apply here.

The reaction so far within the grammaticalization community to these problems has been gradually to widen its field of application, with the result that the notion of grammaticalization is being hollowed out from the inside. This has considerably damaged its strength. It was not for nothing that Givón (1995a: xvi) wrote that functionalists must tighten up their 'analytical rigor', their 'scrutiny of method'. What needs to be further investigated is whether the discourse-pragmatic type of grammaticalization and the syntactic fixation of word order fits the present theory of grammaticalization. If it does not, we may simply be dealing with a different type of change. If it does, the theory needs to be tightened up, to show that it does. More on word order and discourse-pragmatic change will be found in Chapters 5 and 6.

Another important concept that plays a role in grammaticalization on the level of language is the notion of clines or hierarchies. These are also unidirectional, and can be observed diachronically as well as synchronically. Hopper and Traugott (2003: 6) describe a cline as a 'natural "pathway" along which forms evolve, a schema which models the development of forms'. They stress that clines 'are metaphors for labelling grammatical phenomena, not putative neurological or other elements of the language capacity'. Since the description given of a cline involving the noun *back* on the same page (and see also p. 85, and Heine *et al.* 1991a: 161) involves a metaphorical path from concrete (body part) > spatial > temporal > quality, it seems rather strange that clines are only considered to be relevant on the language level and not on the speaker level, where metaphor plays such a crucial role (see below). The metaphorical cline is a functional one, all other clines recognized in Hopper and Traugott are formal ones, such as the noun- and verb-to-affix cline (which are both examples of the 'cline of grammaticality' (p. 7)), the clause-combining cline, and the categoriality cline. It rather looks as if the fact that most of these clines are formal has led Hopper and Traugott to the conclusion that clines are merely diagnostic for the process of grammaticalization. This is also the opinion of Heine *et al.* (1991a: 168), who write 'once a transfer from one [semantic] category to another takes place this is likely to affect the status of the word type used to express that concept as well. ... Thus, the change from a noun *back* to a postposition meaning 'behind' might be viewed as the result of an activity which aims at restoring a one-to-one relationship between cognitive and linguistic structure'. Again the formal change is believed to trail behind. Paradigmatic relationships are not considered, for example the possibility that because a body-part noun like *front* had already moved into a lower formal category (adverb, particle, or pre/postposition) that for that reason another body-part *back* might join the same formal paradigm.

Next we must look at the kind of factors that have been recognized in grammaticalization on the level of the speaker. Most of these are functional and relate to the communicative situation or to the workings of the mind. We have a clear contrast here with generative grammar where the factors are strictly formal. For most linguists writing on grammaticalization, the main mechanisms involved at this level are metaphorical and metonymic in nature (cf. Hopper and Traugott 2003: 84–98).

Metaphorical change is a pragmatic/semantic phenomenon and can be related to the cognitive process of analogy (or the iconic/indexical mode of thinking). It is a type of paradigmatic change whereby a word sign used for a concrete object (i.e. the sign *back* referring to a part of the body) can be reinterpreted on a more abstract level as an indication of 'location', because of some element that these concepts have in common. It is important to note that many metaphorical extensions, especially of a natural (i.e. non-poetic) type are often simultaneously metonymic in character too.[27] Rubba (1994) shows in detail how the extension of the sign for a body part like *back* to a locative noun has as much to do with the relational orientation of the body (i.e. indexical) as with a similarity (iconic) between the back part of the body and the back of some other object. It is a thus a type of inferencing that arises out of the link between ourselves, our own bodies in space, and the way we conceptualize and order the world around us. Metonymy is also related to 'inferencing', but unlike metaphor (which is analogical and paradigmatic), it functions strictly on the syntagmatic (associative) plain and has to do with cause and effect, with associations between objects rather than similarities. It is part of our indexical mode of thinking.[28] The pragmatic metonymic conditioning factor arises out of the communicative situation, and takes place mainly via the 'semanticization of conversational inferences' (Hopper and Traugott 2003: 90).

In connection with 'experiential' metaphors (see fn. 27 above) and metonymic inferences, I cannot stress enough the importance of our own body as a most fruitful and indeed a universal source for both. Just as metaphorical extensions and inferences move outwards from the language user's bodily experience (cf. Lakoff and Johnson 1980; Lakoff and Turner 1989), in the same way the concrete human body is the starting point for language learners, and this must also have been the case in language evolution (see §§3.3, 3.4).

Bybee *et al.* (1994: 300) observe more generally in connection with both metaphor and metonymy that 'the push for grammaticization ... originates in the need to be more specific, in the tendency to infer as much as possible from the input, and in the necessity of interpreting items in context'. Likewise, Hopper and Traugott (2003: 92) concur with Heine *et al.* (1991a: 150–1) that 'grammaticalization can be interpreted as the result of a process which has *problem-solving* as its main goal' (emphasis in the original). It is the result of a 'search for ways to regulate communication and negotiate speaker–hearer interaction'.

These two factors, metaphor and metonymy, are discussed strictly from a functional point of view; almost all grammaticalization theorists consider form to be secondary. Thus Hopper and Traugott (2003: 39) write: '[t]hese modifications [i.e. reanalysis and analogy] comprise changes in interpretation ... *but not at first change in form*' (emphasis added). I do not believe that this is the right approach. There are two points at issue here. The first is that this functional approach obscures the fact that metaphorical and metonymic processes are really the same mechanisms as analogy and reanalysis. But because the former are seen as operating on the meaning level, they are seen as 'motivations' (causes) in grammaticalization (ibid.: 71), while the latter, because they operate on form, are seen as mere mechanisms (ibid.: 39). To my mind, both pairs should be considered equal—they are *causal* mechanisms—but operating on different levels of abstraction (see §§3.3, 3.4). Itkonen (2005: xii) also proposes to treat analogy as a 'psychologically real phenomenon which has *causal* efficacy both in language as in culture' (emphasis added), and not just as a 'merely descriptive device', which is how Hopper and Traugott see it.[29]

The second point concerns the nature of the sign. Anttila (1977, 1989: 88–108 and *passim*, 2003) emphasizes that all linguistic signs (words, structures of words) are 'double-edged': they are 'combinations of form and meaning', and that 'similarity relations exist both in meaning and form, and meaning and form are combined in the symbolic colligation'. For Anttila the paradigmatic (similarity) and syntagmatic (contiguity) axes are part of what he calls the 'analogical grid' or the 'warp and woof of cognition' (2003: 426). He adds that 'analogy [i.e. the analogical grid] works both in structure, giving it cohesion, and as a process for problem-solving' (p. 431; and cf. also Itkonen 2005: 12ff.,63–4). By neglecting form, the formal similarity of patterns and the adjacency (contiguity) of signs are neglected as an important formal force in grammaticalization.

Since both analogy and reanalysis, or metaphor and metonymy, are inextricable parts of the analogical grid, I cannot really endorse the suggestion made in Hopper and Traugott (2003: 39, 63–9, and see also Brinton 1996: 53; Campbell 2001a) that reanalysis is primary, and analogy secondary (cf. also fn. 45 below). They see analogy only as rule generalization, in which a new formal structure, caused by reanalysis, spreads to other environments. It only takes place *after* reanalysis has occurred, which itself is the result of pragmatic inferencing. Reanalysis is seen as more important because it is directly linked to function ('it comprises[s] changes in interpretation' (p. 39), and is caused by pragmatic inferencing), while analogy is seen as secondary because it is linked to form ('it modifies surface manifestations' (ibid.)). I think the main problem is, as noted by Itkonen above, that analogy is used by Hopper and Traugott as a useful descriptive term, but not as a psychological process. In the course of this volume, I will show that there are also changes that proceed formally (e.g. the behaviour of the auxiliaries BE, HAVE discussed in Chapter 4); changes where new forms arise (or disappear) because a learner sees a relation between two structures on the formal level. If reanalysis can be said to take place here, it takes place *after* an *analogical process*. I would argue that analogy is primary or at least stands on an equal footing with reanalysis since a reanalysis, both a semantic-pragmatic and a structural one, takes place within the contours of the communicative situation *and* the grammatical system in which a structure operates. The reanalysis will therefore also be confined and shaped by the formal structures that already exist. My hypothesis is that a reanalysis of a structure will not as a rule result in a totally new structure, but in one that is already in use elsewhere (cf. also Itkonen 2005: 110–13). It is the superficial similarity (analogy) that a language user perceives between two structures and between two communicative uses of them that causes a reanalysis in one of them, so as to bring it in line with the other. The *perception of similarity* must be logically primary to the reanalysis.[30] Thus, the reanalysis of *I am going to walk* from [*I am going* [to *walk*]] > [*I am going to* [*walk*]] [I'm gonna walk] may be caused by metonymic and metaphorical inferencing, but it must be caused as much by the fact that the language user already had [Aux V]-type structures in his language system (e.g. a modal verb such as *will* followed by a bare infinitive, expressing future intention). More details on this will be provided below in §3.4.

I will return to the 'analogical grid' below, but first I would like to give a simple example here of how both form and meaning can be at the heart of a change based on analogy. The example involves folk etymology, where a change in form can be driven by meaning, or a change in meaning driven by form (cf. Coates 1987).[31] An example of the former is OE *angnægl*, which became modern *hangnail* because the root **ang* (referring to something tight, painful) was no longer understood (most Old English words that contained it had disappeared), so another form was found close to the old form and one that was meaningful with respect to the object concerned. Problem-solving can be said to drive this change, but, in a sense, even in this example, form and meaning are equally relevant (cf. fn. 31). An example of change driven by form is *belfry* (from OF *berfrey, belfry*), which at first referred to a movable siege tower, but later acquired the meaning of 'bell tower' because of the formal similarity with the English word *bell*. Meaning plays only a subsidiary role here (in that both words refer to 'towers'). Many examples of these kinds of changes can be found in the lexicon of any language. It is definitely not a freak phenomenon, once thought to occur only among the uneducated (cf. Malkiel 1993: 19–20), but one of genuine importance. In a similar way, as I hope to show in the course of this study, form as well as function play an equal role in morphosyntactic change.

3.3 A comparison and evaluation

To facilitate comparison between the kind of 'factors' playing a role in the P&P and the grammaticalization models, I will loosely use as a basis for comparison 'factors' (mechanisms, principles, conditioning factors) distinguished in historical linguistic studies which are not specifically tied to the two approaches compared here, such as Anttila (1989), Milroy (1992), McMahon (1994), Labov (1994, 2001), Harris and Campbell (1995), Lass (1997), and Croft (2000). I will concentrate on those factors that look relevant to morphosyntactic change. At this point, I include all 'factors', formal and functional, internal and external, because they cannot really be disentangled. These are given in column 1 in Table 3.3. Column 2 presents an overview of all the kind of phenomena mentioned in models concerned with grammar/language change that fall under the main factors given in column 1. Column 3, relates the 'factors' to more general, primitive constraints or characteristics that may be said to be present ontogenetically and/or phylogenetically.

I will begin in reverse fashion by looking at column 3 because it is important to know what the preconditions are for language, that is we first need to know how language developed or develops in terms of language evolution and language acquisition. In recent work on the origin of language, a lot of attention has been paid to the social foundations and the cognitive abilities already present in the animal world before a human proto-language developed, and on the characteristics of a proto-language itself. There is fairly general agreement on quite a number of aspects, and it is interesting to note that quite a few of these aspects also apply to the situation of the language-learning child (cf. Deacon 1997; Steels 1997; and the papers in Hurford *et al.* 1998; Dunbar *et al.* 1999; Knight *et al.* 2000; Christiansen and Kirby 2003; and more specifically Arbib 2003; Hauser and Fitch 2003; Hurford 2003).

As far as the social conditions are concerned, primates and many other mammalian species live in cohesive groups, which are characterized by communicative interaction for purposes of internal cooperation and competition and by a sense of group identity towards outsiders (cf. Noble 2000; Dessalles 2000). Part of this communication is the ability to manipulate others, that is to communicate, by means of gestures and vocalization, in such a way as to effect a response in the other. Wray (2000: 289) considers such primitive holistic 'utterances' to have the same function as four of 'Searle's [1979] five speech act classes', that is: 'commissives' (threats and offers), 'directives' (food begging, requests for grooming), 'expressives' (social greetings), and 'assertives' (food and alarm calls). Another important aspect of these social groups is play, and learning through imitation and play, which is observed among animals as well as young children

Table 3.3. *General survey of 'factors' involved in change*

Main 'factors' involved in change	Sub-'factors'	General constraints (primitive, pre-adaptive)
Reduction/erosion, ease of effort, simplification	Phonological loss, morphological loss, lexical and semantic loss (bleaching), fusion, fixation, lexicalization, loss of marked features	Economy/effective processing, ritualization
Phonetic/prosodic changes	Influence on morphological/ syntactic (cliticization) and lexical levels	Economy/effective processing
Analogy	extension, levelling, lexical diffusion, folk etymology, metaphor	Iconicity, centrality of the body/concrete objects
Reanalysis	Parameter shifts, abduction, exaptation, form–function reanalysis, pragmatic inferencing, folk etymology, metonymic process	Iconicity/indexicality (presence of UG)
Isomorphism ('Humboldt's Universal')	avoidance of homonymy, synonymy, polysemy, and of surface ambiguity	Iconicity/indexicality
Chain shifting, drifts	push- and drag-chains, 'divergence' or 'split'(avoidance of homonyms), grammaticaliza- tion clines,'layering', unidirectionality	Iconicity, more particularly isomorphism (to preserve distinctions), desire for symmetry
Borrowing/contact	Prestige, filling of gaps, code-switching, substratum	Imitation, type and length of contact, immigration
Frequency	Type/token frequency, repetition, imitation, syntactic priming, formulaic phrases, automatization	Economy/effective processing, imitation, memory constraints, ritualization, calls/ gestures
Communicative factors; expressiveness	Preservation of redundancy; creativity; desire for novelty; salience, repetition	Iconicity, effective processing, play/ competition
Social factors	Social networks, standardization, age, sex, class, status, style- and code-switching, face/politeness	Type of society (literate/ preliterate), type of speaker, group identity, identity of self, communicative competence

Psychological/ emotional factors	Subjectivity, body (identity and locality), animateness/agency; politeness strategies, discourse fillers, hedges	Communicative competence, manipulation, identity of self
Perceptual factors	Repetition (resumptive pronouns), type of embedding, linear order, adjacency	Effective processing; memory constraints; perceptual constraints

(cf. Knight 2000: 106ff.; Dąbrowska 2004: 62–5). Children and apes share these features, but in addition, children appear to have 'a highly precocious' sense of self, which so far has only been found to be latently present in chimpanzees (Vihmann and DePaolis 2000: 131). This sense of self is necessary to develop the ability to share attention with others, which according to Tomasello (2003a, 2003b) is a necessary condition for symbolic communication to become possible.[32] Tomasello notes that children develop this in their second year and then know how to communicate *intentionally*. Chimpanzees are also believed to be able to communicate intentionally but not, it seems, through calls, only through gestures (Tomasello 2003b: 99).

The *means* of communication used are again similar for both very young children and many mammalian species. Both possess involuntary vocalizations (e.g. alarm and food calls) and make use of gestures. There is of course an enormous difference in the vocal abilities of humans and mammals. This is the result of the different ways in which the larynx, the tongue and the vocal tract have evolved between species (cf. Hauser and Fitch 2003), but Hauser and Fitch (p. 170) also note that a categorial perception mechanism (necessary for speech) is not special to humans but developed long before humans began to produce speech.

There is fairly wide agreement on the importance of gestures, and it is quite generally accepted that part of the language development can be explained as a gradual shift from visual to vocal gestures as follows: holistic manual gestures > facial gestures (in combination with vocalizations) > mouthed gestures, that is vocalizations (cf. Burling 2000; Corballis 2003). Gestures still play a very important part in communication nowadays in the way in which they accompany our vocalizations (cf. Arbib 2003: 199). A compositional analysis of the holistic phrases is believed to have taken place at a later stage. Gestures are necessarily holistic, and most scholars believe that proto-language as a development of earlier gestures and vocalizations, did not have syntax but consisted of holistic or formulaic phrases (cf. Carstairs-McCarthy 1999, 2000; Knight 2000: 101; Wray 2000; Arbib 2003: 183–7).[33] Indeed some linguists argue that most of language is still formulaic, consisting of automated phrases. One study even suggests that more than '70% of our adult native language may be formulaic' (quoted in Wray and Perkins 2000: 2). This of course depends on how one defines formulae, but it is clear that a large part of our everyday language consists of fixed phrases and is not nearly as creative and novel as generative theory assumes.[34] It is also quite possible that children's comprehension and production of first words and phrases is holistic (cf. Vihman and DePaolis 2000: 135; Clark 2003: 171, Tomasello 2003a: 36–40, 101, 112) but more work needs to be done here. Clark does note that for children at the two-word stage 'there is little evidence that word order has any grammatical role', and Perkins (see Wray and Perkins 2000: 19) has noted a 'curious appearance, disappearance and reappearance of formulaic sequences during language acquisition'.[35]

The frequent repetition of intentional gestures and automated speech also has an effect on the way these gestures or vocalizations are executed, that is they become reduced. Scholars writing on ritualization or conventionalization, as this reduction is called in language, usually refer to the seminal article by Nico Tinbergen (1952). He showed that many gestures and vocalizations in the animal world started off as purely instrumental acts (of aggression, subjection, anything to do with the process of living). For example when a dog bites, it first bares its teeth so as to be ready to bite. Another dog who sees this might run off, thus avoiding being bitten. An aggressor may eventually discover that just snarling is enough to make the other dog understand the message, and thus, the instrumental act may become a communicative signal (with a clear iconic/ indexical base) over time. Haiman (1993, 1994, 1998, 1999) shows that ritualization is a fact of life in many social and cultural areas, and in language too.

Haiman (1999) works out the trajectory of ritualization and its reduction in language in great detail for the instrumental act of self-abasement. For instance, in order to show deference or subjection, one might prostrate oneself upon the floor, thus making oneself look small. In many societies, this was soon reduced to kneeling and later bowing. The same act can also be expressed vocally by using a special 'small' voice or an accommodating rhythm (Haiman 1999: 38 notes that a high-pitched falsetto is a conventional sign of politeness in languages like Tzeltal, Tamil, and Japanese). Another more purely verbal way to express smallness is by using phrases such as 'I am your servant/slave', or addressing the other as 'your highness', etc. Further reduction may then take place by using diminutive nouns or modal constructions to express distance. The trajectory thus followed shows a cline from a purely physical to a purely verbal act, which is accompanied by a loss of iconicity and a loss of sincerity. The form becomes more and more reduced, so that eventually not much of it and of its original intention is left over. It is in many ways, similar to the cline of grammaticalization, and it is one way in which more iconic signs may have changed into arbitrary symbols.

Ritualization and grammaticalization are also connected to economy and communicative efficiency: why should one be elaborate when 'less' will do as well? Since, however, the process also involves a loss of expressivity (sincerity), it is not surprising that the process is cyclical. New ways of expressing oneself (i.e. new forms but usually in already existing patterns) will always be found when someone needs to show that he or she really means it, or when someone wants his or her intentions to be absolutely clear.

Returning now to children, Burling (2000: 31–2) argues that children's 'arms-up' gestures can be explained in the same instrumental way: children learn to use it because it is indexical/iconic to the way in which their arms automatically go up when adults lift them. There is one important difference, however, and that is that the 'arms-up' gesture is not instinctive but learned, unlike the snarling of dogs (Burling 2000: 32). The ritualization of animal gestures from instrumental acts to communicative signals only occurred through 'the long process of natural selection', while the communicative signals represented by human gestures can become ritualized (or conventionalized) 'within the lifetime of a single individual' (ibid.: 31). Burling believes that a similar instrumental origin may have been the basis for the early word-like signs in language evolution, and that these could have conventionalized rapidly since these too came to be learned. Haiman's (1999) study of the ritualization of self-abasement is most interesting in this respect because he shows that the physical and verbal gestures of forms of self-abasement were all present in one and the same (literary) text.

A final link between the evolution of language and language acquisition, concerns the cognitive abilities of both young children and other mammalian species. The most important change in the evolution of language according to Deacon (1997, 2003) is the step from an indexical and iconic use of signs to symbolic (arbitrary) reference.[36] (For Tomasello (2003a, 2003b), this step is linked to children's ability to 'read intentions', an ability not present in apes.) It is well-known that signs used by non-human mammals and animals in general are in some way motivated (i.e. they are iconic and/or indexical): in their *natural* surroundings, animals do not use symbolic signs. Although it has been possible after prolonged and intensive training to teach chimps and bonobos symbolic word reference (but not grammar!) (cf. Deacon 1997: 65ff.), this ability, according to Deacon, usually demonstrates no more than a mechanical form of reference, which only works for as long as the animal is *externally stimulated* to produce those signs.[37] When writing about the emergence of symbolic reference, Deacon (1997: 74–5, 99) suggests that it is connected to iconic and indexical reference in a *hierarchy*:

(2)   THE ICONIC-INDEXICAL-SYMBOLIC HIERARCHY (Deacon 1997: 75).
    Symbolic relationships are composed of indexical relationships between sets of indices and indexical relationships are composed of iconic relationships between sets of icons .... This suggests a kind of semiotic reductionism in which more complex forms of representation are analyzable to simpler forms. In fact, this is essentially what occurs as forms are interpreted. Higher-order forms are decomposed into (replaced or represented by) lower order forms. Inversely, to construct higher representation, one must operate on lower-order forms to replace them (represent them).

Symbolic reference is the most complex form of interpretation, which process occurs only in human languages. From an evolutionary point of view, it is clear that the human brain has evolved furthest in the hierarchy given in (2). The hierarchy also makes clear that symbolic reference *can* only take place on the basis of the two other forms of reference, the indexical and the iconic. Thus, iconic and indexical reference are evolutionary earlier and form the basis for *all* interpretation.

Another important cognitive ability and one closely related to iconicity is that of mimesis. In order to be able to imitate, one needs a sense of self. As we have seen above, children develop this early, while, so far, it has only been seen to be marginally present in chimpanzees and dolphins. Mimesis quite clearly plays an important role in the development of language in our ancestors (cf. Vihman and DePaolis 2000: 139–42). Vihman and DePaolis show that mimesis developed via all kinds of group activities such as tool making, drawing, etc. Communicative signs (gestures, grunts) used during such activities came to be imitated as signals 'lead[ing] to a group repertoire of meaningful symbolic forms stabilised through [the implementation and] action of [an] articulatory filter' (Vihmann and DePaolis 2000: 140–1). Arbib (2003: 184) lists 'parity' or the 'mirror property' (also referred to as the mirror-neuron system) as one of the pre-properties necessary for language to develop. To use language, one must be able to reproduce what someone else has said. He shows that such a mirror system is present in monkeys for grasping, and he believes that 'a key area in the human language system is a possible mirror system for grasping' (ibid.: 189). Note that this provides another link between the motor system and language, the other one being the use of gestures. As far as language acquisition is concerned, it has been noted above that children's learning begins with imitation.

To sum up so far, when we consider the above abilities in connection with what may be significant preconditions or pre-properties for language learning, we may distil the following as crucial. For comprehension, we need a perception mechanism capable of distinguishing between all kinds of speech sounds, we need to be able to hear what is different and what is the same (iconicity), and we need to see a link between objects or actions talked about, and signs used to refer to those objects (indexicality). All these abilities are already present in at least a basic form in (higher) mammals. For speech production, there are requirements on the shape and position of the larynx, the tongue and the vocal tract. These are lacking in mammals (cf. Corballis 2003; Hauser and Fitch 2003), and present in human adults, while in children these organs develop the required position, proportion and agility early in life. The other requirements for production are mimesis (including a sense of our own body in relation to others and the world) and comprehension. We have seen that the former is rudimentarily present in apes in the form of mirror neurons for grasping. In addition, in both comprehension and production, repetition (frequency) is crucial for learning. Another prerequisite, missing in most animals, is an eagerness to learn without reward or punishment (cf. Holyoak and Thagard 1995: 81) and the willingness/ability to take the perspective of the other person (i.e. Tomasello's [2003a, 2003b] 'intention reading').

Thus the most basic cognitive abilities for language learning, are imitation (repetition), intention reading, and iconic and indexical thinking. As far as iconic and indexical thinking is concerned, Holyoak and Thagard (1995: 81 ff.) have shown that very young children and apes have the same abilities to begin with but that at year 1 children are already in the lead, and after the age of 3–4, children still progress and apes stand still. Itkonen (1994: 45), too, emphasizes that both animals and children learn '[t]he properties of co-occurrence and succession, and in particular the causal properties, of things and events ... on the basis of analogy'. In order to survive in this world, they have to become aware of the iconic relations (similarities and differences) between one object and another, and learn the indexical relation between an object and its function/use, so that they know what is good to eat and what to avoid, which animal to trust and which to flee. In a next stage, the *repeated correlation* between an object and its use leads to a higher-order level of iconicity. It is a higher, more abstract level, because they learn by an analogical generalization that *any* object that looks like object *x* with a function *y*, is also bound to have function *y*. The comparison is now no longer based only on the immediate context but also on a collection of *past* experiences, on an abstraction. They begin to learn to recognize *types* from past *tokens*.

All this is still part of animal brains as well as ours. Symbolic representation is one step further still in that at this level the combined iconic/indexical relation begins to be used *separately* from the individual context, object, or occasion in which it was first learned. Symbolic reference happens when we can transfer the referential functions from one *set* to another. In the earlier learning there was iconic overlap between the members within a set; at the higher symbolic level we distinguish a pattern that distinguishes a set as a whole, and we can then apply this same pattern to another set. Holyoak and Thagard (1995) have called this 'system mapping'. It is once more a form of analogy but again on a higher level. On p. 46, they present us with a simple example: humans can see a similarity between a sample presenting, for example, two trees and a sample presenting two frogs (as in Figure 3.1). The pattern that they discern is the isomorphism of the *combination* of *two of the same things*.

Humans would *not* see an analogy between a sample presenting two trees and another one presenting a frog and an apple (Figure 3.2) because here the higher order pattern 'two of the same' does not apply.

Figure 3.1.

Figure 3.2.
Source: Holyoak and Thagard (1995: 50).

Non-human primates, on the other hand, are not able to see this higher, more abstract analogy without extensive training, which crucially involves language training (Holyoak and Thagard 1995: 50). Children begin to understand this relation- or system-mapping from the age of about 3 onwards and would be able to solve the above analogy without help by about age 4 (ibid.: 87ff.; Gentner 2003).

It is clear that imitation and repetition are intimately bound up with the iconic and indexical modes of thinking. Repetition is necessary in order to imitate well, and imitation, of course, leads to repetition. In this light, it is remarkable that the frequency of occurrence of lexical items or constructions did not play much of a role until recently in most theoretical writings on language change. Frequency is not regarded as a factor in generative studies of grammar change. Lightfoot (1979) does not give it a mention in his 'theory of change', but it begins to play a role on the level of the PLD in his later work (1991, 1999), where more attention is given to the triggers in the PLD that might lead up to grammar change. Similarly in Hopper and Traugott's first edition of *Grammaticalization* (1993), frequency is only briefly mentioned as a heuristic tool which 'demonstrates a kind of generalization in use patterns' (p. 103); it is 'associated with unmarked segments' (p. 146), and provides 'evidence for the degree of grammaticalization' (p. 110). In their (2003) edition, however, frequency has been upgraded, and gets a whole section to itself (§5.6). It is no longer just a 'valuable tool', or a 'concomitant of grammaticalization', but it has 'assumed an important place in the empirical study of how lexical forms move into grammatical roles' (pp. 126–7). A number of diachronic functional linguists had already pointed to its importance much earlier, notably DuBois (1985: 359–60), who wrote: 'recurrent patterns in discourse tokens exert pressure on linguistic types', and see also Hook (1991: 65–6), Thompson and Mulac (1991), and Fischer (1994a: 154). In neuronal grammatical models, frequency also plays a crucial role, as I indicated in §2.3 with a reference to Pulvermüller (2002: 19, 163).

In connection with imitation, the phenomenon of 'syntactic priming' should be mentioned, which entails that the act of processing an utterance with a particular form facilitates processing a subsequent utterance with the same or a related form. Pickering and Branigan (1999: 136), in their overview of evidence available for syntactic priming, show that 'speakers tended to repeat syntactic form when producing sentences that were not related in meaning'. In other words, it was not so much the lexical or metrical correspondences that led to imitation but the structure of sentences. Pickering and Branigan see this priming as a by-product of syntactic processing, but they remark that it also has a functional role in that it reduces the computational load and thus facilitates the use of dialogue. Tannen (1985) provides additional evidence of syntactic priming, but also points to the priming of sounds and rhythmical structures. Both types of priming provide evidence for the importance of form as an independent phenomenon, while syntactic priming, in addition, presents direct rather than indirect evidence (as is the case in generative grammar, which relies on intuitive judgements) of what syntactic constructions are considered to be related.

3.4 Concluding remarks

It looks as if factors found to be relevant for learning, in both language evolution and acquisition, are the *iconic* and *indexical* reference systems, in combination with *repetition* (frequency) and *imitation*, all within the context of a social community and individuals who can take a perspective on others.[38] It is clear that the capacity to imitate is itself based on iconic recognition, and that repetition is necessary to entrench the iconic and indexical links in one's experience and to enable a higher form of thinking, such as abstract or symbolic thinking. Given that the same primitives play a role in the two areas of language evolution and language acquisition, it is likely that they should also play an important role in language change. An advantage of this approach is that these primitives are part of the biological endowment inherited from our non-human forebears, and play a role in other, non-linguistic cognitive domains as well. If we can next link these primitive features to features of a neuronal theory of grammar, it would further strengthen our proposal to consider them crucial. In this connection I would like to stress that both reanalysis and isomorphism, two other factors listed in column 1 of Table 3.3, are dependent on iconic/indexical modes of thinking, which would further reduce the number of factors. It is noteworthy too that, in general, the more external, perceptual, social and cultural, factors in column 1 can also be related to the same four, more primitive features operating in a social community.

3.5 A sketch for an analogy-based learning mechanism for language

Before we round off this chapter, I would like to present a highly simplified practical model which attempts to connect language acquisition with change. In the sketch for language learning to be produced below, Anttila's 'analogical grid' (Anttila 2003, discussed in §3.2) and the connectionist model (discussed in §2.3)—and with it the factors of frequency and entrenchment—play a primary role. The same system would also be at work in language change since I assume that the way in which language changes is guided by the same learning mechanisms that help us to acquire language. This does not mean that the sort of changes (or mistakes) that young children make in their language output must be the same as what is seen in language change. Obviously, changes which are made by adults are produced by a learning system that operates on a far greater corpus of linguistic data than is the case for children. Similarly, the structural patterns or 'construction-types' used by adults will not yet all be fully developed in children. This means that the analogical sets on which the mechanisms work may change over time, some of these indeed will become strengthened by use (automated), and hence the learning mechanisms will produce different results.[39]

Since we are here concerned with morphosyntax, the model will skip the comprehension and production of signs which begins to take place at an earlier stage of the acquisition period, at the phonetic/phonological level (for an example of how this first stage may be analysed, see Peters 1985; Guasti 2002). Essentially, though, learning to differentiate between linguistically relevant sounds and non-sounds, between allophonic and phonemic sounds, and learning to recognize and use the typical syllabic and intonational patterns of one's native language should be no different from the way differences and similarities between syntactic structures and morphosyntactic categories are learned, except for the fact that the latter learning takes place on a concrete *and* on more abstract levels, and is, consequently, much more complex. We will also skip the stage where a combination of signs may still be processed holistically. Even though holistic and compositional learning will probably go hand in hand, I will here simply describe what may take place on the basis of words, once compositional learning begins. In all cases of lexical and morphosyntactic learning, it is assumed that form and function go hand in hand.

The idea of a learning system based on analogical sets and indexical and iconic relations is taken from work on analogical sets in morphology (cf. Skousen 1989; Baayen 2003; Chapman and Skousen 2005);[40] it is inspired by the 'Operating Principles' suggested by Peters (1985) and Slobin (1985a) (briefly discussed in §2.2.2, and fn. 44 below), which show how language learning may take place via developmental 'bootstrapping' (cf. also Slobin 1997: 314ff.), by the connectionist neuronal model by Pulvermüller described in Chapter 2, and by a more recent renewed interest in analogy in the cognitive sciences (cf. Hofstadter 1995, Gentner *et al.* 2001). Last, but not least, it is influenced by a very long and fruitful tradition of analogy in historical linguistics (for an overview see Itkonen 2005: ch.2).

The analogical, 'atomistic' (cf. §2.0 above) approach to language involves a continuous learning process rather than the use of a fixed rule system; it is process-driven, invoking procedures and schemas rather than rules. The advantage of postulating a rule system is of course that it minimizes the number of procedures (rules) and simplifies contextual specification. The disadvantage of a rule system, however, is that it is not clear where the rules come from in the first place, and that next to the rule system, one needs a separate lexical system to account for all the exceptions to the rules. In an analogically based system, there is only one system. The disadvantage of an analogical system is that one needs more fine-grained lexical categories (based on semantic and formal criteria) and more 'construction-types'. Pulvermüller (2002: 192–3), however, expects that the number of lexical categories would not exceed 100. In his proposal of a neuronal grammar, he reckons that a few million connections linking input units (starting from the assumption that about 100,000 input sets are needed for lexical items) would be necessary, but since 'most cortical neurons have above 10^4 synapses,[41] the large number of connections should not constitute a problem' (2002: 193). It is interesting to observe in this connection that the logical-formal rule models of language are a product of the fact that the computer in the 1960s did not have enough memory capacity, and so the linguists working with these models 'ele-vat[ed] economy of storage to a central theorem' (Baayen 2003: 230). More recent studies on the workings of the mind/brain emphasize that retrieval from memory is the preferred strategy, and that people are able to store vast numbers of prefabricated units (cf. Dąbrowska 2004: 27).

I shall try to make the idea of an analogical learning system a little more concrete by a simple example of how the model may be built up. I will use the terms 'token' and 'type' to refer to substantive linguistic signs and abstract categories respectively. A 'token-set' constitutes a set of tokens that form a paradigm either semantically or formally. The formal shape of the token (such as specific inflections) may help to identify a 'type', while the communicative context may identify the semantic-pragmatic features of that same type (e.g. the paradigm of (subclasses of) nouns or verbs). In the same way, a combination of tokens, or tokens and types, may form a set with other similar combinations, which I will call a type-set. Such a type-set in fact constitutes a 'construction-type' on the syntagmatic level, that is a schema consisting of a particular configuration of types or of particular tokens and types.

Figure 3.3 shows how one token, *apple*, is iconically (via similarity of function) related to a lexical set containing tokens of other kinds of fruit (*pear*, etc.) and at the same time indexically related to other kinds of iconic sets containing tokens with which it collocates (*eat* etc., *red* etc.). In terms of a neuronal grammar, both these sets would be linked to the primary unit (*apple*) and to each other by so-called neuronal sequence sets, which are specialized in defining a sequence feature. Thus, 'each lexical category label ... would be analogous to a sequence set' (Pulvermüller 2002: 191, and see §2.3). This would ensure that a particular transitive verb (e.g. *peel, pick*) is preceded by a noun which is [+ animate/human] and [+agent] and followed by a noun which also obeys particular features. The relations between tokens and token-sets in Figure 3.3 are still on the concrete

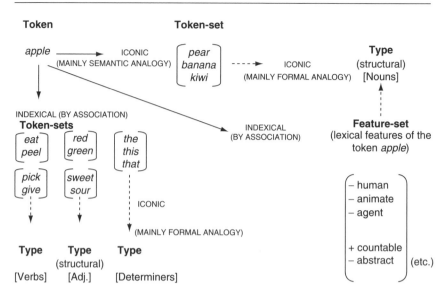

Figure 3.3. *Possible paradigmatic (iconic) and syntagmatic (indexical) relations between the sign* apple *and other linguistic signs forming token-sets and types.*

token-level, but the formation of a paradigmatic *set* of tokens in itself is already on a (semantic and morphosyntactic) type-level (a set is indicated by its inclusion in square brackets); e.g. *peel* and *pick* are both verbs, they may take verbal inflections, they are both transitive and telic, they both require an animate subject NP, etc. Apart from that, the token *apple* is also indexically (via function) related to a set of lexical features, which will in turn, and eventually, help to define the formal type 'Noun' (this is done via subsets of Noun, such as 'Count Noun', 'Inanimate Noun', 'Abstract Noun', etc.) This set of lexical features itself is built upon the learner's experience with lots of other tokens with their contiguous tokens, and all these tokens together are in turn related to more abstract construction-types, which give information about what categories (or types) typically follow or precede a Noun (or a Verb), or at a higher level what phrases typically follow or precede a Noun Phrase. All this cannot be shown in Figure 3.3, which just indicates a first stage of (neural) connections (iconic and indexical) between one word token and other token-sets (represented by black arrows), and between these and other types (represented by broken arrows).

The sets are thus formed on the basis of functional as well as formal analogy, and the links between the tokens, the token-sets and the more abstract types, type-sets and construction-types are indexical as well as iconic. On a higher abstract level, the morphological types (representing categories such as Noun, Verb, etc.) can then be further combined into structural syntactic types: NP construction-type, VP construction-type, etc., and from there, again via frequent collocations of tokens with their sets attached, into larger structures (clause construction-types). Structures or collocations, both at token- and at type-level (or a combination of the two) that occur frequently may become automatized because neuronal sequence sets (i.e. token-sets, types or construction-types that are connected to a particular token when it is used) are strengthened every time they are fired. This creates not only formulaic phrases on the token-level (fixed collocations, idioms, etc.), but also morphological and syntactic 'formulas' on increasingly higher type-levels, for example the typical feature-set of a Noun, the familiar structure of NPs and VPs, and the familiar word orders that obtain within a particular language (e.g. the typical [NP$_S$ VP NP$_O$] sequence of English declarative sentences).

How may change occur in a system that is based on this kind of analogical/indexical learning? In the eyes of most linguists, generative or otherwise, analogy is an inadequate tool to explain change. Harris and Campbell (1995: 51) avoid the term because 'it has been used to cover so many different sorts of phenomena', but they do admit that 'analogues' (which they define as 'structural similarities') are 'a frequent cause or stimulus of change'. Lightfoot (1979: 343ff.) provides a useful and extensive discussion of analogy, admitting its importance but stating at the same time that it is 'too general a notion and cannot be used as the basis for a predictive theory'.[42] In a way, his Transparency Principle has taken over the function of analogy, and he admits that this principle is 'inextricably intertwined with what others have called analogical extension', that is to say it 'sometimes takes the form of extending already existing patterns' (1979: 348). At this point analogy has to do with the *form* a change takes, not with its cause. The cause is the Transparency Principle which explains why reanalyses take place in language, which may take the form of analogical extensions (cf. pp. 344, 348). However, on p. 365, we read that analogy is 'essentially a causal notion', and on p. 373 it is described as 'an explanatory principle for historical change'. It seems then that for Lightfoot too analogy is more than merely form.

A similar dependency of analogy on reanalysis can be found in Hopper and Traugott's (2003: 39) grammaticalization model (and see also Traugott

1995: 1). They consider 'two general mechanisms by which grammaticalization takes place: reanalysis *primarily*, and analogy *secondarily*' (emphasis added). So, as in Lightfoot, reanalysis is 'a prerequisite for the implementation of the change through analogy', or put differently 'analogy ... modifies surface manifestations and in itself does not effect rule change', it only effects 'rule spread' (Hopper and Traugott 2003: 39). In both grammaticalization theory and the P&P approach, reanalysis and analogy are mechanisms, in both reanalysis is primary, and in both the deeper 'causes' for change lie elsewhere (in the pragmatic-semantic forces at work (problem-solving) in the process of grammaticalization, and in the parameter shifts forced by the PLD cues and UG in the P&P model).

I have myself suggested in an early article (1989: 163–6) that analogy may be both a mechanism *and* a cause. I did this on a rather thin basis, having only looked at a small number of instances of language change. I think my early idea can now be strengthened with the help of investigations carried out in the field of language evolution, and language acquisition as noted above, and by our deeper understanding of the importance of (diagrammatic) iconicity in language and its link with indexicality.[43] Recent works on language change also emphasize the importance of analogy as a primary *motive* for change, notably Joseph (2003), Deutscher (2005: 62, 71–2, and especially ch. 6), and Itkonen (2005). Linguists working in language acquisition (cf. Tomasello 1992, 2003a, 2003b, Slobin 1985a, 1985b, etc.) also believe that linguistic abstractions of the type we find in morphosyntax, that is the recognition of different morphological categories and syntactic structures, can be largely built up via an initial concrete base (of at first token- and later type-recognition), starting with signs referring to concrete objects and activities in concrete situations, sorting these into sets and generalizing slowly type-by-type from there.[44] This development from concrete to abstract in grammar also correlates well with the idea that the body is used as the centre from which we learn (as argued in §§3.2 and 3.3). Unlike the principles of UG, it does not start off with abstractions, but it follows the cognitive development of the child in other areas.

I am suggesting here, following linguists such as Anttila (2003), Itkonen and Haukioja (1997), and Itkonen (2005) that by far the most important primitive factor in morphosyntactic change and the acquisition of syntax is the iconic/indexical mode of thinking (cf. Anttila's (2003) 'warp' and 'woof', of his 'analogical grid'). As shown in an admittedly still primitive way in Figure 3.3, this combined mode of thinking leads to the ordering of signs (tokens) into analogical token-sets, and the further symbolic type-ordering into categories and higher syntactic structures, that is what Holyoak and Thagard (1995) have termed system-mapping (cf. §3.3).

I believe that the looseness of analogy, which was seen as such a problem before, will be much constrained if one thinks of analogy as taking place on different levels and of tokens and types being ordered into sets. This means that Kiparsky's tongue-in-cheek example of the kind of impossible novelties that analogy predicts, cannot really occur under this stricter definition.[45] Kiparsky's (1974: 259) *ear* : *hear* = *eye* : X, where the analogy principle would predict *heye* for X, is impossible, first of all because it confuses the morphological level with the phonological one. A misanalysis of a phoneme within one morpheme on the token-level does not occur as far as I know; the most that occurs is a misanalysis of a phoneme between two morphemes on a type-token level,[46] as happened in the case of *a nadder* > *an adder* (discussed in §1.1.2). This change could take place only because the phoneme [a] was also a morphological token (it was a member of the type-set of Determiners). Secondly, the outcome of the analogy, which takes place on the token level, would have to refer to the semantic and structural analogical sets in which each token plays a role. *Eye* and *ear* would be in one set with *nose* and *chin*, and *hear* would be in another set with *see*, *feel*, *touch*, etc. There would be no X to be filled because the position was already filled by *see*, which, with its high frequency, would never allow an analogical newcomer.

Kiparsky's syntactic example is rather similar. He argues that analogy would predict the structure *Mary, who John knows Bill and* on the basis of a proportion such as: *John knows Mary* : *Mary, who John knows* = *John knows Bill and Mary* : X. In this instance, the token-level gets completely confused with the type-level. On a token-level *John* could be replaced by *Fred* or *Peter*, and *knows* could be replaced by *sees* or *recognizes*, or, on a type-token level the Proper Noun type (*John*) could be replaced by an NP (which is equivalent to it in type), and the token *and* could be replaced by another token from the type-set Coordinator, for example *or*. On a higher type-level still, the whole coordinated phrase 'NP$_1$ *and* NP$_2$' could be replaced by another NP$_x$. It is, however, impossible to extract one token (e.g. *and*) out of a higher NP-type, and create a new NP-type with it (*Bill and*), which, in addition, is not supported by any analogical construction-type ('*Bill and*' is not a possible construction-type). In other words, since *and* is *part* of a higher type, the coordinated NP, it can only be replaced on a token-level. The hierarchy between the tokens, the token-sets, and the various levels of types/construction-types must be preserved.[47] In addition, since signs also carry semantic information, Kiparsky's new 'analogical' token here would be completely ill-formed.

In other words, the analogical possibilities are tightly constrained by both the token sets, the type-sets of lower (categories) and higher levels (syntactic constituents and constructions), and the iconic and indexical connections between sets. In addition, the possibilities are also constrained by the fact that the sets are organized both semantically and structurally since each sign or token (because of its binary nature) is part of a formal (structural) as well as a semantic set. Thus, a change can take place first on a semantic token-level, which may cause this token to join another set, after which it may also take over some of the characteristics of this set, through the indexical link it has with a certain syntactic structure type. This is, for instance, how the infinitival clause-type spread from verbs of physical perception to those of mental perception in Old English (cf. Fischer 1989: 160–1). This would be an example of a syntactic change spreading via lexical diffusion. What happened is as follows: the verbs of physical perception form a set. Some of these join the set of verbs of mental perception (via metaphor, i.e. semantic analogy). They join a new set bringing along their clausal structure, thus enabling the other verbs of the new set to acquire the same structure by analogy. A change may also take place on a formal token-level, for example a particular verb may become a noun; this would be an instance of conversion. When a change starts on a higher type-level, the effect of it will not be lexical but syntactic. For example, if the position of an object vis-à-vis a verb changes for perceptive or communicative reasons (salience, weight, animacy, etc.), this might lead to a new construction-type, perhaps starting with certain objects which belong to one and the same token- or type-set.

Looking at these indexical/iconic learning mechanisms, and their possible role in change, it seems clear that a theoretical model that does not deal with function and form on an equal footing, would not fit this proposal. Dependency grammars, such as LFG and HPSG, Role and Reference Grammar (Van Valin and LaPolla 1997; Van Valin 2005) and Construction Grammar (cf. Goldberg 1995; Croft and Cruse 2004), in which lexical features as well as syntactic constructions play a role, and in which surface sequence is important, easily fit this framework, and so does the type of neuronal grammar discussed in §2.3. As briefly indicated above, in Pulvermüller's proposal for a neuronal grammar, the semantic and structural token-sets, types, and construction-types would all be separate neuronal sets, linked by neuronal sequence (detector) sets, which are equivalent to the indexical links. In Construction Grammar, a distinction is also made between what I have called tokens and types. In this model, tokens are substantive constructions (which may be atomic, as in morphemes or words, or complex, as in phrases or idioms) while the more abstract or schematic constructions would be equivalent to types. Croft and Cruse (2004) make clear that constructions may range from fully substantial to fully schematic. Presumably this cline is linked up with the way language is analogically acquired, with types being learned only after the substantive tokens have been fully acquired through frequent use (cf. Goldberg *et al.* 2004).

The two models discussed in this volume can be aligned with this analogical model only with difficulty since in them either form or function is neglected. I would like to note, however, that some of their principles could well be accommodated within the model, such as the structure-preserving sequence of constituents defined by the X-bar principle, or the hierarchies of construction-types defined by government and C-command (cf. Chomsky 1981: 162 ff.). Similarly, the clines and hierarchies distinguished within grammaticalization, would also conform to lexical sets linked in order of abstraction. As heuristic devices, therefore, these 'factors' are all very useful. And, indeed, they may be easier to work with for a researcher, because they supply 'handy terms' to the different levels and hierarchies that have to be distinguished. However, the use of such terms at the same time obscures how the grammatical system really works, because they begin to lead independent lives. They are no longer connected to the primary force of the 'analogical grid' and hence, cause the connection between grammar and the other (linguistic) domains to be moved out of sight.

An additional advantage of this analogical learning system is that there is only one system to begin with, that is a lexical one. There are no separate systems for the lexicon and the syntactic rule module, as in generative linguistics. It is therefore more parsimonious from an evolutionary point of view, and it better fits the neurological findings reported on in §2.2.2.

There is a similar advantage as far as language change is concerned: the same mechanisms are now available for morphosyntactic and lexical change. This links up with the views expressed by grammaticalization theorists, namely that grammaticalization and semantic change are intimately linked. If there are pathways of change to be found in grammaticalization, then one would expect similar ones to be found in semantic change. This is indeed the theme of Traugott and Dasher's (2002) study on semantic change, that is that semantic change shows regularities and direction which in many ways are similar to grammaticalization.

I think this approach may also clarify the difference and the similarity between lexicalization and grammaticalization. Lexicalization takes place strictly on a token-level, while grammaticalization takes place on a combination of token- and type-level, or on a type-level only. If grammaticalization affects only one particular token which happens to be a member of a paradigmatic token-set that also functions as a grammatical type (as in the case of *while*, a subordinator), then as a token it may undergo the same changes that a lexicalized compound undergoes, namely semantic and phonetic reduction (e.g. *foresail* > [fɔːrsl] *waistcoat* [weiskəut], [wɛskət], OE *þa hwile þe* > *ME while*).[48] In other words, this instance comes very close to a simple case of lexicalization. Usually, however, grammaticalization involves a token, which is part of a more abstract type syntagmatically and paradigmatically, as illustrated by the development of BE + *going to* + infinitive. Here, the token *going to* becomes lexicalized into *gonna* but it becomes also, due to its compulsory syntagmatic combination with the copula BE and an infinitive, part of a more abstract construction-type, which itself is a part of a paradigmatic type-set, formed by other auxiliaries combined with infinitives. It is its similarity to other tokens in the auxiliary type-set that causes deeper grammaticalization. In grammaticalization, deeper paradigmatic entrenchment leads to semantic bleaching of the token involved (because the paradigm that this token joins is abstract, belongs to the type-level); in lexicalization, the same process—further entrenchment into a paradigmatic set—leads to semantic narrowing (because the paradigm the token joins is a token-level one).[49]

Other lexical changes, in terms of metaphor and metonymy, or amelioration and pejoration, would be explainable on the token-level;[50] they would constitute a shift of a token to another lexical token-set as a result of the loss or addition of some lexical feature, which itself is caused by some new indexical link created by speakers in connection with their perception of the outside world. Structural semantic change within a particular lexical field would be related to what is already present within some token-set. If a new token joining a set is too much like an existing token in that set, and if the set itself is tightly structured, the older token may be pushed out of the set. This happened, for instance, in the English set of tokens for the four seasons and in the set of words referring to 'marriage', as described by A. Fischer (1994, 1997). In a similar way, the discourse-pragmatic change from propositional to epistemic can be related to change on a higher type-level. This will be further discussed in Chapter 6.

It remains to be seen and further worked out how much such an analogical model may account for all types of changes. In my comparison of explanations given for changes from both a P&P and grammaticalization point of view in Part II, I will further consider its applicability. For the moment it is clear that the 'analogical grid' learning of this framework would cover reanalysis, analogy, parameter resetting, and abduction, since they all involve shifts between token- and type-sets, which had already been formed. It is also to be noted that reanalysis in fact does not occur in the physical sense of the word. When a construction like *I am going to get some water* is 'reanalysed' from 3(a) to 3(b):

(**3a**)   [I am going [to get some water]]
(**3b**)   [I am going to [get some water]]

it in fact joins another token-set. It leaves the construction-type of [V [*to* INF]] and joins the construction-type of [Aux V]. An advantage of the analogical model, is that the (a) and (b) constructions of BE + *going to* may continue to occur side by side as part of two different token-sets representing two different construction-types. Which one is used in any particular instance then depends on the other contiguous tokens within the larger construction. It explains the graduality of the change as it goes through the various type- and token-levels. Once, however, the BE + *going to* occurs as the new construction-type [Aux V] frequently, it is to be expected that it will take on some of the other formal characteristics of this construction-type (the Aux may become fixed in form), and it will also join in the sequence of tokens, features or types connected with [Aux V], that is it may begin to occur with an inanimate subject noun, it may come to be used in an epistemic sense, etc.

Notes

1. Still, we must not underestimate the value of a 'description' because (1) a description already orders the facts according to some (low-level) theoretical view point, and (2) a description of this kind remains readable long after some temporarily fashionable theoretical model may have died out. A good data collection, in other words, can be used again and again—as has happened for instance with the data on English periphrastic *do* gathered by Ellegård (1953), re-used by Kroch (1989a, 1989b)—while other studies conducted within a now lost framework—e.g. the study also of *do* by Haussman (1974)—have lost their value. The reason for this is that too often the description of the data in the confines of a more abstract theory shows (unconscious) manipulation of the data themselves towards the theory.

2. Other grammaticalization theorists who specifically emphasize the role of the speaker are Haspelmath (1999) and Kuteva (2001).

3. Lightfoot (1979: 121) describes this principle as follows: 'The Transparency Principle requires derivations to be minimally complex and initial, underlying structures to be 'close' to their respective surface structures . . . ; it helps to define what constitutes a possible grammar of a particular language'. The Transparency Principle is clearly related to the notion of abduction, which plays an important part in child language acquisition.

4. This is often referred to as the 'uniformitarian principle' which is observed in most diachronic research. Lass (1997: 265) describes this as follows, 'the principles governing the world (= the domain of enquiry) were the same in the past as they are now'. That is, principles applying to a language or grammar at one historical stage also apply at some later or earlier stage. Lass adds (p. 26) that this principle 'is a technique for boundary setting, not a law governing all details of past states', i.e. it does not 'rule out historical novelty'. Hurford (2003: 51) also stresses that 'uniformitarian assumptions' cannot be applied to the early stages of language evolution. Labov points to problems with it from the point of view of societal change. He also gives a useful review of the historical development of the principle in science, and its relation to gradualism vs. catastrophism (Labov 1994: 21–5).

5. Anttila (2002: 236) notes that relatively little work has been done on the 'interface between grammar and external factors' (but cf. Gerritsen and Stein 1992) and also that it would be of interest to know why some cases of variation linger while others move quickly towards a categorial resolution (p. 213). The development of a theory of change would be useful here, it might discover general constraints operating on variation and change of a sociolinguistic nature. Chambers (2002: 349) observes in this respect that 'language change . . . is one type of linguistic variation, with particular social properties'. Similarly, Trudgill (2002) discusses societal factors and their influence on change.

6. Cf. McMahon (2000: 115): 'The more general question arising from these analyses is whether linguistic change can be modelled, and explained, in formal theories at all'. She believes that explanation can be improved by taking formal and functional factors into account: 'Progress in terms of external explanation can only be achieved if functional considerations are incorporated into the [formal] model, or if it is accepted that such considerations are relevant and remove explanation of at least some change types from the scope of the formal theory involved' (p. 125).

7. The same description is still used in a recent article (Lightfoot 2003: 120), except that the phrase 'some parameter of UG is fixed differently', has been replaced by 'some theoretical choice has been taken differently' because in Lightfoot (1999) the notion of parameters has been replaced by the cue-based approach.

8. In the impersonal example above it is the simultaneous changes which are said to be unrelated. We will see in Chapter 4, that in the case of the radical change in English modals (cf. Lightfoot 1979: 98 ff.), the simultaneous changes were all related, while the non-simultaneous triggers (the changes that led up to it) were considered to be not related. We will discuss this problem there. What is crucial at this point is that the bundling of changes together on the surface may point at a grammar change. Lightfoot (1991: 167) indeed only mentions 'a cluster of simultaneous surface changes', while in (1999: 105) he refers to the cluster as 'apparently unrelated changes'.

9. Vincent (2001: 28–9) remarks that Allen comes to similar conclusions with respect to Lightfoot's scenario of the loss of impersonals: 'Once again it required careful detective work on the part of Cynthia Allen (1986) [and see also Allen 1995] to show that the details of the change do not correspond to the broadbrush scenario sketched by Lightfoot. Not only do nominative experiencers only arise with *like* in the fourteenth century even though the word order change is dated to the twelfth century, but other verbs undergo the same shift both earlier and later'. It should also be noted that not all historical linguists agree with Allen's analysis of this case, e.g. van Kemenade (1998) does not fully accept Allen's conclusions on the indirect passive.

10. The X-bar principle holds, stated informally, that all syntactic categories have similar projections and that within one language they tend to branch out in the same direction. The Subjacency principle limits the distance to which an element can be moved. It is believed to be related to the strength of reverberation of neuronal sets, and to the limits of the 'active memory'.

11. Quite a few scholars, often from outside linguistics proper, believe that the universals of UG cannot be confined to formal linguistic ones. According to Deacon (2003: 120), symbolic representation in linguistics is not 'a primitive psychological operation, but a consequence of a semiotic construction process', i.e. 'symbolic competence must be constructed from more basic non-symbolic referential relationships, including icons and indexes'. Similarly, Tomasello (2003b: 101) writes: 'I do not mean to imply that there are no linguistic

universals, of course there are. But these do not consist of specific linguistic categories or constructions; they consist of general communicative functions such as reference and predication, or cognitive abilities such as the tendency to conceptualize objects and events categorically, or information processing skills such as those involved in dealing with rapid vocal sequences'.

12. Van Gelderen (2000) proposes an explanation for this change in terms of a Minimalist framework. She connects the loss of the 'simple' reflexive pronouns with the loss of inherent Case, the loss of pro-drop, and a change in the 'strength' of person and number 'features'. There are quite a few problems, however, with this account. First of all, the case for pro-drop in Old English and early Middle English is not very strong (cf. also Hulk and van Kemenade 1995), and indeed many of her early Middle English examples (p. 138ff.) involve coordinate clauses where pro-drop is usual also in non-pro-drop languages (e.g. exx. (64), (65), (67), (69), (71), (75)) or are clear misreadings of the text (e.g. (63), (74), (77)). Secondly, the use of the new compound reflexive with *self* occurs earlier in the third person, which clashes with the fact that the third person retains inherent Case longer.

13. It is important to stress that these 'triggers' involve all aspects of the PLD. The type of triggers I am concerned with here are the ones involving minor changes.

14. The problem with this is that the nature of the parameters, rules, and principles of UG are not (yet) fixed. Newmeyer (2003: 59–60) notes that '[t]he properties of UG are ... anything but clear. There are more than a dozen different and competing theories, each of which presents a different explanandum for the language ... researcher'. Newmeyer (2004) adds other problems, such as the great number of (micro)parameters that would be needed to account for all syntactic (typological) variation. Penke and Rosenbach (2004: 510–12) note, on the positive side, that since Minimalism there has also been a lot of effort from within the generative school to minimize the number of domain-specific principles and parameters.

Note that the change involving the English modals (to be discussed in Chapter 4) was first seen as a category 3 change (cf. Lightfoot 1979), with all the characteristics of such a change (i.e. a simultaneous cluster of changes and chain reactions) but later became a category 2 change (Lightfoot 1991: 141ff.), presumably because it could not be seen to involve a parameter shift.

15. According to this hypothesis, the trigger can only consist of unembedded material, more precisely 'it is restricted to data occurring in an unembedded binding Domain' (Lightfoot 1991: 32), i.e. it includes embedded COMPs and Subjects of non-finite clauses (cf. p. 78). For an extensive discussion of this hypothesis, which is seen as interesting but very problematic, see the commentary in *Behavioral and Brain Sciences* 12 (1989): 334–75.

16. Coordinate clauses can be both main and subordinate, depending on whether the first clause of the coordinated set is itself main or subordinate. This distinction is often not made. It was not made, for instance by Mitchell (1985) in his Old English grammar (cf. Ohkado 2005).

17. A possibility of accounting for structures produced by both sides of the parameter so to speak, has been suggested by Pintzuk (1991) using the notion of 'competing grammars' (also called the 'double base hypothesis'). Lightfoot (1999: 92) makes use of these ideas. The advantage is that OV exceptions that occur too late in comparison to the parameter resetting can then be accounted for. However, this looks a little *ad hoc* (see §2.2.3).

18. According to Dawkins (1986: 236, 240–1), their (1972) article did not, but in later writings they widened the gap between gradualists and punctuationists by selling their ideas as being radically opposed to Darwin's. Dawkins (1986: 250–1) believes that they were 'helped' in this by journalists, supporters of Intelligent Design, and creationists even though Gould himself was strongly opposed to these ideas. If Dawkins is correct, this would be another example of a difference of opinion exacerbated into a conflict by reductionism (cf. §2.3).

19. For an excellent discussion of the differences and similarities involved between language evolution and biological evolution, and a consideration of the usefulness of a comparison, see McMahon (1994: 314–40; 2000: 137–51) and Croft (2000: 9–41); for a brief review and warning, see also Labov (2001: 3–15).

20. Lass (1997: 140) writes, 'Change is not "catastrophic", but takes time. (Often centuries ...). The time is occupied by a process of variation: primitive and apomorphous [derived] states coexist, with cumulative weighting heading towards categorical implementation of the latter'. Labov (1994: 23–4) does not deny the possibility of catastrophic change but links it to external causes (invasions, migrations, massive immigration). He believes internal changes to be gradual. Croft (2000: 49–51) also favours the gradual-change scenario, since he believes that it is adults rather than children who cause language to change. Anderson (1993: 1) believes that most changes involve 'minimal incremental or decremental modification' and more specifically that radical restructuring is most unlikely with categorial changes in a restrictive theory which makes use, as his does, of a limited number of notional features to define categories.

21. Scope is a problem in grammaticalization theory since in some processes scope becomes more limited, while in others it widens. As we will see in §3.2, this is related to the way scope is interpreted by grammaticalization theorists, e.g. Tabor and Traugott (1998) define it in terms of C-command, whereas most other linguists within this school, follow the less abstract (but not very clearly defined) definition of scope used by Lehmann (1995 [1982]).

22. One of the strongest advocates of unidirectionality is Haspelmath (1999). In Hopper and Traugott (2003: 99ff.), unidirectionality is also considered to be a strong hypothesis: it is presented as systematic with very few counterexamples, which are mostly argued away. In all accounts that support the principle of unidirectionality, it is connected only with the language level. As far as I know, no research has been done to show that it also works on the speaker level with the notable exception of Roberts and Roussou (2003). In this model unidirectionality automatically follows from their structural definition of grammaticalization; this is indeed one of their strong points. For methodological and

theoretical problems connected with the unidirectionality hypothesis, see Newmeyer (1998), Lass (2000), and the special issue on grammaticalization edited by Campbell (2001a).

23. Cf. also Heine *et al.* (1991b: 9), who write that 'Meillet followed Bopp rather than Humboldt in using grammaticalization as *an explanatory parameter* in historical linguistics' (emphasis added). The authors themselves seem to follow this line too (1991b: 11).

24. In many linguistic (but especially in formal) models the faculties of language production and language interpretation are treated as more or less equal, and not as in any way different. In other areas of linguistics, i.e. in language evolution and language acquisition, special attention is paid to comprehension, because one would have to comprehend first *before* one can speak. Speaker interaction is therefore foregrounded, its function, its situational context, etc., which all help towards comprehension. Also frequency, repetition and imitation are considered to be highly important to stimulate and form the comprehension and later production of language. On the priority of comprehension in language evolution, see Burling (2000: 27–9, 38), and in language acquisition, see Clark (2003: 127–30). On the importance of comprehension in terms of language *processing* and the different constraints production and comprehension are subject to, see Baayen and Schreuder (1996).

25. For this description I have used part of the introduction I wrote together with Anette Rosenbach for a book on grammaticalization (Fischer and Rosenbach 2000).

26. I follow here the interpretation of layering given by Hopper and Traugott (2003: 49), which is based on changes in form undergone by one single source word. In Hopper (1991: 22–3) layering is considered from a functional point of view, i.e. it refers to the layer that exists within one functional field. In this interpretation, *is going to* is not layered with *gonna*, but *gonna* is layered with *will* because the latter two forms express the same function of future. Both interpretations of layering are relevant, since they will be of influence in grammatical developments. For example, it is possible that at some stage the newly grammaticalized form (*gonna*) replaces the older form (*will, 'll*), which may happen if the old form loses too much substance to be still viable as a grammatical marker. Brinton (1996: 54) accepts both interpretations of the term layering.

27. Heine *et al.* (1991b: 50, 60) indeed distinguish two types of metaphor. The type that occurs in grammaticalization, they call 'experiental' or 'emerging' metaphors because these metaphors arise out of context (this indicates their indexical or metonymic nature). They contrast these with 'conceptual' or 'creative' metaphors, which are much more likely to contain conceptual 'jumps' and cannot be predicted in any sense. They have made use of recent studies on metaphor (e.g. Lakoff and Johnson 1980; Lakoff and Turner 1989), which show that there is no simple linear iconic link between vehicle and tenor, rather it is two conceptual schemas that are linked. This considerably widens the

'creative' possibilities and also draws attention to the fact that it is not just the similarities seen between two schemas that lead to the creation of a metaphor, but also their differences. For an excellent and detailed overview of theories of metaphor, see Hampe (2005).

28. It is not possible always to make a strict separation between metaphor and metonymy, especially where it concerns 'experiential metaphors', the type most common in ordinary language, as was already indicated in fn. 27. E.g. the off-print of a foot in the sand, may be considered metonymic (an index; i.e. it has been *caused* by a foot) as well as metaphorical (an icon; i.e. it *resembles* the shape of a foot).

29. Note that an even more superficial way of looking at analogy seems to be usual in generative models. It is interesting to note the definition in the generatively inclined *Lexicon of Linguistics* by Kerstens *et al.* (1996–2001), '**Analogy:** MORPHOLOGY: a diachronic process which changes words after the model of other forms', after which follows an extensive example explaining how in Gothic the noun meaning 'foot' shifted from one noun-class to another due to the fact that the accusative form became indistinguishable from the accusative form of another class. Here analogy seems to be reduced to just one level, that of morphology, and applies only to changes in concrete forms, not to more abstract structures.

30. In fact it may not be so much the *perception of a similarity* between one form and another that causes the speaker to make one structure/form analogous to another. Rather, it may be the fact that the speaker does *not* see a difference between the two forms/structures (because they are much alike), and therefore by *misperception* as it were, makes the one form analogous to the other. This would explain why such analogies (or reanalyses) occur so easily in language (change). Deacon (1997: 74) describes this inability to see a difference as the basic process of iconic reference, for further discussion see Fischer (2004b).

31. Coates (1987: 322) states that the formal similarity is more important than the semantic one, concluding on p. 324 that 'the most interesting consequence to emerge from examining this data [i.e. examples of folk etymology] is that the influence of meaning is never a necessary condition for A[nalogical] R[eformation] to take place', while 'formal similarity *is* a precondition' (emphasis added).

32. Tomasello (2003b: 98) writes: 'a strong argument can be made that children can only understand a symbolic convention in the first place if they understand their communicative partner as an intentional agent with whom one may share attention'.

33. Bickerton (2003) disagrees with this assumption because he believes that holistic phrases present a difficulty of comprehension. However, like other generative linguists he ignores the fact that these holistic phrases are uttered in a contextual situation, which is concrete and present and that comprehension is helped by acoustic signals, accompanying gestures (pointing, direction of gaze) and frequent repetition, which are other aspects of learning usually

ignored by this school (cf. most of the comments on language learnability in *Behavioral and Brain Sciences* 12: 321–63). Concerning language acquisition, Clark (2003: 138 and *passim*) notes that young children learn in concrete situations, with concrete objects being talked about, and that the context supplies meaning. Similarly, Tomasello (2003b: 104, and in earlier work) shows that 'young children's early language is not based on adult-like abstractions, innate or otherwise'. Instead he hypothesizes that 'children's early grammar [can] be characterized as an inventory of verb-island constructions (utterance schemas revolving around verbs), which then defined the first syntactic categories as lexically based things such as "hitter", "thing hit", and "thing hit with" '.

34. For a lucid account of the role played by 'creativity' in generative grammar, of the changing ways in which the notion has been used (i.e. the question whether it relates to physical properties of forms, or to more abstract patterns), and its relation to the property of 'recursion', see Itkonen (2005: 69–71).

35. Baayen and Schreuder (1996: 3) write (in a study on morphological processing): 'whether a construction is stored as a construction or as consisting of its constituents depends crucially on the (relative) frequency of the complex word' and on 'the cost of computation'. They show, that because of this, even fully regular complex forms may be stored as one unit. Thus, although memory-based processing precedes rule-based processing, it is not the case that memory-based processing coincides with irregular forms, and rule-based processing with regular ones, as Pinker (1991) had suggested with his 'dual-mechanism model'. Children at the language acquisition stage are still building up their computational system. It is not surprising therefore that the processing of morphologically complex forms may alternate between compositional and formulaic, even when a construction seems completely regular from the linguist's point of view.

36. Bickerton (2003) doesn't agree with Deacon. He believes that the divide between humans and other mammals is not the development of symbolic thinking but the development of syntax. Deacon, however, is at great pains to show that any symbolic abilities that animals have developed is only possible through intensive training, that it is usually linked indexically with rewards, and that the number of symbolic items thus learned remains very small.

37. Since the animal loses the connection when the symbolic sign is no longer externally stimulated, it means that the animal doesn't rise above the indexical stage, as indicated in the hierarchy given in (2) below.

38. Haspelmath (2003) argues that frequency is even the most important factor in change because it creates more economical patterns. He notes that economical patterns arise in three different ways: 'by (i) **differential phonological reduction,** (ii) by **differential inhibition of periphrasis/grammaticalization,** or by **analogical change**' (p. 1). I argue here that frequency and analogy are equally important, and I note that Haspelmath's first two factors are in fact related to the metalinguistic *iconic* (i.e. analogical) 'principle of quantity' (cf. Givón 1995b:

49), according to which more or less coding is used for something that is more or less meaningful.

39. This, for instance, explains why Bybee and Slobin (1982) have found that the generalizations or schemas used to produce the English past tense forms develop and change with age.

40. Note, however, that the analogical work done in the area of morphology by Skousen and others is directly based on linguistic tokens, i.e. on phonologically quite concrete similarities and differences. My point here will be that the analogical process works both on a concrete token-level and on a more abstract type-level, with the latter based on the former. In a sense one could say that even a comparison on a token-level involves an abstraction since two apparently same tokens are in fact never exactly the same (cf. the philosopher Peirce, who stated that true or perfect icons do not exist), but are always based on a *conception* (by the learner) of the same. This is presumably the reason why Itkonen's (2005: xiii) treatment of analogy, if I understand him correctly, concerns only rule-based analogy.

41. Signals are passed between neurons via contact buttons, which are called synapses, which can be found on all parts of the nerve cell (see Pulvermüller 2002: 10–13).

42. By now it seems that most linguists, formal and functional, have given up the idea that language change can be *predicted* (cf. the change in Lass' position (Lass 1997: 330–1) on what counts as an explanation). The most that can be done is to provide an explanation afterwards in terms of some theory and/or frequency counts and entrenchment. McMahon (2000: 124) notes in this connection that 'Lightfoot's ideas on the explanatory scope of his theory seem to have modified over the years'. Whereas in his earlier work (1979, 1981), he was looking for principles within the theory that would explain and predict change, he now seems to accept that 'explanation lies ultimately in the changes in the triggering experience, which [he] accepts he cannot deal with at all' (ibid.). I have noted above that the distinction between 'triggers' (i.e. changes in the PLD) and 'real' changes is very difficult to make because ultimately it depends on the theory one uses. This, of course, considerably weakens the explanations offered for the 'real' changes, i.e. the grammar changes. For this problem of change on two levels, see also McMahon (2000: 123), Croft (2000: 50), and Matthews (2003).

43. On the important role played by iconicity in language see the papers collected in Haiman (1985), Hinton *et al.* (1994), Simone (1995), Landsberg (1995), Nänny and Fischer (1999), Voeltz and Kilian-Hatz (2001), Fischer and Nänny (2001), Müller and Fischer (2003), Maeder *et al.* (2005), and in the collected work of Fónagy (2000). For the indissoluble link between index and icon, see Deacon (1997, 2003) and Anttila (2003).

44. Cf. the type of operating principles suggested in Peters (1985) and Slobin (1985a), which are part of the L(anguage)M(aking)C(apacity), a device similar to the generative LAD, but one which does not presuppose a ready-made

grammar module. The learning device allows for developmental changes taking place in children: it takes into account the increase in processing capacity, and cognitive developments which influence the way in which children perceive the world around them. Instead of on innate principles, children are said to rely on developmental 'bootstrapping'. This means that children exploit existing resources or capabilities to raise themselves to a new situation or state; they 'pull themselves up' from what they already know (i.e. starting with tokens they hear), and by doing so, get to a higher more abstract stage (types, i.e. morphological categories and syntactic constituents) and thus create more resources by which to pull themselves up even further (structural rule types).

45. But cf. Kiparsky (in press), who argues that analogy can be constrained when considered as a case of grammar optimization. Interestingly, he also suggests that analogy is more important in grammaticalization than reanalysis (contra Campbell 2001a, Hopper and Traugott 2003, cf. the discussion at the end of §3.2 above), even going so far as to state that 'labelling a change as a reanalysis, innovative or otherwise, doesn't get at its nature or motivation. For now, the claim that grammaticalization is reanalysis remains virtually a tautology' (p. 19).

46. The token is *nadder*, the type is the determiner set consisting of the tokens *a* and *an*, which are each associated indexically on the phonological level with initial consonant and initial vowel respectively.

47. Harris and Campbell (1995: 101), who use the term 'extension' rather than analogy for the analogical mechanism, also suggest a constraint on extension, which is similar to the one suggested here in that it too is based on *already existent structures*. They write that 'observed extensions generalize to a natural class based on categories already relevant to the sphere in which the rule applied before it was extended'. In a similar way, but more generally, Aitchison (1987: 19) points to already existing structures in combination with natural tendencies as being crucial to the way languages change: 'At every stage, any language has a set of options which it can take, which in turn affect its future options'. She adds that the existing structure and the options 'are overall governed by certain relatively fixed abilities, such as computational ability, memory limitations and so on', as I have also suggested here.

48. This unified way of looking at lexicalization and grammaticalization also offers a solution to such problematic cases of grammaticalization as found in the development of conjunctions like *since* and *while*. Traugott and Hopper (2003: 81–4) treat this development as a regular case of grammaticalization in spite of the fact that it does not show many of the usual characteristics. Haspelmath (1992: 343), indeed, wonders where the evidence is that the case of *while* has 'anything to do with grammaticalization'? Since the change here takes place essentially on a token-level, it is indeed much closer to lexicalization than to grammaticalization. The link to grammaticalization is only weakly present in the token-set of subordinators, which grammatically is still a relatively open class. The analogical model used here makes clear that lexicalization cannot so

easily be separated from grammaticalization, and that the differences between them form a continuum.

49. In Traugott and Dasher (2002: 84–5), of the six characteristics associated with grammaticalization, three are said partly to overlap with those of lexical change, while three others are said to be more typical only of grammaticalization (e.g. reanalysis and fixing of a construction) but yet associated with the first three. This is a little bit confusing. If, however, we distinguish between lexical change and grammaticalization as taking place on different levels, as suggested here, the characteristics or mechanisms will be found to be the same for both, only the results may differ depending on what level the change takes place.

50. Although here too type-sets may be involved, e.g. nouns of a particular semantic set that have concrete as well as abstract meanings may, as a set, affect a new noun that joins the group.

Part II

Case Studies

4

A paradigm case: the story of the modals (and other auxiliaries)

4.0 Introduction

In many ways, the story of the modals in English could be said to constitute a paradigm case. From the moment that Lightfoot wrote his influential article on the development of the English modals in 1974, it has inspired a steady spate of studies on the history of the English modals both within the generative and the grammaticalization schools of thought.[1] Lightfoot indeed called the modals his paradigm case when he introduced the notion of the Transparency Principle and 'radical change' in his study on diachronic syntax (1979). Unlike some of his other examples of radical change, this particular case seemed to follow most neatly the scenario in which a number of unrelated, superficial changes lead to an opacity in the grammar system, which then, as a result of the application of the Transparency Principle, undergo a 'catastrophic' change, evidenced by a number of simultaneous, related changes (cf. the third category in Table 3.1).

Within grammaticalization too, the modals are often seen as a 'model' change. In Plank's (1984: 308) words: '[t]he development of the English modals is a paradigm case of grammaticalization, showing in an exemplary manner how more or less ordinary lexical items are appropriated for the grammatical system, with the linguistic forms involved being gradually adjusted to the functions that transparently motivate them'. Even though Plank and Lightfoot's ideas about the evolution of the modals are in almost all respects diametrically opposed, Plank fully agrees with Lightfoot that the English modal history is 'highly instructive for anyone interested in how the immutable bears upon the transitory in grammar and lexicon, and in what the observation of the latter reveals about the former' (ibid.). Grammaticalization theorists devoted many pages to this case (see fn. 1), and quite a number of these studies are indeed a reaction to the 'radical' proposal put forward by Lightfoot.

Since both approaches have claimed the modals as their prime (or pet) example and defended its special position within their respective theories with so much energy, it is appropriate for me to start the second part of this volume, containing a comparison of a number of phenomena studied within both frameworks, with the modals (Chapter 6 in fact deals with phenomena mainly investigated by functional linguists; I discuss them in this volume because a formal approach may throw more light on their development.) There is an additional reason why I want to give pride of place to the modal auxiliaries. Within grammaticalization, the auxiliaries present in themselves quite a few of the *types* of grammaticalization processes that have been distinguished. As I already mentioned in §3.2, it has been difficult to gather all these types into one theoretical model. The parameters and principles suggested by Lehmann and Hopper work quite well for the regular development of grammatical morphemes out of lexical material, but they apply much less comfortably to other processes, which are also believed to be part of grammaticalization, such as the fixation of word order, clause combining, and the development of syntax out of discourse. All these topics are covered by Hopper and Traugott's (2003: 19) general definition of grammaticalization as 'the study of the development of grammatical forms', and indeed they are all included in their survey. Each of these processes ultimately involves lexical elements, but they are looked at from different 'heights'. The 'traditional' type of grammaticalization considers the reduction of substantive lexical elements, while the three more marginal types consider in all cases combinations of elements (both substantive and abstract), be it on the level of the clause (how does a sequence of words turn into grammar), between clauses (how do clausal relations become more grammaticalized), and on the level of discourse (how do free discourse elements become part of grammar). It may turn out to be impossible to think of grammaticalization as a unitary process, also because changes on the level of the clause and higher need not all be directly concerned with the actual increase of *grammatical* forms.

I will illustrate in this and the ensuing chapters that (modal) auxiliaries offer a good example of the regular lexical > grammatical category cline, with various verbs undergoing (stages of) this formal cline: full verbs > concatenatives > auxiliaries > clitics > affixes > zero. The auxiliaries also show the phenomenon of clause combining at work, and the impact that the fixation of word order may have on grammar. Word order fixation was one of the main types of grammaticalization distinguished by Meillet (1912). In addition, this case can be used to focus on the discourse origins of syntax and morphology (cf. Givón 1979: 209). Finally, modal auxiliaries have been adduced as a prime example of the subjectivity cline in which expressions develop from propositional > textual > epistemic via semantic-pragmatic inferencing in discourse.

For this chapter, I will concentrate on the category shift, on the pragmatic-semantic changes that auxiliaries are said to undergo, and on the role played by the fixation of word order, leaving the issue of clause combining to Chapter 5. All these phenomena are closely related. When a lexical verb becomes reanalysed as an auxiliary, it loses the formal properties of lexical verbs, both concerning its morphological paradigm (inflections disappear and there is a movement towards a single, fixed form) and its verbal accoutrements, that is the arguments and verbal complements it takes. In other words, it no longer defines a clause but it is defined by it (this often entails a reduction in clause structure, from biclausal to monoclausal). The issue of fixed word order and frequency plays much less of a role in most of the discussions on the auxiliaries mentioned in fn. 2 below, even though it is important, as we will see in §4.3.2 (more details can be found in Chapters 5 and 6).

4.1 The English modals as a radical category change

I will only sketch the bare bones of the story here since it is readily available both in its original form (Lightfoot 1974, 1979: 98ff.) and in many of the studies that reviewed it (most conveniently in Warner 1983; Plank 1984; Goossens 1987; Nagle 1989; Denison 1993; McMahon 1994). I will concentrate on the details of Lightfoot's proposal in connection with the available empirical data and the comments given. The essence of his proposal is that the Old English verbs *sculan 'to be obliged to', cunnan 'to know, be able', magan 'to be able', *motan 'to be allowed', willan 'to wish, want'; and, somewhat less centrally, þurfan 'to need', agan 'to have, owe', and *dearran 'to dare' started off originally as main verbs and became recategorized as auxiliaries at some stage in the history of English.[2] Below I will simply refer to these verbs as 'modal verbs' or 'modals' without implying any particular categorial status.

Lightfoot proposed a scenario for this change as follows. He believes that a radical restructuring took place at the beginning of the sixteenth century, by which these verbs underwent a category change from Verb to Aux(iliary). This recategorization was preceded by five independent and gradual surface changes (1), which set the scene, and followed by five (or seven) related simultaneous surface changes (2), which provide evidence that a (deep) grammar change has taken place.

(1) CHANGES PRECEDING THE RADICAL CHANGE IN THE ENGLISH MODALS BEFORE 1600
    (i)   loss of constructions where the modal takes a direct object argument
    (ii) loss of the preterite-present verbs that did not become modal auxiliaries
    (iii) loss of past tense function for the past tense forms
    (iv) the introduction of a special rule feature for epistemic modals[3]
    (v) no adoption of to-infinitives as was the case with other verbs

(2) SIMULTANEOUS CHANGES INVOLVING THE MODALS AFTER 1600
    (i)   loss of infinitival forms of modals
    (ii) loss of present participle forms of modals
    (iii) loss of two modals used consecutively
    (iv) loss of past participle forms of modals
    (v) negative not could no longer be placed after main (i.e. non-aux) verbs
    (vi) main (non-aux) verbs could no longer be inverted
    (vii) the development of new periphrastic modals to fill the gaps created by (i–iv)

We shall first go through the difficulties that have been observed with respect to this proposal. These concern gaps in the empirical data, the timing of the changes, and the semantic cohesion of the verbs in question. After that we can have a look at some of the revisions and counter-proposals, which are partly the result of these (additional) findings, but which can also be connected with a different theoretical outlook on change.

Timing is a very serious matter since the proposal hinges on it. If the Transparency Principle is responsible for the radical change, as is Light-foot's early hypothesis, then we must find, on the one hand, changes leading up to the categorial reanalysis making the construction more and more opaque—these, preferably, should not be related nor simultaneous—and, on the other, changes following the reanalysis—which must be both related and simultaneous. In other words, the two series should be maximally dissimilar because, if the first batch of changes is in character and timing too much like the second one, then the second batch cannot be explained by the first: by a build-up of opacity and as a necessary consequence of some 'deep' change caused by this build-up. As far as timing is concerned, there are three main problems: the first concerns each individual change, the second the relation between each change and each individual modal, while the third applies to the relation between the changes of (1) and (2). Most of the details here come from Aitchison (1980), Warner (1983, 1993), Plank (1984), Goossens (1987), Nagle (1989), and Denison (1993).

In connection with the individual changes in (1) and the behaviour of each modal with respect to each change, we may note as to (1i) that direct objects are found long after 1600 with some of the modals, notably with *can* and *will*. Concerning (1ii), most of the non-modal preterite-present verbs (these are given in fn. 2) indeed eventually disappeared but, if they survived, it was their preterite-present morphology that disappeared. *Wit* survived as a main, weak verb into the nineteenth century. Some verbs (*dugan, þurfan,* and *munan*) disappeared from the standard but persisted as *modal auxiliaries* in some dialectal areas, as Lightfoot duly notes. The interesting thing here, however, as Nagle (1989: 72) pointedly observes, is that this survival pattern indicates 'the abduced semantic character of the paradigm'. It is indeed remarkable that *wit*, being without modal connotations,[4] is pre-served as a main verb, even acquiring some main verb inflections (see *OED* s.v. *wit* v[1], A 2c), while the other three dialectal verbs, which semantically *were* like modals, have survived syntactically as modal auxiliaries and not as main verbs. The loss of the past tense meaning mentioned in (1iii) is a very slow affair. It was already underway in Old English, while even in modern use some of their pastness is still preserved. Again, this loss is different per verb. Goossens (1987) shows it is early with **sculan*, while *could* and *would* have preserved some past tense use up till now. An interesting aspect of this loss of the past tense is that there may be a link with the preterite-present character that all these verbs share. It is possible that the past-present 'confusion' has been typical of these verbs all along, which would mark them off as a special group from the very beginning. I will return to this in §4.2.2.

The change in (1v) is somewhat more complicated. First of all, it has to be noted that there were other verbs that took a bare infinitive in Old English (physical perception verbs and some causatives), which like the modals kept this infinitive in Middle English and beyond. Bock (1931: 121, and see also Chapter 5 in this volume) suggests that the use of the bare infinitive in Old English already suggested a closer link between matrix verb and infinitive, thus marking off these matrix verbs as a special group. More important perhaps is the fact that there was no simple replacement of bare infinitives by *to*-infinitives in Middle English, as is usually assumed. In Fischer (1995, 1996b), I have suggested that there is a functional difference between *to* and bare infinitives, in that *to* indicates an indirect relation (one of non-actuality) between the matrix verb and the infinitive, while the bare infinitival form involves entailment and unity of tense-domain between matrix verb and infinitive (for a similar difference in Present-day English, see Mittwoch 1990 and Duffley 1992). Fischer (1995) and Los (2005: chs 7, 8), in particular, show that the increase of the *to*-infinitives was not at the cost of the bare infinitive, but at the cost of 'that'-clauses containing a verb in the subjunctive. This latter point is of interest. It fits the fact that finite 'that'-complements were rare after all Old English modal verbs, except after *willan* (Ono 1975 and Goossens 1987 give no examples after *cunnan*).[5]

Finally what is missing in the story of loss, is the gradual disappearance of the subjunctive (due mainly to phonological attrition) as an important factor in the whole development. The relation between the increase in the use of modals and the loss of the subjunctive mood is not discussed at all in Lightfoot (1979),[6] but is stressed by all the later commentators on Lightfoot's proposal. In sum, all the changes in (1) (leaving out (1iv) as irrelevant) could also be used to show that these verbs were already rather exceptional in Old English and that they formed a subgroup. This is indeed what many of the commentators have done.

Concerning the changes involved in (2), again the empirical findings do not show such neat timing. As to (2i), infinitival forms, except with *cunnan* and *willan*,[7] were rare from the beginning of the Old English period and, strangely enough, they became more frequent only in the Middle English period. The same is true for the other non-finite forms of the paradigm, mentioned in (2ii) and (2iv) (cf. Mitchell 1985: §993, Warner 1993: 100–2).

This shows that there was no sudden loss, but rather a wave-like development: rare in Old English, appearing more in Middle English, slowly disappearing in Modern English. As to (2iii), two consecutive modals are attested in Old English again only with *cunnan*. They became somewhat more regular in Middle English. These findings can probably be related to the fact that periphrastic tense and aspect constructions became more and more usual in Middle English (with the 'future' auxiliaries *will/shall*, the perfect auxiliaries *have* and *be*, and some aspectuals such as *ginnan* 'to begin'), which led to a need for participles and infinitives of all verbs, including the modals. This would not be a problem for Lightfoot's proposal, since in his view the modals were still verbs in Middle English. On the other hand, the rise of these periphrastic constructions itself, which usually involved two consecutive verbs, may *by itself* have induced a reanalysis.[8] Lightfoot does not mention the rise in frequency as a factor. Roberts (1985: 34, 55) does (but only in passing), and so does Warner (1993: 193–4), who links frequency with salience and prototype formation, which together more sharply defined the properties of the modals as a group. In Chapter 3, I argued that frequency is one of the most crucial factors in change, I will return to this issue in §4.3.2 below.

Before I turn to the other changes in (2), I would like to pause briefly at the behaviour of the modals *cunnan* and *willan*. It is quite clear from the discussion so far that these two verbs were more fully lexical or verb-like than the other core modals **sculan*, *magan*, **motan*. The following differences can be listed:

(3)   VERB-LIKE BEHAVIOUR OF *willan/cunnan* IN OLD ENGLISH AND BEYOND
   (i)   they more frequently take direct objects in OE and keep them longer in ModE
   (ii)   they preserve some past tense uses up to the present moment
   (iii) they regularly have infinitive forms in OE (with *willian/(ge)wilnian* as substitutes for *willan*)
   (iv)   impersonal constructions occur with some modals in ME (cf. Warner 1993: 102, and §4.2.2), but not with *cunnan* and *willan*
   (v)   'that'-clauses in OE and beyond occur regularly only with *willan*; *cunnan* here has a substitute in *witan* (see fn. 4 above)
   (vi)   present participles occur regularly only with *willan*; *cunnan* has a substitute here in *witan*
   (vii) a combination of two modals occurs regularly only with *cunnan*; *willan* has a substitute here in *(ge)wilnian/willian*

(viii)   *willan* was an anomalous verb in OE but not strictly a preterite-present verb

(ix)   semantically, *willan* and *cunnan* do not belong to the performative core of the modality field (see §4.2.2)

Thus, in many respects, *will* and *can* remain verb-like much longer than the other modals, while *must* and *shall* 'seem to have attained unequivocal modalhood much sooner', with *may* 'fall[ing] somewhere between the two pairs' (Denison 1993: 336). It is interesting to observe too that a similar pattern is observable for the Modern Dutch cognates. *Zullen* 'shall' is the least verb-like: it has no past participle, it does not appear as an infinitive in combination with another modal, it cannot take a direct object, a directional adverb without infinitive, or a finite complement clause, and it is rare in ellipsis. *Moeten* 'must' and *mogen* 'may' follow next: a past participle is found, but very rarely, and they are also rare with a direct object (*moeten* more so than *mogen*), directional adverbs are possible but finite complements do not occur. *Willen* and *kunnen* are the most verb-like, being quite regular with direct objects, directional adverbs and, especially *willen*, with finite complements.

To return again to the changes in (2), the phenomena mentioned in (2v–vi) are undisputed in so far as almost all linguists working on this agree that these two developments are directly linked to the emergence of an auxiliary position. The evidence for this comes from the fact that the use of an empty periphrastic verb *do*, which became gradually current in all types of clauses in the fifteenth century, with a peak around 1560, became gradually restricted to and obligatory in (negative) interrogative clauses and somewhat later in negative declarative clauses in the course of the seventeenth century (see Ellegård 1953: 159–60, Warner 1993: 220 ff.). It is difficult, however, to consider the changes in (2v–vi) to be on a par with the first four of (2) because the use of *do* to prevent inversion and the avoidance of *not* after main verbs is rather later than the losses in (2i–iv), while at the same time, as Ellegård (1953: 161) clearly indicates, the frequency of *do* in interrogative and negative clauses was always higher than in affirmative clauses from the beginning. If the radical change took place around 1600, we have no explanation for this early preponderance of *do* in interrogative and negative clauses in the fifteenth–sixteenth centuries. There is a similar problem with (2vii) in that most of the new periphrastic modals (*be to, be going to, be able to, have to, be boun(d) to*, etc.) already begin to occur in the late Middle English period, while one would expect, as Warner (1983: 199, fn.9) correctly observes, this development to be tied to the other losses taking place at stage (1). Krug (2000: 89, 95–6) shows, moreover, that the new construction with *have to* was at first used more often in the finite form, that is where it functioned as an equivalent of the core modal *must* rather than as a gap-filler. It appears therefore that all the changes in (2) were more or less gradual and that some began to manifest themselves too early to be able to speak of a radical change.

This brings us to the relation between the changes in (1) and those in (2). What is really tricky here is that most of the changes in both categories concern losses, which are very hard to pin down to a date. Many of the 'losses' given in (2) could also be said to be characteristic differences (in the form of their absence) between modals and other verbs in Old English. The reason Lightfoot put four of the losses in (2) is presumably because the constructions given in (2i–iv) only became more current in Middle English (when the modals seemed in some ways to become more rather than less verb-like), and therefore their loss was later too. The increase in periphrastic constructions overall must be responsible for this, as I argued above. The difficulty of dating losses and the similarity between the losses of (1) and (2) (*all* losses serve to make the modals more distinctive as a class), however, makes one wonder about Lightfoot's (1979: 109) claim that the changes given in (1) were 'independent'.

The changes in (1) cannot be related, according to Lightfoot, because modals and other verbs still formed one class. These preliminary changes, in other words, only *accidentally* isolated the modals *from* this unitary class. If, however, as most linguists have argued, the modals were already recognizable as a (semantic) subclass, then the changes in (1) would be related because, like the losses in (2), they all serve to make the modals more distinct. Lightfoot thus exaggerates the modals' verbal 'ordinariness' and plays down the formal and semantic differences between modals and verbs in Old English, and also the formal and semantic differences among the modals themselves. This is not surprising, of course, in a theory that works with firmly fixed, non-gradable categories. It could be said that his framework forces him to ignore differences within categories or crossovers between categories. The conclusion that can be drawn for this account of the change is that the behaviour of the modals has not been scanned carefully enough.

4.2 The English modals: other accounts

It helps to look at formal differences in order to establish formal categories and differences between categories, as Lightfoot does. It also helps to look at semantic differences and differences in frequency in order to discover further differences in form and to establish patterns of formal variation. In order to be able to categorize a particular set of elements, one has to scrutinize the variation that occurs between the forms and the particular frequencies with which each variant form occurs. One also has to take into account other constructions that may be considered to be formally and/or functionally equivalent to the new emerging constructions. What I mean is that it is not enough to look only at changes in the behaviour of the modals. Functionally equivalent ways of expressing modality must be considered too. This is where the loss of the subjunctive and the rise of the *to*-infinitive (as a replacement for subjunctive 'that'-clauses, see above) come into play. Critics of Lightfoot's proposal have taken variation, frequency, and functional factors into account in their description of the modals' development.

Before we turn to the semantic/functional factors of this case, and to the way in which the grammaticalization school has dealt with it in §4.2.2, I would like to consider other more or less formalist accounts, and their views on the causes and the nature of the change. It is interesting that linguists such as Roberts, Nagle, and Warner, who have insisted, like Lightfoot, on the importance of the formal variables, nevertheless do not agree with him concerning details of the cause, the path, or the categorial nature of the change. They also pay attention to the role played by the semantic cohesion of the modals, especially Warner. After a discussion of their work in the next subsection, I will also briefly go through Lightfoot's own revisions, which were made in reaction to these critical comments.

4.2.1 Further formal accounts

Roberts (1985) agrees with Lightfoot that there was a radical change, but in his view this change did not concern the categorial status of the modals *an sich*. In addition, the cause of the change is not seen as a gradual increase in opacity, isolating the modals from the rest of the verbs, which was solved by interference from the Transparency Principle. Roberts virtually ignores what happens to the modals and concentrates on changes (2v–vi). These are explained by a parameter shift involving a change in 'government'[9] from a morphological agreement system to a syntactic agreement system. He believes that his explanation is superior to Lightfoot's because he does not need an extra principle of the theory of grammar (i.e. the Transparency Principle).[10] According to Roberts (1985) the modals belonged to the class of Verbs in Old English, and they continue to do so in Modern English, that is to say there was no category change from V to Aux, and not even the addition of the feature [+Aux] to the modals.[11] He does not need a category change because the changes that occur with respect to the modals (i.e. the changes in (1) and (2i–iv)) and with respect to main verbs (i.e. (2v–vi)) do not, strictly speaking, depend on each other. Another difference with Lightfoot is that he assigns a central role to the loss of the subjunctive mood, and sees the modals as their functional equivalents. The close link with the subjunctive ('the core lexical meaning of modals facilitated' their 'substitute[ing] for the subjunctive', p. 42) presumably means that in his view the modals already functioned as a notionally coherent class.[12]

The essence of Roberts' (1985, 1993a) claim is that finite verbs (including the modals) in Middle English were still morphologically governed (and could thus assign θ-roles) *because* they had person/number/tense/mood affixes to attach to in INFL when they moved from VP to INFL. When verbs lose their inflections, and hence can no longer move to INFL, government by morphological agreement is no longer possible. In order to be able to assign θ-roles, such verbs must now be syntactically governed.

The first part of Roberts' account concerns the loss of the subjunctive mood. The subjunctive inflection system was moribund, and the modals came to be used as functional substitutes some time in the Middle English period (1985: 34).[13] The subjunctive was present in the form of agreement features on the verb, which are placed in INFL, an ungoverned position because subjunctive inflections cannot assign θ-roles to the Verb (1985: 42). The idea is that the modals, as functional substitutes, therefore also ended up in the ungoverned INFL position, and hence lost the ability to assign θ-roles. An additional reason why they ended up in INFL, is their own lack of agreement features (1985: 34). (Note that this makes the argument appear rather circular: was it their lack of agreement features that made them end up as operators in INFL or the need to act as substitute for the subjunctive?) In Roberts (1993a: 315, 320) the story is slightly different because he now wishes to take the modal developments in the Modern Scandinavian languages into account. The latter remain verb-like *in spite of* their lack of inflections. For this reason, Roberts suggests that the reanalysis of the modals occurred because of the fact that the inflectional infinitive marker was lost (in this respect English was different from Modern Scandinavian). This lack of morphology forced the modals into the T position (the older INFL node is now split into AGR[eement] and T[ense]).

The second part of Roberts' story concerns the main verbs. Indicative agreement inflections 'had almost disappeared by the mid-sixteenth century' (1985: 43). This made V-movement to INFL (V-to-I) impossible because, if the Verb moved, it could no longer assign θ-roles, which it obviously did. V thus remained *in situ* and was governed by syntactic rather than morphological agreement. Dummy *do* as a semantically empty tense carrier, is, like the modals before, forced into INFL because it assigns no θ-roles. In that position, *do* became a periphrastic substitute for Tense; it could now conveniently take over the role of the tense features which the main verbs, which could no longer move to INFL, had lost. So *do* fills the gap left by the loss of V-to-I.

A number of aspects make the argument awkward. First of all, only the plural indicative inflections were lost by the mid-sixteenth century; in the singular present the second and third person were still intact and distinct from the first, in the past only the second person was still distinct. More distinction was lost only when *thou* fell into disuse in the course of the seventeenth century (cf. Barber 1976: 235–7 for details). In other words, there is no simple link between loss of V-to-I and the loss of inflections. Secondly, and more importantly, there is no neat co-occurrence of the loss of θ-roles in modals, the loss of their inflections, the loss of the infinitival ending *-en*, and the replacement of the subjunctive mood by modals. Some modals already functioned as subjunctives in Old English when they were also still used as full verbs, in both cases *with* their inflectional endings. Modals could thus replace the subjunctive with their agreement features intact. This appears in contradiction to what Roberts (1985: 42) states: 'if modals are semantic substitutes for the subjunctive, they have the same θ-properties as the subjunctive (i.e. none), then they must not be governed or *show agreement*' (emphasis added).

Less satisfactory also is the absence of a direct link between what happened to the modals and the rest of the verbs. In Roberts, it is the loss of verbal inflections that is the cause of two separate changes, which just happen to reinforce each other (through the appearance of modals in INFL and hence an increase in periphrastic constructions, the way was paved, as it were, for the appearance of *do*).[14] The two separate changes drive verbs and modals apart, but yet they still belong to the same category in Roberts' (1985) view. Roberts' explanation may be superior from the point of view of his framework (no extra principle), but it clearly lacks the clarity of Lightfoot's proposal, and seems less concerned than Lightfoot about the empirical data, the actual behaviour of modals and other verbs in Old and Middle English.

Of all the formal approaches to the story of the modals, Warner's (1983, 1990, 1992, 1993) is the most careful and the most detailed. He takes much more of the available empirical detail into account, and he links the development of the modals to other verbs that were likewise developing auxiliary-like behaviour (i.e. *habban* 'have', *beon/wesan* 'be' and *weorðan* 'be(come)'). His story is richer, more complex and consequently much less smooth and simple. His main argument is that the modals were already exceptional in Old English, whereby he does not just refer to the losses in (1) above, which he believes affected them because they were a semantically coherent class, but also to some other exceptional features that bound them together with other 'auxiliaries', such as their occurrence in elliptical constructions (Warner 1993: 110ff.) as illustrated in (4), their transparency to impersonal verb constructions (see §4.2.2 below), and their similar behaviour, where phonetically possible, concerning the cliticization of the negative onto the finite verb (compare *nyl*, *nolde* 'not-will, not-would', *nat*, *nyste* 'not-know, not-knew' to *nis*, *næs* 'not-is, not-was', *nabbe* 'not-have').

(4)   se ðe   wille godcundne wisdom secan ne   mæg he hine wiþ ofermetta
                            (Bo 12.26.22m Warner 1993: 114)
      he who will   heavenly   wisdom seek, not may he it   with arrogance
      'He who wishes to seek heavenly wisdom, cannot [do so] with arrogance'

Warner (1993: 101–2) also pays attention to the verb-like characteristics of the modals in Old English, noticing that, rather than becoming less verb-like, they tend to become more verb-like in the Middle English period, with some of them developing new main-verb present-tense inflections (e.g. *sculleþ* and *cunneþ* for earlier *scullen* and *cunnen* (< OE *sculon* and *cunnon*), and new non-finite forms.[15]

What Warner notices overall is that there is a slow gradual development in the subclass of verbs that later became auxiliaries (this includes the modals) to a formally more coherent class, and that in this development the 'semantic properties are less determining of the status of an individual member than formal properties' (1993: 104). Warner does not deny the possibility of semantic interconnections between members of a set (e.g. between the modals), but he believes that in general the semantic equivalence between members is overridden by their formal (including distributional) properties. In his 1993 full-length study of the English auxiliaries, Warner takes great pains to show that modals and other auxiliaries have moved together, sharing formal and distributional properties, such as position and the development towards 'anaphoric islands', that is as morphologically opaque forms. The fact that all auxiliaries (modal as well as non-modal) move formally to a more coherent class, shows that it cannot be semantic properties alone that decide on class membership (1993: 49ff.).[16] It is interesting to observe in this connection that Miller (1997) found that the French verbs *avoir*, *être*, and *faire*, which all showed auxiliary-like behaviour in their syntax in Older French, also all lost this again in Modern French, in spite of the fact that these verbs do not belong to a semantically unified field.

In his discussion of class membership, Warner is much less categorical than Lightfoot. Making use of Eleanor Rosch's (1978, 1988) prototype theory, he suggests (Warner 1993: 209 ff.) that the Old and Middle English modals and the other auxiliaries belonged to a less distinct subordinate-level category, where boundaries are still ill-defined, and that they gradually changed towards an intermediate, basic-level category, where, according to Rosch, category structuring is clearest. Rosch explains this in terms of cognitive economy. To distinguish a 'chair' (a basic-level term) from a 'kitchen chair' (a subordinate-level term), one needs fewer but more precise or contextual criteria than to distinguish a 'chair' from the superordinate-level term 'furniture', which needs more and rather general criteria. It is therefore at the basic level that category structuring is most economic in terms of ease and economic pay-off.

From this point of view, it is not surprising that some crucial and possibly more rapid changes took place when the auxiliaries had reached a basic-level category status. Warner believes that this happened by about 1500, when the defining features of the auxiliary group had become more or less distinct for that group alone. At that time some further formal changes, isolating auxiliaries from verbs, took place (Warner 1993: 206ff.), which are not mentioned by Lightfoot. These are: (i) the movement of lightly stressed adverbs (also mentioned by Roberts 1985), (ii) the appearance of 'tag questions', (iii) the appearance of a series of clitic forms, and (iv) the appearance of contracted negatives in *-n't*. Note that these changes are not losses but new constructions, and even though they are not all so easy to date (belonging to a more colloquial form of language), they provide much safer cut-off points than losses do. Warner notices that there is a pick-up of speed with these latter changes. However, it has to be stressed that Warner does not follow Lightfoot's concept of radical change. Instead, he explains the more rapid, later developments as a natural result of the differences between auxiliaries and verbs becoming more and more pronounced.

Nagle (1989) takes up a middle position between Lightfoot and Warner. The change as a whole he considers to be more gradual than Lightfoot does because he recognizes two stages in the modals' change rather than one. Thus the modals are involved first in a subcategorization change in early Middle English (1989: 71), and later in a category change to Aux at the beginning of the sixteenth century (1989: 82ff.). He stresses that, on the surface level of the output, the changes which are the effect of the underlying grammar change in the first stage diffuse quite gradually. And even in the second stage the changes are not said to be abrupt, they just diffuse more quickly than in the first stage. This is because at stage one, there was only 'weak abductive inference' (1989: 92), while at stage two we witness the operation of 'strong abduction', which is 'a type of abduction propelled by inductive weight' (1989: 122). It seems to me that this is rather similar to Warner's idea that a change becomes more rapid when a category becomes formally more sharply defined. The difference between Nagle's and Warner's positions, however, is that Warner does not recognize an underlying deeper change. This is possible because he observes a Roschian, more analogue view of categories rather than a digital one.

Nagle favours the idea of gradual change because this is what is visible on the surface (1989: 54), but at the same time he posits an underlying change because he is unhappy with Aitchison's (1980), Warner's (1983), and Plank's (1984) gradualist descriptions of the modal change. According to him, the latter remain mere descriptions; they have no direction, and hence offer no explanation, as Lightfoot's model does. Unfortunately, simply positing underlying changes which diffuse gradually (in all senses of graduality, not just a socio-geographical one, cf. the discussion of Bennett (1981) in §3.1), does not really support the reality of such an underlying change. Nagle (1989: 45) realizes 'that the gradual versus abrupt issue in surface change is largely one of theoretical orientation'.

He thus opts for a theory that offers explanations, even though the empirical data, as he states himself, do not clearly support abruptness.

By wishing to enhance the non-explanatory gradualist position into an explanatory one, Nagle seems to have fallen between two stools. Yet we should be grateful to all linguists who have concerned themselves with this case because it is thanks to their eye for formal details that more and more subtleties with respect to the modals and the other auxiliaries are coming out into the open, making the issues involved in morphosyntactic change slowly become clearer. Both formal morphosyntactic differences as well as evidence of gradual diffusion need to be taken seriously, so that either the discovery of further, more fine-grained formal distinctions may make clear that the changes are chain-like, diffusing slowly via lexical or syntactic features (as is done in LFG and HPSG frameworks, see Chapter 3), or, alternatively, that we may come to the conclusion, in the absence of such a discovery, that we are indeed dealing with a rapid or radical type of change. More knowledge of the micro-stories and more interdisciplinary research, as argued for in Chapter 3, is the only way to help solve the issue of the nature of morphosyntactic change.

A detail revealed by micro-stories is the role played by frequency. Both Roberts (1985: 34, 55) and Warner (1993: 193, 213, 238) refer to an increasing frequency of periphrastic constructions. Roberts mentions it as a causative factor only in passing, but provides no further background information. Warner mentions it in relation to Rosch's suggestion that frequency and salience are related to prototype formation but he adds that she does not link it to change. Warner states his position towards the possible effect of frequency carefully. He sees 'a potential relation' as far as change is concerned, which seems 'straightforward': 'as modal group verbs became more frequent and salient, because of the decline of the subjunctive or their expressive utility in other respects, this will have promoted the formation of a prototype based on their "family resemblance"' (1993: 193). He does not mention the possible role of word order fixation in connection with frequency, although it is clear from word order studies that the juxtaposition of auxiliary and main verb became more and more the norm towards the end of the Middle English period. It seems to me that this is another formal pattern-type that could have been influential in the change. I will come back to this point in §4.3.2 below.

Before we move on to another type of gradualist view of the change, that is a functional one, I will briefly discuss Lightfoot's own revisions of the modal story in reaction to the (critical) evaluations of his first proposal. Lightfoot wrote on the modals again in 1991 (141ff.) and 1999 (158–67; 180–97).[17] The most striking aspect of these revisions is that the story as a whole becomes more gradual and that he recognizes that there is more relation between the changes given in (1) and (2) above.

The changes in (1) were already considered gradual, but Lightfoot now admits that (1i) should go with the changes given in (2i–iv), showing that at least one of the changes in (1) can be seen to refer to the modals as already a distinct subclass. Similarly, (1iii) is now explicitly related to the loss of the subjunctive (Lightfoot 1991: 142, 148; 1999: 184), which thus ties the early modals closely to the area of modality. He maintains, however, that the modals were 'just another class of verbs' in Old English (1999: 183) and that the changes they underwent (before recategorization, which was effectively complete by the sixteenth century) were *not* simultaneous and *not* related (it was in their *combination* that they 'had the effect, in many ways accidental, of making the premodals into a small and distinctive class', 1991: 148).

A second alteration is that the changes given in (2i–iv) (now together with (1i)), are no longer considered so simultaneous. Lightfoot (1991: 142) admits that 'this change may not have been as cataclysmic as I claimed in 1979': a few verbs continued to have verbal characteristics longer and some verbs may have been recategorized before others. In his second revision (1999: 88), he describes the recategorization of the modals as 'piecemeal'. This of course entails that some of the changes in (2) could now be seen as equivalent to the gradual changes in (1) since it is difficult, as I noted above, to date any of these losses precisely. Since the ones in (2) are related, this makes the likelihood that there is also a relationship between all the changes in (1) and (2) much more likely, but Lightfoot does not take this step. He does not conclude that the modals were already a 'peculiar' subclass of verbs in Old English, as Warner argues.

A third shift away from the original story is his proposal for two distinct stages of simultaneous and related change rather than one, the first involving changes (2i–iv, and 1i) and the second (2v–vi)—change (2vii) is no longer in sight. Note that this alteration, too, makes the six changes in (2) less simultaneous. The first stage involves recategorization of the modal verbs as INFL (here he effectively follows Roberts 1985), complete by about 1600, while the second stage concerns the loss of V-to-I movement, which 'seems to have been completed only at the end of the seventeenth century' (Lightfoot 1991: 143).[18] In addition, Lightfoot (1991: 149) stresses that the loss of V-to-I itself was gradual: 'For some 200 years verbs could continue to move to this position, if it was empty'. The loss of V-to-I was the direct result of the fact that the 'verbal position in INFL was appropriated by the modal verbs and *do*' (1991: 149). Lightfoot now also links the change in adverb position, noted by Roberts, to this second stage. This is indeed an interesting co-occurrence, which I will come back to in §4.3.2 below.

Another interesting difference between Lightfoot's and Warner's approaches is the position of the auxiliaries *have* and *be*. They are ignored in Lightfoot's early story, but in Warner they are seen as part of the auxiliary development from the beginning. Lightfoot (1991: 143) describes the loss of V-to-I as a structural change in which the '*non-modal* verbs lost the ability to move up to the *v* position in INFL and ... to interact with the inversion and negation properties' (emphasis added). Since *be* and *have* cannot possibly be classified as modals, it rather looks as if in this account they are still classed as main verbs even though they clearly did not lose the ability to move to INFL. In his second revision (1999: 185 ff.), Lightfoot does consider the 'awkward' behaviour of *have* and *be*. He accepts Warner's (1993: 41 ff., 1995) conclusion that the different morphological auxiliary forms of *be* and *have* (e.g. *is, was, be, been, being, has, have, had*, etc.) developed into 'anaphoric islands' (see also below). Anaphoric islands are holistic, non-decomposable words, verb forms that are not associated with the regular paradigm of full verbs in spite of some similar endings (in the case of *have* and *be*: third person -*s*, participles-*ing*, -*en*/-*d*, etc.). On the basis of Warner's findings, Lightfoot distinguishes a third stage in the process of the auxiliaries, which now also includes the non-modal ones.

This third stage is linked to the two earlier ones in that it is the result of the effects that the modals' development and V-to-I loss had on *be* and *have*. The V-to-I loss isolated *be* and *have* further as verbs—Warner 1993 shows that, like the modals, they were already auxiliary-like in Old English—because they now occurred in a position that was otherwise open *only* to modals and *do*. Warner argues that as a result of this increased isolation, the forms of *be* and *have* began to behave like 'islands', like autonomous forms, just as the modals had done before (see the changes in (2) and Warner 1993: 189ff.; 1997). They became impervious to normal paradigmatic behaviour, so that *was* was no longer construed as [*is*+past] (in contrast to full verbs: *walk-ed* is construed as [*walk*+past], *went* as [*go*+past]). Warner explains a number of nineteenth-century changes as due to this new construal, such as *be/have*'s exceptional behaviour in ellipsis (compare older (5a) to newer (5b) and to unchanged full-verb (5c)), the loss of some forms of the paradigm of *be to* (5d), some new subcategorization restrictions (5e), the rise of the new progressive *is being* replacing the old progressive passive, which was active in form (5f), etc.

(5a)   I wish our opinions were the same but in time they will
            (Jane Austen *Emma*, 1816, from Warner 1995: 537)

(5b)   I wish our opinions were the same and in time they *may / may be

(5c)   I wish our opinions matched, and in time they may

(5d)   You will be to visit me in prison with a basket of provisions
            Jane Austen, *Mansfield Park*, 1814, Warner 1993: 64)

(5e)   One day being discoursing with her upon the extremities they suffered
            (Daniel Defoe, *Robinson Crusoe*, 1719, Warner 1993: 63)

(5f)   At the very time that this dispute was maintaining by the centinel and the drummer (PDE: was being maintained)
            (Laurence Sterne, *Tristram Shandy*, c.1760, Warner 1993: 63)

What we see then is that a fuller and more detailed assessment of the data in combination with a wider sweep of data (involving additional auxiliary-like verbs and constructions in which these auxiliary-like verbs operate) has led to a considerably more gradual account of the change. Instead of one 'radical' change, we now have three (i.e. the three stages described above), while the subchanges, which form part of the three main shifts, are themselves gradual, often taking as long as one or two hundred years to reach completion.

So far, we have virtually ignored the semantic-pragmatic aspects of the modals. These in turn may fill in some of the still remaining gaps or unearth further links. In the next subsection we will consider the accounts of the modals put forward within a grammaticalization framework. These concentrate on semantic-pragmatic developments and on functional and typological universals. They open up new vistas but these are often gained at the cost of the role played by form. They largely ignore what happens to the verbal constructions formally in the wider context of the synchronic grammatical system in which they function.

4.2.2 Grammaticalization accounts

A point made by all but the most formal linguists is that the modals form a unified group semantically. It is difficult, however, to give a satisfactory definition of this notional field. Bybee *et al.* (1994: 176) refer to earlier proposals which describe modality as 'the grammaticization of speakers' (subjective) attitudes and opinions', but add that 'modality notions range far beyond what is included in this definition', and they conclude that 'it may [in fact] be impossible to come up with a succinct characterization of the notional domain of modality and the part of it that is expressed grammatically'. I will, therefore, not attempt a definition, but I will sum up what in grammaticalization studies are considered the general characteristics of modality systems.

First of all, there is the diachronic aspect, emphasized by Bybee *et al.* (1994), which may help to determine the contours of the field. Many languages develop a grammatical system of modality (e.g. in the form of a closed system of verbs/auxiliaries) out of very similar source-concepts. Bybee *et al.* show (and see also Heine and Kuteva 2002) that the source for 'obligation' is usually verbs meaning 'to owe', 'to need', or 'be fitting', and also general auxiliaries like 'have' and 'be'. The source for 'ability' and 'permission' is generally found in verbs meaning 'to know' and in verbs expressing physical power (e.g. Latin *potere*, English *may* related to *might* 'power'), or attainment ('to arrive at, obtain'). The source for 'futurity' generally comes from verbs meaning 'to come, go' or from verbs expressing a wish or intention, but a future sense also very frequently develops from modal verbs expressing ability, permission, and obligation. In a similar way, verbs expressing 'possibility' are usually a development from the ability and permission verbs.

What is even more interesting than the universality of the source-concepts, is the way the verbs involved in modality follow typical paths into, through, and out of the modality field. From more peripheral areas in the modal field (containing verbs expressing knowledge, desire, physical power, etc.), they may move, depending on the source concept, via the central areas of ability > permission > obligation > promise, and more generally from dynamic and deontic uses (ability, permission, obligation) to epistemic (possibility, necessity) and future uses, and from there to subordinate (subjunctive) uses (cf. Conradie 1987; van der Auwera and Plungian 1998). This typological similarity of sources and paths shows that the semantic field of modality is quite tightly knit.

Another feature that sets off modal verbs from 'normal' verbs is their performative aspect (cf. Searle 1979 and earlier work; Conradie 1987; Traugott and Dasher 2002; on performatives *an sich*, see Austin 1962).

Modality does not involve simple statements of fact but it expresses attitudes of commitment towards facts. It is thus part of a performative context, which involves modal root values in concrete speech acts. Involved in this performative or speech-act function, are the notions of ability, permission, and obligation (in Old English expressed by *motan, magan, and *sculan). Other verbs that may play a role in modality but do not have a core performative function, belong either to the pre-performative field (in Old English such verbs as witan, willan, cunnan, (ge)munan)—they often provide source-concepts for later modal usage—or the post-performative field, which contains epistemic and future 'modals'—these in turn often find their sources in the central performative field (cf. van der Auwera and Plungian 1998). A result of the performative function of modals is that it enforces a number of linguistic conditions on them. Traugott and Dasher (2002: 190) note with respect to explicit performatives (such as, I hereby declare, I baptize you in the name of ... etc.) that they are always in the first person, in the present tense, in the indicative mood, and the active voice. Modal verbs are close to such performatives,[19] and here too the first person (the speaker) and the present-time context stand central.

When the speaker is also the agent of the propositional content of an utterance, as in an explicit performative, the meaning of the modal in the clause is both speaker- and agent-oriented.[20] When the speaker addresses someone else, and it is the addressee that is the subject of the clause, the same modal verb may acquire a rather different meaning. Thus the proposition, I will do that for you, implies an intention on the part of the speaker, who is also the subject (agent), whereas You will do that for me, implies that the 'I', the speaker, tells you, the addressee (and grammatical subject) that you have the intention to do it, which is in fact a rather indirect way of giving a command. The hearer (you) may indeed understand it that way, and interpret the clause as a command coming from the speaker. Alternatively, in the first case, the hearer may understand the clause I will do that for you as a 'promise' of 'future' intent. Note also that an interrogative word order may again change the meaning of the clause: Will you do that for me? is a polite way of inquiring after the intention of the addressee, and thus an even more indirect way of giving a command.

In this way, many of the source-concepts that become modal verbs, undergo similar pragmatic-semantic changes that heavily depend on the context; e.g. in our examples above, will may mean 'intention' (probably the base meaning[21]) as well as 'obligation', 'request' and 'promise' as well as 'future'. Seeing how the verbs work in a performative context makes it understandable that similar source-concepts develop along very similar paths in many languages. This is because the context is quite constrained, unlike in the case of the semantic developments of full verbs (and nouns), where the context may be any word-sign with which the verb may be collocated, or any act in the outside world with which the verb may be associated.

The performative linguistic condition of present time also applies to modals. A past tense of a modal verb, used performatively, does not refer to the past. The hearer may then interpret such a past tense as an irrealis or a very polite rejection. *I would do that for you* (*if I could*) uttered in a present-time context, tends to convey that there *is* an intention on the part of the speaker, but that this intention was not brought to fruition because the conditions were not right for it. Using the same past tense in a second person interrogative, as in *Would you do that for me?*, might then convey an even politer tone than the same example in the present, because here the speaker is suggesting that it might not be possible for the addressee to do what he would like him to do, leaving the choice completely open towards the addressee without any pressure from the speaker.

This suggests that it is not an accident that past-tense forms in the field of modality convey present-tense meaning. In Lightfoot's proposal above, changes (1ii–iii) are considered 'accidental' changes, but this now looks unlikely if it can be shown that the Old English verbs involved here functioned as performatives. That they clearly did can be seen from the fact that their main appearance in Old English is in deontic (obligation, permission) and dynamic (ability, necessity) senses (for more details, see below). It is relevant in this connection that Harris and Campbell (1995: 173–6) note, with reference to the development of the modal verb 'want' in Georgian, that this verb developed a past tense with present meaning in Middle Georgian. Thus, the imperfect *unda* 's/he wanted it' changed into a present-tense modal with the new meaning of 'should, must' expressing deontic obligation or epistemic necessity. At the same time the old form *unda* retained its 'want'-meaning, and developed a new past (imperfect) *undoda* 's/he wanted'.[22]

Let me sum up the findings so far. Evidence from diachrony, from speech-act theory and from typological work on modality, shows that the semantic field of modality is tightly structured and often has the same features across related and unrelated languages. It is not the case, however, that modal auxiliaries have to develop in each language, because modality can be expressed in many different ways. Speech-act theory shows that modality is intimately related to politeness strategies, and such strategies can follow different routes, depending to a large extent on the social-cultural traditions of a particular society.[23] However, if a language uses verbs to express modality, then these verbs are tightly conditioned by the field in which they operate, leading to similarities in their behaviour. With this in mind, let us have a closer look at the semantic behaviour and diachronic development of modals and their relation to grammatica-lization.

Most linguists working on modality distinguish between two types of modals, on both formal and semantic grounds, that is between root modals and epistemic modals, whereby the root modals may be further divided into dynamic and deontic modals. This division is not a sharp one, the borders between the types are fluid. A rough division can be given as follows. Dynamic modals are agent-oriented (but see fn. 20 above), which means that the grammatical subject is also semantically the agent of the verbal action. These modals usually take an animate subject and are in their argument structure closest to ordinary verbs. Deontic modals are speaker-oriented and they generally express permission or obligation towards the addressee. The addressee may be the grammatical subject of the proposition (*You must wash the car*), but need not be (*The car must be ready by ten*). The important difference with the dynamic type is that the agent or source of the modality is not related to the grammatical subject of the proposition.

At a still further remove, the source of the permission or obligation need not be a particular participant in the communicative context, but may be represented by some general authority or a set of moral values. Here we see the link with epistemic modality, where the source of permission or obli-gation has become very much backgrounded so that we speak of possibility and necessity instead. It is now circumstances in the world at large which indicate the likelihood or necessity of the proposition. Since it is necessarily the speaker of the proposition who is behind the statement, such an epistemic modal comes to express the attitude of the speaker towards his statement. It is thus rather paradoxical that the *general*—based on the speaker's logical inference from the evidence in the world around him—becomes *subjective*, due, no doubt, to our tendency to put ourselves in the centre of things (cf. §§3.2 and 3.3).

In grammaticalization theory, these modality types and the lexical sources from which they spring are seen as a unidirectional cline, with lexical root modality at one end, and epistemic modality and (subordinate) mood at the other, see (6) (adapted from Bybee *et al.* 1994: 181, 241).

(6) CLINE OF MODALITY (SEMANTIC):
       fully lexical verbs > root modals: dynamic/ >   epistemic modals/ >
                                            deontic   future
       (subordinate marker/
       subjunctive)

Two further types of unidirectional clines are distinguished in grammaticalization, which apply to the development in modal verbs, a formal decategorization cline (7a) and a discourse-pragmatic cline (7b) (based on Hopper and Traugott 2003: 111–12, and on Traugott 1982: 257; Sweetser 1990: 50ff.; Bybee *et al.* 1994: 176ff.; Brinton 1996: 54–65; Traugott and Dasher 2002: 40, 94ff. respectively):

(7a) CLINE OF MODALITY (FORMAL):
        lexical verb > vector verb > auxiliary > clitic > affix > zero
(7b) CLINE OF MODALITY (DISCOURSE-PRAGMATIC):
        propositional   > (textual)   > expressive/attitudinal/interpersonal[24]
        socio-physical > world of reasoning/ > subjective attitude towards
        world   of speech event   the world
        non-subjective > subjective   > intersubjective

As general tendencies observed in languages and as heuristic devices for research purposes these clines are useful. But it is not possible with the help of these clines, as indeed Traugott and Dasher (2002: 36) also argue, 'to predict precisely under what circumstances and when a change will take place in historical linguistics'. They believe this is impossible because 'change originate[s] ... in language use, i.e. in factors *external to language structure*' (emphasis added) (2002: 35). Form and function are here seen as strictly separate, or, more precisely, form is seen as not influencing function. This position taken by Traugott and Dasher seems a little extreme. Compare this to Bybee *et al.*'s (1994: 40) hypothesis that there *is* a 'non-arbitrary relation between the meaning of a gram [a grammatical morpheme] and its mode of expression'.

There is clearly some correspondence between the formal and the pragmatic-semantic clines in (6–7), in that in both clines fully lexical verbs or propositions are at one end. Also, it is indeed the case, typologically, that agent-oriented modals are most frequently expressed by a full lexical verb rather than an affix, and that future and epistemic modality/mood is more often expressed inflectionally than verbally (cf. Bybee *et al.* 1994: 242). On the other hand, it is decidedly not the case that epistemic modals must be expected, formally, to emerge as clitics or affixes. In order to gain a better understanding of the correspondences, we must therefore also gain a better understanding of the mismatches between the two clines in each particular process of grammaticalization. If we assert, as most linguists working in grammaticalization do (cf. §3.2 above), that meaning change precedes formal change, and hence that form does not itself influence meaning, we will not understand why the two clines do not always simply correspond. We will get better explanations for individual developments, and hence a better sense of how language change works, if we investigate the mismatches. To do this, we need to turn our attention to the form of the contemporary grammatical system in which each development or change takes place, because the formal contours of this system have their own role to play in these individual developments.

Thus, although I agree with Traugott and Dasher in the quotation above that change originates in language *use*, I do not agree that it is therefore 'external to language structure' because, as I argued, this use has formal as well as pragmatic-semantic parameters. To my mind, it is a missed opportunity not to tie formal change to meaning change on an equal footing. If we wish to know more about why and how morphosyntactic change takes place, and especially why in one language the modals become more auxiliary-like than in another, even though they undergo the same semantic changes, one must consider those pragmatic-semantic changes together with their formal expressions within the wider grammatical system of that language.[25]

The grammaticalization approach to change also misses the boat in another way. By concentrating on (unidirectional) *meaning* changes, one does not discover the relation between the developments of the modal verbs and that of the other auxiliaries in English (or, for that matter, the relation between the semantically different (auxiliary) verbs *faire* and *avoir/être* in French, cf. Miller (1997), touched upon in §4.2.1). Grammaticalization theorists miss this link because there is no overlap in meaning to alert them to it. Nor would they discover the relation in English between the development of auxiliaries and the loss of the inversion (V-to-I) rule for main verbs, again because there is no *meaning*ful relation between the two.

Another difficulty that crops up because of the apparent correspondence between the formal and semantic clines of (7) is the awkward behaviour of scope. I have noted above in §3.2 that one of the unidirectional grammaticalization parameters distinguished by Lehmann is that of the reduction of scope. Tabor and Traugott (1998) (followed by Roberts and Roussou 2003), however, established that in some grammaticalization clines, there was an increase rather than a reduction in scope. Thus, (7a) seems to indicate scope reduction, while (7b) indicates the opposite. The confusion arises because in grammaticalization all clines are seen as equivalent. Scope should therefore work the same way in all these clines.

However, these clines are clearly not equivalent when one looks at it from an analogical-learning point of view. Formally, it makes an enormous difference whether a cline deals with single tokens, with single low-level types (morphological categories), with composite tokens, with higher-level composite tokens that are part of a construction-type, or with high-level construction-types. Scope will usually be reduced when tokens or low-level types grammaticalize, but this is less likely when higher-level construction-types are involved. Scope in (7a) works on a morphological categorial type-level, it does not look at what happens in terms of constructions, while in (7b) it looks at the pragmatic-semantic functions of larger structures, which relate to a higher syntactic construction-type.

Scope seems even more of a problem in (6), presumably because (6) is a mix of semantic and formal characteristics. On the surface, this cline appears to have scope increase first, followed by scope decrease at the end. The change in the modals from deontic/dynamic to epistemic in (6) concerns semantic-morphological types involved in higher level construction-types, that is, it is not the morphological type alone which becomes epistemic. The fact that the morphological type functions on a higher syntactic level explains the increase in scope. Since this involves the grammaticalization of structures in discourse, I will discuss this aspect in more detail in Chapter 6. The change from epistemic modality to subordinate mood marking—which may be expressed by a modal verb,[26] but usually takes the form of a subjunctive affix—looks again like a decrease in scope. The mood marker in the subordinate clause fully depends on the matrix clause predicate, and no longer has scope over the whole proposition. The reason for this decrease is the fact that this time the morphological mood marker (free or bound) itself undergoes grammaticalization and not some higher construction type in which it is involved.

The 'subordinate' last stage on the cline in (6) presents a problem in some other ways. I have put it in brackets since it does not necessarily represent a neat development through all the earlier stages. Bybee *et al.* (1994: 241) make clear that the subordinate marker may also be directly derived from the dynamic/deontic stage. So there is no monotonic bleaching in this case. The cline suggests, too, that the source concept for the subordinate marker is a modal *verb*. Bybee *et al.* (1994: 224–5, 230ff.), however, show that in many cases the subjunctive ending derives from an older indicative or future affix. (One may wonder whether this could still be called grammaticalization; it looks more like 'exaptation' (Lass 1990), or what Croft (2000: 127–8) has called 'hypoanalysis'. They give examples of how, through the use of new forms for future tense or indicative mood in main clauses, the old future and indicative forms may become isolated in subordinate clauses and then reanalysed as marking subordinateness (see also Kuryłowicz 1964: 136, Haspelmath 1998: 41ff.). Other frequent sources for the subjunctive affix are complementizers used in adverbial clauses of concession or purpose, which express non-actuality (Bybee *et al.* 1994: 225–30). It is interesting to observe in this connection that the subjunctive affixes of Germanic cannot be traced to some lexical source. They derive from an Indo-European optative, which in turn may be derived from a past indicative form, the aorist (cf. Kuryłowicz 1964: 136–8).[27] On the other hand, the loss of these mood affixes did lead to a new cycle of lexical verbs being chosen to indicate modality in many Indo-European languages. In other words, there is a (cyclical) connection between mood affixes and lexical (modal) verbs, even if not a straightforward one.

Having looked at some of the problems that the grammaticalization approach presents in connection with their neglect of form, let me now give a résumé of the general understanding we may gain from their functional way of looking at language use and change, as far as modal verbs are concerned. We have already seen that the functional approach makes clear that the modal verbs form a closed field, and that a change in one verb will cause ripples in the rest of the field. Changes such as the ones given in (1) and (2i–iv) above, are therefore expected to be related rather than unrelated. Secondly, a relation between the loss of the subjunctive and the rise of new modal elements is foreseeable (and indeed common knowledge in traditional accounts, cf. Visser 1963–73: §836) because again they function within the same semantic field. The subjunctive endings form the last stage in the cline of (7a). Because modality is now reduced to affixes, these affixes tend to generalize and lose their meaning altogether, which then leads to a new cycle of lexical modality.[28] Thirdly, knowing the path that verbs may travel once they have come to be used in the performative space, as well as the contours of the pre- and post-performative space, helps us to spot the type of lexical verbs that may become modals and to establish the difference between the epistemic uses of modals and their earlier dynamic/deontic ones. It also clarifies the subtle meaning changes in modals and between modals since the meaning of a modal varies, as we have seen above, depending on which 'person' is the subject of the utterance. Fourthly, we are no longer surprised that preterite-present verbs have performative characteristics, and that they may develop new past tenses in cycles, when these verbs are used as modals but continue to be used as main verbs.[29] It seems that this cycle is only broken when the modals in question no longer look like verbs, as happened in English. Fifthly, it is also not surprising that the number of modals dwindles once they grammaticalize, since grammatical forms whose referential meaning has bleached have no need for synonyms.[30] Thus the loss of the other preterite-presents in English in change (1ii)—which were all part of the larger modality field (cf. fns 2 and 4 above)—was very much to be expected.

A final point of insight via semantics which I have not yet discussed, is that there appears to be a natural link between modals and impersonal verbs. Warner (1993: 100–2) mentions as part of the development of verb-like characteristics of the modals in Middle English that quite a few of them on occasion joined the class of impersonal verbs (and see also Denison 1993: 314–15). Warner notes that impersonal constructions are found with *ouen* 'ought', *mot* 'must', *dar/þarf* 'need', *douen* 'avail, be capable'; the case of *may* is uncertain.[31] He also remarks on the development of OE *behofian* 'to fit', which acquired modal sense in the shortened and non-inflected form *bus/bos* in Middle English, as is clear from (8a). We can add the verbs *neden* and *mister* here (both derived from substantives), which in modal use are regularly found as impersonals in Middle English (8b–c). Interesting too is the verb *want*, which only became a modal when it acquired an infinitival complement in Early Modern English, but which was used as an impersonal in Middle English, as Krug (2000: 119ff.) shows.

(8a)   þe [DAT] bos do als Crist counseiles
                (OE Legends Horstmann 27, Visser §33)
          thee behoves do as Christ advises
          'You should do as Christ advises'

(8b)   her [DAT] nedede no teres for to borwe (Chaucer *T&C* V, 726)
    'she needn't borrow tears'

(8c)   What mystris   þe[DAT],   in gode   or ille,   of me   to melle þe
                                      (*MED*, York Plays 37, 54)
    What needs   thee   in good   or ill   about me   to concern thyself
    'Why need you be concerned about me in good or bad (times)'

I think (and cf. also Plank 1984: 323) that there is a case for seeing the use of the impersonal as a strengthening of the modal rather than the full-verb quality of these verbs, for two reasons. First of all, as I have noted in fn. 20, the subject of the modal verb in the performative space is thematically more of an experiencer than an agent, and it should therefore not be surprising to find the subject in the dative case rather than the nominative. It is interesting in that respect that the more marginal modals, *witan*, *willan*, and *cunnan* (for their behaviour see §4.1) do not occur as impersonals in Middle English; presumably because their subjects are higher in agency or more in control (they do not belong to the prototypical 'psych verbs', cf. McCawley 1976). Likewise the lexical meaning of *magan* 'to have physical power' also requires an agentive subject. Secondly, many other languages (related and unrelated) show verbs related to modality in impersonal use (cf. the impersonal use of the Old Georgian verb *unda*, discussed by Harris and Campbell 1995: 174ff., and the impersonal use of some Modern Greek modal auxiliaries, discussed by Tsangalidis 2004: 203–4). In some cases they have an expletive subject as well as a dative experiencer, as in French (9); in other cases there is only an oblique experiencer, as in Latin (10):

(9a)   Il   faut   te   calmer
    It   needs   you   calm down
    'You must calm down'

(10a)   tibi[DAT]   per   me   ire   licet (Woodcock 1959: §123)
     to-you   for   me   go   is-permitted
     'you may go as far as I am concerned'

(10b)   oportet   nos[ACC]   patriam amare (Woodcock 1959: §123)
     behoves   us   fatherland love
     'we should love our country'

The presence or absence of an expletive subject, is related to whether a language is pro-drop or not. In Old English, subjectless sentences were still possible with impersonals, but these all eventually disappeared before the modern period, and were replaced by constructions with an expletive subject or with a reanalysed dative or accusative experiencer (which became the grammatical subject). Another difference in the use of these impersonal constructions is the nature of the complement, which could be finite as well as non-finite. I will come back to both these points below and in §6.1.

4.3 The two approaches combined

4.3.1 More on the English modals

Once these general semantic distinctions have been made, it is easier to establish (additional) formal differences in the use of modal and non-modal verbs, and to find out what exactly happened to them diachronically. It is not surprising that Warner (1993) found more formal distinctions than previous linguists because he worked from the assumption that semantically the modals form a coherent class and he linked the development of the modals to other developments taking place in English, notably that of other auxiliaries. With the help of these new formal features, he was able to build up a story that does more justice to the historical facts and also makes sense in explanatory terms.

It is clear that in contrast to modern usage, some Old English modals could still be used as ordinary lexical verbs with agentive subjects (*agan*, *cunnan*, *willan*, **dearran*), but deontic and dynamic uses were already prevalent with **sculan*, **motan*, and *magan*. Some verbs were 'impersonal' in their usage in that they did not normally take an animate subject (e.g. *dugan* 'avail') or they varied between personal and impersonal use, like *þurfan* 'need' and the related predicate *is þearf* 'is need'. It is interesting to look in some more detail at *þurfan/is þearf*. The instances shown in Table 4.1 are found in The Dictionary of Old English Corpus (which contains virtually all known Old English texts).

The performative nature of the verb *þurfan* (in contrast to the 'normal' verb *(ge)fremman*) is clear from the disproportionate number of forms in the first and second person, compared to the third person, and the disproportionate number of present tense forms as compared to past forms. An impersonal construction is found with the noun *þearf*, with or without an expletive subject *hit*, which is frequent with all persons, but especially with the third. In this light, it is also not surprising that in Middle English we often find an impersonal construction with the verb *þarf*, which must be by

Table 4.1. *Constructions with* þurfan/is þearf *in Old English texts (compared with a non-performative verb* (ge)fremman *'to act'*)

Forms of *þurfan* /(*ge*)-*fremman* (indicative only)	Person		Number of instances found	
Singular	1. ic þearf	[ic (ge)fremme]	23	[20]
	2. þu þearft	[þu (ge)fremest]	31	[6]
	3. he/heo þearf	[he (ge)fremeþ]	14	[43]
Plural	1. we þurfon	[we (ge)fremaþ]	27	[0]
	2. ge þurfon	[ge (ge)fremaþ]	6	[1]
	3. hie þurfon	[hie (ge)fremaþ]	16	[17]
BE + *þearf* (noun) + dative experiencer	3 sg.: is, bið, byð, sie, sy, wæs, wære + þearf + dative		122	
hit + BE + *þearf* + dative	3 sg		20	
Past tense all persons	Þorfte, þorfton	[(ge) fremede/-don]	28	[342]

analogy with the earlier nominal construction. Presumably *dar*, which belonged to the same semantic set as *þarf*, followed it analogically, also beginning to occur in an impersonal construction in the same period.[32]

Next to the above lexical, deontic, and dynamic meanings, some modals had also developed epistemic uses (in OE *magan*, *sculan, *willan*). This can be shown on the basis of the formal constructions in which they occur. Modals with first or second person subjects are usually dynamic/deontic, but use with the third person is more ambiguous. It may be the report of some performative act with a speaker as source (which would make it deontic), but the source may also be vague and general. This is especially true when the subject is an inanimate noun. From such constructions, new structures develop with empty (11a) or expletive subjects (11b, 11c) or with 'raised subjects' in combination with impersonal verbs as in (11d), which shows that the modal in question is transparent, has no subject of its own. These structures usually require an epistemic reading since there is no addressee and hence no clear speaker-source.

(11a) Eaðe *mæg* gewurðan þæt þu   wite   þæt ic nat, …
                                   (ApT 21. 10, cf. Warner 1993: 166)
    easily can become   that thou know that I not-know
    'it may easily be the case that you know what I don't know'

(11b) hu   hit gewurðan *mihte* þæt Samson se   stranga swa ofslean mihte
how it   become   could that Samson the strong so   kill   could
an   þusend   manna mid   þæs assan   <cinbane> (Judg 15.21)
one   thousand of-men with   the   ass's   chinbone
'how it could come about that Samson, the strong one, could thus kill
a thousand men with an ass's bone'

(11c) &   þy   hit is on worulde aa   swa lencg   swa wyrse, &   swa hit
and thus it   is in   world   ever so   longer so   worse, and so   it
sceal nyde ær   Antecristes tocyme yfelian swyðe. (WHom 20.1.3)
must needs before Antichrist's coming worsen very
'and so in this world it grows ever from bad to worse, and thus it shall
necessarily grow still worse before the coming of the Antichrist'

(11d) hine   *sceal* on   domes   dæg gesceamian beforan gode
(HomU 37 (Nap 46)161, cf. Warner 1993: 123)
on-him must   on   Doom's   day   shame-fall   before   God
'he shall be ashamed before God at Doomsday'

When the subject of the modal clause is a third person animate noun or
pronoun, the nature of the modal is hard to decide because the subject may
be a 'reported' addressee (i.e. the performative act is reported and not a
direct address). Thus, *He must be ready by ten*, may convey that some
speaker had ordered the subject to be ready at that particular time. It may
also mean, however, that the speaker infers from the circumstances or from
general knowledge that the subject will be ready by ten, which makes it
epistemic. When the subject is an inanimate noun, it cannot be an addressee
with some kind of agentive function, but the whole clause may still be a
reported performative act addressed to an implicit agent, as in *The car must
be ready by ten*. So again both readings are possible here. Only context can
decide in these cases, and this is hard because there is often not enough
context to go by in historical texts, with the additional problem that the
inferences we make (which make the modal epistemic) are built upon socio-
cultural presuppositions, which we do not always know enough about.
Unambiguous examples of epistemic modals with animate and inanimate
subjects are still difficult to find in Old English. The contrast between the
examples in (11) and the more lexical/dynamic modals given in (12) is,
however, very clear. Not only do the examples in (12) have subjects that are
higher in control, but the modals are also accompanied by a direct or
prepositional object argument rather than an infinitive, which makes the

clause more transitive and hence the subject higher in agency (cf. Hopper and Thompson 1980).

(12a) &   gyf hwa   oðrum   *sceole* borh oððe bote
      and if anyone to-other(s) owe   debt or compensation
      æt woruldlicum þingum, gelæste hit him   georne ær   oððe æfter
      in worldly   things (he) pay it him/them eagerly before or   after
                                              (LawICn17.3, cf. Warner 1993: 98)
      'and if anyone owes (an)other(s) some debt or compensation in worldly
      affairs, he should pay it to him/them eagerly before or after'

(12b) Symble he bið   ælmihtig god, forðan ðe he symble *wyle* god
      Always he will-be almighty God, because he always will good
      and   næfre nan   yfel (ÆLS (Christmas) 49, cf. Warner 1993: 98)
      and   never no   evil
      'He will always be an almighty God because he always desires good and
      never any evil'

(12c) Ðæs   ilcan[GEN] lecedom *mæg*   wið   ðeh   wærce
                                                (Med 5.10 (Schauman-Cameron)6).
      From-the   same   medicine has-power against hip   pain
      'in the same way, this medicine helps against hip pain'

Example (11b) shows that the modal *mihte* (the second occurrence of *mihte*) could also be used dynamically with an infinitival construction, which thus functions as an intermediate construction between the other examples in (11) and those in (12). Since the infinitive itself must have been a 'deverbative abstract noun' in the earliest stages of Germanic (Kuryłowicz 1964: 158, and cf. Los 2005: 155ff.), it is easy to see how the dynamic uses in (12), with a direct object, were formally similar to the *mihte ofslean* construction in (11b). It was only when the abstract noun became truly verbal,[33] that these constructions began to look rather different from the ones in (12). This shows that there may have been other incremental changes, not mentioned by Lightfoot nor in grammaticalization studies, which eased the transition from full verb to auxiliary.

One point on which the two approaches seem to agree (but for different reasons) is that the development of the modals was one that went mono-tonically (unidirectionally) from full verb to auxiliary. In their concern to follow what is suggested by their respective theories, both schools tend to see only the macro-story, with the effect of simplifying the actual path followed, smoothing out or ignoring what Joseph (2004: 63) has called the 'blips'. Lightfoot is concerned to show how ever-increasing opacity leads inexorably to radical change, while the grammaticalization story of the modals dutifully follows the grammaticalization clines given in (6) and (7), with the semantic changes always steering the syntactic ones (as is most clear in Plank 1984: 308; Brinton 1988: 105).

Warner has shown that the micro-story is much more complex: instead of becoming steadily more Aux-like, the modals also developed some verb-like properties. The facts that he discovered are easy to miss when it is not what your theory expects. It means that the modals could also have gone the other way, becoming more fully verbal rather than less (as happened in Dutch and German). Warner's findings are not a real problem for the P&P framework, which does not make use of unidirectional principles, but it does upset the simplicity of the build-up towards radical change. They are perhaps also not a real problem for grammaticalization, if the phenomenon of layering is taken into account, that is positing a stage where the old and the new forms may coexist for a while (cf. Hopper and Traugott 2003: 49), or if we posit divergence (a lexemic split) in the modal verbs, which in fact is what Warner (1993: 202) proposed for *dare*, *need*, and *can*.[34] Still, it makes the modal development far less neatly unidirectional, and it makes the Dutch/German case an unlikely happening since it does not follow Hopper and Traugott's (2003: 122) typical grammaticalization schema of 'A >A/B > B', but instead seems to follow A > A/B > A. It makes us aware that the development can be messy and that reverse movements are always possible. One such reverse example is given by Burridge (1998), who shows that in Pennsylvania German the past tense of the modal auxiliary *welle* 'will', that is *wotte* (> *wollte*), has become a main verb replacing earlier *winsche* 'wish'. In this instance, special socio-cultural circumstances led to it. In general, it may well be the case that special circumstances are necessary (of an internal or external nature) for reversals to take place, cf. Plank (1995) on reversals in the English's genitive, and Fischer (1997, 2000a) on the *to*-infinitive.

4.3.2 Some more general properties of auxiliaries in auxiliary development

In this subsection, I want to consider a number of formal aspects related to the development of the modals in English and auxiliaries in general, which have not yet been paid much attention to and which are of interest within an analogical approach to change. These are (1) fixed word order, (2) frequency, (3) the INFL position of Aux., and (4) the link with modal adverbs. Two other developments, namely clause combining and subject raising, apply to the auxiliaries too. These will be discussed in Chapter 5, which deals with syntax arising out of discourse.

For auxiliaries to develop, there are some necessary preconditions. One is, as has already been stated above with a reference to Bolinger (1980) (see fn. 8), that we need two verbs, a main verb and an infinitival complement. When these verbs combine, it is unlikely that both verbal elements will keep their own argument structures: one verb will usually lose its independence to the other. This loss will be further reinforced if the two verbs are generally adjacent, and especially if their adjacency is always in the same order. This enables the language learner to analyse the verbs not as two separate tokens, but to analyse them on a higher level as one construction-type. The more often a fixed order of the two verbs occurs, the more likely it is that this analysis on a type-level will take place.[35] The analysis on the type-level will be further enhanced if the paradigm of tokens involved in the construction is small and/or is characterized by the same internal (semantic and/or formal) attributes.

In the case of Old English verb combinations, type-recognition is helped by the fact that the first verb (the later auxiliary) belongs to a small class (the modals and *habban* 'have', *beon* 'be', and *weorðan* 'be/become'), and that the second verb has only five possible tokens as endings, representing only two types (in Old English either the past participle inflections *-en/-ed/-od* or the infinitival inflections *-an/-ian*). For the Old English modals, type-recognition was facilitated by the fact that, as a class, they shared formal and semantic characteristics. This did not apply to the three other verbs. On the other hand, type-recognition in Old English is hindered by the fact that the two verbs are usually not adjacent, that they do not necessarily occur in the same order, and that most members of the small (auxiliary) group also still occur in constructions with their own argument structures.

A number of changes then took place in Middle and Early Modern English which were not directly related to the budding auxiliaries but which greatly helped to make them stand out as a type. This is the fixation of word order to SVO in both main and subordinate clauses, which began already in Old English and can be said to be more or less complete by 1500 (except in cases of Subject-Verb inversion, i.e. V-to-I movement), accompanied by the loss of Verb-second.[36] These two changes ensured that the two verbs now always occurred together (except when separated by *not* or light adverbs), with the exception of interrogative clauses, and always in the same order. Another change is the increasing frequency of verbal combinations due to the loss of inflections, so that periphrastic construction developed in rapid sequence. Thus, the combination with modals became more frequent due to the loss of the subjunctive, and the perfect and ingressive (with the verb *ginnen*, especially the past form *gan*) became more frequent due to the loss of aspectual prefixes (cf. Funke 1922; Brinton 1988, 1996: 67–83), followed later also by the rise of the progressive.[37] The increasing frequency of a combination of two verbs and the much enhanced type-recognition led to automatization, that is to petrification of the type in question and to the loss of verbalness in the first element of the pattern, the auxiliary verb, since it had now become a mere dependent of the main verb; its original verbal nature was no longer necessary for type-recognition. The fossilization of the modal auxiliary took place first and eventually also affected the auxiliaries *have* and *be*, as Warner (1993, 1997) illustrates convincingly. The latter verbs took longer because they were less easily recognizable as a type both semantically (the modals formed a clearer unit here) and formally (the modals stood out as preterite-presents and were only combined with one complement type, that is bare infinitives, while *have* and *be* did not belong to the preterite-present group, and in Middle English could take more complement types, that is past and present participle and *to*-infinitives). As I argued in §3.3, in analogical learning, sequence and token frequency are crucial to type-formation.

String frequency and adjacency also played an important part in the development of the Romance future as described by Fleischman (1982) and many others before her (the earliest being Hermann Paul in 1880). It is now generally accepted that the future affix in Romance language (e.g. French *parler-ai, parler-as, parler-a*; Italian *parler-o, parler-ai, parler-a*) is a development from present-tense forms of the Latin verb *habere* preceded by a bare infinitive (French *avoir: (j')ai, (tu) as, (il) a*; Italian *avere: ho, hai, ha*, 'I have, you have, he has', etc.). The semantic development to future takes place via an intermediate obligative stage (as still visible in English *have to*). What makes the Romance case rather interesting from an analogical learning point of view is the fact that Fleischman makes quite clear that the reanalysis of *habere* into an affix only took place (i) when *habere* and the infinitive were strictly adjacent, (ii) when they occurred in the order infinitive +

habere, and (iii) that it could become an affix only because Romance already had suffixes.

As to (i), Fleischman (1982: 72–4) shows that other constructions which contained *habere* and a marked infinitive (an infinitive introduced by a preposition), such as French *j'ai à travailler* 'I have work to do' and Italian *ho da cantare* 'I have to sing', remained analytic, and kept a dynamic (i.e. agent-oriented), obligative meaning. Note that in Italian an object may occur between *ho* and *da cantare*, and it cannot be used to issue an order. Similarly, constructions in which *habere* and the infinitive were separated by clitic object pronouns (which were less frequent) disappeared, except in Portuguese, where it is now also declining.

With respect to (ii), Fleischman (1982: 113ff.) hypothesizes that the new future construction must have occurred when Latin was still an SOV language, that is when the finite verb still followed the infinitive. This would explain why *habere* + past participle did not become a synthetic perfect in Romance, since this took place later when the language was already SVO. Note also that the development of a perfective *prefix* out of *habere* + infinitive, which is possible on the basis of the word order, is unlikely due to the fact that French does not have any other inflectional prefixes in its system. It is difficult, due to lack of data from Vulgar Latin, to come up with firm proof, but it is interesting to see that Fleischman (1982: 56) also indicates that the (future) infinitive + *habere* construction is at first found most frequently in subordinate clauses, where SOV remained much longer.

As to (iii), it is interesting to note the difference between the Romance futures and the English future. In the Romance languages *habere* could develop into a suffix, because it was in the right position (behind the infinitive) and because the language still had many verbal suffixes. In English the new future auxiliaries, *shall* and *will*, both developed into the clitic *'ll*, but this did not proceed to the next, affixal, stage on the cline given in (7a) above; presumably, because English had lost most of its verbal and nominal inflections, and *'ll* was in the wrong position to attach to the verb as a suffix. Development into a verbal prefix is unlikely because English does not possess prefixal inflections. The construction *'ll*, in fact, cliticizes instead onto the subject and not the verb, usually a pronoun (although a full noun phrase is also possible). It cannot easily fuse with the pronoun because tense is an attribute typical of verbs and not of pronouns. The most likely route, therefore, is that it will in time be reduced to zero,[38] with other future expressions such as *going to/gonna* taking over its role. This shows again, how important the state of the synchronic system is for the grammaticalization process.

Having discussed fixed word order (1) and frequency (2), let us next have a look at point (3) mentioned at the beginning of this subsection, the INFL position of Aux. In generative analyses the creation of an auxiliary is often seen as a movement to a higher INFL position in the abstract structure of the clause. It is evident that in an analogical framework a movement rule is impossible, since it all depends on surface sequence.[39] How then can the auxiliary end up in a higher position? In answer to this question, I would like to stress that the position of the finite verb (which includes the later auxiliary) has in fact not changed in surface structure (cf. Brinton 1988: 104; Krug 2001: 326). It appeared most commonly in second position, usually after the subject, already in Old English in all main clauses, and also gradually more and more in subordinate clauses. As to frequency, this SV_{finite} order must have been the most usual order very soon. The second position of the finite verb remains the most usual order in Middle and Modern English; what changes is the position that could be taken by the finite *main* verb. The fact that the finite verb was more and more often the later auxiliary, automatically meant that children were confronted with an [S Aux V]-type most of the time and with [Aux SV] in questions. The [VS]-type became simply too infrequent to be maintained, also because at the period of change this type was rarer still through the optional use of dummy *do*, which further increased the [Aux SV]-type. Similarly in negative sentences, the order [S Aux *not* V] was becoming the rule and slowly ousted [SV *not*].[40] Type-recognition through frequency thus led to the loss of the [VS] and the [SV *not*] types with main verbs, and movement is not necessary to account for the position of Aux.

We have come to the last of the four points. Quite a few commentators mentioned the changes in adverb position that seemed to accompany the last changes that Lightfoot connected with the modals (given in (2) in §4.1). Ellegård (1953: 183) shows that the regular position of adverbs was after the finite verb (whether modal or full verb) in Middle English (Chaucer), while in subordinate clauses it could occur both before and after the finite verb. This changed in Modern English in the sense that light adverbs began to appear more and more in the position *before* the matrix lexical verb, whether finite or not.[41] Quirk *et al.* (1972: 438ff.) show for Present-day English that the so-called 'intensifier adjuncts', which include emphasizers (*definitely, actually*), amplifiers (*completely, quite*), and downtoners (*hardly, almost*) are adverbs that now, as a rule, occur before the main lexical verb in Present-day English.[42] These adverbs tend to be subjective or evaluative in nature, that is they share a modal aspect. Other adjuncts, for example of manner, place, time, etc., do not normally occur here, unless they can be interpreted subjectively.[43] Thus, we now have *He hardly saw it* as against *He acted gracefully*. When both positions are possible, as in *He clearly told them* against *He told them clearly*, the former implies subjective judgement ('It was clear that he told them') while the latter is descriptive ('he told them in a clear way'). Some intensifiers may also occur in final position, such as the amplifiers. Quirk *et al.* (1972: 450–1) note that one group of amplifiers—the maximizers—prefer final position in positive declarative clauses and also when they denote the upper extreme on the scale. Thus the maximizer *completely* in *He denied it completely* more or less denotes a fact, whereas in *He completely denied it*, it comes closer to a booster, meaning 'He strongly denied it'. Similarly, a subjective element is also more clearly present in the interrogative version: *Did he completely deny it?* Quite clearly here too the preverbal position is related to greater subjectivity or speaker involvement.

Some linguists linked this change in adverb position to the rise of *do*. Ellegård (1953: 180–7) considered this possibility but saw nothing to support this claim (others such as Kroch 1989b, however did). He makes two interesting remarks, however, that may be relevant. First, he notes that the less likely an adverb appeared in pre-finite (main verb) position (i.e. the still unusual position in main clauses at that time), the more likely it was that *do* was inserted (note that the insertion of finite *do* in fact puts the adverb back in its old position, i.e. after the finite verb!). In other words, [NP$_S$ *do* Adv V] only occurred when the adverb was felt to be in an awkward position. Secondly, he remarks that this [NP$_S$ *do* Adv V] construction was not long-lived.

A tentative hypothesis can now be set up with reference to this change in adverb position, and the loss of the [NP$_S$ *do* Adv V] construction, but more empirical research is clearly needed. First of all, as noted above, the re-positioned adverbs are related to subjectivity; adverbs of other semantic classes do not seem to change position so easily. With their subjective/evaluative/attitudinal sense, these adverbs are semantically close to epistemic modal verbs, which by this time (circa 1600) have fully developed. Both are an expression of modality, of the speaker's attitude towards the situation described. Besides, formally, the modals now look more like adverbs than verbs since they had lost almost all inflections.[44] In other words, in both form and sense these auxiliaries were very close to modal adverbs. Children learning the language, might draw such analogical conclusions.[45] Noticeable from the historical record is that all the subjective modal elements (adverbs and verbs) begin to occur in the same position, that is before the main lexical verb. For this reason they would be recognizable as a construction-type. If the adverb was indeed recognized as a modal Aux-like element, then there was no longer a need for the [NP$_S$ *do* Adv V]-construction, which Ellegård regarded as a construction to solve the problem of an awkwardly placed adverb. Leaving out *do* brought the construction analogically in line with the now regular [S Aux/Adv V]-construction. It could therefore disappear, having done its duty in creating a smooth transition.

Intertwined with this development is the position of *not*. In Old English the sentential negative marker *ne* was always positioned before the finite main verb (typologically the most natural position). In late Old English and early Middle English *ne* came to be strengthened by other negative 'intensifier adjuncts', such as *nawiht, naht, noht > not* 'nothing', and *næfre* 'never' placed in the usual adverbial position, that is *after* the finite verb, which was then still most frequently the main verb. The reanalysis of the modals as non-verbs, really meant that the sentential negative marker (which function was now carried by *not* alone) was back in its natural position in all the clauses that contained a periphrastic verbal construction, namely *after* the finite auxiliary but *before* the lexical main verb. In other words, the loss of *ne* at this time also helped to mark the modals as non-verbs since the new sentential negative *not* in its old position preceded not the modal but the main verb. This position of *not*, which was itself originally an 'intensifying adjunct', may also have eased the placement of other intensifying adjuncts before the lexical main verb, while at the same time, the new sentential status of *not* may explain the preservation of the [NP$_S$ *do* Adv V]-construction *only* with the adverb *not*, and not with the other intensifying adverbs.

The new sentential status of *not* (leading to further grammaticalizion and clitic status, just like *ne* before it) in turn is connected to two other phenomena, which may strengthen the hypothesis of Aux becoming an adverb. Warner (1993: 3–4; 1997) and Plank (1984: 330–1) note the development of auxiliaries into anaphoric islands, and the creation of more and more idiosyncratic forms (involving phonetic changes in the stem), especially in combination with negative *not*. The contraction of *not* to *n't* begins to occur from about 1600 onwards, and significantly, is mainly found with auxiliaries and the copula *be* (cf. Rissanen 1999b).[46] About the same time or somewhat later, we see the appearance of phonetically irregular forms: *will not* becomes *won't*, *cannot* becomes *can't*, and similarly *aren't*, *ain't*, *shan't*. It seems then as if the position of the auxiliary next to the adverb *not* came to be interpreted as just one Adverb position, since the two elements were semantically and formally close. If this is correct, we may conclude that the frequency of the construction-type [S Aux/Adv V] led to the fusion of the Aux and the adverb *not*.[47] The much later contraction of modal phrases like *had better/had rather/had sooner* to *'d better*, etc., and even to simply *better* would also fit this development from Aux to adverb.

Another development that is of interest is the use in some non-standard American, Northern English, and Scots varieties of modal auxiliaries in combination with another modal. The first modal here tends to be epistemic, the second not. Labov (1972a: 59), Plank (1984: 315) and others suggested that the first modal functions rather like an adverb. There have also been suggestions that they are both auxiliaries. Whatever their nature, it is clear that they are not some archaic left-over from Middle English, where such combined modals occurred as verbs. Nagle (1994, 1997) shows convincingly that they must be seen as innovations. A final point which shows that epistemic modals are close to adverbs, is the development of quite a few of them into clear adverbs, some even sporting adverbial endings, cf. English *maybe*, and archaic *mayhap*, Swedish *kanske*, Norwegian *kanskje* (both 'mayhap'), French *peut-être*, Dutch *mogelijk,* German *möglicherweise* (the latter two derive from adjectives that consist of *may* + affix, affixes normally only used with nouns and adjectives), Danish *mon* and archaic Swedish *månne* (from the Old Norse modal verb *munu* 'shall, will', both used as modal particles with the approximate sense of 'yet').

4.4 Concluding remarks

The story of the English auxiliaries tells us that for an insightful explanation of what happened we need to take both form and meaning seriously. We have seen that forms may be changed through analogy with other forms, without meaning playing a role, as in the case of the development of *have* and *be* into 'anaphoric islands', in which they followed the modals. We have also seen that the position of an element does not easily change, but that the function of that element may change, as happened with the modal verbs. They remained in position, but no longer as verbs. On the other hand, there is clear evidence that meaning plays a role in the way the modals developed as a group. All these developments together only become clear and understandable when one has an eye for the historical details, for the role played by sequence (and string frequency), and for the synchronic grammatical system in which the changing elements or constructions function. Hypotheses provided by a theory are useful heuristic devices, but they are not laws directing and explaining change. Through the historical details, we can establish the contours of the grammatical system that operated in a particular language at a particular time. This language-specific system is very influential in shaping developments—which may also be subject to some general properties established by the theoretical framework—as they take place. I have tried to show that an analogical learning system which makes use of token- and type-recognition (relating newly emerging tokens and types to existing ones, similar in form and function) and which is sensitive to sequence and frequency can account for the surface developments in the English auxiliary system.

Apart from iconicity, indexicality, and frequency, economy may also play a role in the sense that less frequently occurring types or tokens will tend to adapt themselves to more frequent types, provided there are enough links between them, either in form or function or both. Plank (1985: 155) writes in this connection that in a grammar '*erweiterte* und *markierte* Konstruktionen so weit wie möglich analog entsprechenden *einfachen* und *unmarkierten* Konstruktionen strukturiert sind', that is that there is a strong tendency in language for extended and marked constructions to conform analogically to simpler and unmarked ones. Hawkins (2004) puts forward similar arguments in his defence of the principle of 'Minimize Forms'. He writes:

Minimizations in unique form–property pairings are accomplished by expanding the compatibility of certain forms with a wider range of properties [meanings]. Ambiguity, vagueness, and zero specification are efficient, inasmuch as they reduce the total number of forms that are needed in a language. (Hawkins 2004: 40)

He continues that this minimization is connected with the frequency of the form and/or the processing ease of assigning a particular property to a reduced form. The ambiguity that arises is no problem since '[t]he multiple properties that are assignable to a given form can generally be reduced to a specific P[roperty] in actual language use by exploiting "context" in various ways' (2004: 41; these ideas are rather similar to Goldberg's (1995: 67–8) principles of 'maximized expressive power' and 'maximized economy', both minimizing the number of constructions in a language as much as possible). In §6.1, I will suggest that the more marked and extended epistemic modal constructions eventually conformed in their structure to less marked verbal constructions, for reasons of economy and frequency.

Through a better understanding of what happened to the English auxiliaries, and in particular the modals, we may also gain a clearer understanding of auxiliary developments in other languages. It is evident, for instance, that there are clear similarities between the English modals on the one hand, and the modals in Dutch, German, and the Scandinavian languages on the other. In both cases the modals developed epistemic and future senses. But there are also differences, and these differences may tell us more about causative factors than the similarities. The Dutch, German, and Scandinavian modals became, like the Middle English modals, more verb-like (they generally possess infinitival and past participial forms, most have 'real' past tenses and can take a direct object or directional adverb), but unlike the later English modals, they continued on this path. Why? The main difference between these languages and English is that they kept the V2 rule (Dutch and German also did not undergo the SOV > SVO change), so that word order did not become fixed to one pattern in all types of clauses:

(**13a**) main clause   (Dutch):   Zij *kan* dat niet *begrijpen*
                           (German): Sie *kann* es nicht *verstehen*
                           (Swedish): Hon *kan* det inte *förstå*
                           She can that not understand
(**13b**) subordinate clause (Dutch):   ... als zij dat niet *begrijpen kan/kan begrijpen*
                           (German): ... wenn sie das nicht *verstehen kann*
                           (Swedish): ... om hon inte *kan förstå*
                           ... if she not can understand/understand can

Thus, in main clauses, due to V2, the modal and the main verb are generally not adjacent, except when there is no object or when the object is a clause. When the subject is not in first position, which is frequent in these languages, the modal and infinitive are never adjacent (e.g. Dutch *Dat* **kan** *zij niet* **verstaan** 'that can she not understand') because the subject intervenes.

In subordinate clauses, main verb and modal are adjacent but the order is reversed compared to the main clause in German (V-Aux instead of Aux-V); in Dutch there is a choice; only in Scandinavian has the order become fixed to Aux-V. Consequently, modals and verbs did not become adjacent in all cases, and did not develop one fixed order. This meant that the language learner could not abduce a new type-pattern of [S Aux V], in which the Aux loses its verbal nature. To put it somewhat bluntly, in Dutch, German, and Scandinavian, the modal remained a verb because of a lack of adjacency between it and the main verb.

The case of the auxiliaries has also made clear that we must be careful not to press our general findings, principles, and constraints (based on our theories) too hard on any particular case. Grammaticalization may follow regular, unidirectional paths, but these paths need not be followed in each case. In the same way, the notion of a deep parameter shift should not make us blind to historical surface details that may have been crucial for the development. We must leave room for these details to tell their own story. In Chapter 5, we will look at clause fusion, which has been suggested by Harris and Campbell (1995) as an important factor in auxiliary development. I will argue there that this should only be considered relevant in any one case, if the characteristic features that have been established on the basis of cases investigated earlier, do indeed apply. If these are absent, we must not force the issue but look for further evidence. In this way we may discover further features that may be relevant for clause fusion, or ones that may be relevant to show that there was no fusion. Building up hypotheses and applying them to new cases of change is necessary and useful, but in each case it is the historical details that should have the final word. These then, in turn, help to shape up and refine our hypotheses about change and our hypotheses about the form of the grammar, the learning system.

Notes

1. Other formal studies on the development of (English) modals and/or auxiliaries are by Steele *et al.* (1981); Roberts (1985, 1993b: 238ff.); van Kemenade (1985, 1992); Miller (1997); Roberts and Roussou (2002, 2003); and further treatments by Lightfoot (1982, 1991, 1999, 2003). Grammaticalization and functional approaches to modals and auxiliaries can be found in Traugott (1982, 1989);

Plank (1984); Bybee *et al.* (1984: Chapters 6, 7); the papers in Harris and Ramat (1987); Goossens (1987); Brinton (1988); Sweetser (1990); van der Auwera and Plungian (1998); Kuteva (2001); Traugott and Dasher (2002: 105–47; 190 ff.); Bybee (2003); Tsangalidis (2004). More 'neutral' discussions can be found in Warner (1993); Nagle (1989); Denison (1993: 292ff.); McMahon (1994: 116–29). There are also quite a number of detailed reviews of Lightfoot (1979) by (historical) linguists, see Bennett (1979); Aitchison (1980); Fischer and van der Leek (1981); Romaine (1981); Wasow and Akmajian, Appendix B, in Steele *et al.* (1981); Warner (1983).

2. *motan*, *sculan*, and *dearran* are starred because no infinitival forms have been attested in Old English (here I follow Warner 1993: 145); with most of the other verbs (with the exception of *cunnan*), they are quite rare too. These verbs are part of a group called the preterite-present verbs because the forms in the present tense paradigm were originally past tense forms. The only exception is *willan*, which however began to join the preterite-present group in form already in Old English (cf. Warner 1993: 142). A few other verbs belonged to the preterite-present group, most of which got lost (but see below): *witan*, *unnan*, *(ge)munan*, *dugan*, and anomalous *uton* 'let's'. Note that all these verbs share some of their meanings with the core modals, *witan* 'know' is close to *cunnan*, *unnan* 'grant, wish' is close to *willan*, *dugan* 'avail, be capable' is close to *magan*, and *munan* 'be mindful of, remember' is close to both *willan* (cf. fn.4) and *cunnan/magan* (in its sense of 'to have mental power').

3. In Fischer and van der Leek (1981: 341, fn. 3), we called (iv) a 'highly dubious proposal', since unlike the other changes in (1), it does not concern a surface change (on the surface nothing changes!) but a theory-internal motivation, which one can only accept if one does *not* accept NP-Preposing as part of the grammar of Old English. In the same article (1981: 325ff.), we provide evidence that NP-Preposing *was* possible in Old English, and that therefore change (iv) is vacuous. In later revisions (1982, etc.) Lightfoot has left (iv) out.

4. The reason that *witan*, unlike *cunnan* (both had the meaning 'to know'), remained outside the modal group may be threefold. First of all, the meaning of 'mental power or knowledge' is situated on the edge of the modal semantic field (see §4.2.2). Secondly, and more importantly, *witan* derived from the lost verb *wītan* 'to see' (a cognate of Latin *videre*), and it is quite likely that the sense of visual perception persisted, just as the complementation pattern of the physical perception verbs persisted with this verb in Old English (cf. Ono 1975; Fischer 1989: 199–202). Linked to this is the fact that *witan* unlike *cunnan* could not appear with a same-subject bare infinitive (I owe this observation to Anthony Warner p.c.). Thirdly, when the modals develop into a distinct category (when they grammaticalize), it is to be expected that the paradigmatic choice of verbs within this category will become restricted (this is one of Lehmann's parameters, discussed in §3.2); *witan* was too close to *cunnan* to survive as a modal. In a similar way, we see that ON *mun* 'will, may' (the cognate of *munan*), is, unlike *vilja* 'will', part of the subgroup of modals in Old Norse

(see Faarlund 2004: 129). It presumably ousted *vilja* (which shared some of the subgroup's characteristics, see Faarlund 2004: 51, 123, 159) because they, too, were too close, *mun* like *vilja* expressed intention. Note that in English *will* ousted *mun/mon* in the standard language.

5. There are some examples after *magan* but they are different because they involve a discourse structure in which *magan* functions as an epistemic verb (see further §§5.3 and 6.1).

6. In Lightfoot (1974: 247), it is relegated to a footnote, i.e. (18).

7. *Willan* as an infinitive is rare. In the York-Toronto-Helsinki parsed Corpus of Old English prose, I have only found one instance (ÆCHom I, 38:511.119). The infinitival form used is almost always *(ge)wilnian* or *willian*.

8. Cf. Bolinger's (1980: 297) perceptive remark with respect to a sequence of two verbs: 'the moment a verb is given an infinitive complement, that verb starts down the road of auxiliariness'.

9. I.e. this refers to the technical sense of government as defined in the then current version of GB-theory. For the details, see Roberts (1985: 25–35). In Roberts (1993b: 244, 255), the parameter involved has changed but the effect of it is the same in the sense that it still is concerned with agreement features and the assignment of θ-roles.

10. It must be stated, however, that with hindsight Roberts' parameter was as short-lived as Lightfoot's Transparency Principle. In his later work, he ascribes the development of the modals as due to grammar simplification (which comes close to a Transparency Principle!) and the nature of the feature F* (see §3.1).

11. This is stated in fn. 1, on p. 21. However, on p. 34 Roberts indicates that modals no longer assigned θ-roles when they 'were *reanalyzed as auxiliaries*' (my italics), and the term 'reanalysis' with respect to the modals is used throughout. One wonders what the reanalysis involves, if at the same time they remain Verbs. I am not the only one confused, as is clear from Denison (1993: 331–3). Note that Roberts (1993a: 309) does accept that the modals (formerly raising/control verbs) became auxiliaries in the early sixteenth century.

12. In this respect, it is strange that Roberts (1993a: 311) assumes that there was *no* relation between the reanalysis the modals underwent and the modality they expressed. This makes the fact that only the modals replaced the subjunctive (p. 316) a total accident.

13. There is a good discussion of this in Nagle (1989: 65 ff.), who, however, places the beginning of the replacement of the subjunctive by modals in late Old English. In that period, the indicative and subjunctive inflections were still fully distinctive in the present tense, except in the first person sg, but somewhat less distinctive in the past tense, mainly due to the collapse in late Old English of the phonetic distinction between the indicative pl. *-on* and the subjunctive pl. *-en* endings. The use of modals probably started for expressive reasons, and their use became slowly more obligatory when the subjunctive endings became more and more indistinguishable. It is difficult therefore to date the replacement precisely.

14. Lightfoot (1991), in his revision of the modals, takes over quite a few of Roberts' ideas, such as the link between modal and loss of subjunctive, the idea of two separate changes, and the movement of modal verbs to INFL. Unlike Roberts, however, he preserves a clear link between the two changes by stating that the movement of modals to INFL led to the appropriation of the INFL position by the modal verbs, causing the loss of V-to-I (1991: 149). See also below.

15. As another verb-like characteristic, Warner mentions the fact that some of the Middle English modals joined the class of impersonal verbs. However, this fact can also be interpreted the other way round, as we will see below in §4.2.2.

16. To emphasize the importance of form, Warner (1993: 107) further refers to studies on children's acquisition of word classes, which show that formal errors based on semantic misclassification are rare. In the same vein, I pointed out above (§3.2, fn. 31) that Coates (1987) noted that misanalysis as found in folk etymology is primarily based on form not meaning, and that syntactic priming may take place regardless of semantic content (see Pickering and Branigan 1999, quoted in §3.3).

17. He also discusses it in Lightfoot 1982 (159–65) and 2003 (107–19), but these accounts are virtually the same as the 1979 and 1999 ones respectively.

18. In Lightfoot (1999: 163, 185), this is pushed back even further, completion is now reached only in the eighteenth century.

19. Modals are often used as a watered-down version of explicit performatives because the latter, as in e.g. *I order you to go*, are often too direct and authoritarian. This grammatical rather than lexical status of modal verbs makes them less direct (cf. Traugott and Dasher 2002: 192).

20. Agent- and speaker-oriented modality (beside epistemic modality) are terms used by Bybee *et al.* (1991, 1994) to distinguish, very roughly, between 'dynamic' (ability, volition) and 'deontic' (permission, obligation) modality. As terms they are not entirely felicitous. First, because the 'agent' is often more of an 'experiencer'; secondly, because it suggests a sharp division between these two types; and thirdly, because epistemic modality could also be said to be speaker-oriented. Bybee *et al.* ignore the role that the category of 'person' plays, which may be crucial in deciding whether deontic or epistemic modality is involved. Van der Auwera and Plungian (1998) use the terms 'participant-internal' and 'participant-external' modality for these two types. It has to be noted that all these terms do not completely cover each other. Since no terms serve to make all distinctions clear, I will stick to Bybee *et al.*'s terms here because they are useful when talking about the performative function. Further down I will also make use of the terms 'dynamic' and 'deontic'. The discussion of the examples here and below should make clear what type of modality is intended.

21. Bybee *et al.* (1991: 25) note that agent-oriented modality is closer to lexical semantics, and that it always precedes the (more) speaker-oriented types of modality, i.e. deontic and epistemic modality. Similarly, Traugott and Dasher

(2002: 195) write that verbs with speech-act functions are typically derived from those without, and they also note (2002: 198 ff.) that explicit speech-act verbs are typical of the written mode, they occur in institutional texts (contracts, wills, etc.) and tend to be formal.

22. This went hand in hand with changes in the clausal construction (which made it possible to distinguish the two *unda*s). I will return to the relevance of this in Chapter 5.

23. It is well-known that politeness may be expressed via the use of formal greetings (cf. the custom of *aisatu* in Japan, described in Traugott and Dasher 2002: 215 ff.), via vocalizations (cf. Haiman 1999: 38), via the use of honorifics or special lexical elements or inflections to express deference (Haiman 1999), or via the use of plural and/or third person pronouns to create distance as can be seen in French *tu* vs. *vous*, Dutch *jij* vs. *jullie*, German *du* vs. *Sie*, Italian *tu* vs. *Lei*. These strategies can become quite complicated, e.g. with special lexical signs used for the same referent in different social situations, as in Javanese or Korean (for details see Crystal 1987: 44, 99).

24. Traugott (1989) suggests that there need not be a strict linear order, i.e. the interpersonal stage may also be derived directly from the propositional one (see also Brinton 1996: 111; Traugott and Dasher 2002: 94ff.). Brinton (1996: 113) shows in connection with the development of the pragmatic marker *anon* in Middle and Early Modern English that although the textual function need not be an intermediate stage for the interpersonal function to develop, in terms of chronology the interpersonal function is the last to appear. Concerning another pragmatic marker, i.e. OE *hwæt*, however, she notes (1996: 200) that the textual function may be later than the interpersonal one. It may in fact be difficult to distinguish between the textual and interpersonal as separate stages since they may be connected with a written vs. an oral style. More on this in Chapter 6.

25. e.g. the two clines do not provide any understanding of the differences between the behaviour of Dutch/German modal verbs and English ones. They underwent very similar semantic changes, travelling similar paths, but why did the former diverge towards full verb status, functioning in virtually full verbal paradigms, while the latter devolved towards auxiliaries, fixed and inflectionless?

26. For instance, it has been noted that *should* in Modern English functions as an empty subordinate marker in clauses such as, *The police are expecting that the Lybians should make the first move.* Any sense of weak obligation (still present, but already pleonastic, in *It is essential that on this point the churches should learn from each other*) is impossible here (the examples are from Bybee *et al.* 1994: 215). This development is rather similar to what happened to the subjunctive *affix* in Old English. From an epistemic marker after matrix verbs expressing a subjective opinion, modern *should* and the Old English subjunctive came to be used after evaluative verbs, which state an opinion as a fact. Thus, this diffusion via different semantic classes of matrix verbs causes an increase in frequency of the marker (*should*/the subjunctive affix) and concomitant bleaching of their original mood meaning, usually resulting in zero marking.

27. The derivation of a present subjunctive ending from a past tense, shows again the interesting connection between modality and pastness that is also visible in the origin of many modals as preterite-present verbs.

28. This also happened in Old English. The subjunctive form occurred in subordinate clauses expressing epistemic modality, but through an increase in the frequency of this form (see fn. 26), it spread to other subordinate clauses slowly losing its subjective quality and becoming purely conventional. It was often used conventionally in reported speech and as a type of concord after another clause in the subjunctive (cf. Mitchell 1985: §877ff.).

29. It can therefore be no accident that two unrelated languages like Georgian and English both make use of preterite-present verbs as modals. No doubt more evidence of this will be found in other languages that possess both an inflectional tense system and a modal verb system. For Georgian, see Harris and Campbell (1995: 173ff.).

30. I strongly disagree therefore with Lightfoot (1991: 147) when he writes rather scathingly that 'it has sometimes been hinted that semantic factors determined which of these verbs [i.e. the other preterite-presents mentioned in (1ii)] were lost, but these factors have never been properly articulated'. He thus ignores the widely available evidence of the increase in paradigmaticity (one of Lehmann's parameters, see Table 3.2 above) in processes of grammaticalization.

31. Warner (1993: 252, fn.12) does not accept the occurrence with *may* in the *MED*; Visser's (1963–73: §33) only example is also dubious.

32. The Old English verb *niedan/nydan* 'need' is a different case yet again. In Old English it was not used with a personal subject in the sense of 'need'. That sense was only found in the impersonal construction *me, þe*, etc. *is neod* 'to me, you ... is need'. Only in Middle English do we begin to find personal *neden*, and the verb itself has now also acquired impersonal use.

33. I agree with Los (2005) that both the bare and the to-infinitive show verbal characteristics in the earliest stages of Old English since no examples have been found of these infinitives with an object in the genitive. This makes it clear that they were not completely nominal, as Lightfoot (1979: 186 ff.) has suggested (for a rebuttal, see Fischer and van der Leek 1981: 318ff.). It is not clear, however, to what extent the Old English infinitives retained some of their nominal characteristics. Probably the bare infinitive was more verbal than the *to*-infinitive, which retained a dative ending until the end of the period, and which could be coordinated (although this was rare) with a prepositional noun phrase (cf. Fischer 1996a). Anderson (1993: 12–16) also suggests that both types of infinitive had verbal and nominal characteristics in Old English, and that the bare infinitive was more advanced towards a verbal category than the *to*-infinitive.

34. For the wavering behaviour of *dare* and *need* that continues up to the present day, see Beths (1999) and Taeymans (2004).

35. On the importance of string frequency and adjacency for grammaticalization, see also Krug (2000, 2003). Hawkins' (2004: 42, 63, 81 and *passim*) principle of

'Minimize Forms' is intimately related with frequency, economy, ease, and grammaticalization. On the repetition of adjacent elements and its influence on constituent formation, see Bybee and Scheibman (1999), Bybee (2002).

36. In an analogical framework the sequence Verb-Subject would be learned as a separate type, presumably linked to an interrogative function. That main verbs lost the ability to appear in this position, is related to the factor of frequency. With more and more periphrastic constructions appearing and with dummy *do* joining this group, the main verb simply no longer occurred enough in this position to be visible to the learning child. Its position, to use Lightfoot's (1991: 149) words, was indeed 'appropriated' by the new auxiliary.

37. It is quite possible that in its early use, dummy *do* also functioned as a perfective aspect marker. Denison (1985) presents a convincing case for this on the basis of co-occurrence restrictions in Middle English, pointing also to parallel perfective uses of a *do*-like verb cross-linguistically. Further support for a 'perfective' *do* can be found in Fischer (1992b: 274).

38. It is interesting in this connection to observe the remark made in Hopper and Traugott (2003: 141) in connection with morphologization: 'modal auxiliaries in English are grammaticalized out of earlier full verbs, but they have not (yet) become affixes'. It seems to me that it is unlikely they ever shall considering the system they function in.

39. In a similar way, empty slots are not possible, nor functional heads that are not lexically filled. This should not present a problem, however. Pickering and Barry (1991) show in connection with *wh*-movement and NP-movement that a 'gap-free' theory like Categorial Grammar accounts for the processing of gaps more successfully than a generative theory that works with movement and traces. In language processing hearers do not wait until a gap appears but associate the filler (the moved argument) immediately with the verb, whose argument it is. This leads to much less memory-overload, and it explains why some gapped structures are more likely to occur than others. The article also shows how important intonation is for gap recognition.

40. The old construction remained longest with verbs like *to know, doubt, believe*, etc. It may not be a coincidence that these verbs are all closely related to the modality field. In Fischer (1998: 77–8), I discussed the residual late position of *not* with these verbs in the light of negative raising. It was shown there too that the phenomenon of negative raising is itself closely related to modality (politeness).

41. The positioning of the adverb is probably related to the fact that VO began to be treated more and more as a unit. Warner (2004) shows that this need for V and O to be adjacent induced the increase of the propverb *do* in certain types of interrogative clauses, where the inversion of V and S led to the non-adjacency of V and O. By using *do* here, the order of VSO (where V is followed by two NPs) could be avoided, changing the order to *do* SVO.

42. This does not mean that some other adverbs cannot occur there too, but when they do they are usually in focus, compare *He came into the room then/Then he*

came into the room with *He thén came into the room* (and see also fn. 43). It is also possible that more and more adverbs will be drawn to this position (by semantic or structural analogy) once it has become a possible position for a number of adverbs that occur frequently. More research will be needed to make this clear.

43. Quirk *et al.* (1972: 458) write that time frequency and time duration adjuncts are often used as 'homonyms' for intensifiers. Not surprisingly such temporal adverbs also appear in the position typical for intensifiers.

44. The only ending still in use was *-st* with the second person singular *thou*, which at this time was being replaced by *you*.

45. Warner (p.c.) wonders whether such an analogical abduction is likely, mentioning the position of modals in interrogative clauses, where it is clearly different from adverb position. Acquisition studies might help to answer these questions. What needs to be investigated is how often the modal appears in questions (i.e. we need frequency counts of both types), and also whether questions and declaratives might be learned as separate construction types (cf. the Construction Grammar type of approach). Another feature preventing abduction could be the fact that the third person singular in standard English still has an inflectional *-s* when combined with an adverb, but not when combined with a modal. Note that the negative clauses are not a problem in this respect since the modal + negative were becoming what Warner has called 'anaphoric islands', together they could therefore be interpreted as one form (one adverb), see further below.

46. The contraction with *not* may have been even earlier (first half of the sixteenth century) as Rissanen (1999b) has suggested, based on compound spellings such as *didnot*, *shallnot*, and on the changing order of pronominal subject and *not* with auxiliaries, i.e. the change from *Did I not send* ... to *Did not I send* ...

47. An anonymous reviewer asks why, if this is the case, we do not also begin to 'find *n't* attached to adverbs (*John alwaysn't eats chocolates)'. The reason for this is that the *alwaysn't* slot has already been taken by other adverbs like *never*, preventing an analogical process.

5

From discourse to (morpho)syntax and vice versa: the case of clause fusion

5.0 Introduction: the Pragmatic and the Syntactic Modes

The approach in this chapter and the next will be a little different from the one taken in the previous chapters, in that I will concentrate on a number of problems in the grammaticalization approach, which I will discuss from a more formal point of view. In other words, I will use a formal approach more as a perspective on grammaticalization than as one contrasted with it. The reason for this is that some of the issues presented in these chapters are simply not part of the core concern in formal models. Where possible, however, the formal treatment of the topics will also be presented. Chapter 5 will be mainly concerned with the process of clause fusion, while Chapter 6 will deal with subjectification and the problem of scope.

The two theories under discussion approach the phenomenon of syntax in entirely different ways, which inevitably reflects on their stance towards discourse. Grammaticalization theory is primarily interested in how syntax arises out of the use of language (discourse) in communicative settings, while generative theory sees syntax as a basic schema of sentence formation, an 'already given', which gets fine-tuned into individual grammars with the help of the PLD a child is confronted with. The contrast between the two views on syntax in relation to discourse can be most simply stated as dynamic vs. static. From this point of view it is not surprising that the question of how discourse feeds grammar is only asked within the grammaticalization school of thought. It is probably correct to suggest that within the generative approach, the idea is that discourse feeds off syntax: that is sentences are primary and discourse follows from there.[1]

More agreement may be found between the two approaches when it comes to the evolution of syntax in proto-language. Newmeyer (2003: 74) remarks that syntax must have gradually evolved in the early period of language development and that one of the forces determining grammatical form may well have been 'discourse pressure', with the order of grammatical elements being mainly pragmatic to begin with; the other forces he recognizes are 'structure-concept iconicity' (form–meaning alignment), later followed by 'parsing pressure' (economy).[2] Such an evolvement of syntax can also be read in proposals by linguists such as Pinker (1994: 365ff.) and, more tentatively, Briscoe (2003), who believe that the LAD developed by gradual genetic assimilation.[3] Any such agreement, however, would only cover the initial stage, the idea being that once the LAD was in place, it was fixed, and grammar building would take place on the basis of this innate device and no longer *directly* from discourse and the context of situation.

Grammaticalization linguists concur with the generative linguists just quoted that grammar building emerged slowly in the course of evolution but in their view it *continues* to depend on discourse and context, both during the period of language acquisition and beyond (see e.g. Givón 1979: 4, 50ff., Deutscher 2000, Tomasello 2003a). For the adherents of Emergent Grammar (cf. Hopper 1987, 1998), this is indeed the only influence. Most functional linguists, however, do not deny the influence of some formal system of grammar, but only as one that is transmitted culturally and not genetically. This would leave quite some room for the renewed influence of discourse on language learning and language use, but it also entails that the conventional rules of language that have developed in each language over time play a crucial role, in the sense that children learning the language will discover these rules via the PLD offered to them (in §§3.3 and 3.4 above, I suggested that this may take place via token and later type-analogies).[4]

In this connection, Givón (1979: 223) has made a distinction between the 'Pragmatic Mode' and the 'Syntactic Mode', which represent two extreme poles in the mode of communication. Givón states that every human language knows both extremes and also the stages in between; in other words the two modes are *synchronically* present.[5] Besides this, Givón also argues that the same continuum functions diachronically in syntacticization and in first-language learning (for the latter, see Tomasello 2003a). There is a danger involved, however, in the adoption of this continuum as a unidirectional principle of syntacticization (=grammaticalization) in *language change*. It is important to provide proof by means of actual data that any such development indeed occurred. In other words, the intermediate historical stages between the pragmatic and the syntactic mode must be empirically traceable, and the grammaticalization itself must have left visible marks on the language output. The investigation must show that the (morpho)syntactic structure that arises is not simply a variant existing next to the old structure (used in different modes) but is actually *new* and has become an obligatory element of the language system in question; that is, it must show that the old (pragmatic mode) construction has been replaced also at the pragmatic pole of the continuum. For example, if it is correct that the Modern English genitive -*s* marker (which is now a clitic but was an inflection in Old English) indeed developed from a possessive pronoun *his/her*,[6] this can only be considered a case of grammaticalization if the new -*s* inflection has become an integral part of the grammar replacing the older construction in all modes. (Note that 'divergence' is different from this case: in divergence two forms also continue to exist side by side, but this variation is not one in 'mode' because the two variants have developed different grammatical functions, as in the case of the English numeral *one* and the indefinite article *a(n)* both from OE *ān*).

In this chapter we will look at a number of phenomena connected with the relation between discourse and grammar. Central in the discussion will be the issue of clause combining or clause fusion, which plays an important role in grammaticalization theory, but also in diachronic generative grammar, even though it is used for entirely different purposes and approached from entirely different angles.[7] To grammaticalizationists clause combining is of interest because it sheds light on historical processes of grammar building and on the existence of synchronic and typological variants within and between languages. Within this approach, clause combining involves both clause embedding as well as the chaining of clauses by means of parataxis, coordination, and hypotaxis.[8] This will be discussed in §5.1. In generative grammar clause fusion is first and foremost a (technical) process on the synchronic plane that takes place in the generation of sentences itself when surface structure or 'PF' is derived from a more abstract level of grammar (via such devices as Movement, Raising, Merge, etc.). Since generative grammar is mainly concerned with sentence grammar, the emphasis here is on clause embedding, the phenomenon of ellipsis in coordinated clauses, and the way relative clauses are linked to the main clause.[9] In §5.2, we will concentrate on clause embedding because there is an interesting link here with the historical grammaticalization approach in that the more abstract (underlying) structures are often a reflex of earlier historical stages.[10] Methodologically, this may be compared to the way underlying phonological structures were used in earlier generative phonology, as proposed in Chomsky and Halle's *The Sound Pattern of English* (1968). Here, modern surface forms like *wise/wisdom*, *divine/divinity* were said to have an underlying structure with a long [i:] vowel in the second syllable in order to account (by means of a more general rule) for the split into [ai] [w**ai**z] and [i] [w**i**zdəm]. Thus, the underlying or 'abstract' vowel in deep structure reflects an earlier diachronic stage, before the so-called Great Vowel Shift and a shortening-rule took place (both before 1500), which caused earlier [i:] to split up into [ai] and [i] respectively.

A number of side issues related to matters of discourse and grammaticalization are: the unexpected phenomenon (unexpected from the point of view of the grammaticalization principle of unidirectionality) of scope increase rather than decrease in the discourse-pragmatic subjectification cline (see the questions raised in §§3.2 and 4.2.2) and, in connection with subjectification, the development of conjunctions and pragmatic markers. These issues will be the subject of Chapter 6. The conventionalization and rigidification of word order, another important phenomenon in the shift from the pragmatic mode to the syntactic mode, will be touched upon in this chapter in connection with clause fusion and the development of auxiliary verbs (see §5.3), but the importance of word order will be further highlighted in Chapter 6.

5.1 Grammaticalization and clause combining (or clause fusion)

Matthiesen and Thompson (1988) argue that there is a fundamental analogy between the rhetorical structure of a text and the way clauses are combined. They hypothesize that '[c]lause combining in grammar has evolved as a grammaticalization of the rhetorical units in discourse defined by rhetorical relations' (1988: 301). Similarities are found both in structure and in scoping. In both, the elements that combine are interdependent, either as members of a list (in grammar shown as coordination or apposition) or as satellites dependent on a nucleus (in grammar shown as hypotaxis or subordination). Whether the nucleus or the satellite has scope over the other (or one satellite over another satellite) depends in both cases on the semantic nature of the relation. For instance, it is typical for relations of a 'rhetorical type' (expressing subjective attitudes having to do with felicity and persuasion) to have scope over the whole text or sentence (1988: 298).

This analogy between discourse and grammar is first of all important from a synchronic point of view. It shows differences in how one can build up a text or piece of discourse. One can make relations between clauses or 'idea units' (Chafe's (1985) term for 'clauses' in spoken discourse) explicit by means of lexical elements (complementizers, coordinators, resumptive pronouns), specific intonation contours,[11] or differences in word order,[12] all of which may join clauses together in one sentence-unit, or one can leave the relations implicit by letting the clauses function as grammatically independent units. Structural marking of (inter)dependency may also take place by means of adverbial or deictic particles, which leave the clauses structurally independent, but make the semantic relations between them explicit.

Variation in the use or non-use of structural marking is found most clearly between written and spoken discourse. Quite generally (and somewhat roughly) it can be said that there is a continuum in clause chaining from:

(1) (i) mere juxtaposition (parataxis, no marking) > (ii) juxtaposition with adverbial or deictic particles or resumptive (anaphoric) elements > (iii) hypotactic integration > (iv) complete integration (embedding)

with spoken discourse placed closer to the left end of the continuum, and written discourse to the right. The positions on the continuum could be, somewhat simply, illustrated as follows:

(2i)   I saw John at the garden centre—you know—John was buying flowers
(2ii)   I saw John there. He was buying flowers
(2iii) I saw John when he was buying flowers
(2iv)   I saw John buying flowers

Put in another way (cf. Givón's distinction mentioned above), one could say that spoken discourse is more strongly characterized by the 'pragmatic mode' and written discourse by the 'syntactic mode'. In the former, word order is looser (based on highlighting units of information rather than making use of conventional syntactic word order), and cohesion is achieved through the repetition of core sentence elements, loose connectives in the form of pragmatic markers like 'I mean', 'you know' (cf. Erman 1986), and through paralinguistic and prosodic cues. Another characteristic of spoken language is the focus on personal involvement, expressed also by pragmatic markers ('I think, I mean', etc.). Both these characteristics are clear from (3), representing snatches of dialogue taken from a BBC radio program:

(3)   I mean I think for example the polls the poll in the Sunday Times last weekend for example which showed that I think something I think like sixty-two percent of people believe that believe then that the Government would privatize the health service. ... In terms of people more and more people are going into the private sector encouraged by the Government encouraged by the kind of statement that John Major made two weeks ago. (ICE-GB: S1B-039 #47, #88)

Written discourse, on the other hand, is focused more on subject matter, and cohesion is both lexicalized and grammaticalized according to strict conventional rules (cf. Tannen 1985). Loosely connected sentences; like the main (*I mean* ...) and the *which*-clause at the beginning of (3) (the main clause is left 'dangling'), and the listing of two non-finite clauses by means of the repetition of *encouraged* rather than the use of a coordinator, are not found in written texts. Tighter cohesion in the written mode is thus achieved by the introduction of more explicit marking (e.g. via the grammaticalization of pragmatic markers and discourse particles into co- and subordinators, the conventionalization of word order, etc.) but also by the deletion of redundant elements, such as lexical repetitions and resumptive pronouns (cf. the discussion in §1.2.2).

Similar differences in 'mode' can be found typologically, diachronically, and ontogenetically. Mithun (1988), writing on coordination, notes that all languages show similar intonation patterns and intonation breaks to indicate unitary events and events that are conceptually distinct, but that languages may differ greatly in the amount of explicit structural marking. She believes that there is a connection between explicit marking and the development of literacy.[13] Written texts require additional signalling since they go beyond the immediate context of utterance. Intonation and paralinguistic devices have to be replaced by lexical elements, and idea-units have to be explicitly linked since the text must also be understood by a more general audience, who are not aware of the cultural and pragmatic circumstances and presuppositions on which the discourse is based. Mithun shows by means of examples mainly from Amerindian languages how such explicit markers develop out of frequently used general discourse particles, which are optional at first but later become obligatory. For example, in many languages, a completive particle meaning 'already' comes to be used to indicate sequential actions. Through frequent usage, the particle may become fixed in position and increasingly compulsory and begin to function like a conjunction, effectively integrating the two idea-units into one sentence-unit (Mithun 1988: 343). The grammatical conventions that thus develop depend on the form, the frequency, the meaning, and the position of the original particle, as well as on general formal characteristics of the language in question. In many cases too, oral languages, when they develop a written form, borrow markers from neighbouring languages which are already literate, as happened, for example, with English *because*, adopted from French *cause* via the hybrid phrase *by cause that* when a new written standard developed in the Middle English period (it replaced earlier, less fully developed phrases that could be used as adverbials as well as conjunctions, see fn. 22 below).

In the process of language acquisition, children first learn to communicate in concrete situations where the pragmatic mode is sufficient because the things talked about are directly present in the situational context (cf. Clark 2003; Tomasello 2003a). The more symbolic syntactic mode only fully develops after the age of 5 when children begin to tell stories (Tomasello 2003a: 270ff.). They then learn how to use tense and aspect, and complex constructions to comply with the demands of narrative discourse. Linguistic forms that have been learned before, but only with exophoric reference (i.e. with direct reference to something present in the contextual situation) now acquire endophoric reference. For example, pronouns, which were at first only used deictically (Tomasello 2003a: 205–7), now begin to be used anaphorically. Tomasello adds (p. 275) that the use of such 'devices are uniformly late acquisitions, and may even depend to some extent on the acquisition of *literacy skills during early schooling*' (emphasis added).

Building up a typology of clause linkage by looking at both written and spoken modes of a language, at typologically different languages and at different historical stages of a language, as for example Lehmann (1988) has done, is in itself a neutral exercise. The parallel clause-linking continua that Lehmann sketches have two poles, a pole of maximal compression and a pole of maximal elaboration. It is easy to see, however, how a continuum, such as indicated in (1), comes to be considered a historically necessary, *unidirectional* development in a grammaticalization context, where, as we have seen in §3.2, the *reduction* of linguistic elements (in form, in scope, in meaning) is considered a common property of all *clines*. The question that arises is, is a reduction in clause structure (a construction-type), indicated as a possible path in (1), similar to the reduction of fully referential lexical elements (i.e. tokens) into grammatical ones, which forms the core of the diachronic notion of grammaticalization?

A unidirectional development in clause-chaining or clause combining, based on the continuum in (1), might be justified in cases of language change where there is enough philological evidence for such a process. Grammaticalization research has produced a number of 'successful' diachronic cases (e.g. the development of relative clauses out of main clauses with a deictic marker, cf. Hopper and Traugott 2003: 197, and for more references, Heine and Kuteva 2002: 115). Whether these cases really stick remains to be seen. Deutscher (2001) has pointed out that this particular scenario does not work in Akkadian, and he doubts whether it works in the Germanic languages.[14] In most cases discussed so far there are simply not enough empirical details to prove such a development. Yet, this has not stopped linguists from also applying this cline to cases where no historical stages are available at all. Thus, because of the similarities that are found between the diachronic stages in one language and the linguistic variants found typologically, the cline comes to be treated as a tool for (cf. Hopper 1991: 20; Heine and Kuteva 2002: 1) or even a principle in diachronic reconstruction. The danger is then that a particular integrated or compressed clause structure in a language is interpreted as the last stage on the clause-combining cline, and that, on that basis, an earlier biclausal or paratactic structure is assumed, for which there is no empirical evidence.[15] In Heine and Kuteva (2002), for instance, only the immediate structural context, the synchronic source concepts and the semantic-pragmatic role that lexical elements play are considered for many of the examples of grammaticalization paths they have collected in their *Lexicon*. By placing such synchronic instances under one heading with historical developments that have taken place with similar source concepts/structures in other languages, the suggestion is made that all these developments follow the same paths. The idea of a general unidirectionality is further strengthened by Source-Target lists given in their Appendix. Other formal properties of the language systems concerned, which may also influence the way a construction develops or has developed, are not considered. More problematic is that these postulated reconstructions may in turn get used to provide proof for the reality of the clause-combining cline itself, making the exercise dangerously circular.

What gets snowed under in such a set-up is the possibility of clause elaboration. Lehmann's clause-linkage continua scheme (1988: 217) leaves open the possibility that clauses may become elaborated as well as compressed, that is that the continuum may go both ways.[16] A good example of elaboration is discussed by Lambrecht (1988) concerning a change that has taken place in spoken French (and to some extent also in other Romance languages), whereby the original main clause, with a typical SVO structure as in (4), has been replaced by a cleft *bi*clausal construction as in (5):[17]

(**4**) Les   yeux   me   font   mal
        The   eyes   me   cause   pain
(**5**) J'ai   les   yeux   qui   m' font   mal
        I have   the   eyes   that   me cause   pain
        'My eyes hurt' (cf. Lambrecht 1988: 137)

A linguist with no knowledge of the history of French, and armed with a unidirectional principle of clause combining, might easily conclude that (5) must be an older stage than (4), because (4) shows 'reduction'. Another example of clause elaboration is given by Keller (1998: 221ff.), who shows that Modern German *weil* 'because', is undergoing a development from a subordinating conjunction into a coordinating one. This is shown by the word order of the *weil*-clause, which as a coordinating clause has developed a Verb-second structure, usual only in main clauses and coordinated main clauses (see also Chapter 6). A rather similar thing may have happened with English *for* in an earlier period, which according to Jespersen (1940: 392) at first was a subordinating conjunction, and later in Middle English came to be used as a coordinator. Mitchell (1985: §3037), however, believed that it could already occur in both functions in Old English. A possible case of clause elaboration of the gerund will be discussed below in §5.3.

Deutscher (2000) discusses a case of clause elaboration in the history of Akkadian, (a North-Eastern Semitic language), over a period of 2000 years (2500–500 BC). He shows that in the oldest stages there were very few finite complements, and that more elaborate clausal strategies began to replace earlier nominal strategies. Most importantly, he makes clear that this particular development should be seen as structural *replacement* rather than a structural unidirectional development since the replacement takes place within a functional domain. What could follow from this is that the continuum given in (1) is likely to work structurally in only one direction, with the reverse direction involving functional replacement rather than structural change. In another case he shows that complement clauses arose not from earlier paratactic clauses, as is often presumed, but from subordinate adverbial clauses (see also fn.14).

A similar process may be involved in the acquisition of complex sentences by children. Van Valin (2000) shows that children acquire non-finite complement clauses before finite ones following what he has termed the 'Interclausal Relations Hierarchy' (IRH). According to this hierarchy, 'junctures involving sub-clausal units [i.e. involving the predicate ('nucleus') or the predicate with its semantic arguments ('core')] will appear before those involving whole clauses' (2000: 519). He tests the IRH on a number of language acquisition databases in seven languages (from different language families), and finds in all cases that subclausal levels of juncture will appear before clausal ones, and that the semantic relations coded on this subclausal level are also conceptually the tightest relations (i.e. relations involving causation and desire), thus providing an iconic relationship between syntactic and semantic bonding. Conversely, the loosest types of semantic bonding (e.g. sequential actions) are the first to appear on a clausal level.

The discussion of the clause-combining cline and the grammaticalization of clause linkers in Hopper and Traugott (2003: 176ff.) both strongly suggest—through the emphasis on clause fusion rather than clause elaboration—that the most integrated clause-types are historically later. They provide examples from the history of English, Akkadian, and Hittite (one of the oldest Indo-European languages) of finite complements and relative clauses 'show[ing] a clear continuum from looser to tighter syntactic structuring' (2003: 194). They conclude that '[t]here is substantial evidence that in most languages and most instances there is a continuum of development from less to more unified clause combining' (2003: 209), 'from less to more bonded' (2003: 211). In the light of this discussion, one almost automatically reads their examples given here in (6), which initiate the topic of clause combining but are not explicitly discussed in terms of a pathway, as instances of a similar cline:

(**6a**)   We realize that you have to make a profit.
(**6b**)   His wife only pretended to believe his implausible story.
(**6c**)   Portia really enjoys walking along the beach.
(**6d**)   Numerous witnesses heard the bomb explode.

(Hopper and Traugott 2003: 179)

What we see here, too, is how the verb in the finite complement clause (6a) loses its verbal features of tense, agreement, etc., and becomes more and more reduced, from a *to*-infinitive (6b), to an *-ing* form (6c), and finally to a bare stem (6d).

The *general* idea that a non-finite complement originates from a biclausal structure is clearly advocated in Givón (1979: 214), who writes: 'The complement verb in many languages is non-finite, as in English, and this [i.e. the development from a subordinate finite clause into an embedded non-finite one] involves a marked reduction in the tense–aspect morphology, lack of subject agreement, and often some special infinitival-nominal morphology', and 'the possibility is still open that *all* equi-NP verb complements in language arose via such a process [i.e. from a loose, paratactic concatenation via syntacticization into non-finite embedding]'.

Of course, in order to show that cases such as (6) do represent a grammaticalization path, one would have to look much more closely at the behaviour of each single matrix verb (or of each—semantically and syntactically—coherent class of verbs) and its complementation patterns, and one would want to see a development where the various stages emerge in a chronological order. I will indicate some of the problems concerning (6) with some verbs and their complements from the history of English. When we consider the possible stages of (6) in the light of the diachronic development of (physical) perception-verb constructions in English (a final stage for these is given in 6d), we note that already in Old English, types (6d),

(6c), and (6a) co-existed after this verb-class, and that they still do in Present-day English. In this case there is therefore not much historical evidence for a *path* from a loose construction to a tight one (see also below).

Similarly, when we look at the behaviour of another group of complement-taking verbs in the earliest stages of the English language, that is the verbs of persuading and urging, we find that they occur both with a *þæt*-clause and a *to*-infinitive (cf. types 6a, 6b), as shown with the verb *nydan* 'urge, compel' in (7a–b) respectively (cf. Los 2005: ch. 8). It is unlikely, however, that the *to*-infinitive is a stage on the path away from the *þæt*-clause. Rather, as argued by Los (2005: 45–6), the *to*-infinitive is a development from a purposive *to*-PP consisting of a verbal noun, as illustrated in (7c).

(7a) Þær hy   mon nydde þæt hy   deofulgyld[ACC SG/PL] weorðedon.
                              (Mart 5 (Kotzor)Oc 8, A.5, cf. Los 2005: 200)
      there them 'one' forced that they devil-worship   worshipped
      'there they were forced to worship idols'

(7b) Ðone nydde Decius se kasere   deofolgeld[ACC SG/PL] to begangenne[INF]
                              (Mart 5 (Kotzor)Se 14, A.2, cf. Los 2005: 200)
      him forced Decius the emperor devil-worship   to practise
      'the emperor Decius forced him to practise idolatry'

(7c) Þa yrsode se dema ... ond hine þa nydde to deofolgylde[GEN PL]
      then raged the ruler ... and him then forced to devil-worship
      begonge[DAT].
      practice (Mart 5 (Kotzor)Ap28,A.6, cf. Los 2005: 200)
      'then the ruler became angry and forced him to the practice of idols'

Los makes clear that the *to*-infinitive came to be used more and more as a replacement of both the verbal noun PP and the *þæt*-clause because it had a number of advantages over the other two constructions. Unlike the verbal noun, the infinitive was not constrained by the 'random workings of derivational processes' (Los 2005: 201) so that any verb could be selected in the *to*-infinitival structure. In the *þæt*-clause, tense and agreement were expressed lexically but this did not give it an advantage over the *to*-infinitive in that both tense and agreement were fully controlled by the tense features and the matrix object of the main clause. It became thus more 'economical' to use a *to*-infinitive once this infinitive had acquired verbal features (for this, see below). Moreover, the mood of the complement clause after these verbs was often in the subjunctive, and the sense of 'potentiality/uncertainty' that it conveyed could be carried as well by the future-oriented (purposive) *to*-infinitive.[18]

We would have to conclude then, taking these details of the Old English system into account, that there was no straight, unidirectional pathway from *þæt*-clause to *to*-infinitive. What we have here is structural *replacement* (and not structural *development*) within a functional domain (cf. Deutscher 2000 above). The *to*-infinitive became an option under rather precise conditions, one of which was the replacement of the more awkward *to*-PP. The similarity of the *to*-PP and the *to*-infinitive (which was originally an action noun in the dative) makes it highly likely that analogy played an important role in this replacement.

There is perhaps more evidence for a grammaticalization path in the development of 'that'-complements from independent clauses in Old English, which Hopper and Traugott (2003: 190–4) use as an illustration of a clause-fusion pathway. They argue that the older constructions are of the type illustrated in (8), and that a new complex clause-type (9) developed from there:

(8)   Ða   on morgenne gehierdun þæt þæs   cyninges þegnas þe   him
      then in morning   heard   that of-the king   thanes who him
      beæftan wærun þæt se   cyning ofslægen wæs[INDIC],
      behind were that the   king   slain   was,
      þa   ridon hie þider. (ChronA(Plummer)755.23)
      then   rode they thither
      'Then/when in the morning the king's thanes who had been left behind heard (that) that the king had been killed, then they rode up there'

(9)   ...   þohte   gif he   hi   ealle ofsloge[SUBJ] þæt se   an   ne
      ...   thought if he   them all   slew   that that one not
      ætburste þe   he sohte. (ÆCHom I 5 219.72)
      escape   whom   he sought
      '... thought that if he slew them all, the one he sought would not escape'

Evidence for this development they see in the fact that in (8) a demonstrative pronoun *þæt* is still present in the main clause with the result that the complement, also introduced by *þæt*, is not (yet) embedded into the main clause. This 'extra' pronoun is absent in (9). Further evidence for clause fusion, they find in the fact that the complement clause in (9) has a subjunctive verb, *ofsloge*, which is a mood typical of subordinate clauses, while the equivalent clause in (8) has an indicative verb, *wæs*.

Neat as this may look at first sight, there are quite a few problems connected with the presumed development. First of all, no quantitative evidence is provided that the 'double *þæt*' construction (8) occurs more frequently in earlier than in late Old English. Secondly, it is quite possible that the 'extra' *þæt* in (8) is used in this particular example for processing reasons since there is quite a gap between the matrix verb *gehierdun* and the complement clause. Thirdly, the use of the subjunctive in (9) is in itself not very telling: after a subjective verb like 'think' (expressing uncertainty), a subjunctive is more likely to occur than after a more factual verb like 'hear' used in (8). Fourthly, the possibility is not discussed that the different structures of (8) and (9) may be due to differences between the spoken and the written mode rather than to a chronological development. Philologists have shown that (8) occurs in a text that goes back to an oral story. Other oral features, such as the confusing use of the pronoun *hie* 'they' to refer to three different groups of people in the story, indeed speak for an oral source.[19] Moreover the use of an extra (pleonastic) pronoun *it* or *that* still occasionally occurs in spoken English today, as the instances in (10) show:

(10a)   I felt the need to express *that* <,> *that* I was concerned
                                        (ICE-GB s1a-060-165)

(10b)   ... if you got *that* accepted *that* that pavilion was sacrosanct to the men
                                        (ICE-GB s1b-021-039)

(10c)   and I repeat *it* *that* I believe it starts in a conscious way
                                        (ICE-GB s1b-070-146)

Because of the focus on a grammaticalization path and the neglect of other formal factors present in the grammatical system at the time, other possible causal factors are not considered. What needs to be investigated is the possibility that a double *that* may have come to be avoided in English as a result of the word order change from SOV > SVO, which took place around this time. In the new SVO order, the demonstrative pronoun *that*, as the object of the main verb, would normally appear right in front of the *that*-complement. This not only produces an awkward 'echo',[20] it also renders the use of *that* unnecessary in terms of processing ease since the complement now immediately follows. It is noteworthy in this respect, that a double use of *dat/daß* 'that' (or 'it' + 'that') is more natural in spoken Modern Dutch and German, where the two 'that's do not as a rule occur together in sequence:[21]

(11)	Ik	heb	*dat/'t*	steeds	gezegd	*dat*	ik	dat	nog	doen	moet
	Ich	habe	*das*	immer	gesagt',	*daß*	ich	das	noch	tun	muß
	I	have	*that/it*	always	said	*that*	I		that	still	do	must

'I have always said that I must still do that'

Note that the double use of *that that* in phrases such as *He thought that that's the one* is still quite common, but here the two *that*s are phonetically dissimilar, the second *that* is always strongly stressed.

One of the problems concerning the 'pathway' Hopper and Traugott accept with reference to (8)–(9), is that this grammaticalization only concerns a reduction in clause structure. Since it involves an abstract 'type' (a rule, schema, or superset) and not a 'token' (the 'core' verb may be different each time), the usual grammaticalization reduction features, such as semantic bleaching, phonetic reduction, decategorization, scope decrease, etc. are more difficult to discern in this process. Even though most functional linguists accept that a construction-type has some semantic content (cf. Langacker 1987, 1995; Croft 1991; Goldberg 1995; Tomasello 2003b: 99; Croft and Cruse 2004)—and it is even an axioma in Construction Grammar—it would still be a content of a rather general nature and therefore difficult to 'reduce' except by some form of ellipsis. Similarly, it is difficult to see how there is a change in scope. Hopper and Traugott (2003: 185) seem to suggest that there is an *in*crease in scope, contra the usual unidirectional cline leading to scope decrease (cf. Table 3.2 above). They write: 'typical of hypotactic developments … is the recruitment to connective function of deictics and other demonstratives. The motivation here is the extension of deictic reference from entities referred to in the non-linguistic world to anaphors and cataphors of NPs and then to anaphors or cataphors of propositions (clauses)'. This suggests that they recognize an increase in scope ('extension of deictic reference') concerning the element *þæt* from single 'NPs' to 'propositions' when *þæt* becomes a 'connective'. It seems to me that the use of a demonstrative pronoun like *þæt* in (8) could always refer to an object *or situation* in the non-linguistic world, and hence also to a proposition (an idea-unit) as well as an NP, so that the change from (8) to (9) cannot really be seen as an increase in scope.

It might be argued that the clause linker, *þæt*, itself grammaticalizes from a demonstrative pronoun to a phonetically reduced connective (or 'complementizer'), bleached of its deictic sense. Two comments may be made here. First, it is quite possible that both *þæt*s were already reduced in this construction (both elements are reduced in Modern German and Dutch in (11)), and that quite simply one of them was dropped. Secondly, it is also possible that the second *þæt* in (8) never was a true demonstrative. It may simply have been correlative with the first *þæt* to indicate a link; a (deictic) device, in other words, to monitor the flow of speech (rather similar to the use of Tok Pisin *ia* illustrated in (21) in §1.2.2). In Old English such correlatives were still in frequent use to indicate clause linkage, for example *þa/þonne ... þa/þonne* 'then ... then'/ 'then ... when'.[22]

If we grant that the reduction of *þæt* may not be so relevant in this particular case (but see for some other cases of the 'grammaticalization' of clause linkers below), then the grammaticalization involves mainly the integration of the second clause unit into the first one. What change does that involve? Does it involve changes typical for grammaticalization, as distinguished in §3.2? It could be argued that in our Old English case, it involves a change in word order, that is the new 'complement' acquires the word order typical of subordinate clauses. But, if there was a word order change, the question arises whether it was directly linked to the grammaticalization. Hopper and Traugott (2003: 191) note that in the early example (8) with double *þæt* the word order was already 'something more than merely paratactic'. They imply that the word order change is part of the grammaticalization process but that the earlier stage with the still paratactic order has been lost to us. In connection with this, I would like to draw attention to two things: (i) to the word order change itself and (ii) to the nature of the 'grammaticalization' of the clause linker, in combination with some examples that seem to contradict a close link between its 'grammaticalization' and the word order change.

As to (i), it seems likely that word order in Old English was still pretty much pragmatic, that is that it had mainly an information-signalling function. We see that the order in main and subordinate clauses may differ in Old English, but it is not fully fixed as per clause-type. The order may still be to a large extent discourse-oriented depending on topic-comment rather than on conventional grammatical rules. In such a system subordinate clauses may have a different order for discourse reasons since they usually provide descriptive background information.[23] They are not plot advancing, as main clauses generally are. Probably as a result of literacy and increasing conventionalization and fixation of grammatical rules, the order of different types of clauses and phrases came to be fixed in the form in which they were most frequent, and this could then become a way of differentiating between construction-types. Thus in Dutch and

German, subordinate clauses slowly developed towards fixed SOV, in contrast to main clauses which, although they still show more variety (SVO, OVS, XVS, etc.), are generally V2 (except in questions). In English almost all clause-types eventually became SVO.

What I am suggesting is that the 'grammaticalization' involved in clause combining is difficult to link directly to a change in word order. We see a fixation of a word order that was probably frequent in 'idea-units' of language containing additional background information. The clause in (8), whether syntactically dependent or not, may already have had an order typical for clauses that provide background information. In other words, more complete integration may not have altered the word order at all.

Turning now to (ii), to what extent is the grammaticalization of clause linkers, truly grammaticalization? Is it not rather a matter of lexicalization?[24] Let us have a look at Hopper and Traugott's (2003: 90–2) discussion of the grammaticalization of the noun *while* (OE *hwil* 'time, hour') to a connective. They give an example from an early (12) and a late stage (13):

(**12**) &   wicode þær *þa   hwile* [ACC] *þe*   man þa   burg   worhte
and camped there that time   that 'one' that fortress built
&   getimbrede ...   (ChronA(Plummer)913.3)
and erected
'and camped there during the time that the fortress was built and erected'

(**13**) &   ðæt lastede þa   *xix* wintre   *wile*   Stephne was king
(ChronE(Irvine)1137.32)
and that lasted   those 19   winters while/during time Stephen was king
'and that went on for nineteen years while Stephen was king'

In the early example (12), the word order of the clause introduced by *þa hwile þe* is SOV (*man þa burg worhte*), that is the word order found frequently in subordinate clauses, while in the later example (13) the word order is more typical of that of a main clause (subordinate order would have been *Stephne king was*). This is thus the opposite of what one would expect if the change in word order *is* part of the clause-combining grammaticalization process. The examples seem to indicate that the grammaticalization of the clause linker may have to be considered separately from the issue of clause combining because the only empirical indication of 'combining', that is a change in word order, does not play the role required by the theory. Obviously, more research is necessary to find out whether a link can be established. Concentrating on these two instances, however, it appears that the more important difference between (12) and (13) is the change in the phonetic *shape* of the linker, from *þa hwile þe* to *wile*. If we assume, with the theory, that word order must play a role, then we would have to conclude on the basis of these two instances that the linker in (12) functions as a conjunction, more so than the linker in (13), in spite of the fact that the latter looks more grammaticalized in form because of its reduction. It seems then that the clause combining itself may take place without the phonetic reduction of the conjunction.

If the word order change and the change in the form of the conjunction are separate issues, there seems to be no reason not to treat the change from *þa hwile þe* to *wile* simply as a case of lexicalization. Lexicalization always involves a single token or group of tokens, which, through frequent use or semantic specialization, become a more integrated but at the same time less transparent whole. I fail to see much difference between cases such as *while* and cases such as *cupboard*: both have lost the earlier link to the noun(s) they incorporate,[25] through phonetic reduction and semantic or grammatical specialization. *While* no longer specifically refers to a 'time' or 'hour', and *cupboard* no longer is exclusively connected with 'cups'—since all kinds of things, not just cups, may go into a cupboard—or with 'board', since it no longer refers to the surface on which cups were placed but to a cabinet in which they are placed. The reason why *while* is said to have undergone grammaticalization rather than lexicalization must be because it has been connected to the phenomenon of clause combining. However, if the full phrase already functioned as a clause linker before any other changes occurred, one could simply state that the conjunctive phrase became reduced in a process of lexicalization.

One objection could be made against the idea of *while* as a case of lexicalization, and that is that it involves decategorization (from noun to complementizer), which is typical of grammaticalization and not involved in 'normal' cases of lexicalization. According to Traugott and Dasher (2002: 283) and Brinton and Traugott (2005: ch. 4), lexicalization only involves developments into or between major lexical categories (so they include cases of compounding (*cupboard*) and of what others have called 'degrammaticalization', as in 'to *down* a beer', where an adverb has become a verb), while developments into functional categories must be the result of grammaticalization. According to a more neutral interpretation of lexicalization, such as used by Keller (cf. fn. 25), any item whose meaning can no longer be inferred causally or by association—that is has become more symbolic, non-transparent—is a lexicalized item. Thus, for Keller, lexicalization simply means that that item has become part of the lexicon of a language (this also follows the definition given in the *OED*). The likelihood that lexicalization in this wider sense involves *de*categorization is of course much smaller since fewer items are needed at the grammatical end of the lexicon.

Brinton and Traugott (2005: 89–90) acknowledge this wider sense of lexicalization, which they describe as 'institutionalized adoption into the lexicon'. Seeing the lexicon as an 'inventory' of all forms in a language, this definition of lexicalization would then include forms resulting from grammaticalization. They add, however, that such a broad interpretation 'obscures the differences among types and functions of forms and moreover obscures the processes by which they come to be structured within the inventory. To account for such differences it is necessary to distinguish between lexicalization in a more narrow sense and grammaticalization'. In their discussion, therefore, they stipulate what grammaticalization and lexicalization in the narrow sense entail: 'The output of lexicalization is a "lexical", i.e., contentful item that is stored in the inventory and must be learned by speakers' (ibid. p. 96), while the 'output of grammaticalization is a "grammatical," i.e., functional form' (2005: 99). Similarly, the input to lexicalization and grammaticalization both involve items from the inventory, but in lexicalization these 'tend to be highly specified semantically' (2005: 96), while in grammaticalization they 'must be semantically general' (2005: 99).

The processes that occur in both are described as highly similar, and indeed Brinton and Traugott emphasize the 'parallelism' (see their section 4.4). I think, however, that the differences between the two processes (which they call 'minimal parallelism') can be better explained with reference to the different *levels* on which the processes take place than by stipulating what is 'lexical' and what is 'functional'. Thus, one of their minimal parallels to distinguish grammaticalization from lexicalization is 'decategorialization'. This, however, happens typically with changes on the more abstract token/type-level, and is therefore naturally bound up with the other minimal parallels of 'bleaching', 'subjectification' (because more general meanings are prey to pragmatic inferencing), and with greater 'frequency' and 'productivity'. In other words these differences *depend* on the basic token/type-level that the process starts out from and not on any differences *within the processes* themselves. Brinton and Traugott's discussion of the differences between the two processes is not really convincing because it depends on a too facile distinction between lexical and functional material; in fact the discussion obscures the fact that the processes taking place are to a very large extent the same (cf. Himmelmann 2004).

The whole question of the difference between lexicalization and grammaticalization then becomes a terminological one (cf. also fn. 24); it depends on one's theoretical stance towards the distinction between lexical words and function words. If one believes that there is no clear-cut dividing line between functional and lexical categories, as most functional linguists do, then it seems somewhat illogical to wish to make a strict distinction between lexicalization and grammaticalization in the development of clause linkers such as *while*.

To sum up, lexicalization and grammaticalization clearly have a lot in common. Both involve further symbolization, but the former takes place within the lexicon because it involves tokens and hence the learning of these is item-based, while the latter takes place on a more abstract level (in the system of grammar), since it involves construction-types (which may partly consist of tokens); the learning of this is rule- or schema-based. When tokens only are involved, it makes sense to talk about lexicalization. The important question then in the case of *while* is whether the clause embedding and the change in the token of the complementizer are part of the same process or should be seen as separate. More research is needed here. When abstract types are involved (e.g. a combination of the category Modal and Verb), or a combination of a token and a type (e.g. the combination of the token *going to* with the forms of BE and the infinitive functioning as part of the type), or the combination of a token *mente* with an Adjective as type), we have a more regular case of grammaticalization, provided it observes the relevant parameters in Table 3.2.

In the next subsection I want to look at some phenomena that can be connected with clause fusion in generative theory; cases that have been admitted both as diachronic changes and as synchronic derivational processes.[26] Most of these are also seen as typical cases of grammaticalization within the grammaticalization approach. All of these instances involve tokens that have grammaticalized as part of a construction-type. In this respect they are distinct from the development of the *þæt*-complements, discussed in the present subsection, where it was difficult to link the change in the token directly to a change in clause-type.

5.2 Clause fusion as a synchronic and diachronic process in generative grammar

The generative processes of Subject-raising, Verb-raising, and Equi NP-deletion are all examples of processes whereby elements of an underlying (non-finite) clause become 'expressed' (through movement, fusion, control, or merge) in the sentence-unit on the surface.[27] I will refer to these processes as clause fusion, even though in the generative model, only Verb-raising is seen as an actual case of clause fusion (cf. fn. 7 above). The general idea, whatever the type of generative model being used,[28] is that surface clauses such as *They seemed to understand the situation* and *They tried to understand the situation*, derive from an underlying biclausal structure with the subject of the lower infinitival verb raised into or controlled by the subject position of the higher, matrix verb. Subject-raising takes place when the matrix verb has a structural subject position but does not fill it with an argument of its own because it cannot assign a thematic (or θ-) role to its subject; hence the thematic subject of the infinitive is moved into the matrix subject position. With control verbs there is no movement because both matrix and infinitival verb assign their own thematic subject roles. Because the infinitive has no structural subject position (since it is tenseless), the subject surfaces lexically only in the matrix clause, and controls the empty subject (PRO) of the infinitival complement. Subject-raising is shown in (14) for the P&P and Minimalist models respectively (the structure of control verbs is given below in (15)).

(**14**) $_S$[they$_i$ seemed $_S$[t_i to understand the situation]]

    $_{IP}$[they$_i$ seemed $_{IP}$[t_{i1}[to $_{VP}$[t_i $_V$[understand the situation]]]]]

The underlying biclausal structure is held to be necessary in (14) in order to account for, among other things, the behaviour of reflexives, which require an antecedent within the same clause. The biclausal structure thus ensures that *They seemed to me to understand themselves* is grammatical, while *They seemed to me to understand myself* is not. It is also felt to capture the similarity with the finite clause complement structure *It seemed that they understood the situation* (cf. Radford 1988: 435). In the latter case the biclausal synchronic derivation matches a diachronic process. It is generally agreed by historical linguists that the raised construction with *seem* is historically younger than the biclausal *it*-construction.

Synchronically, however, there may be a problem with a biclausal analysis for both these types because of the fact that the finite and non-finite structures of Subject-raising verbs are *not* so similar semantically or pragmatically, as is clear from a perusal of examples from the ICE-GB corpus. In terms of modality and evidentiality, the *it*-construction is much more strongly impersonal and shows a higher degree of uncertainty than the raised construction. *It seems that they are wrong* could be paraphrased as 'It appears to be the case that they are wrong' (i.e. it is generally thought/ rumoured that they are wrong), while *They seem to be wrong* is more subjective and the uncertainty expressed is hence more open to discussion (the degree of evidentiality is less strong): that is it could be paraphrased as 'I think they may be wrong'. *Seem* in the latter case functions almost like a modal auxiliary, reducing its referential semantic impact, whereas in the *it*-construction *seem* functions like a main verb, with consequently a stronger semantic content. The difference is rather similar to the effect that Negative-raising has: the raised construction, for example *I don't think it's true*, being much less authoritative (more subjective and hence more polite) than the non-raised one, *I think it's not true*.[29] To bring out this pragmatic-semantic difference, it would make sense to see the 'raised' construction as processed monoclausally rather than via an underlying subordinate clause.[30] In an analogical framework the raised constructions would then align with other Aux-Verb constructions in English (e.g. with the epistemic construction *They may be wrong*) to which it is very close both semantically and formally (on the surface, that is), but which are not considered to be biclausal in generative grammar.[31]

Other cases involving clause fusion are Verb-raising and Subject-control. Verb-raising has been suggested as a synchronic process for a number of constructions in German and Dutch, and by van Kemenade (1992) also for some modal-verb constructions in Old English, which other linguists have analysed as Subject-control. I will concentrate on the Old English modal verbs since in that case the *loss* of clause fusion, that is the loss of a biclausal structure (via Verb-raising or Subject-control) has also been used to account for a diachronic process. Most generative linguists (Allen 1975; Lightfoot 1979; Roberts 1985, 1993a, 1993b; van Kemenade 1987, 1992; Roberts and Roussou 2002) have argued that modal verbs in Old English were main verbs functioning as Subject-control verbs in a biclausal structure with an embedded PRO subject, as follows:

(15) ... cp[gif ip[hie ɪ'[ɪ[ɪp[PRO ɪ[þa   blotan]]]   mehten]]]
      ...   if   they   PRO   those   sacrifice   could
      ... 'if they could sacrifice those'(Or 5 2.115.14, cf. van Kemenade 1992: 294)[32]

Van Kemenade (1992: 299ff.) argues that some Old English main-verb modals when combined with an infinitive are better analysed as Verb-raising constructions in order to account for the occurrence of discontinuous infinitival complements such as italicized in (16), which Subject-control structures do not allow (the idea being that subordinate clause constituents cannot be moved across a maximal clause boundary).

(16) ... þæt   he   *þæs* gewinnes   mehte   *mare*   gefremman
                                            (Or 25 4713; Van Kemenade 1992: 300)
      ... that he   that   victory   could   more   achieve
      ' ... so that he could achieve the victory further'

Most generative linguists propose a *monoclausal* structure for the *Present-day* English modals, which implies that they also see, what I have called, clause fusion as a diachronic process. Again the question arises whether these constructions should be considered biclausal in the first place (a question also raised by Denison (1990: 162), but without a definitive answer). I will suggest in §5.4 that the bare infinitival constructions after Old English modal verbs, which were part of a monoclausal structure originally, remained monoclausal all the way through, that is that there is no reason to assume a change of structure from monoclausal into biclausal when the bare infinitive changed from nominal to verbal status. I will also argue that some of the *epistemic* modals may have started off *biclausally*, *pace* van Kemenade (1992), who suggests the opposite in both respects. Her suggestion is that the Old English epistemic modals were already Aux (so monoclausal), and that the root and deontic modals were full verbs operating in a biclausal structure (involving either Raising or Control).

Concerning the structure of these early infinitivals, it is interesting to note that Tomasello (2003a: 245–9) reports that certain types of English infinitival clauses (e.g. with semi-modals such as *have to*, *got to*, *want to* and control verbs such as *like to*, *try to*, etc.) emerge early in language acquisition, long before finite complement clauses develop. Tomasello suggests that these infinitival constructions are processed monoclausally, like modal-verb constructions, and contain only one proposition. In other words, it is not necessarily the case that infinitivals are underlyingly clausal, as seems to be almost automatically assumed within the generative model.

Tomasello's findings indicate that infinitivals need not be complex, and that, therefore, they can as easily stand at the beginning of a clause-combining grammaticalization chain as at the end (*pace* the suggestion raised by the cline in (1) and the examples in (6)).[33] A similar conclusion is reached by Van Valin (2000) as regards language acquisition, and indeed within Role and Reference Grammar 'constructions like *I want to go* and *Bill forced John to leave* do not involve embedding and ... are *not* examples of subordination (Van Valin 2000: 520, and cf. also Van Valin and LaPolla 1997).

The important point to consider then is to what extent clause fusion and/or the change from main verb to Aux, which plays a role in explanations provided by generative as well as grammaticalization models, can be considered to have taken place historically in each such case, and hence can be considered an explanation for the change in question within those models. Before addressing this question in more detail in §§5.4–5.5, it will be useful to look at some other proposals involving clause fusion, provided by historical linguists who belong to neither school.

5.3 Other proposals related to the question of clause fusion and the status of (modal) auxiliaries

Harris and Campbell (1995: 173–91) describe clause fusion as a diachronic process that is typical for full verbs that have become auxiliaries. They argue, in similar fashion to the generative linguists above but with the emphasis on what appears on the surface, that an earlier biclausal surface structure becomes monoclausal, whereby the verb of the matrix clause becomes an auxiliary and that of the subordinate clause becomes the main lexical verb. It is implicit in their discussion, but not expressed, that another corollary of clause fusion is that the former matrix verb becomes transparent to the subject argument of the subordinate verb, that is the subject from the subordinate clause is raised to the subject position of the matrix clause. Although they do not claim that all auxiliary verbs arise out of biclausal constructions (p. 190), they seem to press this point rather, even in cases where there isn't too much empirical evidence for such a development.

They illustrate the process with the help of the history of the Georgian verb *unda* 'want'. In the early situation (cf. stage (17i) below), *unda* (governing a dative subject) can be found with a complement clause introduced by a complementizer followed by a verb in the subjunctive that could have its own subject (in the nominative or narrative case). In a later period (17ii), the subject of matrix clause and subordinate clause became co-indexed. One stage later (17iii), *unda* could turn into an auxiliary (main verb 'want' was also preserved), whereby it acquired a modal meaning 'should'; the complementizer was lost at this point. Later still (17iv), *unda* began to take the nominative or narrative case from the subordinate verb, which remained in the subjunctive.

(17) stage i $[S_{i(DATIVE)}unda_{(V)}) [COMP Verb_{(SUBJUNCTIVE)}PRO_i/S_{j(NOM/NAR)}]]$
      stage ii $[S_{i(DATIVE)}unda_{(V)} [(COMP) Verb_{(SUBJUNCTIVE)}PRO_i]]$
      stage iii $[S_{i(DATIVE)}unda_{(AUX)} Verb_{(SUBJUNCTIVE)}]$
      stage iv $[S_{i(NOM/NAR)}unda_{(AUX)} Verb_{(SUBJUNCTIVE)}]$

The empirical evidence for the development is constituted by the loss of the complementizer, the change in case-form of the matrix subject and the accompanying decategorization of *unda* from Verb to Aux, both syntactically and semantically.

No other verbs are discussed here. Presumably the grammaticalization of the verb *unda* started with this one token verb, which was central in the construction-type, which also involved the complementizer and the subjunctive subordinate verb with its subject. There is no discussion of whether the new construction also spread to other verbs that are similar both syntactically and semantically. Because it involves a token, grammaticalization is relatively easy to establish. I note that other well-established cases of grammaticalization involving reanalysis, such as BE + *going to* + infinitive, also involve a fixed token *going to* as part of a larger type (i.e. the token was preceded by a form of BE and followed by an infinitive), and that such processes generally do not involve other, similar tokens *at the same time*.[34] Usually, the new construction-type is formed on analogy of other construction-types already in existence in the grammar, for example BE *going to* grammaticalized on analogy of other Aux V constructions that were already in the language.[35] (Note that analogy can take place on a token- as well as a type-level, as argued in §3.5 above.)

Harris and Campbell next suggest a scenario similar to the Georgian case of *unda* for the English auxiliaries, including both the modals and also perfect *be* and *have* (and similarly for the development of the Romance perfect). They are all said to have been main verbs to begin with, governing a complement clause. In this they follow the scenario of Lightfoot and most other generative linguists for the modals. It seems to me, however, that there is rather less empirical evidence pointing to an earlier biclausal structure in the development of the English modal and perfect auxiliaries than there is in the Georgian *unda* case. I will discuss the modals in §5.4 and the perfect auxiliary in §5.5.

5.4 The English modal verbs: biclausal or monoclausal structures?

What evidence do we have for a biclausal structure involving the modal verbs in Old English? Should we accept the scenario drawn for Georgian *unda* in (17) also for these modals? In Old English, only the two most lexical modal preterite-present verbs (*willan* and *witan*) could be followed by a *þæt* ('that')-clause, which always had its own subject (PRO subjects do not occur), which was generally not identical to the matrix subject. I have found only a single and rather doubtful example in the parsed York-Toronto-Helsinki Corpus, where *willan* is followed by a *þæt*-clause with a co-indexed subject.[36] In addition, the loss of the complementizer *þæt/that* becomes common only in Middle English, and begins with verbs of 'saying' or 'thinking' rather than with modal verbs (cf. Rissanen 1999a: 284; Brinton 1996: 240–2). The other, more peripheral modal verb, *cunnan*, has not been attested with a *þæt*-clause at all. Although there are some examples with Old English *magan* followed by a *þæt*-clause, I believe they are part of the development of modals to epistemic verbs (I will discuss this further in §6.1).[37]

Another difference with the Georgian case is that the verbs in the finite and non-finite complements were not the same in form originally (in Georgian the verb was and remained in the subjunctive). So none of the characteristics that apply in the Georgian case, apply here. Substituting the infinitive for the Georgian subjunctive, it could be said that *willan* shows instances only of stages (17i) and (iii), while the other modals only appear as stage (iii), and possibly stage (iv) as far as the epistemic modals are concerned (see §6.1). In other words, there is no neat cline or unidirectional development to be discovered here.

Instead, I would suggest that the modal verbs that later became auxiliaries were already part of a monoclausal structure in Old English. As lexical verbs they could be followed by a direct object, and already in the earliest stages this direct object was often an action noun (the bare infinitive) rather than a regular NP. Only in the case of the more marginal (more fully lexical) verb *willan* could this direct object also be a clause. What changed, and this already happened in pre-Old English times, was the syntactic nature of the action noun, which slowly acquired verbal characteristics, such as adjuncts and (in)direct objects. Unfortunately, this change took place in prehistorical times, so that we have no direct empirical evidence for the development. Kuryłowicz (1964: 158) suggests that the bare infinitive (which he classifies as a 'deverbative abstract noun') became verbal when it was replaced by a new verbal abstract noun, as happened in Old English with the introduction of nouns in *-ung* (formed from weak verbs of class 2) and nouns in *-ing* (formed from weak verbs of class 1). This development involving the action noun from a nominal into a verbal category is very similar to the way in which the gerund (deriving from the same OE *-ung/-ing* forms) also acquired verbal attributes in a later period of English (cf. Donner 1986; Jack 1988). Again this latter change may have been caused by the rise of new verbal nouns in *-(at)ion/-ance/-ment*. Note that before the gerund acquired its verbal nature, it could take objects in the genitive case or in the form of a PP. Something similar may have happened in the case of the bare infinitive in a prehistoric period.

However, it is also quite possible that such developments take place spontaneously. Turning again to the development of the gerund, the occurrence of a nominal phrase such as (i) *John's imagining of the Queen's death*, next to (ii) *John imagines the Queen's death* with exactly the same order could easily lead to analogical restructuring via intermediate construction-types such as *John's imagining the Queen's death* (cf. Rissanen 1999a: 292), especially in view of the fact that the verbal construction-type (ii) is much more frequent and more basic. Plank (1985: 158) notes that it is quite usual that marked constructions like (i) reform themselves on the basis of less marked constructions.

It is much less likely that the new verbal nouns in *-ion*, *-ance*, etc., which replaced the nominal gerund in *-ing*, will in turn also become verbs, since, unlike in the cases of the bare infinitive and the gerund, there are too many different forms/suffixes here, reducing their frequency as a token/type and making analogy difficult. My suggestion, therefore, is that the action-noun constituent was replaced by a verbal constituent through analogy, *without* a change in argument status, that is it remained a direct constituent of the matrix verb.

There are a number of other factors that suggest a monoclausal structure for the Old English modals when followed by the bare infinitive, as the more suitable. First of all, there is van Kemenade's (1985, 1992) finding that the Old English modal verbs allowed Verb-raising. Verb-raising implies that there has been a total fusion of the subordinate clause into the main clause, because elements of the subordinate clause have moved inside the main clause across the clause boundary. In other words, Verb-raising is used as a 'trick' to turn a biclausal structure back into a monoclausal one. It would therefore be simpler to assume a monoclausal structure from the beginning. Verb-raising in Old English, and also in Modern German and Dutch, only takes place after verbs that are already auxiliary-like in nature and/or have selected a bare infinitive from the very beginning.[38] In Old English it involves modals, physical perception verbs and causatives, (cf. van Kemenade 1985), while in Modern Dutch and German it spread also to aspectual verbs, verbs that allow Subject-raising like 'seem, appear', and catenative control verbs like 'try, help', etc. (cf. Bennis and Hoekstra 1983: 85–93). I will here concentrate on Dutch because that allows me to work with 'minimal pairs', but similar arguments also apply to Old English and Modern German. Some Dutch examples are given in (18):

(18a)	... dat	hij	*de*	*krant*	probeerde	te	lezen
	... that	he	the	paper	tried	to	read

'... that he tried to read the paper'

(18b)	... dat	hij	*het*	journaal	wilde	zien
	... that	he	the	news	wanted	see

'...that he wanted to see the news'

(18c)	... dat	ze	*op*	reis	blijken	te	gaan
	... that	they	on	journey	appear	to	go

'... that they appear to be going on a journey'

(18d)	... dat	hij	*de*	trein	net	ziet	vertrekken
	... that	he	the	train	just	sees	leave

'... That he is just seeing the train leave'

In all the examples of (18), the italicized NP (or PP), which functions as an argument in the infinitival clause, has been raised into the matrix clause. What is noticeable about the constructions with a bare infinitive (18b, 18d) is that they do not allow infinitival complements with their own tense position, cf. (19), nor the normal extraposition of the infinitival complement (20), which is possible with Control and Subject-raising verbs, as (21) shows:

(19) * ... dat   hij   de   trein   net   ziet   [vertrokken zijn]
      ... that he   the   train   just   sees   (to) have   left
(20) * ...   dat   hij   net   ziet   [de   trein   vertrekken]
      ...   that he   just   sees   the   train   leave
(21) ... dat   hij   hoopt   [(om)   het   te   halen/het   gehaald   te hebben]
      ... that he   hopes   [(for) it   to   pass/it   passed   to have]
      ' ... that he hopes to pass it/to have passed it'

What is also noteworthy is that verbs that take a *te*-infinitive only allow Verb-raising when the *te*-infinitive (cf. fn. 38) is no longer purposive. This is clear from the fact that the 'purposive' strengthening of the infinitive by *om* 'for' is *not* possible in combination with Verb-raising, cf. (22). This shows that Verb-raising is only allowed when the bond between matrix verb and infinitive is a very close one, rendering the matrix verb into an auxiliary or catenative and making the structure to all intents and purposes mono-clausal.

(22a)   ... dat   hij   probeerde   (om)   de   krant   te   lezen
        ... that he   tried   for   the   paper   to   read
(22b) * ... dat hij   de   krant   probeerde om   te   lezen
        ... that he   the   paper   tried   for   to   read
(22c) * ... dat hij   om   de   krant   probeerde te   lezen
        ... that he   for   the   paper   tried   to   read

Other evidence, such as that the subject of the infinitive must be directly governed by the matrix verb (as is the case in Subject-raising structures and ECM constructions), the phenomenon called the IPP [Infinitivus Pro Participio] effect (in which the expected past participle in a perfect construction is replaced by an infinitive, see Bennis and Hoekstra 1983: 87ff. for Dutch),[39] the behaviour of clitics and negative markers (see van Kemenade 1985 for Old English), show that the clause as a whole functions as a single proposition. To assume a biclausal structure here, only to do away with all signs of embeddedness afterwards via a rule of Verb-raising, looks a bit excessive.

   The reason why a biclausal structure is proposed at all is described as follows: the 'object of the embedded infinitival verb receives a semantic role from that verb in a structural configuration' (van Kemenade 1985: 76). That is, if the object *krant*, as, for example, in (18a), does not immediately precede the verb that gives it its semantic role, that is *lezen*, then *krant* cannot receive case, therefore it must receive case underlyingly in a biclausal construction, where it appears directly before *lezen*. Additional reasons have to do with the (syntax-centred) notion of 'economy' favoured by the generative model. Since next to infinitival complements, finite complement clauses also occur—at least with the perception verbs, the Subject-raising verbs and most of the control verbs (core causatives like 'let' generally do not allow a finite clause)—an underlying biclausal construction is deemed to capture a generalization. Secondly, the model also does not favour two different types of control-verbs, one auxiliary-like, and one a full verb. The decision about structure is thus heavily dependent on one's theoretical model.

If, on the other hand, a more surface-type model is used (e.g. as described in Chapter 3), then the verbs in question can be treated as catenatives or semi-auxiliaries when they occur in Verb-raising constructions such as (18). In that case, it is the verb-complex which assigns case. The structure as a whole would be monoclausal to begin with, and case assignment in (18) would not be a problem since the object is directly in front of the verbal cluster, which, as is the rule in Dutch, is verb-final in the clauses given in (18).[40] When the same verb occurs as a subject-control verb (as in 22a), the difference in word order is no problem, since the infinitival complement would be extraposed, in the same way as finite complements. The suggestion then for Modern Dutch is that the infinitival complements of these grammaticalized verbs begin to behave like the infinitival complements of other auxiliaries and allow what has been called 'Verb-raising'. The disadvantage of my proposal is that a verb like *proberen* 'try' must now be classified in the lexicon as two different verbs, as a semi-auxiliary (cf. 18a) and as a control verb (22a). However, since this development with control verbs in Dutch is one that has proceeded (and still does) by lexical diffusion,[41] this idiosyncrasy is no more costly than a general rule of Verb-raising, since this rule, whether obligatory or optional, must also be indicated lexically per verb.

The fact that the spread of a complex-verb construction takes place lexically, also strongly suggests that analogy is here at work: that is when verbs start to behave like (semi-)auxiliaries, they also begin to take over the syntactic structures in which these auxiliaries occur. Since a structure such as (18a) was usual with the modal and the perception-verb complex in Dutch, other verb complexes followed. Interesting in this respect is the spread of the IPP effect. We know little about the origin of it (cf. Kern 1912; de Schutter 2000; van der Horst forthcoming); possibly it arose due to a formal confusion between past participle and infinitive in early Dutch with some verbs (e.g. with most modals, with *zien* 'see' and *laten* 'let'), which then spread via analogy. Entrenchment of the new verb complex definitely played a role since the IPP is now compulsory with those verbs that showed 'Verb-raising' from the beginning (modals, perception verbs, and causatives), as shown by the ungrammaticality of (24b). What also plays a role is position: the IPP effect *may* only take place with control verbs when the two non-finite verbs are adjacent, as in (23a) (and in the case of the 'older' verbs, then it *must* take place, see (24a)). IPP is *not* allowed with control verbs when one of the non-finites is adjacent to the matrix verb and not to the other non-finite (23b), which is also the construction that no longer occurs with the 'older' verbs, cf. (24b):

(23a) Hij heeft het werk proberen[INF] /geprobeerd[PASTPART] af te
      He   has the work try   /tried   off to
      maken[INF]
      finish

(23b) Hij heeft geprobeerd/*proberen het   werk   af   te   maken
      He   has   tried/*try   the   work   off to   finish
      'He has tried to finish the work'

(24a) Hij heeft de trein zien[INF]/* gezien[PASTPART] vertrekken[INF]
      he   has the train see   seen   leave

(24b) *Hij heeft gezien/zien de   trein vertrekken
      He   has   seen/see   the train leave
      'He has seen the train leave'

Another possible factor may have been an abduction (due to analogy) based on another Aux VV construction, which from the beginning (example (25a) is from Middle Dutch) consisted of two infinitives, that is the double V construction after modal verbs in the present tense:

(25a) ghine   selt te hemelrike nit mogen[INF] comen[INF]
                                 (van der Horst 1981: 31)
      you-not shall to heaven   not can   come
      'you shall not be able to go to heaven'

(25b) Hij moet gaan[INF]   solliciteren[INF]
      He   must go   apply (for a job)
      'He must start applying for a job'

(25c) Zij zal hem leren[INF] zwemmen[INF]
      She will him teach   swim
      'She will teach him to swim'

Since Aux VV constructions are not frequent, it is quite possible that they began to be seen as one pattern possibly helped by attraction (a form of copying or morphological harmony).[42] Since the VV complex was separated from the matrix verb in main clauses (due to Verb-second), the morphological form of the infinitival V may have had a stronger attraction on the participial V than the syntactic attraction of the main verb that was further away.

To conclude this excursion into Verb-raising in Dutch, and to return to the Old English modal-verb structure, which typically underwent Verb-raising, I have argued that it is unnecessary and uneconomical to ascribe a biclausal structure to the English modals at any stage of their history. Verb-raising has been shown to be a theory-internal device, which turns underlying biclausal structures back into monoclausal ones; it is clear that it would be simpler to consider them monoclausal in the first place. Furthermore, the originally non-verbal status of the bare infinitive after the modal verbs is shown by the fact that it never had any agreement, tense, or aspect features in the older Germanic languages,[43] and by the fact that finite complements introduced by *þæt/that* did not occur with modals. If the infinitive started off as a(n action) noun, and if the modal verb-complex truly became biclausal in Old English when the action noun developed verbal properties like objects and adjuncts, then it must have lost this clausal status very quickly again: according to Harris and Campbell (1995: 178) 'at least by early Middle English'. It seems a rather unlikely scenario. Bock (1931: 121) notes in this respect that the verbalization of the infinitive in the separate Indo-European languages goes hand in hand with an increasingly narrow syntactic bond between matrix verb and infinitive.[44] My suggestion therefore is that the infinitive after modals in Old English was a direct constituent of the modal, a direct object, which later developed VP properties, but as such remained a direct constituent of the modal V. Bock (1931: 124) describes this verbal object as 'analog zu einem nominalen Objekt'. Through analogy, elaborated constructions like *I must help him* also became possible next to *I help him* and *I must help*. This development, and the loss of direct objects after modals, must have led to the later re-interpretation of modal verbs as auxiliaries, which took place roughly at the end of the Middle English period. The different word orders possible in the modal construction, as described by van Kemenade (1985) in terms of Verb-raising, I would ascribe to scrambling for stylistic or discourse reasons, but this needs further investigation.

5.5 The development of other auxiliaries: biclausal or monoclausal structures?

There are similar difficulties with accepting Harris and Campbell's analysis of the perfect in English and the Romance languages. Again there is no good evidence that in Old English clauses such as *þa hæfdon hie hiera clusan belocene* ('then had they their bolts locked', Or 3 7.62.24), the past participle ever formed a *clause* separate from the matrix verb *habban* 'have'. It appears rather more likely that the past participle was an adjectival phrase which depended on the direct object of *hæfdon*, that is on *clusan*. Note that this past participle was at first declined like an adjective, and that it had no verbal features of mood, agreement, or aspect. Note also that in Old English it was still quite usual for the adjective phrase to follow the head noun when it conveyed new information (cf. Fischer 2000b). In addition, other kinds of predicative phrases can be found here, PPs and APs, as the examples in (26a) and (26b) illustrate respectively,

(**26a**) and *hæfde* hine *to* geferan   þa hwile þe   he lifede (ApT 51.20)
and had   him to companion the time   that he lived
'and had him as a companion as long as he lived'

(**26b**) And se þe   þyses ofteo   *hæbbe*   hit wiþ God *gemæne*
(CH 1660(Rob 60)5)
And he who this   withholds may-have it   with God in-common
'And he who withholds this holds it in common with God'

It is also telling that in rather similar cases with the verb *findan* 'find' and an object plus predicative phrase, we find adjectives (27a), next to present and past participles (27b, 27c), and bare infinitives (27d),

(**27a**) Symle   hy   Guðlac   *gearene* fundon, þonces   gleawne
(Guthlac A/B 913)
Always   they Guthlac   ready   found,   of-thought wise
'They always found Guthlac, ready, wise in thought'

(**27b**) ... and *fundon* hine *licgenne*   on   blodigum limum
(ÆLS(Martin)980)
... and found   him lying   with bloody   limbs

(**27c**) *Fand* þa   *hidde*   in   þa   ealde wealle writes   þet ...
(ChronE(Plummer)963.21)
found then hidden   in   the   old   wall   writings that ...

(27d)	... se	æt	Heorote	*fand*	wæccendne	wer	wiges[GEN]
	... who	at	Heorot	found	watchful	man	battle

bidan (Beo 1265)

abide

... 'who found the watchful man waiting for battle at Heorot'

Moreover, there are no cases found in Old English where the adjective or participle is accompanied by a form of 'to be', making it more fully clausal, as is the case in later English. This suggests that clauses with *findan* and a participle or infinitive were monoclausal in Old English and that a biclausal structure with a *to*-infinitival complement only became possible later (in late Middle English) together with the development of other biclausal constructions, such as the Latin-type accusative and infinitive constructions (see Warner 1982; Fischer 1989, 1992a, 1994b).[45]

It seems to me that the same objections could be raised against a description of the Romance perfect as having developed from a biclausal structure in Latin. Harris and Campbell (1995: 182) write that '[l]inguists have long recognized that this was a biclausal structure'. As evidence for biclausal structure, they mention, among other things, the possibility of having 'distinct subjects in the two clauses' (1995: 183). However, the evidence they give for this consists only of clauses where the 'subject' of the second verb (a past participle) is in fact also the object of *habere*, that is it is not the case that there are *two lexicalized* subject NPs, cf. their example (28).

(28)	in ea	provincia	pecunias	magnas[ACC PL]	collocatas[ACC PL]	habent
	in that	province	moneys	great	placed	have

'They have great capital invested in that province'

(Cicero, from Harris and Campbell 1995: 182)

In (28) the subject of *collocatas*, that is *pecunias* is also the object of the verb *habere*.

Vincent (1982: 80) refers to the Latin participles as modifiers, having the same function that adjectives or prepositional phrases have with *habere* 'have'. Fleischman (1982: 125) makes clear that in the periphrasis, *habere* was first a main verb and then became an auxiliary, but she nowhere states that the past participle had clausal status. Pinkster (1987) describes the perfect as going back to an earlier construction of *habere* + object followed by what he calls a *praedicativum*. Even though this *praedicativum* can in quite a few cases be *paraphrased* by a subordinate clause, this does not prove that it *was* a subordinate clause to start with, and indeed Pinkster does not claim this. Bolkestein (1989) compares the nominal and verbal properties of Latin participles, and also of the *gerundium* and *gerundivum*. She comes to the conclusion that the nominal properties of the participle (i.e. they possess case, number, and can take a preposition) are more prominent than the verbal ones (they lack the features of voice, tense, and person, but they can take an argument and an adverbial adjunct).

An interesting observation in connection with the participles is made by Coleman (1989), who studied the rise and fall of the 'ablative absolute' in Latin. The ablative absolute is a construction that also makes use of an NP accompanied by a participle, but this is not a direct argument of the matrix verb, as is the case in (28). These constructions appear in the various Indo-European languages in either the locative case (Vedic), the dative (Old Church Slavonic, Lithuanian, Old English), the genitive (Greek), or the ablative (Latin). He argues that this construction must have been native to Indo-European. He writes that the Latin construction 'developed by the extension of the predicative verbal constituent to include agent nouns (if this was not intuited) and adjectives ... more important was the increasing exploitation of the verbal properties of the participles. ... This development was due to Greek literary influences and never affected Vulgar Latin, which retained only the basic inherited types, largely in formulaic usage' (Coleman 1989: 353). This strongly suggests that the elaboration of the participles is not part of the spoken language and is stylistically very restricted. It also speaks against a clausal interpretation of the participles. It is interesting too to observe in this connection (cf. Deutscher 2000) that in the well-documented history of Akkadian, the infinitival nominal constructions are much older than the finite complements that later replaced them.

Rather similar in nature is another grammaticalization development that took place in some of the Romance languages with STARE 'stand' + participle (cf. *ser/estar* in Spanish/Portuguese). In Latin, again both participles and adjectives are found here. In Old English, too, *standan* 'stand' is found with a predicative phrase, which may be a present/past participle as well as an adjective.[46]

From an analogical learning point of view, it is much more likely that the constructions with a main verb and a participle are the same as the constructions with a main verb and adjective. There seems no reason to interpret these constructions as biclausal because there is no surface evidence in the contemporary data for their biclausal nature, as there was in the Georgian case with *unda* 'want'. In addition, as already mentioned earlier, Tomasello (2003a) shows that constructions with a participial or infinitival complement appear much earlier in child language than the first truly finite clause constructions. For that reason too, it must seem more than acceptable to analyse the Old English and Latin infinitival, adjectival, and participial complements all in the same way, that is as an object of the main verb or as a modifier to this object.

The same objections could apply to some other instances of auxiliary development in English and Latin where *have/habere* is found in combination with an infinitive. Krug (2000: 53ff.) considers the *to*-infinitive in the Old English constructions of the type,

(**29**)   hæfst ðu æceras to erigenne (ÆGram 135.2)
        'have you acres to plow'

clausal, which makes the whole construction biclausal. Part of the grammaticalization process, according to Krug, is that the construction becomes monoclausal in early Modern English. I would agree here with Bock (1931), however, that the *to*-infinitive in Old English is to be interpreted first and foremost as a modifier of the noun (i.e. very much like the past participle in the Latin construction in (28)). Bock (1931: 128–9) shows that the *to*-infinitive was originally adnominal, and that in Old English poetry the *to*-infinitive occurs almost without exception 'in adnominaler Stellung', that is dependent on nouns (or adjectives) and not on verbs. He remarks that linguists who have interpreted these infinitives as dependent on the verb,

have not at all considered how such a construction would have been possible at such an early time. Historically and when seen in connection with the other uses of the infinitive that have been transmitted, the infinitive in such clauses cannot but be seen as dependent on the nomen in question. To see it in any other way is a modern syntactic interpretation that has been falsely ascribed to the older language.[47]

This dependency of the *to*-infinitive on the noun gradually disappears when the infinitive begins to occur as direct object or subject, and the infinitive itself becomes more verbal when it acquires its own arguments. All this begins to happen in Old English, but it has to be noted that the new auxiliary *have to* only develops in those constructions where the infinitive could be interpreted as depending on the NP object of the matrix verb, as in the construction type given in (29) (and indeed also in (28)). The grammaticalization of *have to* does not take place in sentences of the type,

(**30**)   Ic   hæbbe   anweald   mine   sawle   to   alætanne (Jn (WSCp)10.18)
        I   have   (the) power   my   soul   to   leave

where *hæbbe* and the infinitive each have their own object. In clauses of type (30) 'have' remains a possessive verb and the infinitive retains its modifying function. The change from possessive 'have' to modal 'have to' only takes place (as I have shown in Fischer 1994a) when the middle NP (*æceras* in (29)), which is syntactically the direct object of 'have' but has a semantic role that is often more closely linked to the infinitive, comes to be placed in post-infinitival position after the word order change from SOV > SVO in Middle English. In other words, the ambiguous role of the NP object in terms of its relations to both main verb (a mainly structural relation) and infinitive (a mainly semantic relation), can now no longer be left ambiguous, as was possible in the looser Old English word order. The speaker has to make a choice. If the connection with the infinitive is foremost in his mind, he will reposition the object, on analogy of other SVO structures. If the main verb asserts its pressure, the object may stay where it is (as is indeed still possible in clauses like *I have an apple to eat, I have a paper to write*. Note that this latter choice is usually only made when *have* has a stronger semantic sense, when it expresses an object that the speaker 'possesses' or wishes to 'possess' or bring into existence.) The new word order, *I have to plow acres*, arises when *have* is weak semantically. In this order, it is clearly impossible to interpret *to plow* as a modifier of *acres*, or to see *acres* as an object of *have*. The new adjacency of *have* and the infinitive here leads to the auxiliarization of *have to*. Strong evidence that the grammaticalization into an auxiliary only took place *after* the word order change can be found in the fact that the further effects of the grammaticalization (i.e. the use of *have to* with intransitive infinitives, the use of double *have*, the use of inanimate subjects, *have to* used epistemically), all only appear after the word order change, that is after 1500.

Returning again to the topic of clause combining after this brief excursion, I believe that the change involving *have to* does not involve clause reduction as part of a grammaticalization process, (*pace* Krug 2000), because the construction must be seen as monoclausal to begin with. It is also noteworthy that it does not follow the typical path of a grammaticalization process in that the factors causing it are structural rather than semantic. The deeper cause for the development is the change in word order from SOV to SVO, which caused *have* and the infinitive to occur next to one another, *and* the fact that this new pattern of two adjacent verbs was already a familiar pattern in late Middle English.[48] It is important to note that this development to auxiliary status did not take place on any general scale in either Modern German or Dutch, which remained SOV languages. In other words, to ascribe this change simply to 'grammaticalization' because it is said to show some of the typical characteristics (clause reduction, bleaching of *have*, etc.) is too easy, and not explanatory because it does not account for the differences between German and Dutch on the one side, and English on the other. These differences can only be explained by a closer look at the overall grammatical system in which the auxiliarization took place.

Pinkster (1987: 208–9) suggests a similar development for the Latin infinitive + *habere* construction, which in the Romance languages developed, via an obligative stage (cf. Fleischman 1982: 58–9), into a future tense. Here again, what is crucial, is the fact that there was a single 'shared object' (as in (28)–(29)) and a later word order change, which caused *habere* to be placed consistently after the infinitive so that it could begin to form a fixed unit with the infinitive. Pinkster considers 'the most plausible explanation' for this construction that it developed from *habere* + object + *praedicativum* (which in this case was a *gerundivum*) as in *aedem habuit tuendam* '(a) house he had to look after', where the *gerundivum* was later replaced by an infinitive.[49] Fleischman (1982: 113) notes that the 'crucial factor affecting synthesis must have been auxiliary placement' and she argues that the grammaticalization of *habere* into both a future *as well as* a perfect marker in the Romance languages (i.e. from Lat. *cantare habeo* > Fr (*je*) *chanterai* and from Lat. *habeo cantatu* > Fr (*j'*)*ai chanté*) is due to the fact that the two processes took place at different stages of the language: at the earlier OV stage (*cantare habeo* giving the synthetic future form) and the later VO stage (*habeo cantatu* leading to the periphrastic perfect). Note that the different results (a *synthetic* future vs. a *periphrastic* perfect) are again predictable from the system of grammar out of which these forms emerged. Since the Romance languages have suffixal inflections only, it is unlikely that the perfect auxiliary will ever become reduced to an affix, as has happened to the future auxiliary. Neither Pinkster nor Fleischman go into the question of whether *habere* plus infinitive was biclausal or not. As before, there is no reason to argue for a biclausal structure either diachronically (as an earlier stage) or synchronically (as an underlying structure). According to Roberts and Roussou (2002: 37), however, this construction with *habere* had the same biclausal structure as the Old English modals (2002: 29), whose infinitives were said to be 'at least TPs' (2002: 29).

5.6 Concluding remarks

We may thus conclude that the phenomenon of clause fusion arising out of an historically earlier or a synchronically underlying biclausal structure has been used as a device to explain developments within both the grammaticalization and the generative approach and also as a means to acquire elegant generalizations within both these models. As we have seen, in many of these cases, there is no empirical evidence available to uphold an earlier or underlying biclausal structure. This means that other factors have to be found to explain the diachronic developments or derive the appropriate surface structure. It also means that the assumptions of the theory sometimes obscure what may be the more crucial factors at work in the structure of the grammar or in grammatical change.

It has also been shown that clause reduction or clause fusion is not necessarily unidirectional, and that formally longer and more explicit constructions need not be historically earlier. Thus, after perception verbs, bare infinitives and 'that'-clauses existed from the beginning of the Old English period, while an extended infinitive with *to* only developed at a later period. In a similar way, the bare infinitive after Subject-raising verbs like *schijnen* 'seem' in Dutch, was extended to a *te*-infinitive at a later stage. The reasons for the changes with respect to clause fusion or clause elaboration cannot therefore always be straightforwardly connected to (a unidirectional process of) grammaticalization. It was also found that the development of verbs into (modal) auxiliaries does not necessarily have to be related to a process of clause fusion. In fact, the emergence of a fixed word order (due to frequency and entrenchment), the ensuing adjacency of two verbs leading to univerbation, and the analogical strength of the Aux-V construction-type, may have been more important here.

Notes

1. It is rare to find 'discourse' indexed in generative synchronic or diachronic studies, whereas it is hardly ever absent in functional linguistic studies, whether synchronic or diachronic.
2. For the latter, cf. Givón (1979: 220): '[v]ia syntacticization [which includes the rise of morphological coding] the language loses message transparency while it gains processing speed'.

3. On the other hand, the number of generative linguists who believe in an LAD which emerged rapidly by macro-mutation is perhaps still greater (cf. Chomsky 1988; Lightfoot 2000; Bickerton 2003).

4. The culturally transmitted 'local' patterns of the native language play a significant role in language acquisition. Slobin (2002) shows that children under 2, who are exposed to morphologically rich languages such as Turkish and Inuktitut, use morphology productively, i.e. there is no simple pre-grammar recapitulating proto-grammar. He thus argues against the rather too simple idea of some linguists that 'ontogeny recapitulates phylogeny'. Tomasello (2003a) presents evidence that for the process of language acquisition the primary factors are 'pattern-finding' and 'intention reading', i.e. the ability to understand communicative intentions, to take the perspective of the hearer. He considers pattern-finding subordinate to intention reading, however (2003a: 325). I do not think this is correct. Children are able to recognize formal phonological patterns from very early on. There is evidence that they can do so from age 7 to 8 months (Tomasello 2003a: 28–30; Clark 2003: 68), and infants seem to be able to distinguish their own language from a foreign one as early as four days after birth (Clark 2003: 63). The evidence for the intention-reading ability, however, only emerges near the end of the first year (Tomasello 2003a: 21). In addition, the pattern-finding ability is evolutionary older: unlike intention reading, it is also present in non-human primates (Tomasello 2003a: 4).

5. We will see below that this may not actually be correct, i.e. that the extreme pole of the syntactic mode may be missing in languages that have not developed a written form.

6. This is what happened according to Janda (1980). Janda's story is somewhat complicated in that he considers the use of *his* itself a reanalysis of the earlier morphological genitive in *-es* (slightly changed in Janda 2001); so the *first* part of the development might be said to involve *de*grammaticalization (for a counter view on this first stage, see Allen (1997, 2002), who sees *his* and *-is/-es* as orthographical variants). Norde (2001) writes on the development of the genitive marker in Scandinavian, which like Allen for English (at least for the second stage) she analyses as a case of degrammaticalization. For an overview of the various proposals and yet another interpretation, see Rosenbach (2002, 2004). Whatever the truth of the matter for English, this particular case shows how dangerous it is to use a frequent grammaticalization path followed in genitive development (see Givón 1979: 216–17) as a 'unidirectional principle' in one's search for an explanation. It may lead the researcher to neglect the empirical details which do *not* accord with the 'principle'. This is indeed what Rosenbach (2004: 74) emphasizes: 'in order to understand this development (more fully), it is necessary to look at the broader context of this change, in particular at what else happened in the English NP' (and for a similar attitude as regards Scandinavian and German, see Norde 2001 and Demske 2001 respectively). Note also similar problems concerning the development of the *to*-infinitive in English, discussed in §1.1.2 above.

7. I am using the term 'clause fusion' in quite a loose sense so that I can capture some similar synchronic and diachronic phenomena in the two models. Clause fusion here includes all cases in which the surface sentence-unit (containing one finite verb) is built up out of two (synchronically deeper-level or diachronically earlier) separate clauses, each with their own verbal elements and arguments/ argument positions, disregarding whether the clause is actually fused in generative terms in surface structure (as *is* the case in the process of Verb-raising), or only indicating deeper argument positions by means of PRO or trace (as is the case in Subject-raising and Subject-control).

8. Cf. Hopper and Traugott (2003: 175–211). In their terminology embedding is called 'subordination'; 'parataxis', and 'coordination' involve independent clauses without and with explicit linkers respectively, while 'hypotaxis' refers to dependent clauses, which, unlike embedding, do not constitute an argument in the main clause on which they depend. The definition and use of the term 'hypotaxis' is problematic because functional and structural considerations are confused (cf. Deutscher 2000: 13–14). Hopper and Traugott's 'hypotaxis' refers to a functional rather than a structural dependency.

9. Thus, generative grammar on the whole ignores paratactic and hypotactic clauses, which are more loosely combined with another clause. Most of these clauses are adverbial in nature (they are 'related circumstantially', Matthiessen and Thompson 1988: 277) and like adverbial phrases have been given much less attention in the generative framework. Recent notable exceptions are Haumann (1997), Alexiadou (1997), and Cinque (1999).

10. Cf. Givón (1979: 222): 'the entire process labeled by transformationalists as *embedding transformations* turns out to be a mere recapitulation of attested diachronic changes'.

11. Cf. Mithun (1988: 332), who shows that in spoken texts coordination can be signalled in two ways: by means of a single intonation contour without a break, signalling the coordinated elements to be one conceptual unit, or by separation with 'comma intonation' (which usually includes a pause and a special 'non-final' pitch contour) signalling a list.

12. For instance in Dutch and German, subordinate or hypotactic clause status is shown by the use of SOV order, which is in contrast with the regular SVO(v) order of main clauses. Similarly, conditional clause status may be marked by the inversion of VS, as in English, e.g. ***Should it*** *drop into a second league or tier, much could be lost—including the City's pre-eminence as a European financial centre* (ICE-GB w2e-004 067).

13. Cf. also Kalmár (1985), who notes that hypotaxis (subordination in his terms), which is explicitly marked syntactically and/or lexically, is typical only of evolved languages, i.e. languages that have developed permanent texts. Lack of such subordination is found especially in Australian languages, Uralic languages spoken by Siberian hunters, and in Amerindian languages, such as Ojibwa and Inuktitut. See also the discussion in §1.2.2. Deutscher (2000) argues convincingly that the use of subordination (or of more complex patterns of

communication) is not just related to literacy but, perhaps first and foremost, to the complexity of a society (of which literacy often forms a part). It has to be noted in this connection (cf. Newmeyer 2003: 73–75, and fn. 4 in Chapter 3) that the uniformitarian principle may not hold across the evolution of written language from an oral stage.

14. Deutscher (2001: 410) shows that in Old Akkadian (one of the oldest Semitic languages), the relative clause arose out of a combination of two developments: (i) the extension of the 'genitival complex … to a relative clause', where the 'relative clause is not marked by any independent relative particle, but by the construct state on the head noun' (the 'construct state' is a way of marking the head noun)—this in fact constitutes another example of clause elaboration; and (ii) the use of an appositive construction introduced by the demonstrative *šu*, in which the demonstrative had the same case-form as the head noun. In other words the relative clause did not derive directly from a paratactic construction but via a subordinate, appositional clause. He suggests that something similar took place in Germanic (pp. 415–18).

15. Tabor and Traugott (1998: 240) point to just this danger in connection with Lehmann's (1995[1982]: 64) discussion of the development of the English gerund, where it looks as if the unidirectional cline leads Lehmann to misrepresent the diachronic order in which the various constructions appear.

16. Lehmann (1989a) discusses clause linkage with respect to Latin. Here too the continuum is presented as bidirectional but Lehmann's presentation all through is only in terms of 'reduction', 'desentialization', 'increasing nominality', 'hierarchical downgrading', 'integration of the subordinate clause into the main clause', etc., which definitely gives the impression that the continuum works one way only, from full clausal structure to reduced infinitives, gerundials, gerundiva, etc.

17. The interesting thing about the construction in (5) is that it preserves the basic SVO structure *and at the same time* allows the topic to occur in initial position making the word order conform more closely to the topic comment order typical of the pragmatic mode. Quite possibly (but Lambrechts does not mention this) this construction arose as a reaction to the change in the history of French from a Topic-initial to a (more symbolic/abstract) Subject-initial type of language (TVX to SVO, cf. Vennemann 1974).

18. Indeed, this development may be one of the reasons why the *to*-infinitive in English did not generally become bleached of its future orientation as it did in most positions in Modern German and Dutch. In the latter languages the 'that'-clause is still a frequent construction after the verbs of persuading and urging, there was no wholesale replacement by *to*-infinitives. A number of other facts show the essential difference in the use of the English *to*-infinitive as against the German and Dutch *zu*- and *te*-infinitives. These indicate that *to*, unlike *zu/te*, is more than an empty infinitival marker: (i) the *zu*- and *te*-infinitives are usually supported by *um/om* 'for' to express purpose, while English can make do with a plain *to*-infinitive; (ii) the plain *zu/te*-infinitive may

be used to indicate simultaneity, which is not possible with the Modern English *to*-infinitive: cf. Dutch *Hij lag te slapen* (lit. He lay to sleep), 'he lay sleeping' and German *Er bereut nicht, seine Familie verlassen zu haben*/ Dutch *Hij heeft geen berouw zijn familie verlaten te hebben* (lit. He does not regret to have left his family), 'He does not regret having left his family'; (iii) English *to* may be split off from the infinitive by an adverb, this is not possible with *zu/te*. For more details, see Fischer (1997, 2000a).

19. Cf. Tomasello (2003a: 275) who notes the often confusing use of pronouns by young children who are still in the pragmatic mode.

20. Cf. Menn and MacWhinney (1984: 529): 'strong grounds exist for claiming that there is a general output constraint which tends to prohibit sequences of phonologically identical morphs'. This concerns both bound and free morphs, as their examples show. The constraint leads to the use of omission (as in adverbial *-ly* after an adjective in *-ly*), avoidance (in English for instance *who who* and *which which* are avoided), or suppletion. See also Stemberger (1981), Aitchison (1994).

21. Note also, as observed in §1.2.2, that the so-called *that*-trace phenomenon surfaces differently in English and Dutch. In Dutch, in clauses such as *Wie denk je dat er komt* 'who do you think that will come', *dat* must be present, while in English *that* is generally omitted. The same word order difference may account for this.

22. It is notable that in Old English most of the early sentence linkers developed from originally deictic elements: this is true for *þa/þonne* 'then/when', the relative particle *þe*, and *þæt* itself. Later conjunctions that developed in Old English were usually combinations of these markers with a preposition, adverb or noun as in *for þæm þe* 'because', *(swa) þæt* 'so that', *(to þæm) þæt* 'that' (purpose), *þeah (þe)* 'although', *ær þæm þe* 'before', *þa hwile þe* 'that time that, while', etc. In a similar fashion, Pepicello (1982) shows that the Latin *qui, quæ, quod* (pronominal (deictic) relatives), the coordinating conjunction *-que* and subordinating conjunctions such as *ut* '(so)that', *cum* 'because, when', *quoniam* 'because', etc. all go back to the same Indo-European root. Originally, this root functioned as a general marker of interclausal relationship, marking nothing more than 'textual connectivity or continuity' (1982: 256).

23. The backgrounding and foregrounding of information can be done in different ways but it usually centres on the predicate. It may be done by using different tense and aspect features (as is common in the Romance languages) but also by position. It is also usual to distinguish the focus of a sentence by fronting it (cf. Hock 1986: 315). This has been suggested by Stockwell (1977) as a possible explanation for the V-early position (V1 and later V2) of the matrix verb in Old English main clauses, contrasting with the unmarked V-final position of subordinate clauses.

24. The difference between lexicalization and grammaticalization is probably to a large extent a terminological one. According to some linguists, lexicalization involves the adoption of linguistic elements into the lexicon when their

interpretation/use is no longer transparent, others consider it a possible stage on the grammaticalization path, while for yet a third group lexicalization is the opposite of grammaticalization, cf. the discussion in Lehmann (1989b), Keller (1998), Wischer (2000), Brinton (2002), who distinguishes as many as nine definitions, Brinton and Traugott (2005); for the third interpretation, see especially Ramat (1992: 550–1), who writes 'LEXICALIZATION IS THUS AN ASPECT OF DEGRAMMATICALIZATION ... [it] has to be seen as a process whereby linguistic signs formed by rules of grammar are no longer perceived (parsed) in this way but simply as lexical entries'. The most insightful analysis of the similarities and differences between the two processes can be found in Himmelmann (2004).

25. With Keller (1998) it could be said that both *while* and *cupboard* have lost in diagrammatic iconic reference and have become more 'symbolic' since the link with the original element(s) that make up the lexicalized items has been severed to some extent. Lexicalization thus involves *symbolization*, i.e. using the items in question on a more abstract, more purely linguistic level (cf. Keller 1998: 162–4). All this is rather similar to what happens on the subjectification cline (cf. cline (7b) in §4.2.2), when an item or set of items changes from having reference on a propositional (semiotic, non-linguistic) level to reference on a textual (purely linguistic) level. The first can be inferred on the basis of world knowledge and knowledge of the other symbols that make up the phrase, the second is rule-based.

26. I refer here to 'derivation' in a generative sense: the derivation of a given structure is a representation of the set of operations (depending on the model, this could involve 'movement', 'merge', 'raising', etc.) used to form that structure. Also depending on the model, the derivation could entail different syntactic levels (i.e. deep (underlying) and surface structures) as is the case in the GB model, or be part of the same level, as in the Minimalist model.

27. There have been some changes in form, and variations in terminology. Subject-raising is usually called NP-movement in the P&P model, but is again referred to as Subject-raising in the Minimalist model (cf. Radford 1997: 151). Another term used for it is A[rgument]-Movement. Equi-NP deletion came to be part of Control Theory, with the PRO (the earlier Equi NP) controlled by the matrix subject rather than being deleted. Verb-raising also occurs with control verbs. It only occurs in West-Germanic OV languages, and has always been a rather controversial type of rule.

28. The P&P and the Minimalist models differ only in the status assigned to the non-finite subordinate clause, and in the position of the traces left by the movement of the underlying Subject. In the former model the clause is a bare S (cf. Radford 1988: 435ff), while in the latter it is a maximal projection (IP) (cf. Radford 1997: 175ff.). This difference is related to the status of *to*, which in the Minimalist model has functional content and is situated in INFL (or I).

29. It is notable that in the ICE-GB corpus most of the negative constructions with *seem* show Negative-raising (46 instances) and all these constructions also have

a raised subject (or an empty *it* followed by adjective/infinitive, so no *that*-clause). Only three instances are found with non-raising, and here 'seem' is used as a full verb not as an evidential, with the literal meaning of 'to have the appearance', as in *He seems not to move a muscle in a whole evening* (ICE-GB s1a 045–117). Also very telling is that the more informal and subjective 'raised' construction occurs much more frequently in the spoken part of the corpus than in the written one (57 vs. 29 instances).

30. There is other evidence that makes Raising unlikely and that is that *seem(s) to* behaves like one unit. Krug (2001), and cf. also Plank (1984), refers to the univerbation of the verb and the *to* element in what are often called semi-modals or semi-auxiliaries (Krug calls them 'emerging modals'), such as *have to, used to, need to, try to*. According to Krug a similar phonemic structure has developed in the course of time that is typical for many of these modal groups (of different origins), such as /bɛtə, ni:tə, ju:stə, həftə, ɔ:tə, gɔtə, gɔnə, maitəv, kədəv/ etc. (i.e. '(had) better, need to, used to, have to, ought to, got to, going to>gonna, might have, could have'). (Although Krug does not mention *seem* here, it behaves in many ways like the emerging modals he discusses.) In other words, through analogy of position (a verb before an infinitive) causing seman-tic and phonetic reduction, a two-syllabic phonological form has developed, which in turn seems to function analogically as an 'iconic paradigm', binding these constructions together into a separate 'semi-modal' category. Univerba-tion in *seem to* is also suggested by language acquisition data, cf. Tomasello (2003a: 245–9) mentioned below.

31. Note that a generative type of Raising does not play a role in functional models. Indeed the choice for Raising is ultimately a choice of the theory. In Cognitive Grammar (cf. Langacker 1995) and Construction Grammar (cf. Goldberg 1995; Croft and Cruse 2004), the meaning of a construction is a combination of the meaning of the construction itself and the lexical elements involved in it. The lexical elements themselves do not have a fixed meaning either, rather the construction in which they occur contributes to their overall meaning.

32. Note that there is no agreement among generative linguists concerning the status of the modal verbal complement in Old English. In Allen (1975) and Lightfoot (1979) it is S (which is the same as the later IP). The status in Roberts (1985) is unclear, he wavers between S' (later CP) and VP, but the latter would entail that the modal is not a main verb, which he maintains it is (see §4.2.1). Van Kemenade (1992) argues that it must be a maximal projection C", except for modals used epistemically, since it contains a PRO subject position. Roberts and Roussou (2002: 30ff) argue that modals were biclausal taking a TP complement (similar to IP), and became monoclausal in the sixteenth century.

33. This is not to deny, of course that some of these monoclausal structures may become biclausal in the course of the child's linguistic development. This would account for the emergence of constructions where the infinitive contains a

subject (as in *I want him to* . . .), cf. Tomasello (2003a: 248). Clause elaboration, in other words, could be both an ontogenetic as well as a phylogenetic development (cf. the discussion in §5.1 and fn. 14 above).

34. The grammaticalization of verbal groups such as *be going to*, *be able to*, *have(got) to*, *be to*, *want to*, etc. into 'semi-auxiliaries' all take place at different times and at different speeds in the history of English cf. e.g. Brinton (1988), Danchev and Kytö (1994), Fischer (1994a), Krug (2000).

35. Possibly via two stages of analogy, first analogy with Aux *to* V constructions, and finally analogy via Aux V constructions, resulting in a fusion of *going* + *to* > *gonna*.

36. The example is the following: *Se mildheorta god. wolde ða gyt gebigan. ðæra iudeiscra mod. mid micclum tacnum. to ðam soðum geleafan. gif **hi sylfe woldon. þæt hi**mid dædbote adwæscton heora synna. and asende him to. syllice tacna. swa þæt an steorra stod. se wæs swurde gelic. bufon Hierusalem. beorhte scynende* (ÆCHom II 18.172.105) 'The merciful God wanted then yet (to) bend (convert) the minds of the Jewish (people) with many signs to the true belief, if they themselves wanted. that they through penitence washed off their sins. and he sent to them wondrous signs so that a star stood (still), which like a sword above Jerusalem brightly shone'. The translation is problematic, and it is possible that the *þæt*-clause after *woldon* is in fact a clause dependent on the earlier *wolde*, which has *god* as subject (so no co-indexed subject!), or it is a result clause (with *þæt* meaning 'so that'), depending on the main clause.

37. Denison (1993: 308) mentions two Old English instances of *mæg* followed by a *þæt*-clause but in one case the clause is not a complement directly dependent on *mæg* but is an extension of the direct object pronoun *þæt* : *Ac **þæt** hie magon **þæt** hie þas tida leahtrien* (Or 3 9.74.25) 'But **that** they have-power **that** they these times blame', where in the context the clause is also resultative 'they have only *that* (i.e. such) power that they blame these times'. This is also the function of the clause in Denison's second example: *Hwa mæg þæt he ne wundrie swelcra gesceafta ures scyppendes* (Bo 34.92.7), 'Whoever has-power (such) that he not wonders at-such creations of-our Creator'. Almost all other examples of *magan* followed by a *þæt*-clause occur in glosses and are a translation of Latin *non potest/potuit ut* 'has/had no power so that', where the use of *ut* and the negative also indicates the adverbial, resultative nature of the subordinate clause.

38. Kern (1912: 46–55), Van den Toorn *et al.* (1997: 124–5) and van der Horst (forthcoming) show that most of the verbs that now appear in Verb-raising constructions used to have a bare infinitive to start with. This is true for the modals, for physical perception verbs, for the Subject-raising verb *schijnen* 'seem', and for some control verbs like *wanen* 'think' and *weten* 'know how to'. These verbs only acquired a *te*-infinitive after the marked *te*-infinitive had lost its purposive meaning (and indeed came to be strengthened by *om* in Middle Dutch and early Modern Dutch, cf. Gerritsen 1987) and had thus become more or less identical to the bare infinitive (see fn. 18 above). This latter development must also have helped other control verbs, which had

always required a *te*-infinitive and only became auxiliary-like much later, to allow the same raising construction as was allowed with the early bare infinitival complements. Some of these began to allow Verb-raising from the seventeenth century onwards (*behoren* 'ought to', *pogen, trachten* 'try', *zoeken* 'seek'), many have only acquired it very recently: e.g. *proberen* 'try', *hopen* 'hope', *weigeren* 'refuse'.

39. The IPP effect only appears in Verb-raised constructions after perception verbs, causatives, and optionally with some control verbs in Modern Dutch; in Modern German it occurs too but is much more restricted. Its use is still a bit of a mystery. An example with a control verb from Dutch is:

(a) *De minister heeft een guerillaleider   weigeren*[INF] *te ontmoeten*[INF]
    The minister has   a   guerrilla leader refuse[INF]   to meet

The IPP can only be used when matrix verb and infinitive express the same tense domain. Thus, the IPP cannot be used when the control verb takes a fully purposive *om te*-infinitive. In that case the 'normal' past participle is used:

(b) *De   minister heeft geweigerd*[PASTPART] *(om) een guerillaleider   te*
    The   minister has   refused   (for) a   guerrilla leader to
    ontmoeten
    meet.

The meaning of the two phrases is also not the same (cf. Geerts *et al.* 1984: 581): in (b) the 'meeting' has shifted to a tense domain different from the matrix verb. The IPP construction in (a) expresses 'The minister has refused [a particular meeting with a particular guerrilla leader]', while (b) conveys: 'The minister has refused, in general, [to meet [guerrilla leaders]]', i.e. in the first case the infinitival complement functions as direct object, in the second case it functions as adjunct. It is not surprising therefore that in the object function, the verbal elements may be scrambled since they function as one clausal unit.

40. A possible objection to this proposal could be that different word orders are possible in Dutch and Old English with Verb-raising verbs, which still would make case assignment difficult. Thus in (18a, 18c) the object or PP (*krant, op reis*) may also appear between main verb and infinitive, and this is not possible in (18b, 18d), nor with modals and causative *laten* 'let'. I note that word order is more fixed the older the construction is, i.e. it is more fixed with those verbs that always only accepted bare infinitives. In other words entrenchment plays a role here. Furthermore de Schutter (2000) shows that the many variations that occur in Modern Standard Dutch (both regarding word order and the IPP effect) are due to dialect mixing. To capture all this variation by means of a complex of rules (next to Verb-raising, there is also Verb-projection raising) which are in no way predictable, seems as costly or more costly as simply stating that idiosyncratic lexical variations occur.

41. For instance, the Raising possibility with a verb like *proberen* 'try' or *weigeren* 'refuse' only dates from the nineteenth century, cf. Kern (1912), van der Horst (forthcoming).

42. Another common case of attraction involves what is often called 'proximity concord', i.e. a form of subject–verb agreement, whereby an NP that occurs straight in front of the verb may govern verb agreement even when that NP is not the subject, or whereby the last element in a coordinated NP triggers a singular inflection instead of a plural one. Deutscher (2000: 97) points to the phenomenon of case-attraction in Akkadian, whereby the object of an infinitival verbal noun may be governed directly by the preposition that governs the verbal noun.

43. According to Roberts (1993a), bare infinitivals do have Tense since Tense is associated with the infinitival ending. I find a link between Tense and the infinitival ending hard to accept for two reasons: the *-en* ending, which was lost in Middle English, goes back to the OE *-an* ending, which was originally a nominal ending. It is not explained how this original case ending in time came to stand for Tense. (ii) Roberts explains the rise of the *to*-infinitive (where *to* represents Tense) in Middle English as a replacement of the loss of tense (i.e. the loss of the ending *-en*) in the bare infinitive. It has been shown above (§§4.1 and 5.1), however, that the *to*- infinitive replaced the *that*-clause and not the bare infinitive.

44. In Bock's own words: 'Der Infinitiv der idg. Einzelsprachen erfuhr durch die allmähliche Eingliederung in das Verbalsystem eine stetig fortschreitende Verbalisierung. Gleichzeitig wurde die syntaktische Verbindung zwischen Verb und Infinitiv immer enger, und in seiner Hauptverwendungsart wurde letzterer unter gänzlichem Verlust seiner Kasusnatur schliesslich als fertige Ergänzung einer Reihe an sich unvollständiger Verben gefasst'. He adds that in those cases where a looser link between matrix verb and infinitive was required, a new nominal infinitive developed, i.e. the *to*-infinitive, which as we have seen above, remained nominal much longer than the bare infinitive, but which finally also succumbed to verbalization, just like the gerund later.

45. In contrast to *habban* 'have', there are instances of *findan* 'find' followed by a finite 'that'-clause, but these are very different in nature in that, in all these cases, *findan* describes a mental ('to find out, discover') and not a physical activity (for more differences, see Fischer 1989).

46. Examples can be found in ÆCHom II 126.565 with an adjective (*Seo sunne stod stille on heofonum* 'The sun stood still in the heavens'), in ÆCHom II 116.226 with a present participle (*and eal se munt smocigende stod* 'and the whole mountain stood smoking') and in ÆCHom I 278.96 with a past participle (*. . . godes .æ. þe **stod** on fif bocum awriten* 'in God's law which stood in five books written').

47. 'Man hat dabei gar nicht erwogen, wie ein solcher Gebrauch des Infinitivs zu solch früher Zeit schon hätte möglich sein können. Historisch und im Zusammenhang mit den anderen überlieferten Gebrauchsweisen des Infinitivs

gesehen, kann der *to*-Infinitiv in solchen Sätzen gar nicht anders als in Abhängigkeit von dem betreffenden Nomen gedacht werden. Alles andere ist moderne syntaktische Auffassung und nur zu Unrecht der alten Sprache untergelegt' (p. 129)

48. The adjacency and fixed order of Aux V order became the rule in Middle English main and subordinate clauses, also as a result of the SOV > SVO change and the loss of Verb-second. This meant that this pattern was now highly frequent in all periphrastic verb constructions, unlike in German and Dutch, where the two verbal elements are not necessarily adjacent (they are adjacent only in subordinate clauses and in main clauses without an object, complement, or adjunct), and even if adjacent, do not always occur in the same fixed Aux V order. Note that the *semantic* change from possessive 'have' to obligatory 'have' played much less of a role in the whole development since the Old English constructions of the type given in (29) already conveyed some modal sense, although not necessarily obligative (cf. Fischer 1994a). The same is true for the modern Dutch and German constructions with *hebben/haben* 'have' followed by a *te-/zu*-infinitive; they carry a modal meaning of potentiality, which depending on context, may be obligative.

49. It is most likely that the construction first arose colloquially. For this reason, its origin may be difficult to establish due to a lack of data. Another suggestion has been that it was a calque of a Greek construction (cf. Fleischman 1982: 52–4).

6

Subjectification, scope, and word order

6.0 Introduction

Subjectification (sometimes also termed 'subjectivization') is a phenomenon that often coincides with the process of grammaticalization, especially with the early stages of the process, which according to grammaticalization theorists are characterized by pragmatic enrichment. Traugott (1982, 1989), Sweetser (1990) (and see also the articles in Stein and Wright 1995, and Brinton 1996) show how in many cases of grammaticalization there is a development towards greater subjectivity in that there is a tendency for meanings to become increasingly based in the speaker's subjective attitude towards a proposition. Connections have also been observed between subjectivity and word order. As Finegan (1995: 3) indicates, subjectivity may be marked in many different ways; some languages 'exploit morphology'—but this is often too directly confronting because subjectivity as a modality marker is frequently involved in the expression of politeness—while other languages employ more subtle means, ranging from intonation to word order. Keller (1995), for instance, shows that the different positions of the matrix verb (i.e. Verb-second or Verb-final position) in causal *weil*-clauses in Modern German may mark the difference between a factual and an epistemic stance respectively, while Adamson (2000) shows that the subjective meaning of English adjectives correlates with leftmost position within the NP, and that, diachronically, subjectification of the adjective goes hand in hand with a more leftward position (depending on the model used, this could be seen as leftward movement). This may result eventually in the reanalysis of this adjective into an (adverbial) intensifier.[1] Thus the phrases *long, lovely legs/an old, dirty man* differ from *lovely long legs/a dirty old man* in that only in the latter can the leftmost adjective have scope over the whole phrase (i.e. over the second adjective plus the noun) and be subjective in meaning, whereas in the former the two adjectives have identical scope (they scope over the noun only). This difference is usually indicated by a comma in writing and by a different intonation pattern in the spoken language. For another case of leftward 'movement' and subjectification, involving the English *'s*-genitive, see Rosenbach *et al.* (2000). We will see below that the subjectification of the English core modals is also associated, especially in the generative framework, with leftward movement.

Even though subjectification and grammaticalization are in many ways similar and often develop in tandem, there is a great problem with a difference in unidirectionality of the two clines representing these processes, namely with respect to scope (this was briefly discussed in §4.2.2; the two clines are given there in (7)). In subjectification, that is the discourse-pragmatic type of grammaticalization, there seems to be an increase in scope (cf. Tabor and Traugott 1998) rather than a reduction (the latter is predicted by the grammaticalization parameters put forward by Lehmann, cf. Table 3.2. in §3.2). In §4.2.2, I suggested that this problem may be a consequence of the overemphasis within the grammaticalization approach on the pragmatic-semantic aspects of language in use and of not taking sufficient account of the formal aspects, in particular the form of the synchronic grammatical system of each individual language at the time the change takes place.

For this chapter, I will have another look at the subjectification involved in the development of epistemic modals from dynamic/deontic ones because this too is generally (by both grammaticalization linguists and by generative linguists concerned with the phenomenon of grammaticalization, such as Roberts and Roussou 1999, 2003) considered to involve scope increase rather than decrease. We will see that the phenomenon of clause fusion, discussed in Chapter 5, plays an important part here too, but with a difference. Whereas I argued in §5.3 that there is no evidence for clause fusion in the case of the English modal auxiliaries when they developed from full verbs, nor in the Romance and English development of the perfect auxiliary 'have' from full-verb possessive 'have', I will here suggest that clause fusion does play a role in the development of epistemic modal meaning from deontic/dynamic meaning. This will be the subject of §6.1. Another area where scope increase has been attested in relation to subjectification, is in the development of sentence adverbs and pragmatic markers. Here it appears that position and the occurrence of 'reduced clauses' has been influential. I hope to show by means of a comparison of the way sentence adverbs and pragmatic markers are used in Old English and Modern English on the one hand, and in Modern English and the other Germanic languages on the other, how the loss of the Verb-second rule in English and the overall fixation of word order has considerably changed their deployment in English. This will be the topic of §6.2.

6.1 Subjectification and scope: the development of epistemic modals

Tabor and Traugott (1998: 233ff.) suggest that there is a difference in scope between epistemic constructions such as Present-day English *He must be home by now*/*She may be right*, where the epistemic modal has scope over the whole of the proposition (given in italics in the gloss) and can be paraphrased as 'It is necessarily the case *that he is home by now*'/'It is possibly the case *that she is right*', and dynamic/deontic modal constructions, such as *I must do this first*/*I can drive a combine*, where the scope of *must/can* is restricted to the VP. The point of their article is to show that the modals undergo scope increase when they change from dynamic/deontic to epistemic. I will follow the generative interpretation of scope (i.e. scope in terms of C-command) as used by Tabor and Traugott in their article.[2]

Before we turn to a discussion of scope increase, it must be stated that scope is a notion that is very hard to define. As to its formal properties, the definition heavily depends on the model used since the position of an operator (the element that has scope) in a model's (underlying) structure does not necessarily coincide with the surface position of that element. A semantic-pragmatic notion of scope is perhaps more profitable, but this has been worked out mainly with reference to negatives, quantifiers, and interrogatives. Tabor and Traugott's way of proving scope increase is by means of a method which they call 'diachronic string comparison', that is, a comparison of synchronic structures at periodical intervals to establish change. In order to establish 'scope', they use the generative notion of C-command, with the idea that a node that C-commands another node, also has scope over that node.[3]

The problem with the Tabor–Traugott use of scope here, is that the synchronic stages are described in terms of formal properties of the underlying structure while the diachronic developments are described in terms of the semantic-pragmatic properties of the actual utterances. Two different methods, drawn from the two approaches under discussion here (i.e. the formal and the functional), get mixed up in the application of 'diachronic string comparison'. Grammaticalization looks at the gradual process involving forms or constructions in language change, and it is commonly agreed among grammaticalization theorists that the changes proceed by infinitesimal steps and diffuse so gradually (often via lexical items) that it is difficult, if not impossible, to capture them in hard and fast rules of the type envisaged by generative linguists. Categories too are seen as fluid (cf. the discussion in Chapter 3). What Tabor and Traugott do with their method of diachronic string comparison, is to compare the underlying structures of an early and a later stage; these are clear-cut (because they are formal abstractions), and the differences between the two structures are therefore crystal clear. At the same time, they practise the grammaticalization method in their investigation of the changes visible in the data (in the form of synchronic and diachronic variables) with an eye mainly on the semantic-pragmatic factors involved in the shifts. They are thus using the clarity and the firmness of the generative model for the formal part of the synchronic structures defined for each period and the soft and fluid grammaticalization model for the pragmatic-semantic developments that take place gradually. This mingling makes the argument less than transparent.

Returning to Tabor and Traugott's discussion of scope increase in the English modals, what needs to be looked at is how this change emerged historically both in formal and semantic terms. As far as form is concerned, however, we must turn to the surface forms and not to abstract rules, that is to say, we must look at the variations in form across time. The main question in this development is: is it simply a matter of a modal verb such as *must* changing in meaning, or changing in category, or is there more at issue? To put it differently, is there only a 'token' involved—*must*—or also a 'type', for example the whole category or paradigm to which *must* belongs, or a larger syntactic construction-type in which *must* functions syntagmatically as a token?

Must belongs to the category of core modal auxiliaries in Present-day English, and it seems clear that the epistemic development is typical for all core modals, that is it involves a category and therefore a more abstract type. In other words, this grammaticalization is a true case of grammaticalization and cannot be interpreted as lexicalization, as in the case of *while* described above (§5.1.1), where, as I have argued, *only* a token is involved. The other concern, whether the modal that becomes epistemic forms part of a larger construction, is a trickier one. On the surface, there does not seem to be much formal difference between epistemic and dynamic/deontic modal usage; after all, *He must be at home* can have either meaning in the appropriate context. We will therefore have to look more closely at the historical development of the epistemic modal.

For this, I briefly return to the behaviour of the modal verbs in Old English. It has been shown in §5.3 and in Chapter 4 that the Old English dynamic/deontic modals behave to some extent like main verbs, in that they can take a direct object (which may be an action noun/bare infinitive) or a directional adverbial, and show tense differences. In contrast to most accounts, I have argued that their structure can best be interpreted as monoclausal. Epistemic usage is still rare in Old English, and is, as Warner (1993: 158–9) has made very clear, difficult to establish because the interpretation of epistemicity depends to some extent on contextual and cultural presuppositions.

The only more or less clear epistemic examples from a formal point of view involve 'subjectless' types, that is instances where the modal verb appears without a subject of its own, which makes a dynamic/deontic reading difficult. There are three types, represented by the examples in (1)–(3) respectively. First, there are instances without any subject; these are rare.[4] Second, we frequently find modals combined with an impersonal verb, which seem to have a 'raised' subject (i.e. the 'subject' of the impersonal infinitive, which is usually in the dative, is 'raised' into the matrix clause). The third type is also fairly frequent and concerns a construction in which the modal is combined with an intransitive infinitive, which does not assign a thematic role to its subject, such as copula verbs: *beon* 'be', *gewurþan* 'become, get, happen', etc. Often an expletive subject *hit* 'it' is present. These intransitive verbs are close to impersonal (subjectless) verbs like *gelimpan, gebyrian* 'happen', which may also occur with expletive *hit*.

(1) Eaðe *mæg*, þæt me Drihten þurh   his geearnung miltsigan   wille
                                                            (Bede 3 11.192.5)
    Easily can   that me Lord   through his merit   show-mercy will
    'It is quite possible that the Lord will show me mercy because of his merit'

(2a) þonne *mæg hine scamigan* þære   brædinge his   hlisan (Bo 19.46.5)
     then   can   him   shame   of-the spreading of-his fame
     'then he may be ashamed of the extent of his fame'

(2b) Hwy   ne   sceolde me[DAT] swa þyncan? (Bo 38.119.9)
     Why   not   should   me   so   seem
     'Why should/How could it not seem so to me?'

(3a) Ðeah þe *hit* swa beon *mihte* þæt he þas   blisse   begitan mihte
                                                            (ÆLS (Ash Wed)106)
     Though it so be   could that he those favours beget   could
     'Though it could be the case that he would receive those favours'

(3b) Eaðe *mæg* gewurðan þæt þu   wite   þæt ic nat (ApT 21.10)
     easily may happen   that you know that I not-know
     'it may easily be the case that you know what I don't know'

(3c) Gif hit swa *sceal* gewurðan þæt mann us her finde and
     If it so   must happen   that 'one' us here find and
     mann us for Godes naman to ðam casere   læde (LS 34 (SevenSleepers)415)
     'one' us for God's name   to the emperor lead
     'If it must happen that they find us here and lead us to the emperor because
     of God's name'

We can draw a number of conclusions from these examples. First of all, Old English modal verbs are similar to impersonal verbs. Like some other impersonal verbs in Old English they occur both with animate and inanimate agentive (nominative) subjects (when they are dynamic/deontic), and without a subject, as in (1) and (3b) (cf. Fischer and van der Leek 1983).[5] When the modal verb is used without a nominative (i.e. agentive[6]) NP, the semantic meaning of the verb becomes more general (cf. the different meanings of *ofhreowan* in fn. 5). Thus, *mæg* would then mean 'power exists', *sceal* 'obligation exists', *mot* 'opportunity exists', etc., which would make the meaning of these verbs more dependent on the context and on other available evidence, that is their meaning is established by pragmatic or logical inference: they thus convey general possibility, necessity, etc.

Secondly, it is not surprising to find these non-agentive, non-nominative modals in combination with impersonal infinitives (as in (2)), which likewise can occur without a nominative subject. The constructions of (2) are *structurally* similar to regular monoclausal modal verb constructions, where the nominative subject of the deontic/dynamic modal main verb expresses the same semantic role for both the matrix modal and the infinitival object(-complement). In the same way, a dative/accusative case (or 'subject')[7] expresses an identical role (but here it is experiencer rather than agentive) for both the matrix modal and the impersonal infinitival object, and this case or 'subject' needs to be made explicit only once, as in regular modal verb constructions where the agentive subject is lexicalized once for both the modal and the infinitival object (as in *He can read*).

Denison (1993: 238ff.) and Warner (1993: 129) suggest that the process in the examples of (2) is similar to Subject-raising, but this is not quite felicitous according to the generative definition of Subject-raising. According to this definition, the subject of the infinitival verb (which receives its semantic role from this infinitive) *must* be raised in order to receive Case, and the subject position of the matrix verb (which gives no semantic role to its subject) *must* be filled structurally. There was no need for this in Old English because it still allowed subjectless sentences. Regular cases of Subject-raising, such as with *seem*, *happen*, *chance* only occur from late Middle English onwards, when the language no longer allowed an empty subject position but required an obligatory subject. In Middle English the subject also became more purely structural (i.e. it could express a larger variety of semantic roles, cf. fn. 7) due to the loss of inflectional case. I will therefore call the construction illustrated in (2) a case of 'pseudo-raising' for lack of a better term. In fact, if anything, the construction is more like that of control verbs, except that the infinitive is not clausal (there is no PRO), as I have argued in §5.3 for all the modals.

Thirdly, even though the examples in (2) do not present proper Subject-raising, the exceptional use of this 'pseudo-raising' with impersonal infinitives only, does provide us with indirect evidence that agentive infinitival subjects of 'personal' verbs could not yet be raised: epistemic modals with personal subjects, of the type *He must have forgotten*, could not yet occur in Old English because in this case the modal and the infinitive had different thematic 'subject' roles, expressed by different case-forms. That is, the nominative case expressing 'agentive' arguments with a 'personal' or 'agentive' verb like 'forget' could not be raised to a matrix clause position which required, as an argument of an *impersonal* modal verb, an experiencer 'subject' in the dative or accusative case. Again it is not surprising to find that evidence for an epistemic modal with a personal subject only becomes strong in Middle English, at the same time as Subject-raising structures with verbs like *seem* begin to occur. Under impersonal verbs, I also classify copula verbs like 'to be, to become', which likewise do not assign a thematic role to their subject. This accounts for the occurrence of epistemic modals in (3), where the modal verb is combined with the copulas *beon* and *gewurþan*.

Fourthly, what I find most interesting about the examples in (3) is that the modal verb, followed by the agentless impersonal infinitive, occurs with a *þæt*-clause (note that a *þæt*-clause is also present in (1)). Here we have explicit evidence for a biclausal structure, which (as I have shown in §5.3) could not be found for deontic/dynamic modals. These biclausal constructions are frequent in Old English, especially with *magan*. They suggest that this was the only way to express epistemicity if the infinitival object of the epistemic modal was not itself an agentless or impersonal verb. Note that it is the *þæt*-clause that makes this structure biclausal and *not* the infinitive itself, which I have analysed as a direct object argument of the modal verb, as part of a monoclausal structure. One could say that the structure shown in (3) performed a kind of 'bridge' function: the impersonal modal cannot be easily combined with a *þæt*-clause containing a personal, agentive verb (as we said, (1) is rare and may well be an ellipted construction). The solution, therefore, is to combine the modal with an *impersonal* infinitive, which *can* take a *þæt*-clause.

To come back to the problem of scope increase in the grammaticalization of the modals, I propose, on the strength of the factors given in the four points above, that epistemic usage in combination with personal, agentive verbs arose in Old English via an earlier biclausal structure consisting of an impersonal modal verb (+ impersonal infinitive)[8] + *þæt*-clause, that is type (1) or (3) above. One could also argue that the 'pseudo-raising' constructions of (2) with impersonal infinitives are also originally or underlyingly biclausal. I do not think they are because there is no empirical evidence for this, that is I have not found clauses in Old English such as *mæg þæt hine scamiaþ* ... 'can/may that him is-shame'.

The reason why the epistemic modals become difficult to distinguish in Modern English from the other modal uses, is because they begin to occur in the same type of clauses. The original, epistemic '(It) may be that he comes' construction came to be replaced by the 'He may come' construction. This is due to a formal analogy with the personal construction containing dynamic/deontic modals (the type 'He can/is able to swim') and due to analogy with Subject-raising structures with verbs like *seem*, which in Middle English became possible because of the rise of the structural subject, as noted above, in fn. 7. This analogy must have been greatly helped by the fact that the personal deontic/dynamic modal constructions must have been far more frequent in the PLD available to the language learner. This replacement is largely a question of economy. As Plank (1985) has argued, it is natural for marked constructions to be structured as much as possible analogous to unmarked ones. Since epistemic and deontic/dynamic modality is expressed by the same verbs, and since deontic modals themselves can be *subjectively* deontic (cf. fn. 2), it is not surprising for the epistemically used modals to conform to the structure used for the deontic/dynamic ones. The development also falls in with the 'Minimize Form' principle of Hawkins (2004), referred to earlier in §4.4.

If we accept this development for the epistemic modals, we also have an explanation for the problem of scope because it brings this case in line with the generally accepted behaviour of scope in grammaticalization. From the scenario I have sketched, it follows that the epistemic modal was at first in a higher clause than the actual proposition contained in the (infinitive plus) *þæt*-clause. This naturally entailed that it had scope over the entire *þæt*-clause. With the dynamic/deontic modals the proposition was contained in the infinitive (i.e. the infinitival *object*) alone, which formed part of the matrix clause itself. This means that the scope possibilities of the modal verb with respect to the infinitive were formally the same in Old English, whether it had epistemic or dynamic/deontic sense, but it is only in structures like (3) that the infinitival object of the modal verb includes a *þæt*-clause. Crucially, then, the scope concerns in both cases the immediate constituent of the modal verb.

In Middle English, the epistemic structure of (3) begins to be replaced by the form of that of the dynamic/deontic structure. This formal replacement takes place with the semantics and the scope of the full biclausal *þæt*-clause structure preserved.[9] Since, however, there must have been the biclausal intermediate stage to make this possible, one cannot maintain that this change from deontic/dynamic to epistemic involves scope increase. The scope in fact remains the same. It only *superficially* looks like a case of scope increase, if one ignores the intermediate structure illustrated in (3).

Thus, *if* there is scope increase, it is via an *indirect* route. Lehmann's unidirectional parameter of scope decrease can therefore be maintained in this particular case since the direction of scope has not in fact changed. I therefore disagree with Bybee *et al.* (1994: 198) when they ascribe the English modal shift to epistemic meaning strictly to pragmatic inferencing, and the change in scope strictly to the shift in meaning in the verb. I note that they only give Middle English cases of inferencing (1994: 198–9) and no cases in Old English (1994: 193). Through their emphasis on the discourse-pragmatic nature of the development, they miss the Old English formal (biclausal) structures in which the epistemic meaning could first develop.

It remains to be seen whether the epistemic development of modal auxiliaries in other languages has followed a similar formal path. This question will have to be answered by future research. However, there is additional evidence that the modal becomes epistemic only via a more elaborate construction-type. Boogaart (2004) has argued for the modal verbs in Modern Dutch that they are not polysemous, in the sense that the modal verbs have a deontic as well as an epistemic sense. Rather he suggests a monosemous approach in terms of construction networks, in which the differences in meaning *depend on the construction* in which they occur. He shows by means of corpus evidence that the epistemic sense only occurs in biclausal constructions such as *Het moet/kan (zo) zijn dat* . . . 'It must/may be (so) that . . . '—that is exactly the same type that I have found to be relevant in Old English—and not in constructions such as *Hij moet ziek zijn* 'He must be ill'. If it occurs at all in the latter, it is almost always accompanied by an epistemic adverb/particle such as *wel*, which is difficult to translate but means as much as 'it has to be so'. The use of such particles and of clauses like *Ik denk dat* . . . 'I think that . . . ' are indeed the most usual way of expressing epistemicity in Dutch. Note that in *Ik denk dat*-structures, the epistemicity arises again in a biclausal construction. The same may well be true in the case of particles such as *wel* (they may come from 'reduced clauses'), which I will have a closer look at in §6.2.

A perusal of data from the ICE-GB corpus shows that in actual language use most Present-day English epistemic constructions still concern a modal followed by the infinitive *be* (whether as a copula, or an auxiliary of the progressive/passive/perfect (perfect *have* is also frequent),[10] especially in the case of *must*, somewhat less so in the case of *may*. An epistemic modal followed by a personal *agentive* verb (an active verb with an agentive subject), as in *He must come often*, is much rarer. In other words, an intransitive 'impersonal' infinitive is still usually present. Note that a sentence like *You must be lying/you must have lied* is easily interpreted as epistemic, whereas *you must lie* without *be* sounds strange, and is indeed more easily interpreted as deontic even though this is a strange command (it could be said to a spy who must lie for his country). Epistemic usage of a modal + *be* followed by a *that*-clause is also still common, as in *It may be (the case) that. …* The fact that *may/might* without *be* is somewhat more regular in an epistemic sense, may well be due to the fact that there is hardly any interference here: positive *may* is losing its deontic sense of permission to *can* (negative *may not* is still more usual here), while past *might* has practically lost all deontic meaning. Van der Auwera *et al.* (2005) note in this connection that J. K. Rowling in one of the *Harry Potter* books uses *might* much more frequently than either *may* or *could* for the expression of epistemic possibility (41 instances of *might*, against 21 *could* and 4 *may*)

Note also a clear preference for *biclausal* epistemic constructions in French,

(4) Il   se   peut   qu'elle   vienne[SUBJ][11]
     It   (reflex.) can   that she   come
     'She may come' (i.e. it is possible that she comes)
(5) Il   est   inevitable qu' il se   fasse[SUBJ] prendre un jour[12]
     It   is   inevitable that he   come to grief   one day
     'He must/will come to grief one day'

Monoclausal constructions with modal verbs, on the other hand, always convey only a deontic/dynamic sense, cf.,

(6)   elle peut venire
      she can come (i.e. she is able/allowed to come)
(7)   il doit venir[13]
      he must come (i.e. he is obliged to come)

It is only in constructions where the modal is combined with 'be' (but cf. fn. 13) that it can also have epistemic sense, as in, *Il doit être malade* 'He must be ill'.

Another interesting piece of evidence is the different forms used in some English-based creoles for deontic and epistemic *may* and *must*. Shepherd (1982: 320) indicates that in the Antiguan Creole, *mos* '[is] used exclusively for … deontic meanings', while *mosa* 'is used exclusively for epistemic probability', as her examples in (8) and (9) make clear:

(8)   me mos tap usin   all dark colors
        I must stop wearing all dark colours (because they don't look good on me)

(9a)   A mosa wet deah
        it must-be wet there

(9b)   An ha gol on it an coes five dolla? No, mosa tiif dem from somebody den
        It's gold and costs five dollar? Can't be, must-have stolen it from someone
        then

Shepherd does not mention this, but it seems quite possible that *mosa* is a contraction of earlier (English) *must*+ BE or *must*+ HAVE (cf. the use in Jamaican English of shuda/wuda 'should have/would have' (Silvia Kouwenberg p.c.)). In a similar way, Winford (2000) and Edhard (2004) show that different forms are used in the Suriname creole, Sranan Tongo. Edhard has found unequivocal epistemic uses of both *kan* 'can' and *musu* 'must' only in twentieth-century documents, and in both cases the forms used are part of a larger construction, see (10). Winford's findings from a spoken database (11) are similar:

(10a)   a   musu de taki   a   sondu nanga a   sari di   den
                                              (*Waktitoren*, Edhard 2004: 50)
        it   must be the-case-that the sin   and   the sad that they
        ben   kon   de na ini ...
        been come be at in
        'the sin and sorrow that they had gotten into must have....'

(10b)   a kan de fanowdu fu tan   wakti (*Waktitoren*, Edhard 2004: 45)
        it can be necessary to stay wait
        'it may be necessary to keep waiting'

(11)   a   kan (de) taki   Jan ben   sribi kba (Winford 2000: 94)
        it can (be) the-case-that John PAST sleep already
        'it may be that John was already asleep/John may already have been asleep'

Winford (2000; 72–5, 83ff.), who has looked in more detail at contemporary uses of epistemic *kan* and *musu* in Sranan, has found only a rare use of some counterfactual past tenses (*kan ben/musu ben, ben kan/ben musu*), which may border on epistemic usage (note the use of perfective *ben* < 'been' here). He writes: 'neither *kan* nor *musu* ... seems to have developed clear epistemic senses when used in combination with *ben*, though it is possible that they are moving in this direction' (2000: 84). He continues (2000: 92): 'their [i.e. the modals *kan, musu*] use as auxiliaries in this [epistemic] sense appears to be possible primarily with stative verbs, though even this use is rare in my data. ... However, they appear freely in constructions such as *a kan/musu de taki S*: "it may/must be the case that S" '. In other words, it looks as if Sranan is still at a very early stage of the epistemic use of English-based core modals.

Finally, the occurrence of epistemic adverbs which are a contraction of 'may' +'be', such as Eng. *maybe*, Fr. *peut-être*, Macedonian *možebi*, Polish *może* (< *może być*), Sranan *kande* lit. 'can be', or of 'may'+'happen' as in English archaic *mayhap*, Dutch *misschien* and Swedish *kanske*, or a contraction from 'may'+'that' as in Serbian *možda* < *može da*,[14] shows that the route to these adverbs must also have been similar to the route taken in Old English, that is a modal in combination with 'be, happen' or with the complementizer 'that'.

It seems then that the English modals have developed further towards an epistemic meaning by themselves (i.e. without the support of a 'be'-type of infinitive or a 'that'-clause) than modals in other European languages or English-based creoles. Løken (1997) and Aijmer (1999) have shown, in a comparative study with Norwegian and Swedish respectively, that English uses modal auxiliaries significantly more often than the two Northern Germanic languages for the expression of epistemic possibility. Van der Auwera *et al.* (2005) illustrate a similar tendency in their comparison of English epistemic expressions of possibility (the modals *may/might/could* and the adverbs *maybe/perhaps*) as translated into Slavonic languages, making use of *Harry Potter* translations. Table 6.1 (deduced from their maps) gives the results.

What is interesting about this comparison, apart from the steady decline in the use of auxiliaries towards the south and east of Europe (which may indicate influence of an areal nature), is the fact that as far as the use of epistemic adverbs/particles is concerned, the number of instances is more or less equal in all languages, including English. This is clearly not true for the use of auxiliaries. With 66 occurrences, English uses the epistemic modal

Table 6.1. *The occurrence of epistemic possibility in English compared to Slavonic*

English	West Slavonic			East Slavonic		Northern South Slavonic			Southern South Slavonic	
	Czech	Polish	Slovak	Ukrainian	Russian	Croatian	Serbian	Slovene	Bulgarian	Macedon
Aux 66	42	39	29	31	21	34	34	1	28	25
Adv 21	18	20	16	18	14	19	20	15	15	14
Total 87	60	59	45	49	35	53	54	16	43	39

almost twice as much as the average Slavonic language. When the Slavonic translations use neither modal nor particle, they have recourse to a variety of means, such as simply leaving it out, using a *futurum* or *conditionalis*, or like Dutch, French, and the English-based creoles already mentioned above, making use of mental state predicates in biclausal constructions of the type *I think that* ... (van der Auwera p.c.).

It remains to be seen whether this solution is also possible for other cases of scope increase put forward by Tabor and Traugott (1998), and thus aligning them to the regular grammaticalization pattern. It must be remarked, first of all, that in their article the issue of scope increase is not strictly discussed with respect to the other parameters used by Lehmann to identify grammaticalization. Tabor and Traugott in fact use three, much more general, 'hallmarks' to identify grammaticalization. These involve a correlation between three aspects: the change must be morphosyntactic in nature, it must be pragmatic/semantic, and it must be gradual in the sense that some subtypes appear before others (Tabor and Traugott 1998: 235). This makes a comparison with Lehmann's framework already somewhat problematic and makes a true assessment of the four cases of scope increase that they discuss, problematic too. Indeed, from the point of view of a Lehmannian type of framework some of these cases would not be counted as grammaticalization at all (cf. also Campbell 2001b: 140).

Their first case, the development of the English possessive from an inflectional genitive into a clitic (Tabor and Traugott 1998: 236ff.), has elsewhere been described as *de*grammaticalization (cf. Plank 1995 and others, and see also §5.0, fn.6), where one would naturally expect scope *in*crease, since all of Lehmann's parameters work the other way here. On the other hand, if the clitic developed from the masculine possessive pronoun *his* or an invariant possessive *his*, as Janda (1980, 2001) has argued, then of course the development towards a clitic *'s* would be a regular case of grammaticalization, involving scope decrease, as Tabor and Traugott (1998: 239) indeed acknowledge.

It is difficult to see how their next case, the development of the gerund from nominal to verbal (Tabor and Traugott 1998: 240ff., for more details see also §5.3) can be considered a grammaticalization process: it does not involve any of the other parameters distinguished by Lehmann, such as phonetic reduction, bleaching, etc. There is clause elaboration here rather than reduction, which indeed would go well with scope increase. I have argued in Chapter 5 that clause combining or clause fusion can in some cases be regarded as a process of grammaticalization. It must be clear, therefore, that the *opposite* process of clause elaboration, can hardly be seen as the *same* process. A different way of explaining this particular development is by linking it to the formal falling together of the present participle in *-ende* and the verbal noun in *-unge/-inge* under the general suffix *-inge*, which is known to be at least a contributory factor. If we accept this coalescence, it is not surprising that the original nominal gerund acquired some of the verbal properties of the present participle, since they both have verbs as their stem, and they each have an inflection which is phonetically very much like the other. This is a coincidence rather than a grammaticalization process, a coincidence which leads to analogical change: the *-inge* form, being recategorized as verbal, takes on the verbal features usual for that category.

Their third example, the development of *instead* (*of*) (Tabor and Traugott 1998: 244ff.) looks primarily a case of lexicalization since it involves a single token, not a type, as I have argued for cases such as *while* in §§3.5 and 5.1; its later use as a 'sentence adverb' with subsequent scope increase, in which it resembles the case of *anyway*, their fourth example (1998: 253ff.), will be discussed in the next section.

Before we close the topic of the subjectification of the English modals and move on to a discussion of sentence adverbs and pragmatic markers, we need briefly to return to the already observed link between subjectification and leftward movement. This observation works well in the case of the subjectification of adjectives discussed by Adamson (2000). Roberts and Roussou (2002, 2003) argue, within a Minimalist framework, that a similar link is visible in the grammaticalization of the English modals. They describe how in Old English the modals were still generated in VP position, and how they moved leftwards (or higher up in the tree structure) to acquire Tense. This changes in early Modern English in that the modals now become 'merged' in Tense position, that is they are now permanently on the left side in the clause structure. The situation is altered again when some of the modals undergo 'further reanalysis' and become 'merged in the Mod$_{\text{EPISTEMIC}}$ position' (Roberts and Roussou 2002: 34), in the universal functional clause structure shown in (12) (after Cinque 1999).

(**12**) Mod$_{\text{EPISTEMIC}}$ T(Past) T(Future) Mod$_{\text{IRREALIS}}$ Mod$_{\text{NECESSITY}}$ Mod$_{\text{POSSIBILITY}}$ Mod$_{\text{ROOT}}$

This Merge further leftwards entails that the epistemic modal is impervious to Tense, and it also increases the scope it has over the rest of the proposition. This is an adequate description of the semantic and formal properties of the epistemic modal, where the past tense form does not refer to past time. However, it is also no more than a description. Because of its theory-internal nature (the functional projections given in (12) are simply assumed to be part of UG and not motivated by anything outside the theoretical model), it does not explain *why* there is scope increase. This 'lack' of explanation is related to the fact that, unlike in the case of the adjectives described by Adamson, there is no real change in position on the surface level. In main clauses, the modals still appear in the position they already most regularly appeared in in Old English, that is in second position.[15] Note that the Merging of the modal to the left of the VP in the T position, which took place earlier with the deontic modals, *also* predicts an increase in scope, but, unlike in the case of the epistemic modals, there was no scope increase in semantic terms as far as the deontic modals are concerned. In other words, a position higher up in the syntactic structure need not be automatically linked to a semantic-pragmatic increase in scope.

6.2 Subjectification and scope: sentence adverbs and pragmatic markers

In their challenge of the 'Scope Decrease Hypothesis' (i.e. what is considered the norm in grammaticalization processes), Tabor and Traugott (1998: 244–5) write that the case for scope increase 'will be strengthened if we can show that it characterizes a common kind of grammaticalization episode. A clear example of this sort is provided by a number of adverbial phrases in English which started out as adjuncts of the verb and evolved into sentence adverbs, and in some cases discourse markers' (instead of discourse markers, I will use the term 'pragmatic markers', following Brinton 1996: 29ff.).[16] In this case, too, Tabor and Traugott use the method of 'diachronic string comparison'. I have already described the problems with this method at the beginning of §6.1, and I believe the same reservations apply here, even though the development itself is of a different nature.

There is no space to go into all the details that would be necessary to show how, in the history of English, sentence adverbials and pragmatic markers arose out of verbal adjuncts. More research will be necessary to provide an account that would do justice to both the formal and semantic-pragmatic aspects of the development. My hypothesis is that a closer look at the formal changes from Old to Modern English will show that there is no question of a *direct* scope increase in the cases of grammaticalization (subjectification) involving verbal adjuncts. I propose (this will be worked out further in §6.2.2) that the verbal adjunct (stage i in Figure 6.1) on its way to becoming a sentence adverbial (stage iii) developed via an intermediate stage (stage ii), in which it first appeared in a topic position at the front of the clause, without a change in scope. When some of these sentence adverbials came to be used as a pragmatic marker at an even later stage (stage iv),[17] they did so by filling a position that had already been created by other pragmatic markers, which themselves had often developed from ellipted clausal phrases (reduced modal clauses) that were used as a separate or independent phrase in front of the main proposition and with scope over this proposition.

In fact, the development is rather similar to that of the epistemic modals. In the present case, too, there is no *direct* path of scope increase since the interpretation of the adverbial *as a separate clause* intervenes in the process from verbal adjunct to sentence adverbial and pragmatic marker. My suggestion is that the use of sentence adverbials as pragmatic markers in initial position took place by analogy rather than by an internal semantic-pragmatic development of the adverbials themselves.[18] The analogy was possible due to semantic and structural properties that the sentence adverbials and pragmatic markers shared with the reduced (modal) clauses. In Tabor and Traugott's (1998: 259) formal diachronic string comparison, stages (i) and (iii) are shown but stage (ii) is not. The difference between stages (iiia) and (iiib), which will be discussed below, is not taken into

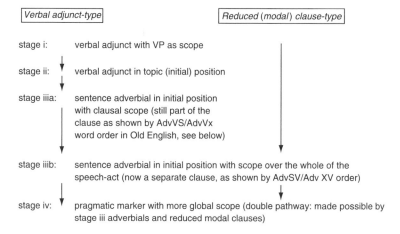

Figure 6.1. *From verbal adjunct to pragmatic marker.*

account. Stage (iv), in which the scope of the pragmatic marker is more global, is reached only via gradual development from stage (iii). The possibility that it is reached via a separate path, that of the reduced, independent clause, which takes up a similar position and shares an epistemic quality, is not considered. By positing only three stages rather than four, and by not taking into consideration the possibility of an extra path, it indeed looks as if the VP adverbs and their metamorphoses into sentence adverbials and pragmatic markers were always part of the same matrix clause, and hence that the grammaticalization and scope increase is a unidirectional and a strictly internally and contextually motivated development.

The idea that some of the verbal adjuncts may have become sentence adverbials or pragmatic markers by analogy rather than grammaticalization has also been suggested by Noël (2005). He proposes that there are two forms of grammaticalization, a slow or gradual type, which is focused on the substantive parts of a construction (which I have called 'tokens'), and a more abrupt type, which is concerned with patterns, that is with construction-types. As support for the latter, he refers to a quotation from Bisang (1998: 156): 'Within a given construction, certain positions can attract further items into a new function by the mechanism of analogy'. In this respect it is indeed notable that some of the sentence adverbs have not been used as VP adverbs at all, for example *presumably*,[19] while others, such as *unquestionably*, have been attested by the *OED* as a sentence adverb earlier than as a manner adverb, or as both at more or less the same time, for example *allegedly*, *admittedly*, *undoubtedly*. This much is clear: some of the sentence adverbials must have arisen by analogy alone.

I will test the above hypotheses on some cases that have been described as undergoing scope expansion, in order to discover the extent to which they can be seen as regular cases of grammaticalization but yet going against Lehmann's parameter of scope decrease. In §6.2.1, I will discuss the development that has led to the 'sentence-adverbial' use of *instead*, as discussed in Tabor and Traugott (1998). The next subsection, §6.2.2, will consider adverbial adjuncts that have developed into sentence adverbials and pragmatic markers, which are said to involve scope increase as well as subjectification (cf. the discussion of *anyway* in Tabor and Traugott 1998, and of *indeed*, *actually*, and *in fact* in Traugott and Dasher 2002: 170ff.). Finally, in §6.2.3 we will look in somewhat more detail at a particular, non-adverbial type of pragmatic marker: *I guess*, *you know*, etc.

6.2.1 The case of instead: a sentence adverb?

Tabor and Traugott (1998) envisage the following development (examples taken from their article):

(13)   GRAMMATICALIZATION OF *instead (of)*

period	grammatical status	example
OE:	noun:	*Iosue on Moyses **stede** ... to heretogan* 'Joshua in Moses's place as leader'
ME:	noun:	*in the **stede** of Pecock*
	complex preposition:	***in stede of** wepynge and preyeres*
eModE:	S-adverb (in the form ('*instead of NP*', p. 250):	***in stead of** doing good*
17th c.:	full-fledged S-adverb (ellipted):	*to have Mr Collins **instead**!*
[18th c.:	conjunction (seen as a separate development):	*you can sit **instead of** stand*]
20th c.:	S-adverb: (heading full clause)	***instead** he began to throw curious...* *glances at ...*

Leaving aside the development into a conjunction, which is seen as a separate strand developing directly from the prepositional phrase,[20] the grammaticalization goes through the following stages: noun (within a PP) > complex preposition > sentence adverb. The development into a complex preposition is a clear one; one, however, that comes close to lexicalization since it involves fixed tokens in a PP construction and is only in a very broad sense a grammatical type.[21] Note that this change is made possible by the fact that inanimate nouns in the genitive were replaced by an *of*-phrase in Middle English when case-forms were lost. When *stead* lost its concrete meaning of 'place' by a metaphorical change and came to be used in a more general sense (probably helped by the use of French *place* which began to replace it in many of its senses), the *of*-construction presumably also became the rule with animate nouns since the genitive phrase came to be restricted to objects that could actually be possessed (cf. OE *Mozes* (genitive) with ME *of Pecock* in (13) above). This entailed that *in stede of* now always appeared in this fixed order without a possessive phrase intervening. It is the fixed order which made the grammaticalization (or perhaps better lexicalization) into a complex preposition possible. This shows again how crucial fixed word order and the form of the overall grammatical system is in individual cases of change.

The development from (complex) preposition into sentence adverb is more complicated and more problematic from a grammaticalization point of view. As a preposition it can be used with all types of nouns, and this includes action nouns such as gerunds. When these gerunds develop direct verbal arguments in the course of the early Modern English period (cf. §5.3), there is in fact no change in the preposition *instead of*. This is clear from the fact that many other prepositions may occur before verbal gerunds too, as illustrated in *by* (*without, through, from, in*, etc.) *giving her a present....* It is because the gerund develops verbal properties, that the preposition may now head a clause-like constituent. This, according to the theoretical model used in Tabor and Traugott, means that the preposition *together with its complement* has now achieved the status of 'sentence adverb' (Tabor and Traugott 1998: 250). Following this line of argument, we would have to accept any *-ing* clause preceded by a preposition (*by, from, without, through*, etc.) as a sentence adverb. This seems to me a step too far. Presumably, the reason why Tabor and Traugott do take this step, is the fact that *instead* by itself, in a next stage, develops into a 'full-fledged' sentence adverb (1998: 251).[22] They provide this as '[f]urther evidence that *instead of* had developed adverbial status'. They add that this new use 'presumably' takes place 'via the ellipsis of the anaphoric *instead of this*' (1998: 250). I think that ellipsis is indeed the crux of the matter. Note that this use of *instead* in a clause such as,

(14)   Michaelis tried to find out what had happened, but Wilson wouldn't say a word—instead he began to throw curious, suspicious glances at his visitors (1925 S. Fitzgerald, *The Great Gatsby*, taken from Tabor and Traugott 1998: 251)

is usually pronounced with a comma-pause and with a different intonation contour. It indicates that it is a reduction of a (participial) clause, and as such, it is not surprising that it has scope over the clause that follows.[23] Again, as in the case of the epistemic modals, the grammaticalization (if that is what it is, see below) does not represent a direct route, but takes place via a new construction-type, which, as a reduced *clause*, has scope over the clause that follows. It preserves this scope when the clause is further reduced to an adverb(ial).

If we consider the case of *instead* (*of*) to be one of grammaticalization, as Tabor and Traugott do, then it is clear that it is not a neat case where we have 'almost a continuum of intermediate phases' (1998: 236). It is true that the elements involved undergo some morphological and phonetic reduction as a phrase (*in (the) stede of* > *instead of*), but this is also characteristic in the lexicalization of phrases or compounds. Moreover the development of the complex preposition *instead of* into the adverb *instead* can hardly be said to be phonetic erosion, rather it is a case of ellipsis.

It is difficult to say that the phrase undergoes pragmatic inferencing leading to semantic bleaching or meaning generalization. The sense of *stede*—'place'—remains part of the meaning of the construction throughout its development. Although the word *stede* 'place' in the prepositional phrase has undergone a metaphorical shift from concrete to abstract (and thus also allowing inanimate nouns to occur with it), this is not something that happens by pragmatic inferencing, but is a typical semantic shift, a regular process of semantic change in lexical items. After this shift, *stede* loses its meaning as a concrete noun indicating a location (as in OE *manega menn siððan gesohton þone stede* 'many men then sought that place', ÆLS (Oswald) 237). Concrete use of the word steadily diminishes and dies out by about 1450 (see the entries in the *OED*), after which it lives on in rather specialized meanings, in poetic diction and in some dialects. The general sense first increases in phrases like *in no stede* 'nowhere', *in eche stede* 'everywhere', and then after 1500 gets restricted more or less to the fixed phrase *in (the) stead.* This process can therefore more correctly be interpreted as a case of lexicalization involving semantic specialization or narrowing than a case of grammaticalization involving pragmatic inferencing followed by bleaching.

When the (complex) preposition *instead of* is followed by a gerund, which in the course of time began to allow verbal arguments, the scope of the preposition is enlarged, but this is true, as I argued above, for all prepositions in this position. Strictly speaking there is no scope increase here since, as before, the node is immediately dominated by the preposition: in other words the preposition has not moved higher or leftwards in the structure. It is only when the gerund itself is ellipted together with *of*, that *instead* begins to look like an adverbial, and as an adverbial, it suddenly looks as if there is scope increase because adverbials normally scope over the VP and not over the whole clause.[24] Note that this ellipsis cannot be said to be a gradual change structurally, nor can I see that there is a semantic change involved, since *instead* as an adverbial still has the same meaning as *instead of*, that is there is no further semantic generalization.

Other parameters of grammaticalization, such as reduction in scope, less paradigmatic choice, a more fixed position within the clause and decategorization towards a more grammatical function, also do not apply here. First of all, paradigmatic choice has not been reduced as far as the prepositional phrase is concerned, we can still use phrases such as *in place of*, *in lieu of* next to *instead of*. Secondly, when *instead* comes to be used in an adverbial position as a reduced clause, its position has become looser rather than more fixed; it can now occur in any position in the clause where subordinate clauses may occur (cf. the schema in (21) below). And thirdly, the change from preposition to adverb(ial) is a change up the categorial cline rather than down, and therefore is, if it involves grammaticalization at all, perhaps more a case of degrammaticalization than grammaticalization.

6.2.2 Verbal adjuncts and beyond

We next turn to the development of sentence adverbials/pragmatic markers from verbal adjuncts. According to Traugott (1995: 1) the development or cline from verbal adjunct > sentence adverbial > discourse (or here: pragmatic) marker is one of the 'staples of grammaticalization theory', even though it violates 'the principles of bonding and reduced scope frequently associated with grammaticalization'. Evidence for grammaticalization is found in the fact that it 'illustrates a cluster of other long-attested structural characteristics of early grammaticalization, specifically decategorialization, phonological reduction, and generalization' and also 'a number of more recently recognized characteristics, especially pragmatic strengthening and subjectification' (1995:1). Below we will have a closer look at the grammaticalization characteristics of this development, but before turning to details, we need to pay a little more attention to the difference between two of the distinct categories on this cline, namely that between sentence adverbials and pragmatic markers.

On the whole, it is not so difficult to distinguish the first stage on this cline from the other two. Verbal adjuncts, especially the ones that turn into sentence adverbials (i.e. mostly adjuncts of manner), behave differently in the sense that their scope is restricted to the VP, which is marked by the fact that their position is within the VP.[25] It is more difficult to see, however, how the development from sentence adverbial to pragmatic or discourse marker presents a *cline* because the difference between the two categories themselves is not clear. When we turn to definitions of these two categories in linguistic dictionaries and specialized studies such as Schiffrin (1987), Swan (1988), and Brinton (1996), we note that very often the same adverbs are classified as both sentence adverbials and pragmatic markers: for example they include both *frankly* and *however*, both *surprisingly* and *nevertheless*. This suggests that layering may be the rule in this case of grammaticalization rather than just a temporary state of affairs in the process, that is the layering is more like a state of polysemy, without much progress (cf. Travis 2005).[26] Thus, *anyway* can still be used in the senses of all of its three stages (cf. Tabor and Traugott 1998); the same is true for *actually* and *in fact*.[27]

Pragmatic markers are said to differ from sentence adverbials in terms of scope—this may be global or local but always extends beyond the immediate utterance they are in—and by their lack of referential content or 'conceptual semantics' (Traugott and Dasher 2002: 152). Schiffrin (1987: 31, 32) describes them as 'sequentially dependent elements which bracket units of talk', which are 'independent of sentential structure', and whose meaning is as much, if not more, determined by discourse position than by its inherent semantics (1987: 63). Thus, on the basis of their presumed lack of referentiality, Brinton (1996: 32) recognizes only a very small inventory of pragmatic markers in English (33 items), while other linguists include as many as 500 (cf. Brinton 1996: 31–2), most of which, not surprisingly, do have fuller semantic content. Pragmatic markers serve primarily to give cohesion to the discourse, to signal the speaker's stance towards what is being said, and to provide interpersonal bonding (cf. Brinton 1996: 30 ff., Traugott and Dasher 2002: 152ff.). Sentence adverbials, on the other hand, are said to have the immediate proposition/sentence as their scope and to be more fully referential.

When we look more closely, however, at a fully referential adverb such as *surprisingly*, which would presumably mark it as a sentence adverbial, we note that its scope may extend well beyond the sentence. In the following example,

(**15**)   Hearing his words is bound to recall the Beat poetry readings of the 50s. I asked him which writers have influenced him most. *Surprisingly, he said, 'I'm incredibly ill-read...'*
       (http://www.josephravens.com/q_voice.htm)

it is clear that the surprise involves the narrator (who is not lexically present in the clause of which *surprisingly* is part) rather than the subject of the proposition, *he*, and that the surprise in the narrator is indeed occasioned by the whole situation that is being talked about (a poet who does not read!), and not just the sentence that it syntactically modifies. *Surprisingly* also expresses the attitude of the speaker here, and could be said to achieve (or call for) bonding between speaker and addressee and provide cohesion in the text (in this example it incorporates the function of *but*).[28]

Consequently it is not easy to distinguish the last two categories on the adverbial cline in terms of scope, cohesion, attitudinal aspects, and bonding (aspects—especially the first two—which do distinguish them quite clearly from the verbal adjunct). It is difficult to say that one or the other has advanced further in subjectification or in terms of a more advanced grammatical function. The amount of 'conceptual semantics' carried by them seems to a great extent determined by the original meaning of the phrase in question, rather than by a process of generalization, which is a hallmark of grammaticalization. For example, an adverbial like *anyway* goes back to an earlier manner adjunct, meaning 'in any mode/manner' and thus had a much more general sense (not in the least through the presence of the quantifier) from the very beginning. Adverbials such as *admittedly* or *surprisingly* have more lexical content because they are derived from verbs with full lexical reference. Clearly, however, both *anyway* and *surprisingly* remained close to their source. It may be likely, therefore, that only the sentence adverbials with a more general sense will end up as pragmatic markers in the more narrow sense of the term.

In other words, the degree of grammaticalization or subjectification possible, depends to a great extent on the semantic contents of the source concept because its semantics is decisive for the relations it can have or develop with other elements in the clause or outside it (cf. also Swan 1988: 10–13, Schiffrin 1987: 63, 267). Another very influential factor in this particular cline is the *position* of the adverbial (cf. Bolinger 1952, Schiffrin 1987, Swan 1988).[29] Traugott and Dasher (2002: 158) note, with many others, that 'the position of an adverb is correlated with difference in meaning'. My suggestion below will be that formal factors such as position and the syntactic nature of the source (an adverbial phrase or an independent, reduced clause), as well as its original semantic content are crucial in the development from verbal adjunct to pragmatic marker, rather than the process of grammaticalization itself, which could perhaps better be seen as a by-product. The phenomenon of subjectification itself, if it can be considered separate from grammaticalization, is more like a general condition behind all communication, which is by its very nature speaker-oriented (cf. the importance of the human body in language processing, discussed in Chapter 3, see Table 3.3).

We will now have a look at the supposed grammaticalization nature of this cline in more detail. The development of *surprisingly, anyway, indeed*, and other adverbials, from verbal adjuncts into sentence adverbials and pragmatic markers is in many ways different from the case discussed in §6.2.1. First of all, the development involves subjectification. Secondly, this case is more interesting because it involves a much larger class of items: the development of *anyway* is rather similar to the development of other attitudinal/epistemic adverbs, such as *anyhow, however, whatever* (often containing quantifiers like *any*, interrogative elements and indefinite pronouns, which all mark non-factuality). Similar developments can be noticed with adverbially used epistemic adjectives ending in -(*a*)*ble* such as *probably, possibly, conceivably, presumably, unquestionably*, and adverbially used descriptive (manner) adjectives and participles, such as *frankly, briefly, surprisingly*, etc.

Yet, this development is also somewhat similar to the one in §6.2.1 in that there is no question of the usual parameters of grammaticalization being at work, such as scope reduction, increasingly fixed position in the clause, loss of paradigmatic choice[30] and decategorization (the first two observations are also made in Traugott 1995: 1, Tabor and Traugott 1998: 254). Furthermore, if one can speak of phonetic reduction at all, it is ellipsis rather than gradual phonetic erosion.

A more important question is, can we speak in these cases of a 'continuum of intermediate phases', typically led by gradual semantic-pragmatic change? Traugott (1995: 8) argues that the concrete PP *in dede* 'came to be endowed with evidential (i.e. epistemic) modal meanings' via inferencing. The first part of the change, however, from 'in the concrete act' > 'in practice' > 'in reality', can also be seen as a regular metaphorical change from concrete to abstract, from locative to spatial; it need not necessarily be a pragmatic inference from the context. According to Traugott (1995: 8), the sense of 'in practice/in reality' led to *indeed* being used as an emphatic assertion, as in (16), and hence, through 'invited inferences of contrast' as an adversative marker, see (17).

(16)   Þat was þe firste wassail in dede (*OED* c1330 R. Brunne, *Chron. Wace*
(Rolls) 7591).

(17)   [He] was iudged to be no man at armes (though in deed he excelled in feates
of chiualrie) (*OED* 1611 BIBLE *Transl. Pref.* 2)

The evidence for the change into an adversative marker via pragmatic
inferencing appears strong, but it has to be noted that *indeed* as a sentence
adverbial or pragmatic marker is still in Present-day English first and
foremost used emphatically, and that its adversative nature still largely
depends on the context, which is often interrogative (*how indeed, why
indeed, did he indeed?*), negative or epistemic. In other words, the change
is not (yet?) part of its semantics. This is also true for the two examples that
Traugott gives of adversative *indeed* as a sentence adverbial. In her first
example (18), it is accompanied by adversative-negative *though* (cf. also
(17) above), and in the second (19) by verbs marked as negative or irrealis:

(18)   somtyme purposely suffering the more noble children to vainquysshe, and, as
it were, gyuying to them place and soueraintie, *thoughe in dede* the inferiour
children haue more lernyng (1531 Governor, from Traugott 1995: 9)

(19)   'It *wasn't* clear to people within the State Department until mid-April that
indeed Bosnia was going to be engulfed in fighting,' he said. 'It *should have
been* clear a month or two months earlier that this was likely' (3 Sept. 1992,
UPI, from Traugott 1995: 9).

Note also that *indeed* in (18)–(19), although classified by Traugott as a
sentence adverbial, is still very close to a VP adjunct, and could be translated
by 'in practice/in reality'. Clearer instances of *indeed* as a sentence adverbial
or pragmatic marker (as a disjunct) with scope over the whole of the speech-
act, including the speaker, are usually indicated by initial position, and if not
initial, by a pause or special intonation pattern, as in (20). Often the marker
is used to note emphatic agreement, enabling the speaker to take his turn,
add something new and yet express bonding (expressing something like
'Yes, indeed (in fact), I agree with you'/'I agree and what's more I ... ')

(20)   Interviewer: What were you doing before you got into computer music?
R.H: I always worked as a pro musician, playing and writing
arrangements
Interviewer: When did you last compose a tune on the C64?
R.H.:   Around 1989 or 1990. I think it was 'Power Play Hockey'
or '1 on 1'.
Interviewer: *Indeed*, do you get fed up with people asking about your classic
C64 compositions?

R.H.:   Well I did back in 1987, but not now. I answer most questions
               looking back with nostalgia. (http://www.freenetpages.co.uk
               /hp/tcworh/int_vide.htm)

Disjuncts, by their very nature, are not an integrated part of the clause (cf. Swan 1988: 224) but form a separate, independent clause. As a disjunct, *indeed* becomes possible in many more positions in the clause than as an adverbial adjunct, since it may now occur in any position in which a parenthetic clause could occur. For instance, the concrete adverbial adjunct *in the act* (indicated by X in (21)) can only occur in a limited number of positions, whereas the disjunct *indeed* or a separate clause like *as we have heard* (both indicated by x) can occur in almost any position in the same clause:

(**21**)   x Yesterday x he x was x caught x X by the police x X

The nature of *indeed* as an independent phrase, (for ease of processing usually placed before the main proposition, cf. Swan 1988: 226) would also explain why there is 'scope increase'. As with the epistemic modals discussed in §6.1, the scope increase does not involve a change in the adverb (or the modal) itself or its use within the clause, but is caused by the fact that *indeed* is now found in a higher clause, which automatically has scope over the rest of the proposition, which constitutes another, separate clause.

The role of pragmatic inferencing in the development of *indeed* into a sentence adverbial and/or pragmatic marker, although present, thus plays a more marginal role here than in the discussions found in the work of Traugott and her associates. My suggestion is, with respect to the stages from verbal adjunct to sentence adverbial (stages (ii–iiia) in Figure 6.1), that the development is linked to a more general semantic (i.e. metaphorical) change combined with the possibility for adjuncts to appear in a topic position (more about this below), while for stages (iiib–iv), its parallel use as a reduced clause and its frequent initial position play a role. Concerning the development of *in fact*, which takes place later than that of *indeed* but is otherwise rather similar, it is likely that the change into a sentence adverbial/pragmatic marker was via analogy with *indeed* rather than via any form of grammaticalization, as the suddenness of the development (in comparison to *indeed*) suggests (as also indicated by Traugott 1995: 10; and cf. Noël 2005, referred to in §6.2 above).

Ellipsis, providing evidence for a status as reduced clause, seems not to have occurred in the development of *indeed*[31] nor in *in fact*, and indeed may be rare in the subcategory of the modal epistemic adverbials (especially the truth intensifiers). In many other cases, however, the change into a sentence adverbial or pragmatic marker can be related to ellipsis, especially where the earliest instantiations with the source concept are exclusively clausal or phrasal. Swan (1988) distinguishes four classes of sentence adverbials (cf. fn. 22) and observes that in Old English only morphologically marked sentence adverbs can be found in the subclass of truth intensifiers (notably *soðlice* 'truly' and *witodlice* 'certainly'),[32] and some in the class of subject-oriented adverbials (notably *riht(lic)e* 'rightly, justly' and *unrihtlice* 'unjustly'), but most adverbials in the latter class are still close to or interpretable as manner adjuncts. Likewise, the adverbs in the class of evaluatives are mostly still used as manner adjuncts or evaluative intensifiers (Swan 1988: 141), while the class of speech-act adverbials does not occur at all (1988: 210). What gets used instead, and this is the point I wish to make, are clauses such as *þæt is sarlic þætte...* 'it is sad/grievous that...', *wæs eac wundorlic þæt...* '[it] was wonderful too that ...' (p. 142), *we secgað ny sceortlice þæt...* 'we will-say now more briefly that ...', *wite ge ðætte...* 'know you that ...' (pp. 211–12), or independent phrases such as *to soðe* 'to truth/truthfully', *mid unrihte* 'with injustice/unjustly', *be gode rihte* 'by good right/justly' (p. 206), *wundorlice gemete*[DAT] 'in a miraculous measure/manner' (p. 146), and even the subject-oriented adverbs *rihte* and *(un)rihtlice* always appear in a fuller phrase (*swiðe rihtlice* or *genoh rihte* 'very rightly/rightly enough') when found in initial position (pp. 167, 172). Even more interesting are a number of occurrences with *rihtlice*, given in (22), where it is preceded by *and* and followed by *swa* 'so' or *þa* 'then'. This clearly indicates its nature as a reduced clause, with *and* initiating the clause and *swa/þa* referring back to an earlier clause.[33]

(22a) On ealdum dagum under moyses æ noldon þa Iudeiscan genealecan þam
       hæþenum, ne mid him gereordian, *and swyþe rihtlice þa*, forþan þe ...
                                                          (ÆLS(Peter's Chair) 178)
       In [the] old days under Moses' law would-not the Jews approach the
       heathens, nor with them feast, and very rightly then, because ...

(22b) ða ða he gelædde þone sceaðan into heofenan rice. ær ðan ðe he lædde
       Petrum. oððe his oðre apostolas; *And rihtlice swa.* for ðan ðe se sceaða
       gelyfde on ðam timan on crist. þa ða his apostolas on mycelre twynunge wæron
                                                          (ÆCHom II,5 46.137–140)

then he led the thief into heaven's kingdom before he led Peter or his other apostles; And rightly so because the thief believed at that time in Christ when his apostles [still] in great doubt were.

These clausal epistemic phrases usually appear in front position in Old English, while the adverbs by themselves mostly do not, except the ones that are already most like sentence adverbials. Table 6.2 shows how many of the *potential* sentence adverbs in the Old English corpus looked at by Swan occur in front position.

It is clear that front position is regular only in column 1. This front position is furthermore linked to a specific word order. It is notable that the usual word order after initial adverbials that are clearly identified as sentence adverbials on semantic-pragmatic grounds (only found among the truth intensifiers in column 1) is SV or XV,[34] that is with the Verb-second position typical of a *main* clause (cf. Koopman 1998: 139). Of the 43 initial instances with *witodlice*, Swan (1988: 106) notes that 33 have SV and only 8 have VS order (with 2 unaccounted for), but in all 8 VS examples, it is another topicalized element that occasions the inversion (cf. fn. 35 below). Similarly, *soðlice* takes SV, except in five cases, in which again another topicalized element causes the inversion (Swan 1988: 92–3). Lenker (2000), who has also studied the behaviour of *soðlice/witodlice*, finds a similar distribution.

This indicates that the sentence adverbial should be interpreted as strictly separate from the matrix clause because it has no influence on the order of its elements. If the adverbial was part of the clause, the regular order would be AdvVS/ AdvVX, due to the Verb-second nature of Old English, and this

Table 6.2. *The number of adverbs* (i.e. possible sentence adverbs on semantic-pragmatic grounds) *that occur in front position in Old English prose texts*

Modal adverbs (truth intensifiers)		Evaluative adverbs		Subject-oriented adverbs	
Front position / Total		Front position / Total		Front position / Total	
witodlice	43/67	positive evaluatives	6/31	*rihte*	8/32[a]
soðlice	30/135	negative evaluatives	3/13	*(un)rihtlice*	5/74
'rest'	13/72			'rest'	15/124
Total	86/274	Total	9/44	Total	28/230

Source: Swan 1988: 135, 145, 154, 166–7, 171–2, 208.
[a] As noted above, all initial occurrences of *rihte* and *(un)rihtlice* are accompanied by another element.

is what we find with the fronted adverbials in columns 2 and 3 in Table 2.6 (see also below).[35] The use of SV/XV word order in Verb-second languages like Old English (and as we will see this works even more strictly for modern Verb-second languages such as Dutch and German) is thus a good indication that the truth intensifier is a separate phrase (i.e. at stage iiib or iv in Figure 6.1), while VS or VX order would indicate that the adverbial is still part of the matrix clause (i.e. at stage ii or iiia). In other words, I hypothesize that the difference in word order indicates a shift from stage (ii–iiia) to stage (iiib–iv). Swan (1988: 223ff.) does not see this shift as crucial. She discusses the occurrence of the different word orders with sentential adverbs and the possible connection to a topic (clause-internal) or disjunct (clause-external) status of the element in question, but in the end decides that she is unable to account for the facts because of the unruly behaviour of the adverbs in column 1 in Table 6.2. I have shown, however, that this behaviour is in fact quite regular, in that VS only occurs when another (topic) element intervenes between *witodlice/soðlice* and the main verb.

The evidence that word order is linked to the status of the adverbial is strengthened by semantic-pragmatic evidence: a sentence-adverbial inter-pretation is strongest for the very adverbs that take SV/XV order. Swan established clear semantic-pragmatic grounds for sentence-adverbial status mainly among the modal adverbs (the first column in Table 6.2). Among the few preposed evaluatives (column 2) discussed by Swan, there are no unambiguous examples of either SV/XV or of VS/VX order; however, all nine preposed adverbs (Swan 1988: 146, 154) can be interpreted as manner adjuncts on semantic grounds (in other words, they would still be at stage ii). As to the preposed adverbs in column 3, for all instances with *(un)riht(lic)e,* word order is ambiguous but the interpretation as a manner adjunct is again possible. In the only two instances I found with SV order in The Dictionary of Old English Corpus (one of which is also in Swan's corpus), a sentence-adverbial rather than an adjunct interpretation is most likely on semantic grounds (both from the *Cura Pastoralis*, CP 13.77.22; 18.139.14),[36] so here too word order, initial position and semantic inter-pretation match in the case of the true sentence adverbial. Of the 'rest' group in this column, most instances are ambiguous as to word order, except three. Two of these are clearly topicalized manner adjuncts followed by VS (23a–b), which is what we would expect on the basis of our hypoth-esis, the third one (23c) looks like a sentence adverbial because here we have SV word order. Semantically, both an interpretation as manner adjunct or as sentence adverbial is possible, as the translation of (23c) makes clear; the word order, therefore, may have been conclusive here for the way it was interpreted.

(**23a**) Swa weorðlice &   swa mildelice wæs Romeburg on fruman   gehalgod
                                       (Or 2 22.39.16, Swan 1988: 187)
        So   worthily and so   mildly   was Rome   in [the] beginning consecrated
    b   & on ðære hwile þe he   þær winnende wæs, frefelice   hiene gesohte
        and in the time that he there fighting was, shamelessly him   sought
        <Minotheo>, seo Sciþþisce cwen (Or 3 9.17.4, cf. Swan 1988: 192)
        Minotheo,   the Scythian queen
    c   Suiðe medomlice Iacobus se   apostol his stirde,   ða   he cuæð:
        Very fitly/justly James   the apostle it steered, when he said:
        Broðor ne beo   eower to fela   lareowa (CP 33.9, Swan 1988: 180)
        Brothers not may-be of-you too many teachers
        'It was fitting that the apostle James guided it [i.e. the possibility of becoming an apostle] OR James guided it in a fitting manner, when he said: brothers not many amongst you will be likely to become teachers'

It is also interesting to observe in this connection the behaviour of Old English *hwæt* (lit. 'what'), which, as Brinton (1996) shows convincingly, is clearly used as a pragmatic marker (it has not developed from an adverb and therefore cannot be a sentence adverbial) to introduce or call attention to a statement (*hwæt* is usually translated by 'lo', 'hear' or 'well'). The examples in Brinton (1996: 181ff.) show that it is always followed by SV/XV order, even when it is used in the fuller phrase *hwæt þa* (cf. the use of *swyþe rihtlice þa* in (22a)). Brinton herself does not comment on the word order because she is primarily concerned with the pragmatic-semantic developments. The fact that all her examples (except four)[37] obey main clause order—even in combination with *þa* (which otherwise as an adverb triggers VS/VX order almost without exception, cf. Swan 1988: 96, Koopman 1998: 144)—shows that *hwæt* itself must be classified as a separate clause, as I argued for *soðlice/witodlice*.

   The situation in Old English thus looks fairly straightforward. Adverbials which function fully as sentence adverbials, and clear pragmatic markers like *hwæt* (i.e. elements whose scope extends over the whole proposition, over the speech-act or beyond) do not show unambiguous evidence of VS order, which strongly suggests that these adverbials constitute *separate* phrases/clauses. In this respect they resemble the fuller clauses that are also used instead of these adverbials, mentioned above. This suggests in turn that there is no *direct* development from VP adverb to IP adverb and to adverb beyond IP level as suggested by Traugott (1995) and Tabor and Traugott (1998). Such a shift only occurs when the original adverbial comes to be used as a separate phrase, which enables it to acquire scope over the main proposition when it is placed above that proposition in a higher (reduced) clause.

The Old English distinction by means of word order has disappeared in Modern English (due to its fixation to SVO order) but is still visible in the modern Germanic languages that have preserved Verb-second. I will show by means of some examples from Dutch that a semantic distinction still exists between adverbials followed by SV/XV order and adverbials followed by VS/VX order. With the first order, the scope of the adverbial is beyond the IP. It includes the speaker if not lexically present in the clause (i.e. the construction is at stage iiib–iv in Figure 6.1) and expresses speaker attitude, while with the second order the scope concerns only the proposition that it is part of or is even restricted to the VP (i.e. stage ii–iiia). In some cases the distinction is neutralized, as we will see below, which may eventually lead to a further blurring of the difference.[38] A distinction along the same lines exists in Modern German, Modern Dutch, and also in Modern Norwegian (cf. some instances given in Swan 1988: 215, 244), but there are small differences in usage between individual cognates. My examples will be mainly from Dutch, for which as a native speaker I have better intuitions. However, I have checked with speakers of German and the Scandinavian languages, and very similar judgements apply there.[39] Obviously more research is necessary in these languages to further test the hypothesized development sketched in Figure 6.1.

First I will give some examples of adverbials that *only* allow VS order. The sentence adverbials here all derive from verbal adjuncts, and in some cases they show their origin as manner adverbial through their suffix (-*wijze, -weise* 'manner' in Dutch and German, respectively).

(24a) Waarschijnlijk *heeft* zij het allemaal opgedronken (Du, VS only)
Wahrschein*lich* hat sie das alles aufgetrunken (Germ, VS only)
Probably has she it all up-drunk
'Probably she has drunk it all'

(24b) Mogelijk(erwijze) *komt* *hij* morgen (Du, VS only)
Möglicherweise *kommt* er morgen (Germ, VS only)
Möjligen kommer han i morgon (Swedish, VS only)

Possibly   comes   he   tomorrow
'Possibly he will come tomorrow'

(24c) *waarschijnlijk   het   kind *heeft hij* niet meer kunnen   redden
       probably   the   child has he   no more been-able save
       'probably he has not been able to save the child anymore'

These adverbials are used as sentence adverbials, but they have not progressed beyond stage (iiia) in Figure 6.1, that is, their most extensive scope is the IP. That they should still be considered an integral part of the clause is clear from the fact that multiple topics cannot occur here as (24c), with an adverbial *and* a topicalized object, shows (cf. n. 35). Example (25) gives examples of sentence adverbials/pragmatic markers where only SV order is found:

(25a) En eerlijk, *ik weet* echt niet of hij de lipstick gestolen heeft of niet (SV).
              (home.wanadoo.nl/prettyblowy/lipstick.html)
      'And frankly/honestly, I do not know whether he has stolen the lipstick or not'

(25b) Kortom, *hij heeft* mij meegesleept door alle 5 verdiepingen, archief in
      en uit, ... (SV)
              (www.bevrijdingskinderen.nl/1984/johnboers/nprc.html)
      'In short, he has dragged me through all 5 floors, one archive after another, ...'

(25c) Hoe dan ook, *ik verbaasde* me erover dat dat weer zolang moet duren. (SV)
              (blog.nder.be)
      'How then also (however it be), I was surprised that again it took so long'

(25d) Jammer, *hij is* niet verstuurd op het moment dat dat beloofd werd
              (forum.fok.nl/topic/687093/2/25)
      'Sadly/unfortunately, it has not been sent at the moment that it was promised'

The sentence adverbials/pragmatic markers in (25) can most easily be linked to reduced clauses; an origin as a manner adverb or intensifier is difficult here from a semantic-pragmatic and/or formal point of view. *Eerlijk* in (25a) is derived from an adjective and is either a reduced form of a clause containing the verb 'be' + *eerlijk* as a predicative adjective or a reduced form of *eerlijk gezegd* 'frankly spoken', with *eerlijk* as adverbial. A very common alternative for *eerlijk* is the phrase *eerlijk is eerlijk*, which still contains the copula and is always followed by SV. In Modern Dutch, the same form *eerlijk* can also be used as a manner (VP) adverb (in Middle Dutch the manner adverb still had an adverbial ending -*e* but this inflection was lost), and then it means 'in a frank/honest way'. As such it may appear in first (=topic) position when emphasized, but then it is always followed by VS order as shown in (26a).[40] The alternative, *eerlijk gezegd* can be followed by both SV and VS even though it is clearly a reduced clause. This is presumably because the fuller phrase, *eerlijk gezegd*, still functions like an adverbial clause, which automatically triggers VS in Dutch, cf. *Zo gauw ik thuis kom, zet ik altijd thee* 'As soon as I get home, make I always tea' (the same applies to German *ehrlich gesagt*). *Kortom* (in 25b) originally meant according to the *WNT* 'short around', that is 'by a shortcut', and is clearly a reduced form; it is always followed by SV (but see n. 39). In origin it is a PP used as an adverbial of place, which came to be used as an adverbial of time. In this case usage as a manner adverb, and hence VS order, is not to be expected. This probably also explains why the form *kort gezegd*, although similar to *eerlijk gezegd* in form, is always followed by SV order, just as the phrase *in het kort* 'in brief'. The expression *hoe dan ook* in (25c) is a reduced clause expressing *hoe het (dan) ook zij* 'however it may be'. As a pragmatic marker it is always followed by SV order. Later the phrase also came to be used occasionally as a manner adverbial 'in whatever way'. When a manner adverbial, it is used in topic position, as in (26b), VS order is the rule; in that case the scope is the VP. *Jammer* in (25d) is originally a noun, and later came to be used as an adjective, but only in predicative position showing its nominal nature; an adverbial origin is therefore out of the question. This makes clear that *jammer* is a reduced clause. Only SV has been attested here. Example (26c) shows that two initial elements are possible here (similar examples could be given with the adverbials in (25a–c), which indicates quite clearly that the adverbials in (25) cannot be seen as an integral part of the clause, since multiple topics are not allowed.[41]

(**26a**)   Eerlijk *heb ik* mijn mogelijkheden afgewogen, ik wist bijvoorbeeld dat ik het Hindi, de religieuze taal van India, zou moeten leren.

        (http://www.refdag.nl/oud/series/predikambt/990819kl07.html)

        'In an honest/open way have I weighed my possibilities, I knew for instance that I would have to learn Hindi, the religious language of India'

(**26b**)   Hoe dan ook *heeft je partner* geen enkele verplichting meer bij de bank of verzekeringsmaatschappij op het moment dat jij zijn helft van het huis van hem koopt.

        (http://www.echtscheidingswijzer.nl/eigen-huis.html)

        'In no way whatsoever has your partner any further obligations with the bank or the insurance company at the moment that you buy half the house from him'

(**26c**)   Jammer,   het   kind   *heeft*   hij   niet   meer   kunnen   redden
        Sadly,   the   child   has   he   no   more   been-able   save
        'Sadly, he has not been able to save the child anymore'

In (27)–(28), I give some more examples of sentence adverbials that can take SV as well as VS order. The difference in usage is quite clear. When VS order is used, the scope of the adverbial does not go beyond the clause, and in some cases the adverbial can still be interpreted as a manner adjunct. When SV order is used, the scope is always the whole speech-act, including the speaker when (s)he is not lexically present in the clause itself.

(27a)   Heel *terecht heeft men* die conclusie het product genoemd van een tweede invalshoek
       (http://www.juridat.be/cass/cass_nl/2002/hoofdstuk/hoofdstuk8.htm)
       Quite rightly has 'one' that conclusion the product called of a second point of view
       'Quite rightly they have called that conclusion the product of a second point of view'
       [they have called it that 'in a correct manner', VP scope, or 'it is right that ...', IP scope]

(27b)   Erwin Kiezenbrink was desondanks zeer trots op zijn finale-plaats, *terecht, hij heeft* er hard voor gevochten en goed zijn kansen benut.
       (http://www.pock.nl/dartist.html)
       E.W. was nevertheless very proud of his place-in-the-finals, [as is] right, he has it hard fought for and well his chances used.
       'E.W was nevertheless quite proud of his place in the finals, quite rightly, he has fought hard for it and used the opportunities well.' [only large scope (beyond IP) is possible here, since it includes the opinion of the writer/speaker and there is a clear link with the previous discourse]

(28a)   Geschrokken slaat ze haar hand voor haar mond. *Gelukkig heeft niemand* het gemerkt.
       (http://www.werktitel.nl/ts2/bijnazomer.htm)
       Startled claps she her hand before her mouth. Fortunate has no one it noticed.
       'Embarrassed she put her hand to her mouth. Fortunately no one had noticed it.'
       [IP scope: 'fortunately for her']

(28b)   *Gelukkig. Ze heeft* het geslikt. Ik dacht niet dat ze zo goedgelovig was eigenlijk.
       (http://www.zweinstein-online.be/fanfictie_lees.php?id=8)
       Fortunate. She has swallowed it. I thought not that she so credulous was in-fact
       'Fortunately, she has swallowed it. I didn't imagine that she would be so credulous in fact.' [only large, speech-act scope possible, since it is fortunate for the narrator not for the subject 'she']

It is clear that the use of the adverbials in (27)–(28) hover between the stages of (ii–iiia) and (iiib–iv) of Figure 6.1. A scope larger than IP is more usual in personal or first person narratives and in spoken discourse,[42] while IP or VP scope is typical of more impersonal, third person narratives. This should not be surprising since in the former the speaker/narrator is more involved in the story/dialogue, and hence any modal or epistemic phrases will automatically be linked to the central character: the speaker. In other words, the amount of subjectification and the difference in word order that expresses it, is closely related to the 'person' (first or third person) the speaker and/or subject appears in. In connection with this it is perhaps also not surprising that, when the subject of the sentence coincides with the speaker, both orders are quite regularly found, since in that case the scope difference marked by VS and SV is largely neutralized, with both word orders expressing the personal interest.

Meinunger (2004) confirms all these facts for Modern German. He notes in addition that a number of sentence adverbials, such as *übrigens* 'by the way', which cannot be used ambiguously both as sentence adverb and VP adjunct, allow both SV as well as VS order (the same applies to the Dutch cognate *overigens*). He writes 'being unable to get a proposition internal reading, these expressions can appear in the Vorfeld [i.e. with V2] without triggering an unwanted interpretation or leading to ungrammaticality' (Meinunger 2004: 77). He likewise notes that semantically ambiguous adverbials (comparable to Dutch *eerlijk* 'honestly' discussed above, cf. (25a) and (26a)) do need to be distinguished by position: 'if the adverbial form is not unambiguously specified for a speech act reading [i.e. by means of SV order], this reading will not emerge. In case a reasonable manner reading (or something similar) is possible, the sentence is grammatical, but only with that reading' (ibid. pp. 76–7). This rather strongly suggests that the unlikely VS order in these cases (unlikely, because these adverbials are very clearly outside the proposition) may have been caused by analogous and frequency factors, since most adverbials at the beginning of the clause in both German and Dutch do appear with VS order. It would be interesting to find out, but this must be left to future research, whether sentence adverbials such as *übrigens/overigens* have diachronically moved from SV order towards accepting also VS order.

The question arises why cases of sentence adverbials originating in VP adjuncts with clear SV order did not yet occur with any frequency in Old English. What may have happened is the following. VP adjuncts could appear in initial position in Old English when they were topicalized, as examples (23a–b) above have shown. It is possible that through this topicalization, some of the adverbials, provided they had the right attitudinal or epistemic quality (i.e. it could happen with adverbs expressing judgement such as *shamelessly*, *justly*, *truly* but not with purely descriptive adverbs such as *slowly*), could begin to change their scope because of their (frequent) position at the beginning of the clause, in terms of what Bolinger (1952 [1972]) has called 'linear modification'. This principle claims that a preposed element will tend to modify everything that follows it due to the fact that we process language utterances in linear fashion.[43] Once this had happened, the same adverbial phrase could also begin to occur separate from the clause—that is with SV order—because it now expressed the attitude of the speaker. The different word order would now also be necessary to disambiguate between the manner reading and the sentence adverbial reading. This stage seems to have been reached in the modern Germanic languages, where both VS and SV order are possible with the same type of adverbs (see the examples in (27–28)). It is clear that with VS order the sentence adverbial has as its scope only the proposition of which it syntactically forms a part (with the exception of the rather special *übrigens* cases discussed above), and in some cases here one can still taste its topicalized use as VP adverb (see the Dutch examples in (26a–b)). When SV order follows, however, the sentence adverbial clearly expresses the opinion or attitude of the speaker or is used to provide cohesion to the discourse. Of great interest also is the fact that when the initial adverbial is clearly a reduced clause (cf. the examples in (25)), SV order is the only possibility (with the exception of cases such as *eerlijk gezegd*, which allow VS order for other reasons, as argued above), indicating the separate or extracyclic nature of the adverbial clause/phrase before SV order.

This development, if it is correct, entails two things. The scope of the original VP adjunct changed presumably through its change in position, and not through pragmatic inferencing of the adverbial itself. Further scope increase was presumably helped by the fact that other initial, reduced-clause adverbials with SV order already had wide scope. For English, this latter factor would have worked even more strongly upon the loss of Verb-second. When Verb-second was lost in the course of the Middle English period, all adverbials would be followed by SV, of whatever origin—that is whether they were originally part of a higher clause or not— and thus their falling together into one category strengthened this category (or 'type') and at the same time weakened the differences that we have observed for Dutch. Secondly, the category itself came to be further isolated as a category separate from other adverbials (i.e. VP adjuncts) in that in English this position—as an unmarked position—became virtually exclusive to (sentence) adverbials as connectives.[44] Upon the loss of Verb-second and the fixation of SVO word order, the appearance of other arguments in this position became rare in English, whereas it remained a regular unmarked topic position for adverbials, and indeed for other types of arguments, in the other Germanic languages as long as they functioned cohesively (cf. fn. 44). The function of these adverbials as a *connective* device helps explain why they were frequent in initial position, and thus why this position could influence the change in scope.

There is a further difference between English and the other Germanic languages, which may also have affected the divergent developments. Only English has a clear, obligatory adverb marker—the suffix *-ly*—a new marker that replaced the phonetically weak OE *-e* ending. This means that the separateness of the sentence adverb is in English sufficiently marked by both position and adverbial suffix. It could have made up for the lack of word order differentiation. This adverb marker also further isolated the adverbial as a category. It is perhaps not surprising, therefore, that English has gained so many more sentence adverbials of the type, *admittedly, presumably* whereas in Dutch these remained clausal or reduced clausal phrases.

From these historical and comparative details, it becomes clear that the wide-scope sentence adverbial/pragmatic marker must originally have been placed outside the main clause, in the form of a prepositional phrase, a reduced clause or a predicative clause followed by a 'that'-complement. In this connection, it is important to point out that the OE *-lic* ending, which accompanied the first true sentence adverbs in Old English (i.e. *witodlice* and *soðlice*, cf. Table 6.2 above), was derived from the noun *lic* 'body', and that it was at first attached to nouns only, conveying that it was like something in body/appearance. In function it thus resembled the preposition *like*, forming a PP with the noun.[45] The adjective *soðlic*, therefore, meant 'truth-like', and was thus rather similar to prepositional phrases such as *to soðe*, which were frequently used in clauses of the type 'I tell you *to soðe* that ...'. These clauses function as sentence adverbials and have scope over the 'that'-clause. When reduced to an adverbial, they would resemble other adverbials but retain their scope over the original 'that'-clause which now becomes the main clause. In turn they could help other adverbials to gain a similar position and function by analogy.

To conclude. I have tried to show that position and word order may have been more influential in the development of verbal adjuncts into sentence adverbials and pragmatic markers in English than hitherto acknowledged within grammaticalization studies. Generative discussions of sentence adverbials clearly pay attention to these formal aspects. Semantic factors are important in so far as the adverbials need to have the modal or epistemic potential to begin with in order to develop into markers of attitude, bonding, and interpersonal relations. This potential also implies, however, that the subjectification development, which is seen as such an important factor in this grammaticalization process, was present 'in embryo' in the adverbials themselves. In addition, as mentioned above, subjectification is a general phenomenon in all spoken forms of communication, where the speaker stands central. At the same time, the fact that these same elements mark cohesion and function as text and discourse connectives, has as much to do with their placement in initial position as with any inferential seman-tic-pragmatic developments. As connectives, they are also more likely to express the attitude of the narrator/speaker than when they are used more purely as manner adverbs or intensifiers, explaining the increase in subjectivity that has been noticed. It has been argued that in the case of certain adverbials this initial position may have become unmarked and frequent, which could make it subject to the principle of linear modification, and hence to scope increase.[46] The use of independent clauses such as 'it is strange', 'it is possible', 'it is true', which were often put in front of the main proposition to express (logical) relations between pieces of discourse uttered by the speaker, also helped—especially when reduced so that they looked like adverbials—to establish an initial position for elements which expressed connections as well as personal opinions and attitudes. In English this first position became further strengthened by the loss of Verb-second, which marked off the pre-S position as one typical for connectives and adverbials. Adverbials themselves also became clearly marked though the increasing use of the -*ly* suffix.

6.2.3 Parentheticals as pragmatic markers

In this section I will have a closer look at another type of pragmatic marker, one that did not develop out of adverbials but for which it has also been suggested that both grammaticalization and subjectification have been at work. Concerning the development of English parenthetic markers such as *I guess* and *I think*, I will compare two relevant investigations: Thompson and Mulac (1991), who have investigated the matter synchronically but also made suggestions as to the historical development of these markers, and Brinton (1996), who analysed constructions of the *I guess*-type diachronically, from Old English onwards. First I will briefly describe their proposals. Next, since the conclusions they draw differ considerably, I will consider developments in Dutch—another Germanic language, close enough but yet different—to find out which of the two hypotheses holds up more generally. Finally, we need to look again at the extent to which this development falls under the rubric of grammaticalization, and how the development of this type of pragmatic marker compares to the one discussed in the previous section.

Thompson and Mulac (1991: 313) suggest that parentheticals, as shown in (29c), have evolved from matrix clause structures such as (29a) via a stage given in (29b):

(**29a**)   I think *that* we're definitely moving towards being more technological
(**29b**)   I think 0 exercise is really beneficial
(**29c**)   It's just your point of view you know what you like to do in your spare time
       I think

They do not investigate the historical shift empirically but deduce it from synchronic quantitative and qualitative evidence. They argue that the grammaticalization of these parentheticals can be shown by means of discourse frequency counts on the assumption that there is a relationship between the frequency of tokens and the emergence of grammar. They base their counts on a corpus of recorded conversations between university students. The reason that they use spoken discourse is because the parentheticals are rare in written language. In their description of the development, (29a) and (29b) are seen as the 'target' constructions from which the epistemic parenthetical (29c) has derived, but (29b) itself can also be seen as an epistemic parenthetical, which makes it the 'bridge' construction that makes the change possible (cf. Diessel and Tomasello 2001: 107–8, who describe the three constructions as a continuum whereby (29b) and (29c) are often difficult to distinguish). Once the parenthetical has evolved, it can be put in any position in the sentence.

The qualitative evidence they present concerns the semantic change of the 'believe-type'-target verb from a verb of cognition (e.g. *think* in the sense of 'to have thoughts') into an epistemic evidential, with *think* expressing 'degree of speaker commitment'. This change is closely related to the frequent use of the verb in combination with the first person (second person is also used but amounts to only 4 per cent of all parentheticals in their corpus), which is in fact responsible for the subjectification that these constructions undergo ('markers of evidentiality and epistemicity are skewed towards first person singular declaratives and second person questions', Thompson and Mulac 1991: 322). It is only in these persons that the verb evolves into a parenthetical at all.

The question arises whether this change is the result of pragmatic inferencing, which is said to play a role in cases of grammaticalization/subjectification, or whether this concerns a case where the verbal expression in the first person (which makes it necessarily subjective from the beginning) becomes formulaic through frequent use. Brinton (1996: 243, 254) clearly opts for the former,[47] while Thompson and Mulac are closer to the latter in suggesting that the phrases are formulaic (cf. also Thompson 2002) and that the development resembles lexicalization (Thompson and Mulac 1991: 324). After some discussion they reject the option of lexicalization, however, because the epistemic phrase is 'still available for ordinary negation and questioning'. I will return to this point at the end of this section.

Frequency is counted on a number of levels. First it is established which target verbs (i.e. verbs expressing belief as a mode of knowing) are overall most frequent. In their corpus, this is the verbs *think* and *guess*, which account for 65 per cent of all believe-type verb occurrences, with the other 42 verbs spread over the remaining 35 per cent. Secondly, it is found that out of the 18 verbs that are in fact used as parentheticals, these two verbs alone account for 85 per cent of all cases. Thirdly, *think* and *guess* occur much more frequently in construction-type (29b), that is with a zero-complement—*think* has a zero-complement 91 per cent of the time, and *guess* 99 per cent—compared to a percentage of 76 per cent of all other tokens. Finally, they count the frequency of first and second person singular subjects. *I* occurs 83 per cent of the time with all target verbs, and *you* 5 per cent, while when used as clear epistemic parentheticals, *I* appears 95 per cent of the time and *you* 4 per cent. These pronominal subjects also occur more frequently when the target verbs are followed by a zero-complement. All these counts together show that the combination *I think* is most likely to occur with a zero-complement 92 per cent of the time.

Thompson and Mulac (1991: 314) see a direct relationship between these various frequencies, which they believe throws light on to how they developed:

the most frequent target clause subjects and verbs are just those which are most frequently found as E[pistemic]PAR[enthetical] expressions, and we suggested that the frequent occurrence of *I* (in declaratives) and *you* (in questions) without *that* in target constructions has led to their re-interpretation as epistemic phrases with verbs expressing belief. ... As epistemic phrases, then, these combinations are free to float to various positions in the clause to which they are providing testimony, as other epistemic particles in English do, such as *maybe*. Again, we found strong correlations between the frequency of the forms found in these EPARs and the frequency of those found in target epistemic phrases without *that*. (Thompson and Mulac 1991: 326)

They therefore conclude (1991: 316) that the blurring of the distinction between the main and the complement clause (through the loss of *that*) paved the way for the rise of the epistemic parentheticals.

Brinton (1996: 239ff.) basically agrees with Thompson and Mulac as far as the semantic-pragmatic development is concerned (but see fn. 47). She further notes that in Middle English, too, there is a synchronic correspondence between structures similar to the ones given in (29). She doubts, however, whether there is a diachronic correspondence, that is whether the Middle English type (29c) also developed from (29a) via (29b). First of all, she does not find a similar neat quantitative correlation for Middle English. This may be due to a lack of the right data (her data, naturally, are only from written sources), but it is telling that the most frequent parentheticals (*gesse*, *leve*, *undertake* 'guess, believe, undertake') do not occur most frequently with zero-complements, as they did in Thompson and Mulac's corpus. On the other hand, the most common parentheticals in line after *gesse*, that is *trow*, *wot* 'trust, know', do occur most frequently with *that*-less clauses. Secondly, she looks at the use of these same verbs in Old English. She does not find the modern construction-types illustrated in (29) there, but other, what she calls 'relative' constructions, remnants of which can still be found in Middle English (Brinton 1996: 240–2). On the basis of these she proposes a different development.

Let us have a look at these Middle English 'relative' constructions (the examples and glosses follow Brinton 1996: 249–50). They are of two types:

(30a) He took me certeyn gold, *that woot I weel* (Chaucer *CT, Shipman's Tale*, 403–4)
       'He brought me a certain amount of gold, that know I well'

(30b)   He lese shal; *therof have I no doute*. (Chaucer, *CT, C. Yeoman's Tale*, 833)
            He shall lose, of that have I no doubt

(31a)   She hath ynough to doone, hardyly/ To wynnen from hire fader, *so trowe I*
                                           (Chaucer, *T&C* bk V, 1124–25)
            'She has enough to do, surely, to get away from her father, so I believe
            [=which I believe]'

(31b)   For thrittene is a covent, *as I gesse* (Chaucer, *CT, Summoner's Tale*, 2259)
            For thirteen is a convent, as I guess [=which I guess]

The first type (30) is described as 'relative structures where the main clause
is pronominalized within the parenthetical with the demonstrative pronoun
that/this, the personal pronoun *it*, or a form such as *therof*, all of which are
anaphoric' (1996: 248). Type (31) concerns parentheticals introduced by *as/
so*. Brinton (1996: 250) writes that *as/so* functions either as a relative
pronoun (in final position), or as a subordinator ('in so far as') in initial
and medial position. She concludes that both types 'contain relative pronouns referring anaphorically to the attached clause' (1996: 251).

The attention Brinton pays to the 'relative pronoun' is important, as we
will see below, but there are also a few problems with this account. First of
all it is not really possible to compare Brinton's Old and Middle English
data directly with Thompson and Mulac's modern data. The latter are
from a spoken corpus, the former from a written one. It is perhaps not
surprising in this respect that Brinton finds more examples in Middle
English than in Old English. A lot of Middle English oral poetry is quite
colloquial (especially Chaucer's *Canterbury Tales* and *Troilus and Criseyde*,
both used by Brinton) whereas the Old English prose texts used by Brinton
are mainly religious or historical works, while the poetry is heavily constrained by the alliterative half lines, both in lexis and grammar, making it
in many ways quite unlike colloquial speech.

Brinton (1996: 240–1), referring to Gorrell (1895), finds some examples
of believe-type verbs in Old English followed by a zero-complement but
remarks that the 'contexts in which omission occurs are quite limited'.
Gorrell (1895: 396–7) however, interprets these examples not as verb +
zero-complement but as syntactically independent clauses, or 'simple introductory expressions like the Modern English "you know" '. Brinton
believes that Gorrell overstates his case here because the omission of *þæt*
'that' is not frequently found after these verbs (however, neither Brinton
nor Gorrell (1895: 348ff.) give any frequencies here to back up their case).[48]
I think, however, that Gorrell may be nearer the truth with his idea that

these introductory phrases function like adverbials such as 'probably'. The fact that zero-complements are not frequent, may be totally irrelevant, if it is indeed the case that these expressions are *independent* syntactic structures from the beginning. Moreover, it remains to be seen whether Thompson and Mulac's hypothesis is correct for the historical development. A problem is of course that Gorrell did not find many such independent structures in Old English, but as stated this may be due to the poverty of the record.

Returning to Brinton's 'relative pronoun'-hypothesis, she draws our attention to a more frequent Old English construction with believe-type verbs presenting 'syntactically complete clauses with an anaphoric demonstrative referring back to the preceding clause, that is relative clauses' (1996: 241), which she believes are the ancestors of the Middle English constructions noted in (30)–(31). These are of the type illustrated in (32) (I have again followed Brinton's glossing here) with *þæs* as the anaphoric demonstrative and *þe* as the relative particle indicating the status of the clause,

(32a)   se hæfde ænne sunu nu for þrym gærum, & se wæs, *þæs þe* ic wene, V winter
(GDPref and 4(C)6.271.18)
he had one son now for three years, and he was, of this which I know, five winters old

(32b)   Petrus cwæð: *þæs þe* ic ongyte, þes wæs mycel wer utan on þam mægnum þe he worhte, ... (GD 1(C)5.47.14)
Peter said: of that which I know, this was a great man on the outside in the strength which he wrought, ...

(32c)   ne sceal þær dyrne sum/ wesan, *þæs* ic wene (Beo A41 270)
nor shall anything there be secret, of this I think

Two things are to be noted here. First of all, Brinton's translations with a relative pronoun are awkward. The reason for this is that the *þæs* (*þe*) structures do not in fact function as relatives in these clauses; they do not introduce a relative clause. They are rather similar to formulae such as *for þæm* (*þe*) (lit. 'for that [reason] (that)' > 'because', 'therefore'), which introduce subordinate clauses or provide adverbial connectives between clauses. These originate from a relative construction, but are no longer used as such in Old English. In addition, all cases given by Brinton concern the genitive object *þæs*,[49] which occurs even with verbs that do not normally govern a genitive (such as *cnawan, deman, cweþan, tellan*, given in Table 6.3, cf. Mitchell 1985: §1092). This shows that the form *þæs* is independent; its case is not dependent on the argument relation it has with the main verb (Thompson (2002: 128ff.) even argues that verbs like *think* do not take an object argument at all). The genitive is often used adverbially in Old English to express extension or duration (cf. *nihtes* 'at night'). All this indicates that *þæs* is not an object but an adverbial expressing 'the measure in/the extent to which', and that *þæs þe*, like *for þæm þe*, introduces a subordinate clause, more precisely what Quirk *et al.* (1972) have called a subordinate clause of proportion. *Þæs* without *þe* connects the clause more loosely by means of an adverbial conjunct, best translated by 'so, thus'. I assume that both the subordinate clause and the more loosely connected paratactic clause could further develop into 'a comment clause', which has a rather independent status. I have found quite a few examples of this type of clause in Old English, but only in texts consisting of or containing many dialogues. Table 6.3 gives an overview of the believe-type verbs found with the *þæs* (*þe*) construction in The Dictionary of Old English Corpus.

This finding makes it likely that the Middle English clauses in (30) and also the ones introduced by *as/so* in (31) are the same as these clauses, that is, they too are not relative clauses. Interpreting *as* as an adverbial rather than a relative, also explains why in the Middle English data we occasionally find examples with inverted word order: next to *as/so I trowe* there is *so trowe I*, and next to *I trowe*, we also find *trowe I* (cf. Brinton 1996: 213).[50] It explains the occurrence of pleonastic *it* in clauses such as *as it semeth me*, *as it thynketh me*, where the occurrence of the pronoun *it* is difficult to explain away as 'a dummy subject with an impersonal verb' (Brinton 1996: 251), since in these clauses the 'relative pronoun' *as* should function as a subject. Finally, it explains examples such as the ones given in (33), which cannot be understood from the point of view of Thompson and Mulac's idea of the zero-complements as a bridge structure. In (33) the 'zero-complement' of the believe-type verb shows all the paraphernalia of a main clause, that is with an

Table 6.3. *Number of Old English constructions of the type illustrated in (32), with the verb in the first person present tense*

þæs (*þe*) ic +V$_{pres}$	*cnawan/ witan* 'know'	*cweþan/tellan secgan/ reccan* 'say, tell'	*deman/ þencan gemunan* 'think, consider'	*geliefan* 'believe'	*hopian* 'hope'	*ongietan/ begietan* 'under- stand'	*wenan* 'believe, expect'
4	7	3	3	1	5	13

NP in topic position followed by inverted word order. This indicates that *I woot* and *I trowe* occur early as separate, independent clauses by themselves,

(33a) I trowe an hundred tymes been they kist (Chaucer, *CT, M. of Law's Tale* 1074)
'I believe, a hundred times did they kiss each other'
(33b) And for I woot wel ingot have ye noon (Chaucer, *CT C. Yeoman's Tale* 1206)
And, for I know well, mould have you none [you don't have a mould]

In other words, there seems to be no need to create an intermediate relative-clause stage in the process sketched by Brinton (cf. (34) below).

Brinton's stages of development, replacing the ones suggested by Thompson and Mulac in (29), are as follows:

(34) DIACHRONIC DEVELOPMENT OF *I guess*-parentheticals according to Brinton (1996: 252)
Stage I: *They are poisonous.* That I think
Stage II: *They are poisonous* {that I think, I think that/it, as/so I think} = which I think
Stage III: *They are poisonous, I think* OR
They are poisonous, as I think = as far as I think, probably
Stage IV: I think, *they are poisonous / They are*, I think, *poisonous*

So now we have two possible sources for the English parentheticals. They may have developed from a main clause introducing a *that*- and later zero-complement, losing its main-clause status in the process and merging with what was originally the subordinate clause. The problem with this is that we have little historical evidence for it, zero-clauses seem to be rare in Old English, while quite a few of the zero-clauses in Middle English still display main clause word order (cf. (33)). Moreover, this development could only take place once the complementizer (*that*) was *regularly* left out. This became the case only at the end of the Middle English period. *That*-loss then steadily increased in the sixteenth century and reached a peak at the end of the seventeenth century (cf. Rissanen 1999a: 284). This loss was greatly helped by the fact that in this same period the typical subordinate clause word order (SOV) disappeared so that there really was very little difference between a clause with and without *that*. These developments, however, are a little bit too late to explain the rise of the parentheticals from zero-complements, since there are already many parentheticals in late Middle English, as Brinton shows.

The other possibility is that they developed from a relative clause as indicated in (34II). Although I agree with Brinton that a development from a clause with an anaphoric element is most probable, I do not think it likely that this was a relative. Rather than as a relative clause, I interpret the Old and Middle English examples as 'subordinate proportional' (Quirk *et al.*'s (1972) term) or as paratactic, independent clauses introduced by an anaphoric connective element in the genitive, which I would classify as an adverbial derived from a demonstrative pronoun.

From the point of view of timing, and also from the evidence that we have from Old English, this second (modified) development may be the more likely one. Of course, if the parenthetical started in this way, it may well have been reinforced in the later period by the rapid spread of zero-complements. In order to get a better perspective on both possibilities, let us have a look at what happened in a closely related language such as Dutch. Here parentheticals of the type *I guess, I think* also developed, but some of the other changes, that is the rise of zero-complements and the fixation of SVO word order did not occur there.

First we will have to establish which of the believe-type verbs have come to be used as parentheticals in Dutch. I will only use synchronic evidence here based on frequencies, which I have established via a quick and superficial (but I think for this purpose adequate) Google search.[51] The count is not precise, but it does give an idea; moreover the parentheticals are more frequent in the highly colloquial webpages than in many other available sources. Clearly, we will need more fine-tuned data, both diachronic Dutch data and typological Germanic data to come to any firm conclusions, but some preliminary ones are possible on the basis of this small pilot. The same frequency counts may help us to establish, following the Thompson–Mulac method, what constructions may have been of influence in the development. In this case, variations in word order, which were not available for Modern English, may help us to arrive at a more detailed picture. Some relevant frequency counts can be found in Table 6.4. I have only considered phrases in the first person singular because it is clear from Thompson and Mulac that second person singular parentheticals are rare.

What can we deduce from this table? *Weten* 'know' is the verb that occurs most frequently in the first person (that is, in the present tense), but a quick perusal of examples confirms that in most cases it is used as a full cognitive verb. The next two most frequent collocations with the first person are with the verbs *vinden* 'find' and *denken* 'think'. What is of interest concerning these two verbs is the fact that the past tense first person is even more common than the present in the most frequent construction,

Table 6.4. *Constructions with believe-type verbs in present day Dutch collected with Google (May 2005)*

Verbs	CONSTRUCTIONS				
	Verb-Subject			Subject-Verb	
	V+ *ik* 'I'	'that' + V + *ik*	V + *ik* + 'that'	*ik* + V +'that' (+ *ik/we*)	*Ik*+V+ Ø+*ik/ we*
bedoelen 'mean'	**276,000**	45,700	18,300	21,100 (785/ 359)	21,100/ 791
[past tense]	[39,200]				
denken 'think'	**893,000**	53,000	265,000	894,000 (306,000/ 101,000)	45,300/ 986
[past tense]	**[905,000]**	[42,500]	[78,100]	[409,000 (68,700/ 10,300)]	[35,400/ 1,140]
geloven 'believe'	**565,000**	29,500	25,500	224,000 (53,900/ 11,100)	12,000/ 34
[past tense]	[9,410]				
hopen 'hope'	**409,000**	23,700	103,000	1,570,000 (136,000/ 40,900	3,770/ 69
[past tense]	[15,600]				
menen 'mean'	**71,100**	12,100	10,100	33,200 (888/ 659)	308/ 1
[past tense]	[11,500]				
verwachten 'expect'	**98,000**	3,800	17,000	51,400 (710/970)	191/ 16
[past tense]	[10,900]				
vinden 'find'	**707,000**	385,000	223,000	550,700 (21,500/ 18,100)	925/ 172
[past tense]	**[1,118,200]**	[104,400]	[52,300]	[80,000 (10,000/ 1,800)]	[735/ 14]
Weten 'know'	**1,040,000**	187,000	142,000	440,000 (77,700/ 5,160)	9,920/ 159
[past tense]	[292,000]	55,800	39,800	[92,200 (27,800/ 951)]	[424/ 28]

the inverted *vind ik/denk ik* 'find I/think I'. This is a very clear indication of the modal use of the past tense, which is regular only with epistemic expressions (cf. the modal use of English *might*, *could*, *should*, etc. which likewise also do not refer to a past time). It shows, in other words, the parenthetical epistemic status of these phrases. Interestingly enough, the past tense with parentheticals is not at all usual in English. The ICE-GB corpus, gives 1655 hits for *I think*, and only 284 for *I thought*, similarly for the other frequent parentheticals (*I mean/meant*: 1417 vs. 24; I suppose/supposed: 212 vs. 5; *I guess/guessed*: 43 vs. 1, etc.).

The next two verbs in line in Table 6.4 are *geloven* 'believe' and *hopen* 'hope'. Past tense use does not confirm parenthetical status in this case. However, their low frequency may well be due to the fact that their past tenses (*geloofde* and *hoopte*) are too long and phonetically awkward (because of the consonant cluster) to be of parenthetical use. Compare this to *vond* 'found' and *dacht* 'thought', which are monosyllabic (cf. on the point of brevity and its relation to frequency/economy, Krug 2001).

Another piece of evidence that may be said to confirm the parenthetical status of these four most frequent verbs (after *weten*, which we have excluded on semantic grounds) is the fact that only these verbs may undergo Negative-raising in Dutch. In Fischer (1998), I have shown that Negative-raising is closely related to modality and politeness. It is altogether clear that when a still fully cognitive believe-type verb is negated, the verb itself is negated. In Negative-raising, however, the parenthetical verb is itself not semantically negative (as a parenthetical verb it has very little referential meaning), but the negative marker is raised from the subordinate-clause predicate, which represents the true negative proposition. Negative-raising constructions, like parentheticals, are most common in the first person, and they both serve to tone down the discourse; they are used as 'stance-verbs' (Thompson 2002: 139) to create bonding.

The next thing to be observed in Table 6.4 is the small number of zero-complement clauses in the last column. In Dutch, unlike in English, it never became usual to drop the complementizer (this may well be related to the fact that the word order in subordinate clauses remained SOV). Indeed at a quick scan, most of the examples here concern a new main clause after *ik +* Verb, shown by the fact that it has SVO word order (the same is true for the structure Verb + *ik*, not shown in the Table).[52] This at least suggests that the Thompson–Mulac scenario cannot be correct for the earlier stages of the development in English, where word order was still more like Dutch. The later *that*-dropping in English may have speeded up the use of believe-type verbs as parentheticals there, but this would need to be shown by a more detailed investigation of the Middle and Modern English periods. My impression is indeed that Dutch makes less use of parentheticals than English, which may well be due to the fact that 'that'-dropping did not become the rule with these verbs. Again, this needs to be investigated further.

A final, most noticeable difference is the large frequency of inverted structures with the Dutch believe-type verbs (columns 1–3) compared to the occurrence of SV orders (columns 4–5). We already noted above that in Middle English both orders still occur, although the inverted order is not frequent (presumably due to the increasing fixation to SVO in this period). The only way to explain the inversion is by accepting that the parenthetical phrase is in fact a main clause. Only main clauses undergo inversion in Dutch. The fact that a structure with initial demonstrative *dat* 'that' (column 2) also occurs fairly regularly, suggests that this VS phrase is a reduced clause introduced by a demonstrative pronoun in topic position, or by some topicalized anaphoric adverb (the combination with *dan/zo* 'then/so'+ Verb+ *ik* 'I', is quite high with *denk ik*: 139,600, less so with *vind ik*: 74,320). This comes close to the Middle English construction *so trowe I/so I trowe* 'thus believe I/I believe'.

If the phrase started off as an independent clause, as Gorrell suggested in 1895 (see above),[53] then the grammaticalization, if that is what it is, does not involve scope increase, since as a clause it would have had scope over the proposition in the next clause or the preceding clause (or both) all along, linked as it was to this clause by the anaphoric/cataphoric demonstrative pronoun or adverb.

This brings us to a discussion of the status of this change. Is it a case of grammaticalization or is it more like lexicalization? Does it involve subjectification? As to the latter, there is no doubt that the parentheticals are subject-oriented, but I would ascribe that simply to the fact that they are a development almost exclusively of first-person verbal phrases. In the same way I would ascribe the conversational implicature of uncertainty, which Brinton (1996: 244) believes becomes fully semanticized in the parenthetical, as another necessary result of the fusion of a believe-type verb and the first person. The use of such a verb in the first person expresses by its very nature uncertainty (*I believe*, *I guess*, *I suppose*), and it is no accident that the phrase *I know* misses out on this development in English as well as in Dutch. If the verb *know* is used epistemically at all, it is mostly in the phrase *Yes I know*, which does not occur, like the other parentheticals, in almost any position in the clause, or in the phrase *you know*. The use of the second person makes it different from the other parentheticals too, which do not frequently occur in the second person.

Thompson and Mulac (1991: 324) believe that the parentheticals represent a case of grammaticalization—although they do not see them as 'a "textbook case" study'—and so does Brinton (1996: 253). They both agree that its development does not follow some of the usual parameters, such as phonetic reduction, morphological bonding, increasingly fixed syntactic position, and decrease in scope. They mark the following characteristics (referring to the principles by Hopper as well as Lehmann, cf. §3.2) as evidence in favour of grammaticalization: decategorialization, specialization, divergence, and persistence.

As to persistence, it is true that the original sense of the cognitive verb persists, but that in itself does not rank something as grammaticalization, since in lexicalization the original sense persists too. In fact the parentheticals preserve more meaning than is usual in the grammaticalization of discourse markers (cf. Schiffrin 1987: 73, 267), which also explains (see below) why their specialization (or in Lehmann's terms 'paradigmatization') is not as severe as with full referential elements grammaticalizing into affixes or auxiliaries. As to specialization, it is correct that only a few of the cognitive verbs are regularly used as parentheticals. However, that does not imply that others cannot still be used as such, as Thompson and Mulac (1991: 319) make clear in their survey: there are still 15 percent of 'other' verbs used as parentheticals, which although less frequent, are as true parentheticals as the more usual *I guess, I think*.

Concerning divergence, it seems to me that there is some contradiction here. If indeed the verbal phrase has decategorialized, that is become a pragmatic marker, a secondary category, as is suggested, then indeed the old and the new forms must have diverged, since *I think* etc. now belongs to two different categories: full verbal phrase and (adverbial) pragmatic marker. But decategorialization and divergence equally apply to the process of lexicalization. For instance, in *today*, which no one would dispute *is* a case of lexicalization, an adverb arises from a noun in a prepositional phrase. Moreover, Thompson and Mulac (1991: 324) contradict themselves when they characterize the development of *I think* as decategorialization and at the same time deny that it can be lexicalization by saying that the 'E[pistemic] P[phrase]s are still available for ordinary negation and questioning (It's cute, don't you think?)'.

Let us now have a look at the case for lexicalization. Many of the features apply to both grammaticalization and lexicalization: divergence and persistence, as we have seen, but also morphological bonding. Brinton (1996: 253) writes that bonding does not apply to this case, but this may be questionable. Since the standardization of the spelling, it has become less likely that separate words will come to be written as a unit. It is of interest, however, that other verbal parentheticals did become a lexical unit in earlier English or in non-standard languages. An example is the phrase *methinks* and *godwot* 'god knows' (according to the *OED* written sometimes as one word), similarly Afrikaans *glo* from earlier *glo'k* < *glo ek* < Dutch *geloof ik* 'believe I', as noted in Thompson and Mulac (1991: 318). Wischer (2000), indeed, characterizes *methinks* as a case of 'syntactic lexicalization' because, as she notes, the two processes of lexicalization and grammaticalization may both be said to be present here.

As to Thompson and Mulac's argument that parenthenticals cannot represent lexicalization because they are still available for negation and questioning, this seems to me not quite correct. The negative *I don't think*, which is always used with Negative-raising, can only occur at the beginning of a clause because it has to precede the subordinate clause that it negates. In other words, unlike the regular parenthetical *I think*, it cannot occur in almost any position in the clause. Similarly, the phrase *do you think* is clearly followed by part of the complement clause in (35):

(**35**)   What do you think this offers? (ICE-GB s1A-001-116)

because it is impossible to put the phrase at the end and preserve the overall construction (see (36)). Example (36) simultaneously shows that the complement is an obligatory argument of the predicate *think* because it cannot be left out. This is quite unlike the use of parenthetical *I think*, which can occur in all the positions indicated by x in (37), but which is not itself an obligatory part of the clause *What this offers*. Hence the clause *What this offers* must appear as a main clause (*What does this offer?*) or must be part of a main clause (*What this offers, is ...*).

(**36**)   *What this offers do you think?
(**37**) x What x this x offers x, is x ...
          x What x does this x offer x ?

Also of interest is that most other common parentheticals do not appear in a negative or interrogative form at all: there are no examples of *do you/I guess, you/I don't guess* in the ICE-GB corpus. This indicates that such examples with *think*, which do occur in the corpus, are not true parentheticals but are closer to expressing a 'mode of knowing' (i.e. Thompson and Mulac's type (29b)). In this light it is not surprising that a complement clause must follow because the cognitive verb (unlike the epistemic evidential) needs a complement and the complement depends on the verb.

Diessel and Tomasello (2001: 106ff.), who have looked at the use of parentheticals like *I think* in child language, distinguish three uses of believe-type verbs: (i) as formulaic parentheticals occurring only in the first person singular present indicative, (ii) as performatives used in direct questions, imperatives, and hortatives, and (iii) as assertives. Only in the latter case are they used as full verbs governing an embedded complement clause. This is the type that does not occur in early child language, and which is rare in spoken discourse (hence not considered in Thompson 2002).

To my mind parenthetical phrases such as *I think*, etc. are best seen as formulaic tokens, undergoing lexicalization rather than grammaticalization. In this process, they lose some referential content, being narrowed down to a more epistemic, evaluative meaning. In non-standardized languages they are likely to form one lexical unit in the course of time, provided they are not replaced by new tokens lexicalized from new believe-type-verbs. As with modal adverbs expressing speakers' stance (*awfully, terribly, gigantically*), they may have a quick turnover since they also serve as markers of personality, group identity, and politeness. I do not believe they originally were part of a complex clause as both Thompson and Mulac, and Brinton have argued in different ways. They probably occurred *both* in independent clauses *and* with complement clauses from the very beginning, the former being most frequent in spoken, the latter in written discourse. The difference is probably one *between* Givón's (1979) pragmatic and syntactic mode, which exist side by side in evolved languages. In other words, this case does not present a *direct* historical development, whereby a construction in the pragmatic mode develops into a syntactic construction. A knowledge of even older historical stages would be necessary to decide on this point for English. It seems to me more likely, however, that Gorrell (1895) is right when he accepts the use of parentheticals already for Old English, and I find it hard to agree with Diessel and Tomasello (2001: 135), who believe that the diachronic development in this particular case is the opposite of the ontogenetic development, where the parenthetical use clearly comes first. It may well have been early diachronically too.

6.3 Concluding remarks

I have tried to show in this chapter that the type of grammaticalization known as subjectification is special in a number of ways. The phenomenon of scope increase, which is the opposite of what one would expect according to the Lehmannian parameters of grammaticalization, is not a direct unidirectional development of the elements that grammaticalize (or lexicalize), but is caused by the fact that the grammaticalizing elements occur originally in a higher or independent clause. This means that scope increase is caused by a change in structure (cf. Deutscher's 'structural replacement' discussed in §5.1, and in fn. 9 above) rather then a gradual change in the lexical elements themselves, which in fact retain the scope they had. I have also tried to show that the semantic-pragmatic development towards subjectification is not so much due to the discourse context in which the elements occur (pragmatic inferencing), but to their own lexical source-concept(s), to general semantic principles of change (notably metaphor), and to the position in which and the collocation with which they occur in the clause. As to position, it is clear that leftwards movement influences scope, as predicted by Bolinger's linearity principle. This principle is more explanatory than the 'move' to or 'merge' in a higher position in the structural tree (which is mostly abstract, i.e. the elements do not necessarily move on the surface) used in the generative model, since this is a theory-internal description. In addition, other changes that take place in the grammar of a language (through external causes—standardization, foreign and cultural influences—as well as internal ones on the syntactic, lexical, morphological, etc. levels) have repercussions on the position of the grammaticalizing or lexicalizing element(s) and on the word order that helps to distinguish this position.

Notes

1. The further development into an adverbial intensifier happened, for instance, with English *very*. In Middle English *verray/very* (< OF *ve(r)rai*, Mod. Fr. *vrai* 'true') was still only used as an adjective.

2. Van Valin and LaPolla (1997: 47–8) follow a similar scope interpretation in their functional model: deontic modality is considered to be an operator on the 'core' (i.e. the predicate and its semantic arguments), while epistemic modality is an operator on the 'clause' (which contains the core plus the 'periphery'). The same distinction is made in Functional Grammar (cf. Dik 1997). There are various interpretations concerning the scope of modals; for a different view, see e.g. Warner (1993:16). In addition, purely deontic modals are in themselves difficult to classify because the interpretation depends on the subject selected. Thus *must*

in *I must go home now*, would have narrow scope (the VP only) because the speaker is also the agent (i.e. the modal is more dynamic), while in *He must go home*, expressing the speaker's will, *must* would have scope over the whole of the proposition, and could therefore be called subjectively deontic.

3. There is an additional problem in using C-command to determine scope. In some of the most recent generative models there is a proliferation of functional heads (cf. Cinque 1999), the order of which is crucial for any decision about scope. The C-command definition of scope is therefore bound up with all kinds of theory-internal motivations, and may not be the best tool to measure scope by.

4. It is possible to construe the *þæt*-clause in this type as a subject. As with impersonal verbs (which the modals resemble, see §4.2.2 and below) the status of the clause is ambiguous. For some discussion, see Fischer and van der Leek (1983: 348–9). According to Bock (1931: 149, 154) the function of both bare and *to*-infinitives, which normally were positioned after the predicate, was still very much one of dependence on the predicate; the same could be said for the *þæt*-clause, which in function correlated with the *to*-infinitive.

5. For instance, the impersonal verb *ofhreowan* 'rew' occurs in three different construction-types (note that the meaning of the verb depends on the syntactic configuration in which it occurs): without a grammatical subject (a), with an inanimate (agentive/causal) subject (b), and with an animate (agentive/experiencer) subject (subject status is indicated by the nominative case),

   (a) him[DAT] ofhreow   þæs   mannes[GEN]
   (ÆCHom I 13 281.12)
   to-him   pity-existed from-the man

   (b) þa   ofhreow   þam   munece[DAT] þæs   hreoflian mægenleast[NOM]
   (ÆCHom I23 369139)
   then brought-pity to-the monk   the   leper's   feebleness

   (c) se mæssepreost[NOM] þæs   mannes[GEN] ofhreow (ÆLS(Oswald) 262)
   the priest   from-the man   felt-pity

   Not all impersonal verbs are found with all three types. This is also true for the modal verbs. They may be used without a nominative NP in both Old and Middle English (e.g. type (a), see Warner 1993: 102 and §4.2.2 above). They occur both with an inanimate subject (type b) and an animate subject (type c), when they are used dynamically. Concerning type (a), this only occurs with a complement clause as 'object', the status of which is difficult to determine since a clause is case-less (cf. Fischer and van der Leek 1983: 348–9; Denison 1990: 140–3). The similarity with impersonals is also not entirely straightforward, but this is because the modal verbs are already semantically idiosyncratic in some respects. Denison (1990: 143) suggests a similar classification for the modals as impersonals but hesitates to accept it fully because of the uncertainty about the existence of a true subjectless (a) type.

6. I use 'agentive' with some hesitation here because the animate and inanimate nominative subjects also carry the thematic role of 'experiencer' and 'cause' respectively. The point I wish to make is that they are both seen as the source of the action expressed by the verb, the means by which an action comes about. In terms of Hopper and Thompson (1980), they are more transitive than the subjectless type, which is intransitive and stative. Following Van Valin and LaPolla's (1997) Role and Reference Grammar, it might be better to refer to this semantic role as a 'macrorole'. There are only two macroroles, viz. ACTOR and UNDERGOER; these are scalar and more structural or abstract than the lower level semantic roles. The role referred to here is that of ACTOR.

7. Although in Old English the nominative subject position was generally filled by the agentive argument (except in intransitive clauses [including passives], where the position could also be filled by the theme/patient argument), we could refer to this dative/accusative case as a 'subject'. Morphologically it is not in the nominative but in some ways (e.g. in coordinate clauses) it already functioned like a syntactic or purely structural subject, cf. Allen (1986, 1995). In Middle English all these non-nominative 'subjects' become true morphological subjects when the subject position is opened up to other semantic roles. Thus, prepositional and dative passives (e.g. *The bed was slept in*; *He was given a book*) only became possible in Middle English (cf. Fischer 1992b: 383–7, Allen 2001). In generative models this is usually seen as a change from inherent Case to structural Case assignment.

8. This includes intransitive verbs like 'be, become' as I have argued above, because these too do not assign an argument role to the subject position.

9. Note that it is not the longer construction itself which is reduced or ellipted, the construction is *replaced* (i.e. Deutscher's (2000) notion of 'structural replacement' applies here rather than 'structural change', cf. §5.1). This is due, as I have argued above, to the much higher frequency of the dynamic/deontic construction, featuring the *same* verbs (analogy), and helped by the fact that the language system now allowed Subject-raising and had acquired a structural subject position that had to be obligatorily filled.

10. For the relation between perfect *have* and evidentiality, see Brinton (1996: 243), who notes that source-concepts for evidentiality include perfects. Noteworthy in this respect are the modal combinations with *have*, such as *must have*, *might have*, *could have*, etc., which are all connected with non-factuality.

11. The use of the reflexive here is interesting because it indicates in clauses like *La branche se casse* 'The branch breaks', that there is in fact no agentive force present, i.e. that the cause of breaking is unknown, not related to anything in the outside world, in contrast to non-reflexive *La branche casse*, where the cause of breaking lies clearly in the outside world and is known from the context. In a similar way, the reflexive pronoun with *pouvoir* in (4) suggests that the act of 'coming' expressed in *vienne* can only be *logically* deduced and not from any direct perceptual evidence (hence the use of the subjunctive).

Hella Olberz (p.c.) mentions that Spanish has a construction rather similar to the French one in (4) but with the expletive subject left out:

(a) Puede   que   haya   un   contexto   que   yo   ignoro
         Can   that   there-is a   context   that I   not-know
         'It may be that there is a context which I am unaware of'

The interesting thing about this construction is that *puede que* has become a fixed formula (clear from the fact that it can no longer be negated) and is developing into an adverb, much like English *maybe* and others discussed at the end of this section.

12. Another way of saying this is *Il risque de se faire prendre*, which expresses a less strong inevitability than (5). This looks monoclausal, but in fact *risquer* like English *seem* is a subject-raising verb. In addition, the infinitival marker *de* makes clear that this infinitive (in contrast to the bare infinitives in (6)–(7)) is clausal in that it functions as a clause boundary and does not allow extraction (cf. Kayne 1981, who showed that French *de* is a complementizer and incompatible with raising). We have seen a similar case with Dutch *om te*-infinitives (discussed in §5.3): in contrast to bare and *te*-infinitives the IPP effect does not occur here because elements cannot be extracted from the *om te* infinitive, cf. also Roberts and Roussou (2002: 30).

13. Another possible meaning of *Il doit venir*, is that 'there is certainty that he comes, because he has said so himself'. In other words, this is also not epistemic. Note that the so-called *conditionnel présent* of these modals can appear in an epistemic sense without 'be' (as in *Elle pourrait venir/Il devrait venir* 'She could come/He should come'), but here the verbal form *itself* expresses potentiality or irrealis, and is therefore epistemic.

14. The Slavonic data are taken from van der Auwera *et al.* (2005). Of interest here is the fact that Dutch *misschien* is still often followed by the complementizer *dat* 'that' especially in the spoken language.

15. The same is true for the case of the gerund, discussed by Tabor and Traugott. They show in their diachronic string comparison (1998: 244) that the *-ing* element has moved leftwards in the structure to a higher position, but there is no surface evidence for this (for the notion of 'diachronic string comparison' see §6.2).

16. Clear terminology in connection with sentence adverbs, discourse markers, and pragmatic markers, is a problem because they often involve the same tokens, they share a number of syntactic positions (especially in English) and they are also very close semantically, as we will see below.

17. There is a clear semantic link between the types of adverbials that may become sentence adverbials and pragmatic markers. Viewpoint or evaluative adverbials, intensifiers, and manner adverbs inherently contain an aspect of subjectivity and/or epistemicity which is missing in e.g. time and place adverbials, which are usually factual. Thus, in communication, these 'judgemental' adverbs implicitly convey the view of the speaker or the narrator, also when (s)he is not

syntactically present in the clause, and hence their scope may involve not just the proposition but the whole of the speech-act. In their function of comment on the speech-act, they may next function as pragmatic markers, whose role is to express a personal response or a reaction to the discourse, and hence give structure to the discourse. Both sentence adverbials and pragmatic markers have an interpersonal and a cohesive function (cf. Brinton 1996: 36ff.). In view of this, it should not come as a surprise that it is often difficult to keep them apart (see also §6.2.2 below).

18. This is how it is described in Traugott (1995: 13) (and see also Traugott and Dasher 2002: 170): 'The developments suggest that there is a diachronic path along an adverbial cline of the type: VAdv > IPAdv > DM' (i.e. verbal adjunct > sentence adverbial > pragmatic or discourse marker), where in 'all cases a meaning change in the clause internal PP [i.e. the verbal adjunct] was required *before the form could become an IPAdv* ... these were prerequisites enabling (but of course not causing) the subsequent changes to occur' (emphasis added). I will argue below that the enabling factors were structural as well as semantic-pragmatic.

19. *Presumably* is used as a sentence adverb from 1846 onwards. The *OED* records one instance of it as a manner adverb (from 1646), but qualifies this use as 'rare' and 'obsolete'. It seems unlikely therefore that this sentence adverb developed from a manner adverb.

20. Note that *instead of* does not really develop into a proper conjunction because it cannot be used before a subject + a finite verbal form. Even though Tabor and Traugott (1998: 251) write that recent types involve 'finite ... VP coordination', they do not give examples of this. Note that *He sang instead of he spoke* is not possible. Examples of *He sang instead of spoke* can be found on the internet and indeed sound more natural. The ICE-GB corpus, however, gives no examples of this, so presumably it is still rare. The corpus has 65 examples of the use of *instead of*: in 32 cases it connects NPs, in 30 cases it connects present participles or gerunds (in two of these instances the *instead of* phrase + *-ing* comes first in the clause and is followed by a finite verb in the matrix clause), in two cases it connects adjective phrases. One example is very interesting because it shows that a finite verb is in fact avoided: *We sit in the car instead of walking* (ICE-GB W2b-022 010).

21. It is clear that grammaticalization and lexicalization are on a continuum (see also the discussion at the end of §5.1 and §6.2.3), and that the processes that lead to it are the same, the results only differ depending on whether we are dealing with a type or a token. Moreover, even if we follow the definitions given in Brinton and Traugott (2005), it is still the case that the category of prepositions is quite an open class (it admits new members quite frequently, which do not necessarily replace old members in the category), so even in their terms, lexicalization may be the more appropriate description.

22. This 'sentence adverb' is clearly different from the usual ones as defined by Swan (1988), to which the authors refer. Quirk *et al.* (1972: 673) indeed classify

instead as an adverbial conjunct, i.e. an adverb used to connect sentences, whereas sentence adverbs in the sense of Swan are called adverbial disjuncts. These disjuncts are of various types, distinguished by most linguists as follows (cf. Swan 1988: 29ff.): (i) evaluative adverbs (speaker-oriented), (ii) modal adverbs (epistemic or truth evaluating), also called truth intensifiers, (iii) subject disjuncts (i.e. speaker- and subject-oriented), also called epitheticals, and (iv) speech-act adverbials (message-oriented). Note that the term 'adverb' refers to a part of speech, while 'adverbial' refers to a particular function that a phrase has in the clause. 'Adverbials' thus includes all adverbs formally marked as adverbs, but it may also include NPs (*yesterday*, *this week*), PPs (of time and place), and lexicalized PPs or longer phrases/clauses, such as *tomorrow*, *indeed*, *nevertheless*, *anon*, *methinks*, etc. In this chapter, I will use the term adverbial when I wish to refer to the whole group as a functional category. I will use adverb if the adverbial is an adverb.

23. The scope would be rather similar to the scope that subordinate clauses have over the main clause when they *precede* the main clause, as is typical for temporal and causal clauses, as e.g. in *When I look around at my friends, virtually all of them seem to have got careers* (ICE-GB w1b-001-200); *Because he refused to disassociate his experience from his belief, he sought to re-think, re-explain and render properly metaphysical doctrines which* ... (ICE-GB w2a-003-051)

24. The scope of adverbials is in fact not easily defined. Note that place or time adverbials may well have scope over the subject in contrast to manner adverbs which are said to scope over the VP only.

25. In terms of the generative model, this means that the verbal adjunct is C-commanded by the matrix verb. This dependency on the verb is shown on the surface level by the fact that the adverbial is usually placed close to the matrix verb. It can also be found in initial or final position in the clause with other arguments intervening, but in these cases the adverbial can be said to have been moved by scrambling or topicalization, which usually results in extra emphasis.

26. On this question, see also Swan (1988: 13–14), who wrote, referring to Greenbaum (1969: 6), 'His conclusion with regard to multi-function adverbs appears to be that they are (syntactic) homonyms: "Items that are identical in their written and spoken forms but that differ syntactically are considered to be 'syntactic homonyms'..." '. Greenbaum's idea comes close to Boogaart's (2004) proposal mentioned in §6.1, which considers the modal verbs to be monosemous, with their different deontic and epistemic senses determined by the (syntactic) construction they appear in.

27. The *OED* senses 3 and 4 for *actually* show that the verbal adjunct use, with the meaning 'in act, in fact' is still current; cf. their example: *The rates of interest actually paid in business vary very much*, where the scope of *actually* is the predicate. The same is true for *in fact*, as is clear from the example in Traugott and Dasher (2002: 157): *Humanity, comfortably engaged elsewhere in the business of living, is absent in fact but everywhere present in feeling*. The use of *indeed*

may now be mainly as a sentence adverbial and pragmatic marker, but as an emphatic marker, as in *He is a painter indeed*, it is still an adverbial with narrow scope.

28. In fact most initial adverbials, whether disjuncts or conjuncts (cf. fn. 22), have a connecting function, due to their first position in the clause, which entails that the line between the two cannot be very sharply drawn in this respect.

29. Not surprisingly, generative linguists have been more aware of the importance of position in the analysis of sentence adverbials/pragmatic markers, cf. Meinunger (2004) and Zwart (2005). I will come back to this below.

30. Swan (1988: 32 and *passim*) gives a fairly extensive list of sentence adverbs, but comments that 'it is not by any means complete, partly because this may be to some extent an open class'.

31. It is possible, however, that the frequent occurrence of *yes indeed/no indeed* as a separate (reduced) clause has played a role in the development of *indeed* as a pragmatic marker by itself with more global scope.

32. Elements like OE *soðlice* and *witodlice* used as pragmatic markers are very hard to translate. Their polysemy is also clear from the fact that both of them translate a large variety of Latin pragmatic markers such as *autem*, *enim*, *nam*, *ecce*, etc. I have here used a literal translation in their propositional use, even though their usage as pragmatic markers is much more frequent. For more information on their usage in Old English, see Lenker (2000).

33. Swan (1988: 176) has classified these as sentence adverbials in sentence final position (which she notes is 'an unusual feature'). However, due to their nature as a reduced clause and occurring between two clauses (as the full examples in (22) show), they could as easily be considered initial, i.e. preceding the next clause. Another interesting example is ÆCHom II, 37 279 215, where *rihtlice swa* is followed by *þæt*, introducing a subordinate clause that depends on it.

34. Examples of XV order only occur when another element than the subject is topicalized in first position, as in:

> **(a)** Soðlice on me earmre is mines fæder nama reowlice forworden (ApT 2.14)
>   Verily in miserable me is my father's name cruelly perished

It may be safely concluded that it is the topicalized element (*on me earmre*) that causes the inversion of subject and verb, and not the sentence adverbial (*Soðlice*) itself, as is still the case for similar structures in Modern Dutch and German (cf. for Old English, Swan 1988: 94, for Modern Dutch, Evers-Vermeul 2005: 23). In addition, as Evers-Vermeul and Swan (1988: 223) also note, a double topic position is problematic from a theoretical point of view, indicating that *Soðlice* is not itself in topic position.

Note that when the subject is a pronoun or when the adverbial is at the head of a coordinate clause, it is difficult to distinguish between SV/XV and VS/VX order, since pronouns, as clitics (cf. van Kemenade 1987; Koopman 1998), do not normally invert, while the subject of a coordinate clause is usually PRO. These examples will be identified as 'ambiguous' in the discussion below.

35. Koopman (1998: 139) writes in connection with word order after *witodlice* (where he found only one case of VS/VX in his corpus against 78 cases of SV/XV with nominal subjects) that *witodlice* is 'probably best interpreted as being outside the syntax of the clause'. Similar descriptions are given for the modern Dutch and German instances of SV or V3 by Zwart (2005), who uses terms like 'extracyclic' and 'extradependent', and Meinunger (2004), who refers to their inability to get 'a proposition internal reading' (p. 77). In this connection it should be noted that inversion of nominal subject and verb after a topicalized element is not fully grammaticalized in Old English (in contrast to modern Dutch/German). Koopman (1998: 136) shows, for instance, that inversion after topicalized objects only becomes the rule in later Old English (in early Old English it occurs 53% of the time, in Ælfric 91%). After prepositional phrases, however, it always was the rule rising from an average of 69% in early Old English to 93% in Ælfric.

36. Most examples are construed with the verbs *secgan* 'say' or *ongietan* 'understand', where the phrase *swiðe rihte* or *genoh rihte* clearly means, that something is said or understood 'in a correctly enough manner'; in the context they cannot be interpreted as 'it is right enough that you say/understand …'. The exceptions from the Cura Pastoralis can both be interpreted as sentence adverbials because they involve the 'passive' verb *hatan* 'to be called', where a manner adjunct is unlikely through the lack of an agentive argument: e.g. *Suiðe ryhte ða sacerdas sint gehatene sacerdas*, 'very rightly the priests are called priests', is most likely to mean 'it is proper that the priests are called priests', and not 'priests are called priests in a proper manner'.

37. The exceptions concern three cases (i.e. her (11b), (12e), and (13f) on pp. 194–7) where *hwæt* is followed by another topicalized element which causes the inversion (cf. fn. 34). The fourth case (12a) is rather special in that it is an existential clause, where the newly introduced subject as a rule follows the verb in Old English (cf. Swan 1988: 94), i.e. the clause has the order, *Wæs sum æðele cyning*… '(there) was a noble king…' rather than *Sum æðele cyning wæs*…

38. It is interesting to observe from the examples I have gathered from the web with Google, that second language learners of Dutch (their L2 status is clear from their weblogs) often make mistakes with the word order after sentence adverbials and/or pragmatic markers, e.g.,

   (a) Eerlijk wil   ik niet per se   naar Armin kijken tenzij er
                (www.tranceaddict.com/forums/showthread/t-181608.html)
       Honest want   I   not specifically at   Armin look   unless there
       een   (kleine) meeting is.
       a   small   meeting is
       'Honestly/frankly I do not specifically want to watch Armin unless there is a small meeting'

In standard Dutch, the word order would have been SV: *Eerlijk, ik wil...*

With *kortom* 'in short', which functions as a pragmatic marker only, I have found 4990 hits with SV order in the combination *Kortom ik heb* ... 'In short, I have...', and only 103 hits with VS order, most of which concern interrogative clauses where VS is the norm. The 'mistakes' with VS order are all from non-standard Dutch texts. For standard usage see the discussion and the examples in (25)–(28) below.

39. The distinction is clearer in the modern Verb-second languages than in Old English, since they are more strictly Verb-second than Old English was. For this reason, Koopman (1998: 14) states that the occurrence of the inversion of subject and verb should not be used as 'a diagnostic test'. However, in combination with semantic-pragmatic information provided by the context and leaving out of account texts heavily influenced by Latin, the nature of the adverbial may be established with quite a bit of confidence.

40. We see exactly the same procedure with other adjectives that can be used both adjectivally as well as adverbially. Thus *vreemd* 'strange' as an adjective and reduced clause (*het is vreemd* 'it is strange' always takes SV, whereas *vreemd* as an adverb (in which case it is often found together with *genoeg* 'enough') is always followed by VS. This also explains why in Norwegian, *Pussig, hun satte seg ned* (with SV) '[It is] strange, she sat herself down', is acceptable while **Pussig, satte hun seg ned* (with VS) 'Strangely she sat herself down' is not, because a manner interpretation is most unlikely here. If the clause had contained the predicate 'looked at him', then a manner interpretation and hence VS order would have been fine.

41. Cases with two initial elements followed by inversion such as, *Hier op deze plaats zal het gebeuren* 'Here in this place will it happen', do not count as multiple topics since here the two topics are clearly one, with *op deze plaats* dependent on or appositional to *hier*. We find something similar in Old English, as is shown by example (22a) above: here 'under Moses law' is an elaboration of 'in the old days'. Note also that in the example given in fn. 34, which concerns a full sentential adverb and not a VP adjunct, the two initial elements can in no way be interpreted as one topic.

42. Indeed many of the examples in the first person that I have found on the web with SV order after *gelukkig* 'fortunately' are accompanied by parenthetic phrases such as 'I think' making the personal stance more explicit; this is not the case with the VS examples where the scope is the IP, which, when used in the first person, *already includes the speaker*.

43. Bolinger applies the principle to explain, e.g., the meaning differences between preposed and postposed adjectives in Spanish, and to some extent in Modern English with adjectives that show variable behaviour, like *responsible*. Fischer (2000b, 2004a) finds that the principle also applies to Old English pre- and postposed adjectives: meaning differences can be established which are similar to the Spanish ones. The principle explains why leftmost position (on the

surface, not as part of an abstract model) often coincides with larger scope. Cf. also the order of adjectives discussed by Adamson (2000).

44. Of course, VP adjuncts may still occur here but only when they provide narrative cohesion; this is the case mainly with time and place adverbials. Descriptive adverbs (e.g. *slowly*, *desperately*) used in English in this position are always emphatic. Note that in Dutch even direct verbal arguments may appear in first position (with VS order) without any extra emphasis as long as they are used cohesively, as in,

(a) Maar wat de oorzaak kan zijn van die bloedklonter *dat heeft hij* niet gezegd. (www.zappybaby.be/forum_all/index.cfm/fuseaction/thread/CFB/1/TID/ 2379815/StartRow/1.cfm)
But   what the cause may be of this blood clot,   that has he not said

This is no longer possible in English, where in a clause like *That he has not said, that* is always emphatic.

45. For the early adverbial behaviour of adjectives in *-lic*, see Fischer (2004a: 9, 25; 2006)

46. Purely descriptive manner adverbs placed in initial or topic position, usually carry emphasis (cf. also Swan 1988: 224), whereas this is not the case for adverbials indicating time or place because these often serve anaphorically to provide cohesion in text. The epistemic adverbials in front position appear to serve a similar role, i.e. like the time and place adverbials they provide *perspective* (i.e. they give structure to the discourse), and hence are often not emphatic in that position.

47. Brinton (1996: 243) writes that the 'conventionalization of a conversational implicature' plays a role in what she sees as a second stage, namely the change from verbs expressing 'a mode of knowing' to epistemic parentheticals. The stage from 'act of cognition' to 'mode of knowing' she considers similar to a metaphorical change. In other words, the first stage is a common kind of semantic change, one involving a change from concrete to abstract.

48. For an overview of the complications arising in trying to decide whether *þæt* is left out, or whether we are dealing with direct discourse, see Mitchell (1985: §§1981ff.).

49. With one exception, i.e. her example (23d), which has *þæt*, but this is a misquotation since The Dictionary of Old English Corpus has *þæs*. A search of this corpus shows furthermore that there is not a single example where a believe-type verb in the first person sg pres. is preceded by the pronoun *þæt* in the accusative, which is the regular case for a verbal direct object.

50. This may also show that the clause is in fact a main clause, because in subordinate clauses adverbials cannot be placed in topic position, since this is already filled by the complementizer. We will return to this question below when we look at Dutch parentheticals.

51. Although not ideal, Meyer *et al.* (2003) show that the web can be usefully searched with public search engines such as Google producing worthwhile results for linguistic study.

52. Note that it is not possible when searching in Google to filter out punctuation marks and capitals, hence no distinction can be made between *I think he is right* and *I think. He is right.*

53. The same verbs with a complement clause introduced by the complementizer 'that' may then have coexisted with the independent parenthetical clause from the very beginning (see also below). In Old English at least both are found.

7

Toward a usage-based theory of morphosyntactic change: summary and conclusions

In this volume I have compared two models for morphosyntactic change which in many ways are each other's opposites. Where grammaticalization theory is primarily interested in shifts in language utterances and in the semantic-pragmatic motivations behind the shifts, the generative model lays great store by the forms and structures of language, and considers the locus of change to be the individual grammar system rather than language output (cf. §§2.1, 2.2). I have tried to show that both approaches have contributed considerably to a better understanding of morphosyntactic change but that the rather one-sided emphasis on *either* form *or* function results in a skewed picture. The two ways of looking at language need to be combined into a single effort in order to advance our understanding of the way the system works and how languages change. In addition, we need to look at other domains in which language plays a role, notably language acquisition, language evolution, and neurolinguistic models, so that the findings there mesh with our findings on change (cf. §2.3).

I have worked from the assumption that form and function are inseparable (cf. §3.5). Both are part of what Anttila (2003) has called the 'analogical grid'. This grid is made up of a contiguity (or indexical) axis and a similarity (or iconic) axis. The system of every language forms a complex network in which each linguistic sign, both concrete and abstract, is organized with respect to all other signs, both within each level and between levels (i.e. the phonetic, the morphological, the syntactic, the semantic-pragmatic, and discourse levels). A shift in one 'box' in the grid may therefore have repercussions on its own level, and on higher or lower levels depending on its function and frequency. Thus a phonetic change usually affects all words that share the same sound in the same or similar surroundings. The sound change may be contained within its own lexical set but it may also force other sets to undergo change depending on how important the sound is in preserving a distinction between sets. If the sound change concerns a frequent sound which carries a grammatical function (e.g. an inflection), it may well have repercussions above the immediate phonetic/phonological or lexical level.

Analogy (both formal and functional), which forms the basis of the analogical grid, is seen as one of the main mechanisms or motivating factors in language learning and change (cf. §§3.2–3.5). When a particular token (an element or string of elements) α changes its meaning or function in the communicative context from x to y, this may have an effect on its form, in the sense that α now becomes realigned with another set of tokens, that is the set that shares the form's new function. Once α has joined this new set, it in turn may begin to affect the forms that already were in the set, or α itself may be influenced by the members of its new set. The perception of similarity, or perhaps better the inability to see a difference (cf. §3.2, fn.30), between two linguistic signs or between two referents, may cause the learner/speaker to shift such an element to another set in his processing system, a set that is functionally or formally close (this mechanism is often called 'abduction').

Not only does similarity play a role in language learning and change, but so also does frequency and what Tomasello (2003a, 2003b) has called 'intention reading', that is the ability and eagerness to share attention in an object or event with others and to understand the communicative intentions of others, and hence to find a meaning in each act of communication (cf. §3.3). Elements that are frequent strengthen or entrench a token, a type (category), or a construction-type (pattern) in the processing system (by which it may become automated). Intention reading often leads to pragmatic inferencing (because we understand an utterance always in context). This may change the meaning of a linguistic token, and hence may affect the indexical relation between a sign and its referent. Frequency has been much ignored in the past, by both models, but is now generally considered to be very crucial. Through the use of corpora, evident in both generative work (e.g. in Kroch 1989 a, b; Pintzuk 1991; Kroch and Taylor 1997; Koopman 1998; Moerenhout and van der Wurff 2000, 2005) and grammaticalization studies (e.g. Fischer 1994a; Krug 2000; Wong 2004; Bybee and

Hopper 2001) frequency has become a factor that can be measured, and it has now been elevated to a high rank in the more dynamic models of grammar and of change.

Frequency determines which linguistic tokens and abstract types (structures) become automated or entrenched within the processing system. When a particular analogical set loses some of its members (tokens) so that it stands out less as a type or pattern, the remaining members may join another pattern that is close to it in either form or function. Thus there is a constant balance between economy (the number of tokens/patterns to be remembered and stored) and expressivity (the necessary distinction between patterns, that is highly marked or infrequent patterns are too costly to be stored separately). In this way, the Modern Dutch suffix -*aar*, which constituted two different types (it is/was used as an (active) agentive suffix and as a passive suffix—for example *wandelaar* 'one who walks', vs. *gijzelaar* 'one who is taken hostage') is slowly losing the passive -*aar*-type because the number of lexical items that belong to this set is quite small and unproductive, while the active -*aar*-set is very large and productive. Thus the 'passive' tokens, *gijzelaar* and *martelaar* ('one who is tortured, a martyr'), are now often interpreted as active ('one who takes hostages, one who tortures'): due to a similarity in form and to the high cost of their computation in comparison to its yield, they have shifted to the set with the more frequent tokens, taking on their meaning.

Language is learned via concrete tokens in concrete situations, probably at first in a formulaic way. For this reason I have placed great emphasis on the necessity to study surface forms (cf. §1.1). Decomposition of these tokens is steered by product frequency and by the cost of computation. On the phonetic level, differences between sounds will in the long run only be recognized in so far as they are meaningful, and hence useful.[1] The phonological distinctions thus learned will help the learner to distinguish between morphemes on a more abstract level. Similarly, complex words will only be decomposed if the derivational or inflectional elements are frequent enough and are seen as functional. In other words, the language learner learns how to decompose the tokens he is confronted with in order to reduce complexity, he learns how to recognize recurrent patterns, both more concrete ones (on the phonetic/phonological and lexical level) and more abstract ones (on the morphosyntactic and discourse level). Decomposition is more likely to occur on the higher, more abstract levels because here the cost of computation would become far too high if all existing patterns (consisting of combinations of tokens) would have to be stored separately by their concrete tokens. Wholesale direct storage will presumably only happen with idiomatic phrases (where decomposition often does not help) or with very frequent collocations (where frequency may indeed lead to lexicalization). Kirby (2000) and Hurford (2000b) (cf. §2.2.2) have shown by means of computer simulation programs that syntax arises automatically in language evolution when the linguistic elements used increase in number if given enough time.

Returning to the force of analogy, this has often been ridiculed in the past (cf. Kiparsky 1974; Lightfoot 2004: 743), or seen as a mere mechanism (cf. §3.5). Like other linguistic rules or principles it cannot be used to predict, and it is clear that it needs to be constrained. Anttila (2003: 435) emphasizes that analogy 'cannot be predicted in advance, [because] [i]t needs the total context as the background'. This 'total context' includes the 'grid', that is the analogically evolved, dynamic system in which a linguistic element functions, but also the socio-cultural communicational setting, the learner's experience of the world (including its language) around him, and the sensitivity of the brain's processing system to differences in productivity. Both the grid and the frequency-sensitive processing system provide the necessary constraints on analogy.

The learner builds up his 'grid' by means of a continuous learning process which is fed by his socio-cultural and linguistic experience. Certain tokens will become entrenched and comprehended/produced wholesale while others may come to be generated via more abstract patterns (or types) as a result of decomposition. Frequency of both tokens, types and construction-types thus leads to automatization and entrenchment. The idea of a usage-based grammar is fruitful for a model of change because it naturally incorporates internal as well as external motivating factors (cf. §1.2). It also entails that learning is schema-based rather than rule-based. A system of *rules*, such as accepted in generative models, does not take account of token- or type-frequencies. Accepting the principles and parameters of UG entails that there will be across-the-board emergence of abstractions related to the domain of a certain parameter, it entails fast and instantaneous generalizations. A schema-based approach predicts that shifts will be gradual rather than abrupt (cf. §3.1), since they will tend to start small and spread out from there. Abstractions will initially be local and piecemeal based on specifiable characteristics of the input (cf. Tomasello's (2003a: 113ff.) suggestion that children's early language is organized by means of 'constructional islands'). I have shown in Chapter 4 that the rule-based explanation used in the English modals story did not really work since the modals did not all change the structures in which they occurred at the same time, nor did they all move at the same speed. With a schema-based approach, we can more easily account for time lags and individual differences in behaviour.

An analogical usage-based model for change has some further advantages. It makes sense in terms of language learning, as we have seen above, and in terms of (language) evolution, since analogy is a basic cognitive ability in all mammals, and it also plays a role in other, evolutionary older cognitive domains, such as vision. Using analogy as the basis for grammar building takes away the difficulty of having to explain when or how a specific grammar module first arose in humans (cf. §2.2.2). The fact that most or all other mammals have no syntax in their communicative system has to do with the human ability to perform analogical abstractions, also called 'system mapping' (cf. §3.3) thanks to their bigger brains and larger memory space.

I have shown in the case studies in Part II that frequency, surface position, and surface adjacency, brought about by the fixation of word order into conventional patterns, play an important role in change. In a similar way, the increasing complexity of societies (cf. Deutscher 2000) and the conventionalization of a written standard (cf. §§1.2.2, 5.1) must have been influential in language change leading to a shift from the pragmatic mode to the syntactic mode (cf. §§5.0–5.1), and causing loss of variation and a certain rigidification of patterns. This development has indeed given the impression that syntax is very rule-like, but this impression is strongly based on the written language, which has been the main source of data for most synchronic generative studies. When this synchronic model came to be used on diachronic data, it inevitably also tried to streamline change and to reduce the variation found in the diachronic data. In a usage-based approach more attention is paid to the 'surface'-data (and to the spoken language), to the amount of variation present, and this has led to less radical, less abstract, and less rule-like explanations (cf. §§4.3.1, 4.4).

In a similar way, principles used within grammaticalization may lead us to ignore the linguistic surface details. It has been shown for instance that position may have been more crucial to the development of pragmatic markers from verbal adjuncts than semantic-pragmatic inferencing and unidirectional notions of subjectification and scope increase (§6.2.2). The elements that subjectified in the course of time usually already contained a subjective epistemic element. In the case of parentheticals, such as *I mean*, *I think*, it is through their collocation (adjacency) with first and second person pronouns that 'subjectification' ensued (cf. §6.2.3). In addition, it was shown in both Chapters 5 and 6 that scope increase is not a gradual subjectification phenomenenon. Rather, it is connected to the fact that formerly independent clauses with scope over preceding and/or following clauses, may come to be construed syntactically as part of the main clause so that it looked as if their scope had increased. Similarly, it was also shown that the scope increase with verbal adjuncts that became pragmatic markers is first and foremost related to initial (topic) position, and develops in connection with what Bolinger has called 'linear modification'. To account for scope increase in terms of leftward movement as is done in generative models (cf. §§6.0, 6.1) is correct in the sense that initial elements tend to have scope over elements that follow. However, this account only works as an explanation when this initial or leftward position also appears on the surface. To 'explain' scope increase by Move or Merge to or in a functional head high in the syntactic tree, only *describes* the increase in terms of the model used, it does not explain the change itself except in those cases where the position has actually changed on the surface.

The idea of an analogical grid and the blurring of a categorical difference between the lexicon and the grammar, also helps to explain why lexicalization and grammaticalization are in many ways very similar, and hence difficult to keep apart. I have demonstrated this with respect to the 'grammaticalization' of clause connectors, the phenomenon of clause fusion, and the development of pragmatic markers (cf. §§3.5, 5.1 and Chapter 6).

Analogy enables us to explain the phenomenon of clause elaboration since most instances of this concern elaborations into a clause construction-type that already existed elsewhere in the system. Thus the change undergone by the gerund from a nominal action noun to a verb (cf. §5.3) is easily explainable from the fact that both verb and action noun contain a verbal stem, and that the verbal arguments were already often present (in the form of a possessive and prepositional phrase) in positions similar to the argument positions of an equivalent verb. The evidence for the opposite phenomenon of clause fusion is more difficult to come by. I have argued that some generally accepted cases of clause fusion were in fact not biclausal to start with (cf. §5.1). Clause fusion did arise in the case of the epistemic modals, as I discussed in §6.1, but here again it concerned a replacement by analogy rather than a direct fusion process. Other attested instances of clause fusion remain dubious. Deutscher (2001) looked at the development of relative clauses in Akkadian, and he shows that it is unlikely that relative markers and clauses developed out of demonstrative pronouns in paratactic clauses; rather they grew out of clauses that were already subordinate. Similar such proposals for English and Hittite (cf. Hopper and Traugott 2003: 197ff.) and other languages (see examples and references in Heine and Kuteva 2002: 113–15) will need detailed research before it can be decided that the fusion of a paratactic clause into another clause probably 'constitutes the most frequent way in which relative clause markers may evolve' (2002: 115). The problem may be that in the case of clause fusion, in contrast to clause elaboration, an analogical pattern may not be so readily available.

The important role played in all these cases by analogy links up with my argument (in §3.2), *pace* Hopper and Traugott (2003: 39), that analogy is primary and reanalysis secondary. Most (all) cases of reanalysis that I have looked at in Part II of this volume concern collocations that were reanalysed on the basis of patterns or construction-types that were already in use elsewhere in the system.

In grammaticalization theory, much attention is paid to unidirectional processes, which are seen as the rule rather than the exception. The more formally inclined linguists believe that such unidirectional processes are epiphenomenal. Depending on what one looks at, both may be partly right. When the grammaticalization process concerns one or more tokens or a combination of tokens and types rather than pure construction-types, we may discern a gradual semantic generalization and phonetic erosion of the tokens involved, which would in most cases be difficult to reverse due to loss of substance. However, the moment more abstract structures come into the picture, the process becomes much more clearly one of structural replacement (by analogy, as we have seen above in the case of clause fusion/ elaboration) because there is no gradual diminution of substance. Formal linguists who concentrate on the system rather than on the output, are also right, however, when they maintain that even such gradual shifts in the forms of the token(s) are *replacements* made by a speaker, because the language utterances themselves cannot 'diminish'. They are, after all, each time they are uttered the *digital* product of a speaker's processing system (one utterance in itself cannot be *analogue*). When one looks at these differences in terms of analogical replacement, however, it is clear that there is a distinction. The unidirectional process of bleaching and phonetic erosion (e.g. of *am/is/are going to* into *gonna*) cannot easily be understood as analogical replacement, while the grammaticalization of pure construction-types can. It is no wonder therefore that the unidirectional principles of grammaticalization theory run into their biggest problems when the grammaticalization concerns pure construction-types. We have seen in Chapters 5 and 6 that it is difficult to see the grammaticalization of clause types in the light of a unidirectional process.

Notes

1. 'Meaningful' primarily refers to sounds that serve to make a system-dependent distinction in lexical meaning, but it may also refer to a social distinction, i.e. it may indicate a difference in accent (dialect or social class).

References

ADAMSON, S. 2000. 'A lovely little example: word order options and category shift in the premodifying string', pp. 39–66 of *Pathways of Change. Grammaticalization in English*, edited by O. Fischer, A. Rosenbach, and D. Stein. Amsterdam: Benjamins.

AHLQVIST, A. (ed.) 1982. *Papers from the 5th International Conference on Historical Linguistics*. Amsterdam: Benjamins.

AIJMER, K. 1999. 'Epistemic possibility in an English–Swedish contrastive perspective', pp. 301–21 of *Out of Corpora. Studies in Honour of Stig Johansan*, edited by H. Hasselgård and S. Oksefjell. Amsterdam: Rodopi.

AITCHISON, J. 1980. 'Review of *Principles of Diachronic Syntax* by D. Lightfoot', *Linguistics*, 18: 137–46.

—— 1987. 'The language lifegame: prediction, explanation and linguistic change', pp. 11–32 of *Explanation and Linguistic Change*, edited by W. Koopman, F. C. v. d. Leek, O. Fischer, and R. Eaton. Amsterdam: Benjamins.

—— 1994. ' "Say, Say It Again Sam": the treatment of repetition in linguistics', *Swiss Papers in English Language and Literature*, 7: 15–34.

—— 2001. *Language Change. Progress or Decay?*, 3rd edn. Cambridge: Cambridge University Press.

ALEXIADOU, A. 1997. *Adverb Placement: A Case Study in Antisymmetric Syntax*. Amsterdam: Benjamins.

ALLEN, C. 1975. 'Old English modals', pp. 91–100 of *Papers in the History and Structure of English*, edited by J. Grimshaw. Amherst: University of Massachusetts, Department of Linguistics.

—— 1986. 'Reconsidering the history of *like*', *Journal of Linguistics*, 22: 375–409.

—— 1995. *Case Marking and Reanalysis. Grammatical Relations from Old to Early Modern English*. Oxford: Oxford University Press.

—— 1997. 'The origins of the "group genitive" in English', *Transactions of the Philological Society*, 95: 111–31.

—— 2001. 'The development of a new passive in English', pp. 43–72 of *Time over Matter. Diachronic Perspectives on Morphosyntax*, edited by M. Butt and T. Holloway King. Stanford: CSLI Publications.

—— 2002. 'Case and Middle English genitive noun phrases', pp. 57–80 of *Syntactic Effects of Morphological Change*, edited by D. W. Lightfoot. Oxford: Oxford University Press.

ANDERSEN, H. 1973. 'Abductive and deductive change', *Language*, 48: 765–94.

ANDERSON, J. 1993. 'Parameters of syntactic change: A notional view', pp. 1–42 of *Historical Linguistics. Problems and Perspectives*, edited by C. Jones. London: Longman.

ANSHEN, F. and ARONOFF, M. 1996. 'Morphology in real time', *Yearbook of Morphology*, 1996: 9–12.

ANTTILA, A. 2002. 'Variation and phonological theory', pp. 206–43 of *The Handbook of Language Variation and Change*, edited by J. K. Chambers, P. Trudgill, and N. Schilling-Estes. Oxford: Blackwell.

ANTTILA, R. 1977. *Analogy*. The Hague: Mouton.

—— 1989. *Historical and Comparative Linguistics*. Amsterdam: Benjamins.

—— 2003. 'Analogy: The warp and woof of cognition', pp. 425–40 of *The Handbook of Historical Linguistics*, edited by B. D. Joseph and R. D. Janda. Oxford: Blackwell.

ARBIB, M. A. 2003. 'The evolving mirror system: A neural basis for language readiness', pp. 182–200 of *Language Evolution*, edited by M. H. Christiansen and S. Kirby. Oxford: Oxford University Press.

AUSTIN, J. L. 1962. *How to Do Things with Words*. Oxford: Oxford University Press.

AUWERA, J. VAN DE and PLUNGIAN, V. A. 1998. 'Modality's semantic map', *Linguistic Typology*, 2: 79–124.

AUWERA, J. VAN DE, SCHALLEY, E., and NUYTS, J. 2005. 'Epistemic possibility in a Slavonic parallel corpus—A pilot study', pp. 201–18 of *Modality in Slavonic Languages. New Perspectives*, edited by B. Hansen and P. Karlík. Munich: Otto Sagner.

BAAYEN, R. H. 2003. 'Probabilistic approaches to morphology', pp. 229–87 of *Probabilistic Linguistics*, edited by R. Bod, J. Hay, and S. Jannedy. Cambridge, Mass.: MIT Press.

BAAYEN, R. H. and SCHREUDER, R. 1996. 'Morphology: Why, how, when, when not, and why not', *Yearbook of Morphology*, 1996: 1–7.

BARBER, C. 1976. *Early Modern English*. London: André Deutsch.

BARRON, J. 2001. 'Perception and raising verbs: Synchronic and diachronic relationships', pp. 73–103 of *Time over Matter. Diachronic Perspectives on Morphosyntax*, edited by M. Butt and T. Holloway King. Stanford: CSLI Publications.

BEHE, M. J. 1996. *Darwin's Black Box: The Biochemical Challenge to Evolution*. New York: Free Press.

BENNETT, P. 1979. 'Observations on the transparency principle', *Linguistics*, 17: 843–61.

—— 1981. 'Is syntactic change gradual?', *Glossa*, 15: 115–35.

BENNIS, H. and HOEKSTRA, T. 1983. *De Syntaxis van het Nederlands. Een Inleiding in de Regeer- en Bindtheorie*. Dordrecht: Foris.

BENSKIN, M. and LAING, M. 1981. 'Translations and Mischsprachen in Middle English manuscripts', pp. 55–106 of *So Meny People Longages and Tonges*.

Philological Essays in Scots and Mediaeval English Presented to Angus Mcintosh, edited by M. Benskin and M. L. Samuels. Edinburgh: Middle English Dialect Project.

BERGEN, B. K. 2004. 'The psychological reality of phonaesthemes', *Language*, 80: 290–311.

BERGH, G. and SEPPÄNEN, A. 1994. 'Subject extraction in English: The use of the *that*-complementizer', pp. 131–43 of *English Historical Linguistics 1992*, edited by F. Fernández, M. Fuster, and J. J. Calvot. Amsterdam: Benjamins.

BERKUM, J. V., ZWITSERLOOD, P., BROWN, C. M., and HAGOORT, P. 2003. 'When and how do listeners relate a sentence to the wider discourse? Evidence from the N400 effect', *Cognitive Brain Research*, 17: 701–18.

BERMÚDEZ OTERO, R. M., DENISON, D., HOGG, R. M., and McCULLY, C. B. (eds) 2000. *Generative Theory and Corpus Studies: A Dialogue from 10 ICEHL*. Berlin: Mouton de Gruyter.

BETHS, F. 1999. 'The history of *dare* and the status of unidirectionality', *Linguistics*, 37: 1069–110.

BIBER, D. 1986. 'Spoken and written textual dimensions in English', *Language*, 62: 384–411.

—— 1991. *Variation across Speech and Writing*. Cambridge: Cambridge University Press.

BIBER, D. and FINEGAN, E. (eds) 1994. *Sociolinguistic Perspectives on Register*. Oxford: Oxford University Press.

BICKERTON, D. 2003. 'Symbol and structure: A comprehensive framework for language evolution', pp. 77–93 of *Language Evolution*, edited by M. H. Christiansen and S. Kirby. Oxford: Oxford University Press.

BISANG, W. 1998. 'Grammaticalization and language contact, constructions and positions', pp. 13–58 of *The Limits of Grammaticalization*, edited by A. Giacalone Ramat and P. J. Hopper. Amsterdam: Benjamins.

BLOOMFIELD, L. 1933. *Language*. New York: Holt.

BOCK, H. 1931. 'Studien zum präpositionalen Infinitiv und Akkusativ mit dem *to*-Infinitiv', *Anglia*, 55: 114–249.

BOLINGER, D. L. 1952. 'Linear modification', *PMLA*, 67: 1117–44.

—— 1980. '*Wanna* and the gradience of auxiliaries', pp. 292–99 of *Wege zur Universalienforschung: Sprachwissen-schaftliche Beiträge zum 60. Geburtstag von Hansjakob Seiler*, edited by G. Brettschneider and C. Lehmann. Tübingen: Gunter Narr.

BOLKESTEIN, A. M. 1989. 'Parameters in the expression of embedded predications in Latin', pp. 3–35 of *Subordination and Other Topics*, edited by G. Calaboli. Amsterdam: Benjamins.

BOOGAART, R. 2004. 'Van modale werkwoorden naar modale constructies', presentation at the 'Coglingdag', University of Utrecht (see also for a forthcoming English version http://webhost.ua.ac.be/tisp/viewabstract.php?id=820)

BÖRJARS, K., VINCENT, N., and CHAPMAN, C. 1996. 'Paradigms, periphrases and pronominal inflection', *Yearbook of Morphology*, 1996: 155–80.

BRAINE, M. D. S. 1988. 'Modeling the acquisition of syntactic structure', pp. 217–19 of *Categories and Processes in Language Acquisition Theory*, edited by Y. Levy, I. M. Schlesinger, and M. D. S. Braine Erlbaum, XX.

BRESNAN, J. and AISSEN, J. 2002. 'Optimality and functionality: Objections and refutations', *Natural Language & Linguistic Theory*, 20: 81–95.

BRINTON, L. J. 1988. *The Development of English Aspectual Systems*. Cambridge: Cambridge University Press.

—— 1996. *Pragmatic Markers in English: Grammaticalization and Discourse Functions*. Berlin: Mouton de Gruyter.

—— 2002. 'Grammaticalization versus lexicalization reconsidered: On the "late" use of temporal adverbs', pp. 86–97 of English Historical Syntax and Morphology. Selected papers from the 11th International Conference on English Historical Linguistics, edited by T. Fanego, M.-J. López-Couso, and J. Pérez-Guerra. Amsterdam: Benjamins.

—— and TRAUGOTT, E. C. 2005. *Lexicalization and Language Change*. Cambridge: Cambridge University Press.

BRISCOE, T. 2003. 'Grammatical assimilation', pp. 295–316 of *Language Evolution*, edited by M. H. Christiansen and S. Kirby. Oxford: Oxford University Press.

BROWN, G. 1982. 'The spoken language', pp. 75–87 of *Linguistics and the Teacher*, edited by R. Carter. London: Routledge and Kegan Paul.

BURLING, R. 2000. 'Comprehension, production and conventionalisation in the origins of language', pp. 27–39 of *The Evolutionary Emergence of Language*, edited by M. Studdert-Kennedy, and J. R. Hurford. Cambridge: Cambridge University Press.

BURNLEY, D. 1992. 'Lexis and semantics', pp. 409–99 of *The Cambridge History of the English Language Vol II*, edited by N. Blake. Cambridge: Cambridge University Press.

BURRIDGE, K. 1998. 'From modal auxiliary to lexical verb: The curious case of Pennsylvania German *wotte*', pp. 19–33 of *Historical Linguistics 1995. Volume 2: Germanic Linguistics*, edited by R. M. Hogg and L. van Bergen. Amsterdam: Benjamins.

BYBEE, J. L. 1988. 'The diachronic dimension in explanation', pp. 350–79 of *Explaining Language Universals*, edited by John A. Hawkins. Oxford: Blackwell.

—— 2001. *Phonology and Language Use*. Cambridge: Cambridge University Press.

—— 2002. 'Sequentiality as the basis of constituent structure', pp. 109–34 of *The Evolution of Language out of Pre-Language*, edited by T. Givón and B. F. Malle. Amsterdam: Benjamins.

—— 2003. 'Mechanisms of change in grammaticization: The role of frequency', pp. 602–23 of *The Handbook of Historical Linguistics*, edited by B. D. Joseph and R. D. Janda. Oxford: Blackwell.

—— and HOPPER, P. J. (eds) 2001. *Frequency and the Emergence of Linguistic Structure.* Amsterdam: Benjamins.

—— and PAGLIUCA, W. 1985. 'Cross-linguistic comparison and the development of grammatical meaning', pp. 59–83 of *Historical Semantics, Historical Word Formation*, edited by J. Fisiak. Berlin: Mouton de Gruyter.

——, ——, and PERKINS, R. D. 1991. 'Back to the future', pp. 15–58 of *Approaches to Grammaticalization*, edited by E. C. Traugott and B. Heine. Amsterdam: Benjamins.

—— PERKINS, R. D., and PAGLIUCA, W. 1994. *The Evolution of Grammar. Tense, Aspect, and Modality in the Languages of the World.* Chicago: University of Chicago Press.

—— and SCHEIBMAN, J. 1999. 'The effect of usage on degrees of constituency: The reduction of *don't* in English', *Linguistics*, 37: 575–96.

—— and SLOBIN, D. I. 1982. 'Rules and schemas in the development and use of the English past tense', *Language*, 58: 265–89.

CAMPBELL, A. 1959. *Old English Grammer*. Oxford: Clarendon Press.

CAMPBELL, L. 2001a. 'What is wrong with grammaticalization?', *Language Sciences*, 23: 113–61.

—— (ed.) 2001b. *Grammaticalization. A Critical Assessment*. Special issue of *Language Sciences* 23: ii–iii.

CARSTAIRS-MCCARTHY, A. 1999. *The Origins of Complex Language: An Inquiry into the Evolutionary Beginnings of Sentences, Syllables and Truth.* Oxford: Oxford University Press.

—— 2000. 'The distinction between sentences and noun phrases: An impediment to language evolution?' pp. 248–63 of *The Evolutionary Emergence of Language*, edited by C. Knight, M. Studdert-Kennedy, and J. R. Hurford. Cambridge: Cambridge University Press.

CHAFE, W. L. 1985. 'Linguistic differences produced by differences between speaking and writing', pp. 105–23 of *Literacy, Language, and Learning*, edited by D. R. Olson, N. Torrance, and A. Hildyard. Cambridge: Cambridge University Press.

CHAMBERS, J. K. 2002. 'Patterns of variation including change', pp. 349–72 of *The Handbook of Language Variation and Change*, edited by J. K. Chambers, P. Trudgill, and N. Schilling-Estes. Oxford: Blackwell.

CHAPMAN, D. and SKOUSEN, R. 2005. 'Analogical modeling and morphological change: The case of the adjectival negative prefix in English', *English Language and Linguistics*, 9: 333–57.

CHESHIRE, J. and STEIN, D. (eds) 1997. *Taming the Vernacular: From Dialect to Written Standard Language*. Harlow: Longman.

CHOMSKY, N. 1957. *Syntactic Structures*. The Hague: Mouton.

—— 1965. *Aspects of the Theory of Syntax*. Cambridge Mass.: MIT Press.

—— 1975. *Reflections on Language*. New York: Pantheon.

—— 1981. *Lectures on Government and Binding*. Dordrecht: Foris.

CHOMSKY, N. 1982. *The Generative Enterprise: A Discussion with Riny Huybregts and Henk Van Riemsdijk*. Dordrecht: Foris.

—— 1988. *Language and Problems of Knowledge*. Cambridge, Mass.: MIT Press.

—— 1991. 'Linguistics and cognitive science: Problems and mysteries', pp. 26–55 of *The Chomskyan Turn: Generative Linguistics, Philosophy, Mathematics and Psychology*, edited by A. Kasher. Oxford: Blackwell.

—— 1995. *The Minimalist Program*. Cambridge Mass.: MIT Press.

—— 2002. *On Nature and Language* (ed. by A. Belletti and L. Rizzi). Cambridge: Cambridge University Press.

CHRISTIANSEN, M. H. and KIRBY, S. (eds) 2003. *Language Evolution*. Oxford: Oxford University Press.

CINQUE, G. 1999. *Adverbs and Functional Heads. A Cross-Linguistic Perspective*. Oxford: Oxford University Press.

CLARK, E. V. 2003. *First Language Acquisition*. Cambridge: Cambridge University Press.

CLARK, R. and ROBERTS, I. G. 1993. 'A computational model of language learnability and language change', *Linguistic Inquiry*, 24: 299–345.

COATES, R. 1987. 'Pragmatic sources of analogical reformation', *Journal of Linguistics*, 23: 319–40.

COETSEM, F. V. 2000. *A General and Unified Theory of the Transmission Process in Language Contact*. Heidelberg: Carl Winter.

COLEMAN, R. 1989. 'The rise and fall of absolute constructions: A Latin case history', pp. 353–74 of *Subordination and Other Topics*, edited by G. Calboli. Amsterdam: Benjamins.

CONRADIE, C. J. 1987. 'Semantic change in modal auxiliaries as a result of speech act embedding', pp. 171–80 of *Historical Development of Auxiliaries*, edited by M. Harris and P. Ramat. Berlin: Mouton de Gruyter.

CORBALLIS, M. C. 2003. 'From hand to mouth: The gestural origins of language, pp. 201–18 of *Language Evolution*, edited by M. H. Christiansen and S. Kirby. Oxford: Oxford University Press.

CRAIN, S. 1991. 'Language acquisition in the absence of experience', *Behavioral and Brain Sciences*, 14: 597–612.

CROFT, W. 1991. *Syntactic Categories and Grammatical Relations. The Cognitive Organization of Information*. Chicago: The University of Chicago Press.

—— 2000. *Explaining Language Change. An Evolutionary Approach*. London: Longman.

—— and CRUSE, A. 2004. *Radical Construction Grammar: Syntactic Theory in Typological Perspective*. Oxford: Oxford University Press.

CRYSTAL, D. 1987. *The Cambridge Encyclopedia of Language*. Cambridge: Cambridge University Press.

—— 1997. *Dictionary of Linguistics and Phonetics*, 4th edn. Oxford: Blackwell.

DĄBROWSKA, E. 2004. *Language, Mind and Brain: Some Psychological and Neurological Constraints on Theories of Grammar*. Washington DC: Georgetown University Press.

DANCHEV, A. and KYTÖ, M. 1994. 'The construction *be going to* + infinitive in Early Modern English', pp. 59–77 of *Studies in Early Modern English*, edited by D. Kastovsky. Berlin: Mouton de Gruyter.

DAWKINS, R. 1986. *The Blind Watchmaker*. London: Longman (Harmondsworth: Penguin 1988).

DEACON, T. W. 1997. *The Symbolic Species. The Co-Evolution of Language and the Brain*. New York: Norton.

—— 2003. 'Universal grammar and semiotic constraints', pp. 111–39 of *Language Evolution*, edited by M. H. Christiansen and S. Kirby. Oxford: Oxford University Press.

DEMSKE, U. 2001. *Merkmale und Relationen. Diachrone Studien zur Nominalphrase des Deutschen*. Berlin: Mouton de Gruyter.

DENISON, D. 1985. 'The origins of periphrastic "do": Ellegård and Visser reconsidered', pp. 45–60 of *Papers from the Fourth International Conference on English Historical Linguistics*, edited by R. Eaton, O. Fischer, F. van der Leek, and W. F. Koopman. Amsterdam: Benjamins.

—— 1990. 'Auxiliary + impersonal in Old English', *Folia Linguistica Historica*, 9: 139–66.

—— 1993. *English Historical Syntax*. London: Longman.

DERWING, B. L. 1977. 'Is the child really a "little linguist"?' pp. 78–84 of *Language Learning and Thought*, edited by J. MacNamara. New York: Academic Press.

DESSALLES, J.-L. 2000. 'Language and hominid politics', pp. 62–80 of *The Evolutionary Emergence of Language*, edited by C. Knight, M. Studdert-Kennedy and J. R. Hurford. Cambridge: Cambridge University Press.

DETGES, U. 2004. 'How cognitive is grammaticalization? The history of the Catalan perfet perifràstic', pp. 211–27 of *Up and Down the cline—The Nature of Grammaticalization*, edited by O. Fischer, M. Norde, and H. Perridon. Amsterdam: Benjamins.

DEUTSCHER, G. 2000. *Syntactic Change in Akkadian. The Evolution of Sentential Complementation*. Oxford: Oxford University Press.

—— 2001. 'The rise and fall of a rogue relative construction', *Studies in Language*, 25: 405–22.

—— 2002. 'On the misuse of the notion of "Abduction" in Linguistics', *Journal of Linguistics*, 38: 469–85.

DEUTSCHER, G. 2005. *The Unfolding of Language*. London: Heinemann.

DIESSEL, H. and TOMASELLO, M. 2001. 'The acquisition of finite complement clauses in English: a corpus-based analysis', *Cognitive Linguistics*, 12: 97–141.

DIK, S. C. 1997. *The Theory of Functional Grammar. Part I: The structure of the clause* 2nd, rev edn., edited by K. Hengeveld. Berlin: Mouton de Gruyter.

DODD, D. and FOGEL, A. 1991. 'Nonnativist alternatives to the negative evidence hypothesis', *Behavioral and Brain Sciences*, 14: 617–18.

DONNER, M. 1986. 'The gerund in Middle English', *English Studies*, 67: 394–400.

DORIAN, N. C. 1993. 'Internally and externally motivated change in language contact settings: Doubts about dichotomy', pp. 131–55 of *Historical Linguistics*, edited by C. Jones. London: Longman.

DRESHER, E. and HORNSTEIN, N. 1979. 'Trace theory and NP movement rules', *Linguistic Inquiry*, 10: 65–80.

DUBOIS, J. 1985. 'Competing motivations', pp. 343–65 of *Iconicity in Syntax*, edited by J. Haiman. Amsterdam: Benjamins.

DUFFLEY, P. J. 1992. *The English Infinitive*. London: Longman.

DUNBAR, R. I. M., KNIGHT, C., and POWER, C. (eds) 1999. *The Evolution of Culture*. Edinburgh: Edinburgh University Press.

EDHARD, A. 2004. 'Semantic modality map for Sranan Tongo', MA thesis, English Department, Faculty of Humanities. University of Amsterdam.

ELDREDGE, N. and GOULD, S. J. 1972. 'Punctuated equilibria: An alternative to phyletic gradualism', pp. 82–115 of *Models of Paleobiology*, edited by T. J. M. Schopf. San Francisco: Freeman, Cooper.

ELLEGÅRD, A. 1953. *The Auxiliary Do. The Establishment and Regulation of Its Use in English*. Stockholm: Almqvist & Wiksell.

ERMAN, B. D. 1986. 'Some pragmatic expressions in English conversation', pp. 131–47 of *English in Speech and Writing. A Symposium*, edited by G. Tottie and I. Bäcklund. Stockholm: Almqvist & Wiksell.

EVERS-VERMEUL, J. 2005. *The Development of Dutch Connectives. Change and Acquisition as Windows on Form–Function Relations*. Utrecht: LOT.

FAARLUND, J. T. 2004. *The Syntax of Old Norse*. Oxford: Oxford University Press.

FEILKE, H., KAPPEST, K.-P., and KNOBLOCH, C. (eds) 2001. *Grammatikalisierung, Spracherwerb und Schriftlichkeit*. Tübingen: Niemeyer.

FINEGAN, E. 1995. 'Subjectivity and subjectivisation: An introduction', pp. 1–15 of *Subjectivity and Subjectivisation*, edited by D. Stein and S. Wright. Cambridge: Cambridge University Press.

FISCHER, A. 1994. ' "Summer Is Icumen in": The seasons of the year in Middle English and Early Modern English', pp. 79–95 of *Studies in Early Modern English*, edited by D. Kastovsky. Berlin: Mouton de Gruyter.

—— 1997. ' "With This Ring I Thee Wed": The verbs *to wed* and *to marry* in the history of English', pp. 467–81 of *Language History and Linguistic Modelling*, edited by R. Hickey and S. Puppel. Berlin: Mouton de Gruyter.

FISCHER, O. 1979. 'A comparative study of philosophical terms in the Alfredian and Chaucerian Boethius', *Neophilologus*, 63: 622–39.

—— 1988. 'The rise of the *for NP to V* construction: An explanation', pp. 67–88 of *An Historic Tongue. Studies in English Linguistics in Memory of Barbara Strang*, edited by G. Nixon and J. Honey. London: Routledge.

—— 1989. 'The origin and spread of the accusative and infinitive construction in English', *Folia Linguistica Historica*, 8: 143–217.

—— 1991. 'The rise of the passive infinitive in English', pp. 141–88 of *Historical English Syntax*, edited by D. Kastovsky. Berlin: Mouton de Gruyter.

—— 1992a. 'Syntactic change and borrowing: The case of the accusative and infinitive construction in English', pp. 16–88 of *Internal and External Factors in Syntactic Change*, edited by M. Gerritsen and D. Stein. Berlin: Mouton de Gruyter.

—— 1992b. 'Syntax', pp. 207–408 of *The Cambridge History of the English Language. Vol. II*, edited by N. Blake. Cambridge: Cambridge University Press.

—— 1994a. 'The development of quasi-auxiliaries in English and changes in word order', *Neophilologus*, 78: 137–64.

—— 1994b. 'The fortunes of the Latin-type accusative and infinitive construction in Dutch and English compared', pp. 91–133 of *Language Change and Language Structure. Old Germanic Languages in a Comparative Perspective*, edited by T. Swan, E. Mørck, and O. Jansen Westvik. Berlin: Mouton de Gruyter.

—— 1995. 'The distinction between *to* and bare infinitival complements in Late Middle English', *Diachronica*, 12: 1–30.

—— 1996a. 'The status of *to* in Old English *to*-infinitives: A reply to Kageyama', *Lingua*, 99: 107–33.

—— 1996b. 'Verbal complementation in Early ME: how do the infinitives fit in?' pp. 247–70 of *English Historical Linguistics 1994*, edited by D. Britton. Amsterdam: Benjamins.

—— 1997. 'The grammaticalisation of infinitival *to* in English compared with German and Dutch', pp. 265–80 of *Language History and Linguistic Modelling*, edited by R. Hickey and S. Puppel. Berlin: Mouton de Gruyter.

—— 1998. 'On negative raising in the history of English', pp. 55–100 of *Negation in the History of English*, edited by I. Tieken-Boon van Ostade, G. Tottie, and W. van der Wurff. Berlin: Mouton de Gruyter.

—— 2000a. 'Grammaticalisation: Unidirectional, non-reversible? The case of *to* before the infinitive in English', pp. 149–69 of *Pathways of Change*, edited by O. Fischer, A. Rosenbach, and D. Stein. Amsterdam: Benjamins.

—— 2000b. 'The Position of the Adjective in Old English', pp. 153–81 of *Generative Theory and Corpus Studies*, edited by R. M. Bermúdez Otero, D. Denison, R. M. Hogg, and C. B. McCully. Berlin: Mouton de Gruyter.

FISCHER, O. 2004a. 'Developments in the category adjective from Old to Middle English', *Studies in Medieval English Language and Literature*, 19: 1–36.

—— 2004b. 'Evidence for iconicity in language', *Logos and Language. Journal of general linguistics and language theory*, 5.i: 1–19.

—— 2004c. 'Review of Tania Kuteva, *Auxiliation: An Enquiry into the Nature of Grammaticalization*', *Language*, 80: 320–4.

—— 2006. 'On the position of adjectives in Middle English', *English Language and Linguistics*, 10: 253–88.

FISCHER, O., KEMENADE, A. VAN, KOOPMAN, W. and WURFF, W. VAN DER 2000a. *The Syntax of Early English*. Cambridge: Cambridge University Press.

FISCHER, O. and LEEK, F. C. VAN DER 1981. 'Optional vs. radical reanalysis: Mechanisms of syntactic change (Review of Lightfoot 1979)', *Lingua*, 55: 301–50.

—— and—— 1983. 'The demise of the Old English impersonal construction', *Journal of Linguistics*, 19: 337–68.

—— and—— 1987. 'A "case" for the Old English impersonal', pp. 79–120 of *Explanation and Linguistic Change*, edited by W. Koopman, R. Eaton, O. Fischer, and F. van der Leek. Amsterdam: Benjamins.

FISCHER, O. and NÄNNY, M. 1999. 'Introduction. Iconicity as a creative force in language use', pp. i–xxxvi of *Form Miming Meaning*, edited by M. Nänny and O. Fischer, Amsterdam: Benjamins.

—— and—— (eds) 2001. *The Motivated Sign. Iconicity in Language and Literature 2*. Amsterdam: Benjamins.

FISCHER, O., NORDE, M., and PERRIDON, H. (eds) 2004. *Up and Down the Cline—The Nature of Grammaticalization*. Amsterdam: Benjamins.

FISCHER, O. and ROSENBACH, A. 2000. 'Introduction', pp. 1–37 of *Pathways of Change: Grammaticalization in English*, edited by O. Fischer, A. Rosenbach, and D. Stein. Amsterdam: Benjamins.

FISCHER, O., ROSENBACH, A., and STEIN, D. 2000b. *Pathways of Change*. Amsterdam: Benjamins.

FLEISCHMAN, S. 1982. *The Future in Thought and Language: Diachronic Evidence from Romance*. Cambridge: Cambridge University Press.

FODOR, F. A. 1985. 'Precis of the modularity of mind', *Behavioral and Brain Sciences*, 8: 1–42.

FÓNAGY, I. 2000. *Languages within Language. An Evolutive Approach*. Amsterdam: Benjamins.

FOOLEN, A. 2002. 'Frederick J. Newmeyer's *Language Form and Language Function*', *Functions of Language*, 9: 87–103.

FUNKE, O. 1922. 'Die Fügung *ginnen* mit dem Infinitiv im Mittelenglischen', *Englische Studien*, 56: 1–27.

GEERTS, G., HAESERYN, W., ROOIJ, J. D. and TOORN, M. C. VAN DE (eds) 1984. *Algemene Nederlandse Spraakkunst*. Groningen: Wolters-Noordhoff.

—— 1993. *The Rise of Functional Categories*. Amsterdam: Benjamins.

GELDEREN, E. VAN 2000. *A History of English Reflexive Pronouns. Person, Self, and Interpretability*. Amsterdam: Benjamins.

—— 2004. *Grammaticalization as Economy*. Amsterdam: Benjamins.

GENTNER, D. 2003. 'Why we're so smart', pp. 195–235 of *Language in Mind. Advances in the Study of Language and Thought*, edited by D. Gentner and S. Goldin-Meadow. Cambridge Mass.: MIT Press.

—— HOLYOAK, K. J and KOKINOV, B. K. (eds) 2001. *The Analogical Mind. Perspectives from Cognitive Science*. Cambridge, Mass: MIT Press.

GERRITSON, M. 1987. Syntaktische Verandering in Kontrolezinnen: Een Sociolinguïstische Studie can het Brugs can de 13ᵉ tot de 17ᵉ Eeuw. Dordrecht: ICG Printing.

—— and STEIN, D. (eds) 1992a. *Internal and External Factors in Syntactic Change*. Berlin: Mouton de Gruyter.

—— 1992b. 'Introduction: On "internal" and "external" in syntactic change', pp. 1–15 of *Internal and External Factors in Syntactic Change*, edited by M. Gerritsen and D. Stein (eds), 1–15.

GIACALONE RAMAT, A. and HOPPER, P. J. (eds) 1998. *The Limits of Grammaticalization*. Amsterdam: Benjamins.

GIVÓN, T. 1979. *On Understanding Grammar*. New York: Academic Press.

—— 1993. *English Grammar. A Function-Based Introduction*. Amsterdam: Benjamins.

—— 1995a. *Functionalism and Grammar*. Amsterdam: Benjamins.

—— 1995b. 'Isomorphism in the grammatical code: cognitive and biological considerations', pp. 47–76 of *Iconicity in Language*, edited by R. Simone. Amsterdam: Benjamins.

—— 2002. 'The visual information processing system as an evolutionary precursor of human language', pp. 3–50 of *The Evolution of Language out of Pre-Language*, edited by T. Givón and B. F. Malle. Amsterdam: Benjamins.

GOLDBERG, A. E. 1995. *Constructions: A Construction Grammar Approach to Argument Structure*. Chicago: The University of Chicago Press.

—— CASENHISER, D. M., and STHURAMAN, N. 2004. 'Learning argument structure generalizations', *Cognitive Linguistics*, 15: 289–316.

GOLDBERG, E. 2001. *The Executive Brain. Frontal Lobes and the Civilized Mind*. Oxford: Oxford University Press.

GOOSSENS, L. 1987. 'The auxiliarization of the English modals: A functional grammar view', pp. 111–43 of *Historical Development of Auxiliaries*, edited by M. Harris and P. Ramat. Berlin: Mouton de Gruyter.

GORRELL, J. H. 1895. 'Indirect discourse in Anglo-Saxon', *PMLA*, 10: 342–485.

GREENBAUM, S. 1969. *Studies in English Adverbial Usage*. London: Longman.

GRICE, H. P. 1975, 'Logic and conversation', pp. 41–58 of *Syntax and Semantics*, vol. 3, edited by P. Cole and J. Morgan. New York: Academic Press.

GUASTI, M. T. 2002. *Language Acquisition. The Growth of Grammar*. Cambridge Mass.: MIT Press.

HAIMAN, J. 1985 (ed.). *Iconicity in Syntax*. Amsterdam: Benjamins.

—— 1993. 'Life, the universe, and human language (a brief synopsis)', *Language Sciences*, 15: 293–322.

—— 1994. 'Ritualization and the development of language', pp. 3–28 of *Perspectives on Grammaticalization*, edited by W. Pagliuca. Amsterdam: Benjamins.

HAIMAN, J. 1998. *Talk is Cheap. Sarcasm, Alienation, and the Evolution of Language*. Oxford: Oxford University Press.

HAIMAN, J. 1999. 'Action, speech, and grammar: The sublimation trajectory', pp. 37–57 of *Form Miming Meaning*, edited by M. Nänny and O. Fischer. Amsterdam: Benjamins.

—— and THOMPSON, S. A. (eds) 1988. *Clause Combining in Grammar and Discourse*. Amsterdam: Benjamins.

HALE, M. 1998. 'Diachronic syntax', *Syntax*, 1: 1–14.

HALLIDAY, M. A. K. and HASSAN, R. 1976. *Cohesion in English*. London: Longman.

HAMPE, B. 2005. 'On the role of iconic motivation in conceptual metaphor: Has metaphor theory come full circle?' pp. 39–66 of *Inside-out and Outside-in*, edited by C. Maeder, W. J. Herlofsky, and O. Fischer. Amsterdam: Benjamins.

—— and SCHÖNEFELD, D. 2003. 'Creative syntax: Iconic principles within the symbolic', pp. 243–61 of *From Sign to Signing*, edited by W. G. Müller and O. Fischer. Amsterdam: Benjamins.

HANSSEN, F. 1910. *Spanische Grammatik auf historischer Grundlage*. Halle a. S.: Max Niemeyer.

HARRIS, A. C. and CAMPBELL, L. 1995. *Historical Syntax in Cross-Linguistic Perspective*. Cambridge: Cambridge University Press.

HARRIS, M. and RAMAT, P. (eds) 1987. *Historical Development of Auxiliaries*. Berlin: Mouton de Gruyter.

HASPELMATH, M. 1989. 'From purposive to infinitive—A universal path of grammaticization', *Folia Linguistica Historica*, 10: 287–310.

—— 1992. 'Review of Traugott and Heine 1991', *Lingua*, 88: 340–5.

—— 1998. 'The semantic development of old presents: New futures and subjunctives without grammaticalization', *Diachronica*, 15: 29–62.

—— 1999. 'Why is grammaticalization irreversible?' *Linguistics*, 37: 1043–68.

—— 2000. 'Why can't we talk to each other?' *Lingua*, 110: 235–55.

—— 2003. 'Creating economical morphosyntactic patterns in language change'. Paper given for the Workshop 'Explaining Linguistic Universals: Historical Convergence and Universal Grammar'. UC Berkeley.

—— 2004. 'Does linguistic explanation presuppose linguistic description?' *Studies in Language*, 28: 554–79.

HAUMANN, D. 1997. *The Syntax of Subordination*. Tübingen: Niemeyer.

HAUSER, M. D. and FITCH, W. T. 2003. 'What are the uniquely human components of the language faculty?' pp. 158–81 of *Language Evolution*, edited by M. H. Christiansen and S. Kirby. Oxford: Oxford University Press.

——, CHOMSKY, N., and FITCH, W. T. 2002. 'The faculty of language: What is it, who has it, and how did it evolve?', *Science*, 298: 1569–79.

HAUSSMAN, R. B. 1974. 'The origin and development of Modern English periphrastic *do*', pp. 159–89 of *Historical Linguistics*, edited by J. M. Anderson and C. Jones. Amsterdam: North Holland Publishing.

HAWKINS, J. A. 2004. *Efficiency and Complexity in Grammars*. Oxford: Oxford University Press.

HEINE, B. 1994. 'Grammaticalization as an explanatory parameter', pp. 255–88 of *Perspectives on Grammaticalization*, edited by W. Pagliuca. Amsterdam: Benjamins.

—— 2003. 'Grammaticalization', pp. 575–601 of *The Handbook of Historical Linguistics*, edited by B. D. Joseph and R. D. Janda. Oxford: Blackwell.

—— and KUTEVA, T. 2002. *World Lexicon of Grammaticalization*. Cambridge: Cambridge University Press.

—— and REH, M. 1984. *Grammaticalization and Reanalysis in African Languages*. Hamburg: Helmut Buske.

——, CLAUDI, U. and HÜNNEMEYER, F. 1991a. 'From cognition to grammar— Evidence from African languages', pp. 149–87 of *Approaches to Grammaticalization Vol. 1*, edited by E. C. Traugott and B. Heine. Amsterdam: Benjamins.

——, ——, and —— 1991b. *Grammaticalization. A Conceptual Framework*. Chicago: University of Chicago Press.

HIMMELMANN, N. P. 2004. 'Lexicalization and grammaticalization: Opposite or orthogonal?', pp. 21–42 of *What Makes Grammaticalization? A Look from its Fringes and its Components*, edited by W. Bisang, N. P. Himmelmann, and B. Wiemer. Berlin: Mouton de Gruyter.

HINTON, L., NICHOLS, J. and OHALA, J. (eds) 1994. *Sound Symbolism*. Cambridge: Cambridge University Press.

HIRVONEN, P. 2005. 'Phonological and morphological aspects of the attrition of Finnish', Talk given at the 2nd International Conference on First Language Attrition, Vrije Universiteit, Amsterdam, August.

HOCK, H. H. 1986. *Principles of Historical Linguistics*. Berlin: Mouton de Gruyter.

HOFSTADTER, D. 1995. *Fluid Concepts and Creative Analogies. Computer Models of the Fundamental Mechanisms of Thought*. New York: Basic Books.

HOLYOAK, K. J. and THAGARD, P. 1995. *Mental Leaps. Analogy in Creative Thought*. Cambridge Mass.: MIT Press.

HOOK, P. E. 1991. 'The emergence of perfective aspect in Indo-Aryan languages', pp. 59–89 of *Approaches to Grammaticalization*, *Vol. 2*, edited by E. C. Traugott and B. Heine. Amsterdam: Benjamins.

HOPPER, P. J. 1987. 'Emergent grammar', *Berkeley Linguistics Society*, 13: 139–57.

—— 1991. 'On some principles of grammaticalization', pp. 17–35 of *Approaches to Grammaticalization, Vol. 1*, edited by E. C. Traugott and B. Heine. Amsterdam: Benjamins.

—— 1998. 'Emergent grammar (revised version)', pp. 155–75 of *The Psychology of Language: Cognitive and Functional Approaches to Language Structure*, edited by M. Tomasello. Mahwah, New Jersey: Erlbaum.

HOPPER, P. J. and THOMPSON, S. A. 1980. 'Transitivity in grammar and discourse', *Language*, 56: 251–99.

HOPPER, P. J. and TRAUGOTT, E. C. 2003 [1993]. *Grammaticalization*. Cambridge: Cambridge University Press.

HORST, J. M. VAN DE 1981. *Kleine Middelnederlandse Syntoxis*. Amsterdam: Huis aan de drie grachten.

—— 1986. *Historische Grammatica en Taaltekens*, PhD thesis, Faculty of Arts, University of Amsterdam.

—— (forthcoming). *Geschiedenis van de Nederlandse Syntaxis*.

HUDDLESTON, R. 1971. *The Sentence in Written English*. Cambridge: Cambridge University Press.

HULK, A. and KEMENADE, A. VAN 1995. 'Verb-second, pro-drop, functional projections and language change', pp. 227–56 of *Clause Structure and Language Change*, edited by A. Battye and I. Roberts. Oxford: Oxford University Press.

HURFORD, J. R. 2000a. 'Introduction: The emergence of syntax', pp. 219–30 of *The Evolutionary Emergence of Language*, edited by C. Knight, M. Studdert-Kennedy, and J. R. Hurford. Cambridge: Cambridge University Press.

—— 2000b. 'Social transmission favours linguistic generalisation', pp. 324–52 of *The Evolutionary Emergence of Language*, edited by C. Knight, M. Studdert-Kennedy, and J. R. Hurford. Cambridge: Cambridge University Press.

—— 2003. 'The language mosaic and its evolution', pp. 38–57 of *Language Evolution*, edited by M. H. Christiansen and S. Kirby. Oxford: Oxford University Press.

—— STUDDERT-KENNEDY, M., and KNIGHT, C. (eds) 1998. *Approaches to the Evolution of Language*. Cambridge: Cambridge University Press.

IJBEMA, A. 2002. *Grammaticalization and Infinitival Complements in Dutch*, Leiden: University of Leiden (LOT Series).

ITKONEN, E. 1994. 'Iconicity, analogy and universal grammar', *Journal of Pragmatics*, 22: 37–53.

—— 2005. *Analogy as Structure and Process*. Amsterdam: Benjamins.

—— and HAUKIOJA, J. 1997. 'A rehabilitation of analogy in syntax (and elsewhere)', pp. 131–77 of *Metalinguistik im Wandel. Die 'kognitive Wende' in Wissenschaftstheorie und Linguistik*, edited by A. Kertész. Frankfurt: Peter Lang.

JACK, G. B. 1988. 'The origins of the English gerund', *NOWELE*, 12: 15–75.

JACKENDOFF, R. 2002. *Foundations of Language. Brain, Meaning, Grammar, Evolution*. Oxford: Oxford University Press.

JANDA, R. D. 1980. 'On the decline of declensional systems: The overall loss of OE nominal case inflections and the ME reanalysis of *-es* as *his*', pp. 243–52 of *Papers from the 4th International Conference on Historical Linguistics*, edited by E. C. Traugott, R. Labrum, S. Shepherd, and P. Kiparsky. Amsterdam: Benjamins.

—— 2001. 'Beyond "pathways" and "unidirectionality": On the discontinuity of language transmission and the counterability of grammaticalization', *Language Sciences*, 23: 265–340.

—— and JOSEPH, B. D. 2003. 'On language, change, and language change—or, of history, linguistics, and historical linguistics', pp. 3–180 of *The Handbook of Historical Linguistics*, edited by B. D. Joseph and R. D. Janda. Oxford: Blackwell.

JESPERSEN, O. 1909–1949. *A Modern English Grammar on Historical Principles*. Vols.I–VII. Copenhagen: Munksgaard.

JOHNSON, P. E. 2000. *The Wedge of Truth: Splitting the Foundations of Naturalism*. Downer's Grove III: InterVarsity Press.

JOSEPH, B. D. 2001. 'Is there such a thing as "grammaticalization"?', *Language Sciences*, 23: 163–86.

—— 2003. 'Some thoughts on optimality, optimization, and analogy: Back to basics (and beyond)'. Lecture given at the Meertens Instituut, Amsterdam, May 26.

—— 2004. 'Rescuing traditional historical linguistics from grammaticalization theory', pp. 45–71 of *Up and Down the Cline*, edited by O. Fischer, M. Norde, and H. Perridon. Amsterdam: Benjamins.

JOSEPH, B. D. and JANDA R. D. (eds) 2003. *The Handbook of Historical Linguistics*. Oxford: Blackwell.

JUCKER, A. H. (ed.) 1995. *Historical Pragmatics: Pragmatic Developments in the History of English*. Amsterdam: Benjamins.

KALLEN, J. L. 1994. 'English in Ireland', in *The Cambridge History of the English Language*, Vol. V, *English in Britain and Overseas. Origins and Development*, edited by R. Burchfield. Cambridge: Cambridge University Press.

KALMÁR, I. 1985. 'Are there really no primitive languages?' pp. 148–66 of *Literacy, Language, and Learning*, edited by D. R. Olson, N. Torrance, and A. Hildyard. Cambridge: Cambridge University Press.

KATZ, J. J. and FODOR, J. 1963. 'The structure of semantic theory', *Language*, 39: 170–210.

KAYNE, R. S. 1981. 'On certain differences between French and English', *Linguistic Inquiry*, 12: 349–71.

—— 1994. *The Antisymmetry of Syntax*. Cambridge Mass.: MIT Press.

KELLER, R. 1994. *On Language Change. The Invisible Hand in Language*. London: Routledge (translated from the German by Brigitte Nerlich).

—— 1995. 'The epistemic *weil*', pp. 16–30 of *Subjectivity and Subjectivisation*, edited by D. Stein and S. Wright. Cambridge: Cambridge University Press.

—— 1998. *A Theory of Linguistic Signs*. Oxford: Oxford University Press.

KEMENADE, A. VAN 1985. 'Old English infinitival complements and West-Germanic "V"-raising', pp. 73–84 of *Papers from the Fourth International Conference on English Historical Linguistics*, edited by R. Eaton, O. Fischer, F. van der Leek, and W. F. Koopman. Amsterdam: Benjamins.

—— 1987. *Syntactic Case and Morphological Case in the History of English*. Dordrecht: ICG Printing.

KEMENADE, A. VAN 1992. 'Structural factors in the history of English modals', pp. 287–309 of *History of Englishes: New Methods and Interpretations in Historical Linguistics*, edited by M. Rissanen. Berlin: Mouton de Gruyter.

—— 1998. 'Review of Allen 1995', *Journal of Linguistics*, 34: 227–32.

—— 2000. 'Jespersen's cycle revisited: formal properties of grammaticalization', pp. 51–74 of *Diachronic Syntax*, edited by S. Pintzuk, G. Tsoulas, and A. Warner. Oxford: Oxford University Press.

—— and VINCENT, N. (eds) 1997. *Parameters of Morphosyntactic Change*. Cambridge: Cambridge University Press.

KERN, J. H. 1912. 'De met het participium praeteriti omschreven werkwoordsvormen in 't Nederlands', *Verhandelingen der Koninklijke Akademie van Wetenschappen*, new series 12: 1–318.

KERSTENS, J., RUYS, E., and ZWARTS, J. 1996–2001 *Lexicon of Linguistics* (online), http://www2.let.uu.nl/UiL-OTS/Lexicon.

KIPARSKY, P. 1974. 'Remarks on analogical change', pp. 257–75 of *Historical Linguistics*, edited by J. M. Anderson and C. Jones. Amsterdam: North Holland Publishing.

—— (in press). 'Grammaticalization as optimization', *Language Universals and Language Change*, edited by J. Good. Oxford: Oxford University Press. (available online at http://www.stanford.edu/~kiparsky/Papers/yalegrammaticalization.pdf).

KIRBY, C. 2000. 'Syntax without natural selection: How compositionality emerges from vocabulary in a population of learners', pp. 303–23 of *The Evolutionary Emergence of Language*, edited by C. Knight, M. Studdert-Kennedy, and J. R. Hurford. Cambridge: Cambridge University Press.

KIRBY, S. and CHRISTIANSEN, M. H. 2003. 'From language learning to language evolution', pp. 272–94 of *Language Evolution*, edited by M. H. Christiansen and S. Kirby. Oxford: Oxford University Press.

KLIMA, E. 1965. *Studies in Diachronic Transformational Syntax*. PhD thesis, Harvard University.

KLOOSTER, W. G. 2000. *Geen. Over Verplaatsing en Focus* ['No(ne). On Movement and Focus']. Amsterdam: Vossiuspers AUP.

KNIGHT, C. 2000. 'Play as precursor of phonology and syntax', pp. 99–119 of *The Evolutionary Emergence of Language*, edited by C. Knight, M. Studdert-Kennedy, and J. R. Hurford. Cambridge: Cambridge University Press.

—— STUDDERT-KENNEDY, M. and HURFORD, J. R. (eds) 2000. *The Evolutionary Emergence of Language. Social Function and the Origins of Linguistic Form*. Cambridge: Cambridge University Press.

KÖNIG, E. and SIEMUND, P. 2000. 'The development of complex reflexives and intensifiers in English', *Diachronica*, 17: 39–84.

KOERNER, E. F. K. 1999. *Linguistic Historiography. Projects & Prospects*. Amsterdam: Benjamins.

KOOPMAN, W. F. 1998. 'Inversion after single and multiple topics in Old English', pp. 135–50 of *Advances in English Historical Linguistics*, edited by J. Fisiak and M. Krygier. Berlin: Mouton de Gruyter.

KROCH, A. S. 1989a. 'Function and grammar in the history of English: Periphrastic DO', pp. 133–72 of *Language Change and Variation*, edited by R. W. Fasold and D. Schiffrin. Amsterdam: Benjamins.

—— 1989b. 'Reflexes of grammar in patterns of language change', *Journal of Language Variation and Change*, 1: 199–244.

—— and TAYLOR, A. 1997. 'Verb movement in Old and Middle English: Dialect variation and language contact', pp. 297–325 of *Parameters of Morphosyntactic change*, edited by A. van Kemenade and N. Vincent. Cambridge: Cambridge University Press.

KRUG, M. G. 2000. *Emerging English Modals: A Corpus-Based Study of Grammaticalization*. Berlin: Mouton de Gruyter.

—— 2001. 'Frequency, iconicity, categorization: Evidence from emerging modals', pp. 309–35 of *Frequency and the Emergence of Linguistic Structure*, edited by J. Bybee and P. J. Hopper. Amsterdam: Benjamins.

—— 2003. 'Frequency as a determinant in grammatical variation and change', pp. 7–67 of *Determinants of Grammatical Variation in English*, edited by G. Rohdenburg and B. Mondorf. Berlin: Mouton de Gruyter.

KURYŁOWICZ, J. 1964. *The Inflectional Categories of Indo-European*. Heidelberg: Carl Winter.

KUTEVA, T. 2001. *Auxiliation. An Enquiry into the Nature of Grammaticalization*. Oxford: Oxford University Press.

LABOV, W. 1972a. *Language in the Inner City*. Philadelphia: University of Pennsylvania Press.

—— 1972b. *Sociolinguistic Patterns*. Philadelphia: University of Philadelphia Press.

—— 1994. *Principles of Linguistic Change. Internal Factors*. Oxford: Blackwell.

—— 2001. *Principles of Linguistic Change. Social Factors*. Oxford: Blackwell.

LAKOFF, G. and JOHNSON, M. 1980. *Metaphors We Live By*. Chicago: University of Chicago Press.

—— and TURNER, M. 1989. *More Than Cool Reason: A Field Guide to Poetic Metaphor*. Chicago: University of Chicago Press.

LAMBRECHT, K. 1988. 'Presentational cleft constructions in spoken French', pp. 135–79 of *Clause Combining in Grammar and Discourse*, edited by J. Haiman and S. A. Thompson. Amsterdam: Benjamins.

LANDSBERG, M. E. (ed.) 1995. *Syntactic Iconicity and Linguistic Freezes. The Human Dimension*. Berlin: Mouton de Gruyter.

LANGACKER, R. W. 1987. *Foundations of Cognitive Grammar*. Stanford: Stanford University Press.

—— 1995. 'Raising and transparency', *Language*, 71: 1–62.

LASS, R. 1980. *On Explaining Language Change*. Cambridge: Cambridge University Press.

—— 1990. 'How to do things with junk: Exaptation in language evolution', *Journal of Linguistics*, 26: 79–102.

—— 1997. *Historical Linguistics and Language Change*. Cambridge: Cambridge University Press.

—— 2000b. 'Remarks on (uni)directionality', pp. 207–27 in *Pathways of Change*, edited by O. Fischer, A. Rosenbach, and D. Stein. Amsterdam: Benjamins.

LEHMANN, C. 1982[1995]. *Thoughts on Grammaticalization*. Munich: Lincom Europa (first published in the series 'Arbeiten des Kölner Universalien-Projektes' 48, University of Cologne).

—— 1985. 'Grammaticalization: Synchronic variation and diachronic change', *Lingua e Stile*, 20: 303–18.

—— 1988. 'Towards a typology of clause linkage', pp. 181–225 of *Clause Combining in Grammar and Discourse*, edited by J. Haiman and S. A. Thompson. Amsterdam: Benjamins.

—— 1989a. 'Latin subordination in typological perspective', pp. 153–79 of *Subordination and Other Topics*, edited by G. Calboli. Amsterdam: Benjamins.

—— 1989b. 'Grammatikalisierung und Lexikalisierung', *Zeitschrift für Phonetik, Sprachwissenschaft und Kommunikationsforschung*, 42: 11–19.

LEHMANN, W. P. 1992. *Historical Linguistics*, 3rd edn. London: Routledge.

LENKER, U. 2000b. '*Soplice* and *Witodlice*. Discourse markers in Old English', pp. 229–49 in *Pathways of Change*, edited by O. Fischer, A. Rosenbach, and D. Stein. Amsterdam: Benjamins.

LIEBERMAN, P. 1991. *Uniquely Human. The Evolution of Speech, Thought, and Selfless Behavior*. Cambridge Mass.: Harvard University Press.

LIGHTFOOT, D. W. 1974. 'The diachronic analysis of English modals', pp. 219–49 of *Historical Linguistics*, edited by J. M. Anderson and C. Jones. Amsterdam: North Holland Publishing.

—— 1979. *Principles of Diachronic Syntax*. Cambridge: Cambridge University Press.

—— 1981. 'The history of noun phrase movement', pp. 86–119 of *The Logical Problem of Language Acquisition*, edited by C. L. Baker and J. McCarthy. Cambridge Mass.: MIT Press.

—— 1982. *The Language Lottery. Towards a Biology of Grammar*. Cambridge Mass.: MIT Press.

—— 1991. *How to Set Parameters: Arguments from Language Change*. Cambridge: MIT Press.

—— 1999. *The Development of Language: Acquisition, Change, and Evolution*. Malden, MA: Blackwell.

—— 2000. 'The spandrels of the linguistic genotype', pp. 231–47 of *The Evolutionary Emergence of Language*, edited by C. Knight, M. Studdert-Kennedy, and J. R. Hurford. Cambridge: Cambridge University Press.

—— 2002a. 'Introduction', pp. 1–19 of *Syntactic Effects of Morphological Change*, edited by D. W. Lightfoot. Oxford: Oxford University Press.

—— (ed.) 2002b. *Syntactic Effects of Morphological Change*. Oxford: Oxford University Press.

—— 2003. 'Grammaticalization: Cause or effect?' pp. 99–123 of *Motives for Language Change*, edited by R. Hickey. Cambridge: Cambridge University Press.

—— 2004. 'Abstraction and performance. a commentary on Fischer', *Studies in Language*, 28: 741–4.

LØKEN, B. 1997. 'Expressing possibility in English and Norwegian', *ICAME Journal*, 21: 43–59.

LOMBARDO VALLAURI, E. 2004. 'The relation between mind and language: The innateness hypothesis and the poverty of the stimulus', *The Linguistic Review*, 21: 345–87.

LOS, B. 2005. *The Rise of the to-Infinitive*. Oxford: Oxford University Press.

LYONS, J. 1970. *Chomsky*. London: Fontana/Collins.

—— 1977. *Semantics*. Vol. I. Cambridge: Cambridge University Press.

MAEDER, C., HERLOFSKY, W. J., and FISCHER, O. (eds) 2005. *Inside-out and Outside-in. Iconicity in Language and Literature 4*. Amsterdam: Benjamins.

MALKIEL, Y. 1993. *Etymology*. Cambridge: Cambridge University Press.

MARCHAND, H. 1969. *Categories and Types of Modern English Word Formation*. München: Beck.

MATTHEWS, P. 2003. 'On change in "E-language"', pp. 7–17 of *Motives for Language Change*, edited by R. Hickey. Cambridge: Cambridge University Press.

MATTHIESSEN, C. and THOMPSON, S. A. 1988. 'The structure of discourse and "Subordination"', pp. 275–329 of *Clause Cambining in Grammar and Discourse*, edited by J. Haiman and S. A. Thompson. Amsterdam: Benjamins.

MCCAWLEY, N. 1976. 'From OE/ME "impersonal" to "personal" constructions: What is a "subjectless" S?', pp. 129–204 of *Papers from the Parasession on Diachronic Syntax*, edited by S. B. Steever *et al.* Chicago: Chicago Linguistic Society.

MCMAHON, A. 1994. *Understanding Language Change*. Cambridge: Cambridge University Press.

—— 2000. *Change, Chance and Optimality*. Oxford: Oxford University Press.

MEILLET, A. 1912. 'L'évolution des formes grammaticales', *Scientia*, 12: 6.

—— 1937 [1903], *Introduction à l'étude comparative des langues indo-européennes*, 8th edn. Paris: Hachette.

MEINUNGER, A. 2004. 'Interface restrictions on verb second', *Linguistics in Potsdam*, 22: 51–81 (also available online at http://www.ling.uni-potsdam.de/lip).

MENN, L. and MACWHINNEY, B. 1984. 'The repeated morph constraint: Toward an explanation', *Language*, 60: 519–41.

MEYER, C. F., GRABOWSKI, R., HAN, H.-Y., MANTZOURANIS, K., and MOSES, S. 2003. 'The World Wide Web as Linguistic Corpus', pp. 241–54 of *Corpus Analysis, Language Structure and Language Use*, edited by P. Leistyna and C. F. Meyer. Amsterdam: Rodopi.

MILLER, D. G. 2002. *Nonfinite Structures in Theory and Change*. Oxford: Oxford University Press.

MILLER, J. 2004. 'Perfect and resultative constructions in spoken and non-standard English', pp. 229–46 of *Up and Down the Cline*, edited by O. Fischer, M. Norde and H. Perridon. Amsterdam: Benjamins.

MILLER, P. H. 1997. 'Auxiliary verbs in Old and Middle French: A diachronic study of substitutive *faire* and a comparison with the Modern English auxiliaries', pp. 119–33 of *Parameters of Morphosyntactic Change*, edited by A. van Kemenade and N. Vincent. Cambridge: Cambridge University Press.

MILROY, J. 1992. *Linguistic Variation and Change. On the Historical Sociolinguistics of English*. Oxford: Blackwell.

—— 1993. 'On the social origins of language change', pp. 215–36 of *Historical Linguistics*, edited by C. Jones. London: Longman.

MILROY, L. 1987. *Language and Social Networks*. Oxford: Blackwell.

MITCHELL, B. 1985. *Old English Syntax*. Oxford: Oxford University Press.

MITHUN, M. 1988. 'The grammaticization of coordination', pp. 331–59 of *Clause Combining in Grammar and Discourse*, edited by J. Haiman and S. A. Thompson. Amsterdam: Benjamins.

—— 1991. 'The role of motivation in the emergence of grammatical categories: The grammaticization of subjects', pp. 159–84 of *Approaches to Grammaticalization*, edited by E. C. Traugott and B. Heine. Amsterdam: Benjamins.

—— 2003. 'Functional perspectives on syntactic change', pp. 553–72 of *The Handbook of Historical Linguistics*, edited by B. D. Joseph and R. D. Janda. Oxford: Blackwell.

MITTWOCH, A. 1990. 'On the distribution of bare infinitive complements in English', *Journal of Linguistics*, 26: 103–31.

MOERENHOUT, M. and WURFF, W. VAN DER 2000. 'Remnants of the old order: OV in the *Paston Letters*', *English Studies*, 81: 513–30.

—— and—— 2005. 'Object-verb order in early sixteenth-century English prose: An exploratory study', *English Language and Linguistics*, 9: 83–114.

MÜLLER, W. G. and FISCHER, O. (eds) 2003. *From Sign to Signing. Iconicity in Language and Literature 3*. Amsterdam: Benjamins.

MUYSKEN, P. 1981. 'Halfway between Quechua and Spanish: The case for relexification', pp. 52–78 of *Historicity and Variation in Creole Studies*, edited by A. Highfield and A. Valdman. Ann Arbor: Karoma Publishers.

NAGLE, S. J. 1989. *Inferential Change and Syntactic Modality in English*. Frankfurt: Peter Lang.

—— 1994. 'The English double modal conspiracy', *Diachronica*, 11: 199–211.

—— 1997. 'What is double about double modals?' pp. 1513–26 of *Language History and Linguistic Modelling*, edited by R. Hickey and S. Puppel. Berlin: Mouton de Gruyter.

NÄNNY, M. and FISCHER, O. (eds) 1999. *Form Miming Meaning. Iconicity in Language and Literature*. Amsterdam: Benjamins.

NEVALAINEN, T. 1997. 'The processes of adverb derivation in Late Middle English and Early Modern English', pp. 145–89 of *Grammaticalization at Work. Studies of Long-Term Development in English*, edited by M. Rissanen, M. Kytö, and K. Heikkonen. Berlin: Mouton de Gruyter.

—— and RAUMOLIN-BRUNBERG, H. (eds) 1996. *Sociolinguistics and Language History: Studies Based on the Corpus of Early English Correspondence*. Amsterdam: Rodopi.

NEWMEYER, F. J. 1998. *Language Form and Language Function*. Cambridge Mass.: MIT Press.

—— 2003. 'What can the field of linguistics tell us about the origin of language?', pp. 58–76 of *Language Evolution*, edited by M. H. Christiansen and S. Kirby. Oxford: Oxford University Press.

—— 2004. 'Typological evidence and universal grammar', *Studies in Language*, 38: 527–48.

NOBLE, J. 2000. 'Cooperation, competition and the evolution of prelinguistic communication', pp. 40–61 of *The Evolutionary Emergence of Language*, edited by C. Knight, M. Studdert-Kennedy, and J. R. Hurford. Cambridge: Cambridge University Press.

NOËL, D. 2005. 'The productivity of a "source of information" construction: Or, where grammaticalization theory and construction grammar meet'. Paper given at the Fitigra Conference, Leuven, Belgium, February 2005.

NORDE, M. 2001. 'Deflexion as a counterdirectional factor in grammatical change', *Language Sciences*, 23: 231–64.

OHKADO, M. 2005. *Clause Structure in Old English*, PhD thesis, Faculty of Humanities, University of Amsterdam.

ONO, S. 1975. 'The Old English verbs of knowing', *Studies in English Literature* (English number), 1975: 33–60.

PAGLIUCA, W. (ed.) 1994. *Perspectives on Grammaticalization*. Amsterdam: Benjamins.

PAUL, H. 1975 [1880]. *Prinzipien der Sprachgeschichte*. Tübingen: Niemeyer.

PENKE, M. and ROSENBACH, A. 2004. 'What counts as evidence in linguistics? an introduction', *Studies in Language*, 28: 480–526.

PEPICELLO, W. J. 1982. 'On the sources of Indo-European conjunctions of purpose, cause and result', pp. 256–64 of *Papers from the 5th International Conference on Historical Linguistics*, edited by A. Ahlqvist. Amsterdam: Benjamins.

PETERS, A. M. 1985. 'Language segmentation: Operating principles for the perception and analysis of language', pp. 1029–67 of *The Crosslinguistic Study of Language Acquisition*, edited by D. I. Slobin. Mahwah, NJ: Erlbaun.

PICKERING, M. J. and BARRY, G. 1991. 'Sentence processing without empty categories', *Language and Cognitive Processes*, 6: 229–59.

—— and BRANIGAN, H. P. 1999. 'Syntactic priming in language production', *Trends in Cognitive Sciences*, 3: 136–41.

PINKER, S. 1991. 'Rules of language', *Science*, 253: 530–5.

—— 1994. *The Language Instinct. The New Science of Language and Mind*. Harmondsworth: Penguin Books.

PINKSTER, H. 1987. 'The strategy and chronology of the development of future and perfect tense auxiliaries in Latin', pp. 193–223 of *Historical Development of Auxiliaries*, edited by M. Harris and P. Ramat. Berlin: Mouton de Gruyter.

PINTZUK, S. 1991. *Phrase Structures in Competition: Variation and Change in Old English Word Order*. PhD thesis, University of Pennsylvania.

—— and KROCH, A. S. 1989. 'The rightward movement of complements and adjuncts in the Old English of *Beowulf*', *Language Variation and Change*, 1: 115–43.

—— TSOULAS, G., and WARNER, A. (eds) 2000. *Diachronic Syntax. Models and Mechanisms*. Oxford: Oxford University Press.

PLANK, F. 1984. 'The modals story retold', *Studies in Language*, 8: 305–64.

—— 1985. 'Prädikativ und Koprädikativ', *Zeitschrift für germanische Linguistik*, 13: 154–85.

—— 1995. 'Entgrammatisierung—Spiegelbild der Grammatisierung?', pp. 199–219 of *Natürlichkeitstheorie und Sprachwandel*, edited by N. Boretzky, W. Dressler, T. Orešnik, and W. U. Wurzel. Bochum: Brochmeyer.

POLLARD, C. and SAG, I. A. 1994. *Head-Driven Phrase Structure Grammar*. Chicago: Chicago University Press.

PULVERMÜLLER, F. 2002. *The Neuroscience of Language. On Brain Circuits of Words and Serial Order*. Cambridge: Cambridge University Press.

QUIRK, R., GREENBAUM, S., LEECH, G., and SVARTVIK, J. 1972. *A Grammar of Contemporary English*. London: Longman.

RADFORD, A. 1988. *Transformational Grammar. A First Course*. Cambridge: Cambridge University Press.

—— 1997. *Syntax. A Minimalist Introduction*. Cambridge: Cambridge University Press.

RAMAT, P. 1992. 'Thoughts on degrammaticalization', *Linguistics*, 30: 549–60.

RIEMANN, O. 1927. *Syntaxe latine d'après les principes de la grammaire historique*. Paris: Klincksieck.

Rissanen, M. 1999a. 'Syntax', pp. 187–331 of *The Cambridge History of the English Language. Vol. III, 1476–1776*, edited by R. Lass. Cambridge: Cambridge University Press.

—— 1999b. '*Isn't it?* or *is it not?* On the order of postverbal subject and negative particle in the history of English', pp. 189–205 of *Negation in the History of English*, edited by I. Tieken Boon van Ostade, G. Tottie, and W. van der Wurff. Amsterdam: Benjamins.

—— Kytö, M., and Palander-Collin, M. (eds). 1993. *Early English in the Computer Age. Explorations through the Helsinki Corpus*. Berlin: Mouton de Gruyter.

Roberts, I. G. 1985. 'Agreement parameters and the development of English modal auxiliaries', *Natural Language & Linguistic Theory*, 3: 21–58.

—— 1993a. *Verbs and Diachronic Syntax: A Comparative History of English and French*. Dordrecht: Kluwer.

—— 1993b. 'A formal account of grammaticalization in the history of Romance futures', *Folia Linguistica Historica*, 13: 219–58.

—— and Roussou, A. 1999. 'A formal approach to grammaticalization', *Linguistics*, 37: 1011–41.

—— and—— 2002. 'The history of the future', pp. 23–56 of *Syntactic Effects of Morphological Change*, edited by D. W. Lightfoot. Oxford: Oxford University Press.

—— and—— 2003. *Syntactic Change. A Minimalist Approach to Grammaticalization*. Cambridge: Cambridge University Press.

Rohdenburg, G. 1996. 'Cognitive complexity and increased grammatical explicitness in English', *Cognitive Linguistics*, 7: 149–82.

—— 2003. 'Cognitive complexity and *Horror Aequi* as factors determining the use of interrogative clause linkers in English', pp. 205–49 of *Determinants of Grammatical Variation in English*, edited by G. Rohdenburg and B. Mondorf. Berlin: Mouton de Gruyter.

Romaine, S. 1981. 'The transparency principle: What it is and why it doesn't work', *Lingua*, 55: 277–300.

—— 1982. *Socio-Historical Linguistics, its Status and Methodology*. Cambridge: Cambridge University Press.

Rosch, E. 1978. 'Principles of categorization', pp. 27–48 of *Cognition and Categorization*, edited by E. Rosch and B. B. Lloyd. Hillsdale NJ: Erlbaum.

—— 1988. 'Coherences and categorization: a historical view', pp. 373–92 of *The Development of Language and Language Researchers: Essays in Honor of Roger Brown*, edited by F. Kessel. Hillsdale NJ: Erlbaum.

Rosenbach, A. 2002. *Genitive Variation in English. Conceptual Factors in Synchronic and Diachronic Studies*. Berlin: Mouton de Gruyter.

—— 2004. 'The English -*s*-genitive: A case of degrammaticalization?' pp. 73–96 of *Up and Down the Cline*, edited by O. Fischer, M. Norde, and H. Perridon. Amsterdam: Benjamins.

ROSENBACH, A. STEIN, D., and VEZZOSI, L. 2000. 'On the history of the *s*-genitive', pp. 183–210 of *Generative Theory and Corpus Studies*, edited by R. Bermúdez Otero, D. Denison, R. M. Hogg, and C. B. McCully. Berlin: Mouton de Gruyter.

RUBBA, J. 1994. 'Grammaticization as semantic change: a case study of preposition development', pp. 81–101 of *Perspectives on Grammaticalization*, edited by W. Pagliuca. Amsterdam: Benjamins.

SAMUELS, M. L. 1972. *Linguistic Evolution. With Special Reference to English.* Cambridge: Cambridge University Press.

SAPIR, E. 1963 [1929]. 'A study in phonetic symbolism', *Journal of Experimental Psychology*, 12: 225–39. (Reprinted in D. G. Mandelbaum (ed.) 1963 *Selected Writings of Edward Sapir in Language, Culture and Personality*. Berkeley: University of California Press.)

SAUSSURE, F. de 1983 [1922]. *Course in General Linguistics, Translated and Annotated by R. Harris.* London: Duckworth.

SCHIFFRIN, D. 1987. *Discourse Markers.* Cambridge: Cambridge University Press.

SCHLESINGER, I. M. 1989. 'Language acquisition: Dubious assumptions and a specious explanatory principle', *Behavioral and Brain Sciences*, 12: 356–7.

SCHLÜTER, J. 2003. 'Phonological determinants of grammatical variation in English: Chomsky's worst possible case', pp. 68–118 of *Determinants of Grammatical Variation in English*, edited by G. Rohdenburg and B. Mondorf. Berlin: Mouton de Gruyter.

SCHUTTER, G. DE 2000. 'Systeem en ontlening in taal: Nog eens het IPP-effect', *Taal en Tongval*, 52: 208–28.

SEARLE, J. 1979. *Expression and Meaning. Studies in the Theory of Speech Acts.* Cambridge: Cambridge University Press.

SHAPIRO, M. 1991. *The Sense of Change. Language as History.* Bloomington: Indiana University Press.

SHEPHERD, S. C. 1982. 'From deontic to epistemic: An analysis of modals in the history of English, creoles, and language acquisition', pp. 316–23 of *Papers from the 5th International Conference on Historical Linguistics*, edited by A. Ahlqvist. Amsterdam: Benjamins.

SIMONE, R. (ed.) 1994. *Iconicity in Language.* Amsterdam: Benjamins.

SINAR, B. 2005. 'Him or himself? On variation in Middle English reflexives', paper given at the 4th York-Holland Symposium on the History of English Syntax. Leiden University.

SKOUSEN, R. 1989. *Analogical Modeling of Language.* Dordrecht: Kluwer.

—— 1992. *Analogy and Structure.* Dordrecht: Kluwer.

SLOBIN, D. I. 1977. 'Language change in childhood and in history', pp. 185–214 of *Language Learning and Thought*, edited by J. T. Macnamara. New York: Academic Press.

—— 1985a. 'Crosslinguistic evidence for the language-making capacity', pp. 1158–256 of *The Crosslinguistic Study of Language Acquisition Vol. 2.*, edited by D. I. Slobin. Mahwah, NJ: Erlbaum Associates.

—— (ed.) 1985b. *The Crosslinguistic Study of Language Acquisition. Vol. 2. Theoretical Issues.* Mahwah, NJ: Erlbaum Associates.

—— 1997 [2001]. 'The origins of grammaticizable notions: Beyond the individual mind', pp. 265–323 of *The Crosslinguistic Study of Language Acquisition. Vol. 5. Expanding the Contexts*, edited by D. I. Slobin. Mahwah, NJ: Erlbaum Associates. (Reprinted in shortened form on pp. 406–49 of *Language Acquisition and Conceptual Development*, edited by M. Bowerman and S. C. Levinson. Cambridge University Press.)

—— 2002. 'Language evolution, acquisition and diachrony: Probing the parallels', pp. 375–92 of *The Evolution of Language out of Pre-Language*, edited by T. Givón and B. F. Malle. Amsterdam: Benjamins.

STEELE, S., with A. AKMAJIAN, R. DEMERS, E. JELINEK, C. KITIGAWA, R. OEHRLE and T. WASOW (eds) 1981. *An Encyclopedia of AUX: A Study of Cross-Linguistic Equivalence.* Cambridge Mass.: MIT Press.

STEELS, L. 1997. 'Synthesising the origins of language and meaning using co-evolution, self-organisation and level formation', in *Evolution of Human Language*, edited by J. Hurford, C. Knight, and M. Studdert-Kennedy. Edinburgh: Edinburgh University Press.

STEIN, D. and WRIGHT, S. (eds) 1995. *Subjectivity and Subjectivisation. Linguistic Perspectives.* Cambridge: Cambridge University Press.

STEMBERGER, J. P. 1981. 'Morphological haplology', *Language*, 57: 791–817.

STOCKWELL, R. P. 1977. 'Motivations for exbraciation in Old English', pp. 291–312 of *Mechanisms of Syntactic Change*, edited by C. N. Li. Austin: University of Texas Press.

SWAN, T. 1988. *Sentence Adverbials in English: A Synchronic and Diachronic Investigation.* Oslo: Novus.

SWEETSER, E. E. 1990. *From Etymology to Pragmatics: Metaphorical and Cultural Aspects of Semantic Structure.* Cambridge: Cambridge University Press.

TABOR, W. and TRAUGOTT, E. C. 1998. 'Structural scope expansion and grammaticalization', pp. 229–72 of *The Limits of Grammaticalization*, edited by A. Giacalone Ramat and P. J. Hopper. Amsterdam: Benjamins.

TAEYMANS, M. 2004. 'An investigation into the marginal modals *dare* and *need* in British present-day English. A corpus-based approach', pp. 97–114 of *Up and Down the Cline*, edited by O. Fischer, M. Norde, and H. Perridon. Amsterdam: Benjamins.

TANNEN, D. 1985. 'Relative focus on involvement in oral and written discourse', pp. 124–47 of *Literacy, Language, and Learning*, edited by D. R. Olson, N. Torrance, and A. Hildyard. Cambridge: Cambridge University Press.

TAYLOR, A. 2005. 'Prosodic evidence for incipient VO order in Old English', *English Language and Linguistics*, 9: 139–56.

THOMASON, S. G. 2001. *Language Contact. An Introduction*. Edinburgh: Edinburgh University Press.

—— and KAUFMAN, T. 1988. *Language Contact, Creolization, and Genetic Linguistics*. Berkeley: University of California Press.

THOMPSON, S. A. 2002. '"Object complements" and conversation. Towards a realistic account', *Studies in Language*, 26: 125–64.

—— and MULAC, A. 1991. 'A quantitative perspective on the grammaticization of epistemic parentheticals in English', pp. 313–29 of *Approaches to Grammaticalization, Vol. 2*, edited by E. C. Traugott and B. Heine. Amsterdam: Benjamins.

TINBERGEN, N. 1952. 'Derived activities: their causation, biological significance, origin and emancipation during evolution', *Quarterly Review of Biology*, 27: 1–32.

TOMASELLO, M. 1992. *First Verbs: A Case Study in Early Grammatical Development*. Cambridge: Cambridge University Press.

—— 1995. 'Language is not an instinct', *Cognitive Development*, 10: 131–56.

—— 2003a. *Constructing a Language. A Usage-Based Theory of Language Acquisition*. Cambridge Mass.: Harvard University Press.

—— 2003b. 'On the different origins of symbols and grammar', pp. 94–110 of *Language Evolution*, edited by M. H. Christiansen and S. Kirby. Oxford: Oxford University Press.

TOORN, M. C. VAN DE, PIJNENBURG, W. J. J., LEUVENSTEIJN, J. A. VAN, and HORST, J. M. VAN DER (eds) 1997. *Geschiedenis van de Nederlandse Taal*. Amsterdam: Amsterdam University Press.

TRAUGOTT, E. C. 1982. 'From propositional to textual and expressive meanings: Some semantic-pragmatic aspects of grammaticalization', pp. 245–71 of *Perspectives on Historical Linguistics*, edited by W. P. Lehmann and Y. Malkiel. Amsterdam: Benjamins.

—— 1989. 'On the rise of epistemic meanings in English: An example of subjectification in semantic change', *Language*, 65: 31–55.

—— 1995. 'The role of the development of discourse markers in a theory of grammaticalization'. Paper presented at ICHL 12, Manchester University. (www.stanford.edu/~traugott/traugott.html)

—— and DASHER, R. B. 2002. *Regularity in Semantic Change*. Cambridge: Cambridge University Press.

—— and HEINE, B. (eds) 1991. *Approaches to Grammaticalization, Vol. 1: Focus on Theoretical and Methodological Issues, Vol. 2: Focus on Types of Grammatical Markers*. Amsterdam: Benjamins.

TRAVIS, C. E. 2005. *Discourse Markers in Colombian Spanish. A Study in Polysemy*. Berlin: Mouton de Gruyter.

TRUDGILL, P. 1974. *The Social Differentiation of English in Norwich*. Cambridge: Cambridge University Press.

—— 1983. *On Dialect. Social and Geographical Perspectives*. Oxford: Blackwell.

—— 2002. 'Linguistic and social typology', pp. 707–28 of *The Handbook of Language Variation and Change*, edited by J. K. Chambers, P. Trudgill, and N. Schilling Estes. Oxford: Blackwell.

TSANGALIDIS, A. 2004. 'Unidirectionality in the grammaticalization of modality in Greek', pp. 193–209 of *Up and Down the Cline*, edited by O. Fischer, M. Norde, and H. Perridon. Amsterdam: Benjamins.

VAN VALIN, R. D. Jr. 2000. 'The acquisition of complex sentences: a case study in the role of theory in the study of language development', pp. 511–31 of *Papers from the Chicago Linguistic Society* 36, *The Panels*, edited by A. Okrent and J. P. Boyle.

—— 2005. *Exploring the Syntax–Semantics Interface*. Cambridge: Cambridge University Press.

—— and LAPOLLA, R. J. 1997. *Syntax: Structure, Meaning and Function*. Cambridge: Cambridge University Press.

VELDE, F. VAN DE 2004. 'De Middelnederlandse onpersoonlijke constructie en haar grammaticale concurrenten. semantische motivering van de argumentstructuur', *Nederlandse Taalkunde*, 9: 48–76.

VENNEMANN, T. 1974. 'Topics, subjects and word order: From SXV to SVX via TVX', pp. 339–76 of *Historical Linguistics* Vol. I, edited by J. M. Anderson and C. Jones. Amsterdam: North Holland Publishing.

VIHMAN, M. M. and DEPAOLIS, R. A. 2000. 'Role of mimesis in infant language development: Evidence for phylogeny?' pp. 130–45 of *The Evolutionary Emergence of Language*, edited by C. Knight, M. Studdert-Kennedy, and J. R. Hurford. Cambridge: Cambridge University Press.

VINCENT, N. 1982. 'The development of auxiliaries HABERE and ESSE in Romance', pp. 71–96 of *Studies in the Romance Verb*, edited by N. Vincent and M. Harris. London: Croom Helm.

—— 1995. 'Exaptation and grammaticalization', pp. 433–45 of *Historical Linguistics 1993*, edited by H. Andersen. Amsterdam: Benjamins.

—— 2001. 'LFG as a model of syntactic change', pp. 1–42 of *Time over Matter*, edited by M. Butt and T. Holloway King. Stanford: CSLI Publications.

VISSER, F. T. 1963–1973. *An Historical Syntax of the English Language*. 3 Vols. Leiden: E.J. Brill.

VOELTZ, E. F. K. and KILIAN-HATZ, C. (eds) 2001. *Ideophones*. Amsterdam: Benjamins.

WARNER, A. R. 1982. *Complementation in Middle English and the Methodology of Historical Syntax*. London: Croom Helm.

—— 1983. 'Review article of D. W. Lightfoot', *Principles of Diachronic Syntax*, *Journal of Linguistics*, 19: 187–209.

—— 1990. 'Reworking the history of English auxiliaries', pp. 537–58 of *Papers from the 5th International Conference on English Historical Linguistics, Cambridge,*

6–9 April 1987, edited by S. Adamson, V. Law, N. Vincent and S. Wright. Amsterdam: Benjamins.

—— 1992. 'Elliptical and impersonal constructions: evidence for auxiliaries in Old English?' pp. 178–210 of *Evidence for Old English: Material and Theoretical Bases for Reconstruction*, edited by F. Colman. Edinburgh: Donald.

WARNER, A. R. 1993. *English Auxiliaries. Structure and History*. Cambridge: Cambridge University Press.

—— 1995. 'Predicting the progressive passive: Parametric change within a lexicalist framework', *Language*, 71: 533–57.

—— 1997. 'Extending the paradigm: An interpretation of the historical development of auxiliary sequences in English', *English Studies*, 78: 162–89.

—— 2004. 'What drove do?' pp. 229–42 of *New Perspectives on English Historical Linguistics. Volume I: Syntax and Morphology*, edited by C. Kay, S. Horobin and J. Smith. Amsterdam: Benjamins.

WEINREICH, U., LABOV, W., and HERZOG, M. I. 1968. 'Empirical foundations for a theory of language change', pp. 95–195 of *Directions for Historical Linguistics* edited by W. P. Lehmann and Y. Malkiel. Austin: University of Texas Press.

WEIß, H. 2004. 'A question of relevance: Some remarks on standard languages', *Studies in Language*, 28: 647–73.

WIEGAND, N. 1982. 'From discourse to syntax: *For* in early English causal clauses', pp. 385–93 of *Papers from the 5th International Conference on Historical Linguistics*, edited by A. Ahlqvist. Amsterdam: Benjamins.

WINFORD, D. 2000. 'Irrealis in Sranan: Mood and modality in a radical creole', *Journal of Pidgin and Creole Languages*, 15: 63–125.

WISCHER, I. 2000. 'Grammaticalization versus lexicalization. *"Methinks"* there is some confusion', pp. 355–70 in *Pathways of Change*, edited by O. Fischer, A. Rosenbach, and D. Stein. Amsterdam: Benjamins.

WISCHER, I. and DIEWALD, G. (eds) 2002. *New Reflections on Grammaticalization*. Amsterdam: Benjamins.

WONG, K.-S. 2004. 'The acquisition of polysemous forms: The case of *Bei2* ("Give") in Cantonese', pp. 325–43 of *Up and Down the Cline*, edited by O. Fischer, M. Norde, and H. Perridon. Amsterdam: Benjamins.

WOODCOCK, E. C. 1959. *A New Latin Syntax*. London: Methuen.

WRAY, A. 1999. 'Formulaic language in learners and native speakers', *Language Teaching*, 32: 213–31.

—— 2000. 'Holistic utterances in protolanguage: The link from primates to humans', pp. 285–302 of *The Evolutionary Emergence of Language*, edited by C. Knight, M. Studdert-Kennedy, and J. R. Hurford. Cambridge: Cambridge University Press.

WRAY, A. and PERKINS, M. R. 2000. 'The functions of formulaic language: An integrated model', *Language and Communication*, 20: 1–28.

WUNDERLICH, D. 2004. 'Why assume UG?' *Studies in Language*, 28: 615–41.

WURFF, W. v. d. 1989. 'A remarkable gap in the history of English syntax', *Folia Linguistica Historica*, 9: 117–59.

—— 1990. *Diffusion and Reanalysis in Syntax*, PhD thesis, Faculty of Arts, University of Amsterdam.

—— 1999. 'Objects and verbs in modern Icelandic and fifteenth-century English: A word order parallel and its causes', *Lingua*, 109: 237–65.

—— 2000. 'Variation and change: Text types and the modelling of syntactic change', pp. 261–82 of *Generative Theory and Corpus Studies*, edited by R. Bermúdez Otero, D. Denison, R. M. Hogg, and C. B. McCully. Berlin: Mouton de Gruyter.

YNGVE, V. H. 1996. *From Grammar to Science: New Foundations for General Linguistics*. Amsterdam: Benjamins.

ZWART, J. W. 2005. 'Verb second as a function of merge', pp. 11–40 of *The Function of Function Words and Functional Categories*, edited by M. den Dikken and C. M. Tortora. Amsterdam: Benjamins.

Corpora used

The York-Toronto-Helsinki Parsed Corpus of Old English Prose (http://www-users.york.ac.uk/~lang22/YcoeHome1.htm)

The Penn-Helsinki Parsed Corpus of Middle English, second edition (http://www.ling.upenn.edu/hist-corpora/)

The Dictionary of Old English Corpus (http://ets.umdl.umich.edu/o/oec/)

ICE-GB: the International Corpus of English: the British component (http://www.ucl.ac.uk/english-usage/projects/ice-gb/)

Name Index

Subject Index